CHILTON BOOK COMPANY

REPAIR MANUAL

DODGE CARAVAN PLYMOUTH VOYAGER 1984-88

All U.S. and Canadian models of DODGE Caravan and PLYMOUTH Voyager

Vice President and General Manager JOHN P. KUSHNERICK
Editor-in-Chief KERRY A. FREEMAN, S.A.E.
Managing Editor DEAN F. MORGANTINI, S.A.E.
Senior Editor RICHARD J. RIVELE, S.A.E.
Senior Editor W. CALVIN SETTLE, JR., S.A.E.

CHILTON BOOK COMPANY
Radnor, Pennsylvania
19089

CONTENTS

SAFETY NOTICE

Proper service and repair procedures are vital to the safe, reliable operation of all motor vehicles, as well as the personal safety of those performing repairs. This book outlines procedures for servicing and repairing vehicles using safe, effective methods. The procedures contain many NOTES, CAUTIONS and WARNINGS which should be followed along with standard safety procedures to eliminate the possibility of personal injury or improper service which could damage the vehicle or compromise its safety.

It is important to note that repair procedures and techniques, tools and parts for servicing motor vehicles, as well as the skill and experience of the individual performing the work vary widely. It is not possible to anticipate all of the conceivable ways or conditions under which vehicles may be serviced, or to provide cautions as to all of the possible hazards that may result. Standard and accepted safety precautions and equipment should be used during cutting, grinding, chiseling, prying, or any other process that can cause material removal or projectiles.

Some procedures require the use of tools specially designed for a specific purpose. Before substituting another tool or procedure, you must be completely satisfied that neither your personal safety, nor the performance of the vehicle will be endangered.

Although the information in this guide is based on industry sources and is as complete as possible at the time of publication, the possibility exists that the manufacturer made later changes which could not be included here. While striving for total accuracy, Chilton Book Company cannot assume responsibility for any errors, changes, or omissions that may occur in the compilation of this data.

PART NUMBERS

Part numbers listed in this reference are not recommendations by Chilton for any product by brand name. They are references that can be used with interchange manuals and aftermarket supplier catalogs to locate each brand supplier's discrete part number.

SPECIAL TOOLS

Special tools are recommended by the vehicle manufacturer to perform their specific job. Use has been kept to a minimum, but where absolutely necessary, they are referred to in the text by the part number of the tool manufacturer. These tools can be purchased, under the appropriate part number, from Owatonna Tool Company, Owatonna, MN 55060 or an equivalent tool can be purchased locally from a tool supplier or parts outlet. Before substituting any tool for the one recommended, read the SAFETY NOTICE at the top of this page.

ACKNOWLEDGMENTS

Chilton Book Company wishes to express appreciation to the Chrysler Plymouth Division, Chrysler Motor Corporation, Detroit, Michigan and the Dodge Division, Chrysler Motors Corporation, Detroit, Michigan for their generous assistance.

Manufactured in the United States of America
1234567890   8765432109

Chilton's Repair Manual: Dodge Caravan/Plymouth Voyager 1984–88
ISBN 0-8019-7931-5 pbk.
Library of Congress Catalog Card No. 88-43173

General Information and Maintenance

HOW TO USE THIS BOOK

Chilton's Repair and Tune-Up Guide for the Dodge Caravan/Plymouth Voyager is intended to teach you about the inner workings of your van and save you money on its upkeep.

The first two chapters will be the most used, since they contain maintenance, tune-up information and service procedures. Studies have shown that a properly tuned and maintained vehicle will get better gas mileage (which translates into lower operating costs) and periodic maintenance will catch minor problems before they turn into major repair bills. The other chapters deal with the more complex systems of your car. Operating systems from engine through brakes are covered to the extent that the average do-it-yourselfer becomes mechanically involved. This book does not cover repairs that the expertise required and the investment in special tools make the task impractical and uneconomical. It will give you the detailed instructions to help you change your own brake pads and shoes, tune-up the engine, replace spark plugs and filters, and do many more jobs that will save you money, give you personal satisfaction and help you avoid expensive problems.

Before attempting any repairs or service on your vehicle, read through the entire procedure outlined in the appropriate chapter. This will give you the overall view of what tools and supplies will be required. Many times a description of the system function and operation is given, helping you to understand what repairs must be done.

Two basic mechanic's rules should be mentioned here. First, whenever the LEFT side of the car or engine is referred to, it is meant to specify the DRIVER'S side of the car. Conversely, the RIGHT side of the car means the PAS-SENGER'S side. Second, all screws and bolts are removed by turning counterclockwise, and tightened by turning clockwise (unless otherwise noted).

Safety is always the most important rule. Constantly be aware of the dangers involved in working on or around an automobile, and take proper precautions to avoid the risk of personal injury or damage to the vehicle. See the section in this chapter, Servicing Your Vehicle Safely, and the SAFETY NOTICE on the acknowledgment page before attempting any service procedures. Pay special attention to the instructions provided.

There are 3 common mistakes in mechanical work:

1. Incorrect order of assembly, disassembly or adjustment. When taking something apart or putting it together, doing things in the wrong order usually just costs you extra time; however, it CAN break something. Read the entire procedure before beginning disassembly. Do everything in the order in which the instructions say you should do it, even if you can't immediately see a reason for it. When you're taking apart something that is very intricate (for example a carburetor), you might want to draw a picture of how it looks when assembled at one point in order to make sure you get everything back in its proper position. We will supply exploded views whenever possible, but sometimes the job requires more attention to detail than an illustration provides. When making adjustments (especially tune-up adjustments), do them in order. One adjustment often affects another, and you cannot expect satisfactory results unless each adjustment is made in accordance with its sequence.

2. Overtorquing (or undertorquing) nuts and bolts. While it is more common for overtorquing to cause damage, undertorquing

can cause a fastener to vibrate loose and cause serious damage, especially when dealing with aluminum parts. Pay attention to torque specifications and utilize a torque wrench in assembly. If a torque figure is not available remember that, if you are using the right tool to do the job, you will probably not have to strain yourself to get a fastener tight enough. The pitch of most threads is so slight that the tension you put on the wrench will be multiplied many times in actual force on what you are tightening. A good example of how critical torque is can be seen in the case of spark plug installation, especially where you are putting the plug into an aluminum cylinder head. Too little torque can fail to crush the gasket, causing leakage of combustion gases, and consequent overheating of the plug and engine parts. Too much torque can damage the threads or distort the plug, which changes the spark gap. Since more and more manufacturers are using aluminum in their engine and chassis parts to save weight, a torque wrench should be in any serious do-it-yourselfer's tool box.

NOTE: *There are many commercial chemical products available for ensuring that fasteners won't come loose, even if they are not torqued just right (a very common brand is Loctite®). If you're worried about getting something together tight enough to hold, but loose enough to avoid mechanical damage during assembly, one of these products might offer substantial insurance. Read the label on the package and make sure the product is compatible with the materials, fluids, etc. involved before choosing one.*

3. Crossthreading. This occurs when a part such as a bolt is screwed into a nut or casting at the wrong angle and forced, causing the threads to become damaged. Crossthreading is more likely to occur if access is difficult. It helps to clean and lubricate fasteners, and to start threading with the part to be installed going straight in, using your fingers. If you encounter resistance, unscrew the part and start over again at a different angle until it can be inserted and turned several times without much effort. Keep in mind that many parts, especially spark plugs, use tapered threads so that gentle turning will automatically bring the part you're threading to the proper angle if you don't force it or resist a change in angle. Don't put a wrench on the part until it's been turned in a couple of times by hand. If you suddenly encounter resistance and the part has not seated fully, don't force it. Pull it back out and make sure it's clean and threading properly.

Always take your time and be patient; once you have some experience, working on your car will become an enjoyable hobby.

TOOLS AND EQUIPMENT

Naturally, without the proper tools and equipment it is impossible to properly service your vehicle. It would be impossible to catalog each tool that you would need to perform each or every operation in this book. It would also be unwise for the amateur to rush out and buy an expensive set of tools, on the theory that he may need one or more of them at sometime.

The best approach is to proceed slowly, gathering together a good quality set of those tools that are used most frequently. Don't be misled by the low cost of bargain tools. It is far better to spend a little more for better quality. Forged wrenches, 6 or 12 point sockets and fine tooth ratchets are by far preferable to their less expensive counterparts. As any good mechanic can tell you, there are few worse experiences than trying to work on a car with bad tools. Your monetary savings will be far outweighed by frustration and mangled knuckles.

Begin accumulating those tools that are used most frequently; those associated with routine maintenance and tune-up.

In addition to the normal assortment of screwdrivers and pliers you should have the following tools for routine maintenance jobs:

1. SAE/Metric wrenches, sockets and combination open end/box end wrenches in sizes from ⅛″ (3mm) to ¾″ (19mm), and a spark plug socket (9/16″ or ⅝″). If possible, buy various length socket drive extensions. One break in this department is that the metric sockets available in the U.S. will all fit the ratchet handles and extensions you may already have (¼, ⅜, and ½″ drive).

2. Jackstands for support.

3. Oil filter wrench.

4. Oil filler spout or funnel.

5. Grease gun for chassis lubrication.

6. Hydrometer for checking the battery.

7. A low flat pan for draining oil.

8. Lots of rags for wiping up the inevitable mess.

In addition to the above items there are several others that are not absolutely necessary, but handy to have around. These include oil-dry, a transmission fluid funnel and the usual supply of lubricants, antifreeze and fluids, although these can be purchased as needed. This is a basic list for routine maintenance, but only your personal needs and desires can accurately determine your list of necessary tools.

The second list of tools is for tune-ups. While the tools involved here are slightly more sophisticated, they need not be outrageously expensive. A basic list of tune-up equipment could include:

1. Tachometer

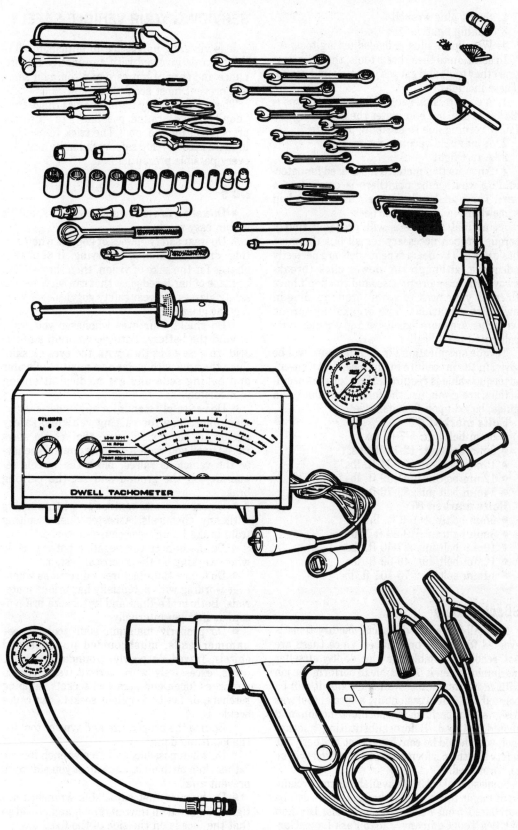

The tools and equipment shown here will handle the majority of the maintenance on your vehicle

2. Spark plug wrench
3. Timing light
4. Wire spark plug gauge/adjusting tools

In addition to these basic tools, there are several other tools and gauges you may find useful. These include:

1. A compression gauge. The screw-in type is slower to use, but eliminates the possibility of a faulty reading due to escaping pressure
2. A manifold vacuum gauge
3. A test light
4. An induction meter. This is used for determining whether or not there is current in a wire. These are handy for use if a wire is broken somewhere in a wiring harness.

As a final note, you will probably find a torque wrench necessary for all but the most basic work. The beam type models are perfectly adequate, although the newer click (breakaway) type are more precise, and you don't have to crane your neck to see a torque reading in awkward situations. The breakaway torque wrenches are more expensive and should be recalibrated periodically.

Torque specification for each fastener will be given in the procedure in any case that a specific torque value is required. If no torque specifications are given, use the following values as a guide, based upon fastener size:

Bolts marked 6T
- 6mm bolt/nut: 5-7 ft. lbs.
- 8mm bolt/nut: 12-17 ft. lbs.
- 10mm bolt/nut: 23-34 ft. lbs.
- 12mm bolt/nut: 41-59 ft. lbs.
- 14mm bolt/nut: 56-76 ft. lbs.

Bolts marked 8T
- 6mm bolt/nut: 6-9 ft. lbs.
- 8mm bolt/nut: 13-20 ft. lbs.
- 10mm bolt/nut: 27-40 ft. lbs.
- 12mm bolt/nut: 46-69 ft. lbs.
- 14mm bolt/nut: 75-101 ft. lbs.

Special Tools

Normally, the use of special factory tools is avoided for repair procedures, since these are not readily available for the do-it-yourselfer mechanic. When it is possible to perform the job with more commonly available tools, it will be pointed out, but occasionally, a special tool was designed to perform a specific function and should be used. Before substituting another tool, you should be convinced that neither your safety nor the performance of the vehicle will be compromised.

Some special tools are available commercially from major tool manufacturers. Others can be purchased from Miller Special Tools; Division of Utica Tool Company, 32615 Park Lane, Garden City, Michigan 48135.

SERVICING YOUR VEHICLE SAFELY

It is virtually impossible to anticipate all of the hazards involved with automotive maintenance and service but care and common sense will prevent most accidents.

The rules of safety for mechanics range from "don't smoke around gasoline", to "use the proper tool for the job." The trick to avoiding injuries is to develop safe work habits and take every possible precaution.

Do's

- Do keep a fire extinguisher and first aid kit within easy reach.
- Do wear safety glasses or goggles when cutting, drilling, grinding or prying. If you wear glasses for the sake of vision, then they should be made of hardened glass that can serve also as safety glasses, or wear safety goggles over your regular glasses.
- Do shield your eyes whenever you work around the battery. Batteries contain sulfuric acid. In case of contact with the eyes or skin, flush the area with water or a mixture of water and baking soda and get medical attention immediately.
- Do use safety stands for any under-car service. Jacks are for raising vehicles; safety stands are for making sure the vehicle stays raised until you want it to come down. Whenever the vehicle is raised, block the wheels remaining on the ground and set the parking brake.
- Do use adequate ventilation when working with any chemicals. Asbestos dust resulting from brake lining wear cause cancer.
- Do disconnect the negative battery cable when working on the electrical system.
- Do follow manufacturer's directions whenever working with potentially hazardous materials. Both brake fluid and antifreeze are poisonous if taken internally.
- Do properly maintain your tools. Loose hammerheads, mushroomed punches and chisels, frayed or poorly grounded electrical cords, excessively worn screwdrivers, spread wrenches (open end), cracked sockets, slipping ratchets, or faulty droplight sockets can cause accidents.
- Do use the proper size and type of tool for the job being done.
- Do when possible, pull on a wrench handle rather than push on it, and adjust you stance to prevent a fall.
- Do be sure that adjustable wrenches are tightly adjusted on the nut or bolt and pulled so that the face is on the side of the fixed jaw.
- Do select a wrench or socket that fits the

Always use jackstands when working under the vehicle

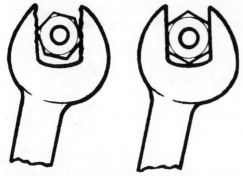

Use the proper size wrench and position it properly on the flats of the nut or bolt

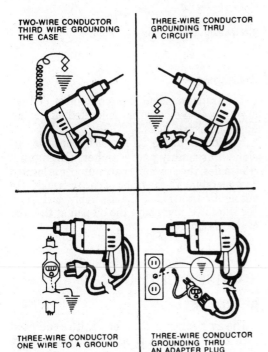

TWO-WIRE CONDUCTOR
THIRD WIRE GROUNDING
THE CASE

THREE-WIRE CONDUCTOR
GROUNDING THRU
A CIRCUIT

THREE-WIRE CONDUCTOR
ONE WIRE TO A GROUND

THREE-WIRE CONDUCTOR
GROUNDING THRU
AN ADAPTER PLUG

Power tools should always be properly grounded

nut or bolt. The wrench or socket should sit straight, not cocked.

● Do strike squarely with a hammer. avoid glancing blows.

● Do set the parking brake and block the wheels if the work requires that the engine be running.

Don'ts

● Don't run an engine in a garage or anywhere else without proper ventilation—EVER! Carbon monoxide is poisonous. It is absorbed by the body 400 times faster than oxygen. It takes a long time to leave the human body and you can build up a deadly supply of it in your system by simply breathing in a little every day. You may not realize you are slowly poisoning yourself. Always use power vents, windows, fans or open the garage doors.

● Don't work around moving parts while wearing a necktie or other loose clothing. Short sleeves are much safer than long, loose sleeves. Hard-toed shoes with neoprene soles protect your toes and give a better grip on slippery surfaces. Jewelry such as watches, fancy belt buckles, beads, or body adornment of any kind is not safe while working around a car. Long hair should be hidden under a hat or cap.

● Don't use pockets for toolboxes. A fall or bump can drive a screwdriver deep into you body. Even a wiping cloth hanging from the back pocket can wrap around a spinning shaft or fan.

● Don't smoke when working around gasoline, cleaning solvent or other flammable material.

● Don't smoke when working around the battery. When the battery is being charged, it gives off explosive hydrogen gas.

● Don't use gasoline to wash your hands. There are excellent soaps available. Gasoline may contain lead, and lead can enter the body through a cut, accumulating in the body until you are very ill. Gasoline also removes all the natural oils from the skin so that bone dry hands will suck up oil and grease.

● Don't service the air conditioning system unless you are equipped with the necessary tools and training. The refrigerant, R-12, is extremely cold and when exposed to the air, will instantly freeze any surface it comes in contact with, including your eyes. Although the refrigerant is normally non-toxic, R-12 becomes a deadly poisonous gas in the presence of an open flame. One good whiff of the vapors from burning refrigerant can be fatal.

NOTE: *The Dodge and Plymouth vehicles described in this Repair & Tune Up Guide are metric-specified. While some inch-standard parts are used, body panels, fasteners, drivetrain components, and tires are all specified according to the Metric System. Dimensions and performance data are also expressed in metric units.*

VEHICLE AND COMPONENT IDENTIFICATION

Vehicle Identification Number (V.I.N.)

The vehicle identification number (VIN) consists of seventeen numbers and letters embossed on a plate, located on the upper left corner of the instrument panel, near the windshield.

Engine Identification Number (E.I.N.)

All engine assemblies carry an engine identification number (E.I.N.). On 2.2 liter and 2.5 liter engines, the E.I.N. is located on the face of the engine block, directly under the cylinder head (left side of vehicle).

On the 2.6 liter, and 3.0 liter engines, the E.I.N. is located on the left side of the engine block between the core plug and the rear face of the block (radiator side of vehicle).

Engine Serial Number

In addition to the previously covered E.I.N., each engine assembly carries an engine serial number which must be referenced when ordering engine replacement parts.

On the 2.2 liter, and 2.5 liter engines, the engine serial number is located on the rear face of the engine block, directly below the cylinder head (below E.I.N.). On 2.6 liter, and 3.0 liter engines, the engine serial number is located on the exhaust manifold stud (dash panel side of vehicle).

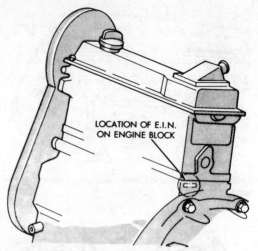

EIN location on 2.2L and 2.5L engines

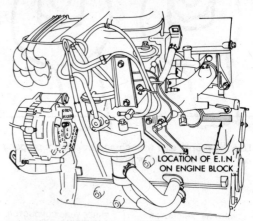

EIN location on 2.6L and 3.0L engines

Transaxle

The transaxle identification number (T.I.N.) is stamped on a boss that is located on the left upper transaxle housing.

In addition to the T.I.N., each transaxle carries an assembly part number. On manual transaxles, the assembly part number is located on a metal tag at the front of the transaxle. On automatic transaxles, the assembly part number is located just above the oil pan at the rear of the assembly.

ROUTINE MAINTENANCE

Air Cleaner

The air cleaner element on vehicles equipped with 2.2 liter engine should be replaced every 52,000 miles. Vehicles equipped with 2.5L, 2.6L, and 3.0 liter engines should be replaced

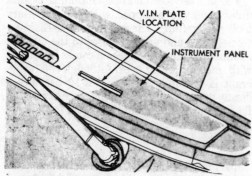

Location of V.I.N. plate

every 30,000 miles. However, if the vehicle is operated frequently through dusty areas; it will require periodic inspection at least every 15,000 miles.

REMOVAL AND INSTALLATION

2.2L Engine

1. Unfasten the three holddown clips and remove the three wing nuts that retain the top of the air cleaner housing.

2. Remove the top of the air cleaner housing and position out of the way with the breather hose attached.

3. Remove the air cleaner element from the housing.

4. Clean the inside of the housing but take care not to allow the dirt to enter the carburetor air intake.

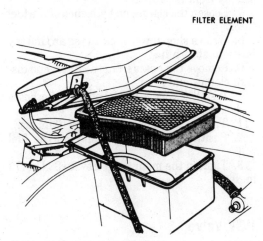

2.2L engine air cleaner filter

2.6L engine air cleaner filter

5. Install a new air cleaner element with the screen side up into the plastic housing.

6. Position the steel top cover so that the hold down clips and support bracket studs are aligned.

NOTE: *The procedures in the next steps should be followed as stated to prevent loosening and air leaks.*

7. Install the wing nuts on both carburetor studs and tighten them to 14 inch lbs. Install the wing nut that attaches the air cleaner tab to the support bracket and tighten to 14 inch lbs.

8. Fasten the holddown clips.

2.5L, 2.6L and 3.0L Engines

1. Unfasten the holddown clips that retain the air cleaner cover.

2. Remove the air cleaner housing cover with intake hose attached and position out of the way.

3. Remove the air cleaner element from the housing.

4. Clean the inside of the air cleaner housing.

5. Install a new cleaner element and position the cover on the air cleaner housing. Secure the holddown clips.

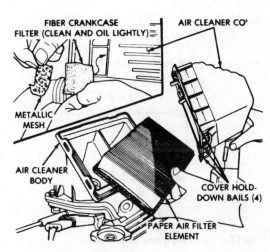

2.5L air cleaner assembly

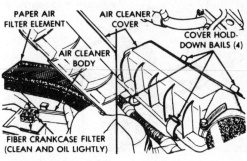

3.0L air cleaner assembly

Fuel Filter

CAUTION: *Don't smoke when working around gasoline, cleaning solvent or other flammable material.*

The fuel system on all vehicles incorporate two fuel filters. One is part of the fuel gauge unit; located inside the fuel tank at the fuel suction tube. Routine servicing of this filter is not necessary. However, if limited vehicle speed or hard starting is exhibited, it should be inspected.

The second filter is located in the fuel line between the fuel pump and the carburetor. Replacement of this filter is recommended every 52,000 miles.

REMOVAL AND INSTALLATION

2.2L and 2.6L Engines

1. Clean the area at the filter and clamps with a suitable solvent
2. Loosen the clamps on both ends of filter.
3. Wrap a shop towel or clean rag around the hoses to absorb fuel.
4. Remove the hoses from the filter, and discard the clamps and filter.

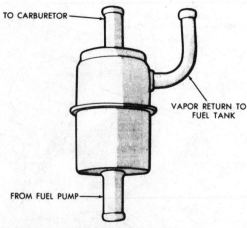

TO CARBURETOR

VAPOR RETURN TO FUEL TANK

FROM FUEL PUMP

Fuel filter vapor separator 2.2L engine

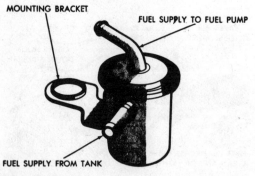

MOUNTING BRACKET

FUEL SUPPLY TO FUEL PUMP

FUEL SUPPLY FROM TANK

Typical inline filter

5. Install the new filter between the fuel lines and clamp.
6. Tighten the clamps to 1 N.m (10 in. lbs.)

2.5L and 3.0L Engines

CAUTION: *Before servicing any components within the fuel system, the system pressure must first be released.*

1. Loosen the gas cap to release tank pressure.
2. On the 2.5L engine, disconnect the harness connector from the injector
3. On the 3.0L engine, disconnect the harness connector from any injector
4. Ground one terminal of the injector.
5. Connect a jumper to the other terminal and momentarily touch the positive terminal of the battery for no longer than 10 seconds. This releases the system pressure.
6. Remove the retaining screw and filter assembly from the fuel rail.
7. Loosen the clamps on both ends of the fuel filter.
8. Wrap a shop towel or clean rag around the hoses to absorb fuel
9. Remove the hoses from the filter, and discard clamps and filter.
10. Install the new filter between the hoses and clamp.
11. Tighten the clamps to 1 N.m (10 in. lbs.).
12. Position the filter assembly on the fuel rail.
13. Tighten the mounting screw to 8 N.m (75 in. lbs.)

PCV Valve

2.2L, 2.5L, and 3.0L Engines

Crankcase vapors and piston blow-by are removed from the engine by intake manifold vacuum. The emissions are drawn through the PCV valve (usually located in the top of the engine valve cover) into the intake manifold where they become part of the air/fuel mixture. Crankcase vapors are then burned and pass through the exhaust system. When there are not enough vapors or blow-by pressure in the engine, air is drawn from the air cleaner. With this system no outside air enters the crankcase.

The PCV valve is used to control the rate at which crankcase vapors are returned to the intake manifold. The action of the valve plunger is controlled by intake manifold vacuum and the spring. During deceleration and idle, when manifold vacuum is high, it overcomes the tension of the valve spring and the plunger bottoms in the manifold end of the valve housing. Because of the valve construction, it reduces, but does not stop, the passage of vapors to the

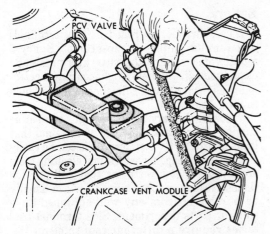

2.2L engine crankcase module and PCV valve

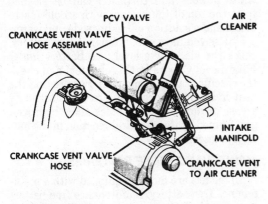

2.5L PCV system

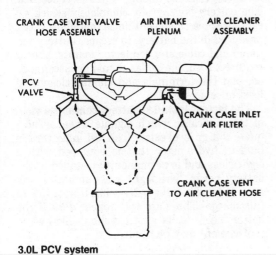

3.0L PCV system

2.6L Engine

Intake manifold vacuum draws air from the air cleaner through the valve cover into the engine, the outside air is mixed with crankcase vapors and piston blow-by and drawn through the PCV valve (located in the top end of the engine cover) and into the intake manifold where it becomes part of the air/fuel mixture. The vapors are burned and expelled with exhaust gases.

TESTING

1. Place the vehicle in Park, or Neutral (if manual transaxle). Set the parking brake and block the wheels.
2. Start the engine and allow to idle until normal operating temperature is reached.
3. With the engine idling, remove the PCV valve, with hose attached, from its rubber molded connector.
4. When the PCV valve is free of its mounting, a hissing noise will be heard and a strong vacuum felt when a finger is placed over the valve inlet. When the engine is turned off, the valve should rattle when shaken. If the valve is not operating properly it must be replaced.

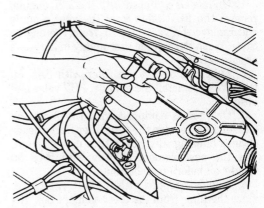

Checking for vacuum at PCV valve

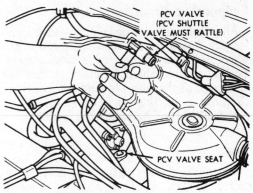

To be considered serviceable, the PCV valve must rattle when shaken

intake manifold. When the engine is lightly accelerated or operated at constant speed, spring tension matches intake manifold vacuum pull and the plunger takes a mid-position in the valve body, allowing more vapors to flow into the manifold.

REMOVAL AND INSTALLATION

1. With the engine off, clean PCV valve area with a suitable solvent.

2. Remove the PCV valve from the mounting grommet on the top cover (2.6L, 2.5L, and 3.0L) or from the vent module (2.2L) engines. Disconnect the hose from the valve.

3. Examine the vacuum hose and replace if the hose is cracked, broken or dried out. Always check the vent hose for clogging. If clogged, replace or clean as necessary.

4. Install a new PCV valve into the hose and install into mounting grommet.

Crankcase Vent Filter

All engines are equipped with a crankcase vent filter which is used to filter the outside air before it enters the PCV system. The filter is located in the air cleaner housing on 2.6L and 2.5L, or in the vent module on 2.2L engines. The filter is located inside the filter element box on 3.0L engines. Replacement should be performed every 52,000 miles.

VENT FILTER SERVICE

1. On models equipped with the 2.2L engine, remove the PCV valve from the vent module and remove the vent module from the engine cover. Wash the module thoroughly in kerosene or safe solvent.

2. Lubricate or wet the filter with SAE 30 weight oil. Reinstall the module, PCV valve and hose.

3. On models equipped with the 2.5L and 2.6L engine, remove the vent filter from the air cleaner housing. Replace with a new element. Wet the new element slightly with SAE 30 weight oil before installation.

4. Models equipped with the 3.0L engine, remove the filter from the filter element box. Renew filter.

Evaporative Charcoal Canister

All vehicles are equipped with a sealed, maintenance free charcoal canister, located in the wheel well area of the engine compartment. Fuel vapors, from the carburetor float chamber and from the gas tank, are temporarily held in the canister until they can be drawn into the intake manifold and burned in the engine.

SERVICE

Periodic inspection of the vent hoses is required. Replace any hoses that are cracked, torn or become hard. Use only fuel resistant hose if replacement becomes necessary.

Battery

Loose, dirty, or corroded battery terminals are a major cause of "no-start." Every 3 months or so, remove the battery terminals and clean them, giving them a light coating of petroleum jelly when you are finished. This will help to retard corrosion.

Check the battery cables for signs of wear or chafing and replace any cable or terminal that looks marginal. Battery terminals can be easily cleaned and inexpensive terminal cleaning tools are an excellent investment that will pay for themselves many times over. They can usually be purchased from any well-equipped auto store or parts department. Side terminal batteries require a different tool to clean the threads in the battery case. The accumulated white powder and corrosion can be cleaned from the top of the battery with an old toothbrush and a solution of baking soda and water.

Unless you have a maintenance-free battery, check the electrolyte level (see Battery under Fluid Level Checks in this chapter) and check the specific gravity of each cell. Be sure that the vent holes in each cell cap are not blocked by grease or dirt. The vent holes allow hydrogen gas, formed by the chemical reaction in the battery, to escape safely.

MAINTENANCE FREE BATTERIES

All models are factory equipped with a maintenance free battery. Maintenance free batteries are as the name implies, totally free of maintenance as far as adding water is concerned. The battery is generally completely sealed except for some small vent holes that allow gases, produced in the battery, to escape. Battery terminal and cable end connector maintenance is required. Also, the cables should be disconnected, and the terminals and clamps cleaned at least once a year.

The factory installed battery contains a visual test indicator which signals when an adequate charge level exists. The test indicator is a built-in hydrometer that is equipped with a sight glass and is permanently installed in the battery cover. The sight glass indicator will show green when the battery has from a 75% to full charge. The glass will appear dark if the battery needs recharging and show yellow when replacement may be needed.

The battery is equipped with a built-in test indicator

CAUTION: *Batteries contain electrolyte, a mixture of sulphuric acid and distilled water. The use of adequate eye protection, and a suitable pair of rubber gloves is strongly recommended when working with batteries. In any event, if battery acid comes in contact with the skin or eyes, flush the affected area with plenty of clear water, and seek medical attention.*

REPLACEMENT BATTERIES (EXCEPT MAINTENANCE FREE)

If a replacement battery of the non-maintenance free type has been installed in your vehicle, be sure to check the fluid level at least once a month. During warm weather or during periods of extended service, more frequent checking is necessary.

The fluid level can be checked through the case on translucent polypropylene batteries. The cell caps must be removed on other styles. The fluid (electrolyte) level should be kept filled to the split ring inside each cell filler opening, or to the line marked or molded on the outside of the battery case.

If the fluid level is low, add water (distilled water only) through the top openings until the correct level is reached. Each cell is separated and must be checked and filled individually.

If water is added in freezing weather, the vehicle should be driven several miles to allow the water to mix with the electrolyte.

SPECIFIC GRAVITY (EXCEPT MAINTENANCE FREE BATTERIES)

At least once a year, check the specific gravity of the battery. It should be between 1.20 in.Hg and 1.26 in.Hg at room temperature.

The specific gravity can be check with the use of a hydrometer, an inexpensive instrument available from many sources, including auto parts stores. The hydrometer has a squeeze bulb at one end and a nozzle at the other. Battery electrolyte is sucked into the hydrometer until the float is lifted from its seat. The specific gravity is then read by noting the position of the float. Generally, if after charging, the specific gravity between any two cells varies more than 50 points (0.50), the battery is bad and should be replaced.

It is not possible to check the specific gravity in this manner on sealed (maintenance free) batteries. Instead, the indicator built into the top of the case must be relied on to display any signs of battery deterioration. Refer to section marked "MAINTENANCE FREE BATTERIES".

CABLES AND CLAMPS

Once a year, the battery terminals and the cable clamps should be cleaned. Loosen the clamps and remove the cables, negative cable first. On batteries with posts on top, the use of a puller specially made for the purpose is recommended. These are inexpensive, and available in auto parts stores. Side terminal battery cables are secured with a bolt.

Clean the cable lamps and the battery terminal with a wire brush, until all corrosion, grease, etc., is removed and the metal is shiny. It is especially important to clean the inside of the clamp thoroughly, since a small deposit of foreign material or oxidation there will prevent a sound electrical connection and inhibit either starting or charging. Special tools are available for cleaning these parts, one type for conventional batteries and another type for side terminal batteries.

Before installing the cables, loosen the battery holddown clamp or strap, remove the battery and check the battery tray. Clear it of any debris, and check it for soundness. Rust should be wire brushed away, and the metal given a coat of anti-rust paint. Replace the battery and tighten the holddown clamp or strap securely, but be careful not to overtighten, which will crack the battery case.

After the clamps and terminals are clean, reinstall the cables, negative cable last; do not hammer on the clamps to install. Tighten the clamps securely, but do not distort them. Give the clamps and terminals a thin external coat of grease after installation, to retard corrosion.

Check the cables at the same time that the terminals are cleaned. If the cable insulation is

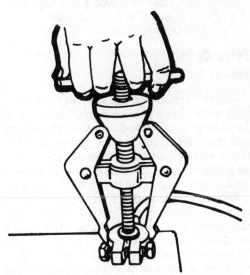

A small puller will easily remove the cable from the terminals

Clean the inside of the terminal clamp

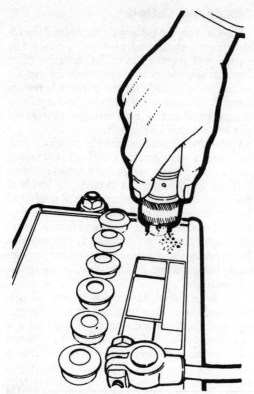

An inexpensive tool easily cleans the battery terminals

cracked or broken, or if the ends are frayed, the cable should be replaced with a new cable of the same length and gauge.

CAUTION: *Keep flame or sparks away from the battery; it gives off explosive hydrogen gas. Battery electrolyte contains sulphuric acid. If you should splash any on your skin or in your eyes, flush the affected area with plenty of clear water. If it lands in your eyes, get medical help immediately.*

Drive Belts
INSPECTION

Check the condition and tension of all drive belts every 12,000 miles, or at least once a year. Loose drive belts can lead to poor engine cooling and diminished alternator, power steering pump, air conditioning compressor, or emission air pump output. A belt that is too tight places a strain on the bearings in the driven component.

Replace any drive belt that is glazed, worn, cracked, or stretched to the point where correct adjustment tension is impossible. If two belts are used to drive a component, always replace both belts when replacement is necessary. After installing a new belt, run the engine for ten minutes, shut off the engine and recheck the belt tension. Readjust if necessary.

CHECKING DRIVE BELT ADJUSTMENT

Two popular methods of checking drive belt adjustment are; the Belt Tension Gauge Method and the Belt Deflection Method. The former requires a special gauge and the latter requires a straight edge and scale or just a good eye for measurement. The deflection method will be used in the following belt replacement instructions. A rule of thumb for checking belt tension by the deflection method is to determine the midpoint between two pulleys of the drive belt and press down at that point with moderate thumb pressure. The belt should deflect to the measurement indicated in the following installation procedures. Adjustment is necessary if the belt is either too loose or too tight.

REMOVAL AND INSTALLATION

NOTE: *Jack up the front of the vehicle, support on jackstands and remove the lower splash shield if access is hampered due to space limitations when changing drive belts.*

A/C Compressor Drive Belt 2.2L Engine

1. Loosen the idler pulley bracket pivot screw and the locking screw.
2. Remove the belt and install replacement.
3. Using a breaker bar and socket apply torque to welded nut provided on the mounted bracket to obtain proper tension.
4. Tighten the locking screw first, followed by pivot screw. Tighten to 40 ft. lbs.

Alternator Drive Belt 2.2L Engines (Chrysler Type)

If removal of the alternator belt is required, the A/C belt must first be removed.

1. Loosen the pivot nut, locking screw, and the adjusting screw.

2. Remove the belt and install replacement.

3. Adjust to specification by tightening the adjusting screw.

4. Tighten the locking screw to 25 ft. lbs.

5. Tighten the pivot nut to 30 ft. lbs.

2.2L Engine BELTS—TENSION CHART and REMOVE/INSTALL-ADJUST

Accessory Drive Belt		Gauge	Deflection	Torque
Air Conditioning Compressor	New	105 lb.	8mm (5/16 in.)	54 N·m (40 ft. lbs.)
	Used	80 lb.	9mm (7/16 in.)	41 N·m (30 ft. lbs.)
Air Pump	New	—	5mm (3/16 in.)	61 N·m (45 ft. lbs.)
	Used	—	6mm (1/4 in.)	47 N·m (35 ft. lbs.)
Alternator/Water Pump "V" Belt and Poly "V"	New	115 lb.	3mm (1/8 in.)	149 N·m (110 ft. lbs.)
	Used	80 lb.	6mm (1/4 in.)	108 N·m (80 ft. lbs.)
Power Steering Pump	New	105 lb.	6mm (1/4 in.)	102 N·m (75 ft. lbs.)
	Used	80 lb.	11mm (7/16 in.)	75 N·m (55 ft. lbs.)

2.2L engine belt tension chart

2.5L Engine BELTS—TENSION CHART and REMOVE/INSTALL-ADJUST

Accessory Drive Belt		Gauge	Deflection	Torque
Air Conditioning Compressor	New	105 lb.	8mm (5/16 in.)	54 N·m (40 ft. lbs.)
	Used	80 lb.	11mm (7/16 in.)	41 N·m (30 ft. lbs.)
Alternator/Water Pump Poly "V"	New	115 lb.	3mm (1/8 in.)	149 N·m (110 ft. lbs.)
	Used	80 lb.	6mm (1/4 in.)	108 N·m (80 ft. lbs.)
Power Steering Pump	New	105 lb.	6mm (1/4 in.)	102 N·m (75 ft. lbs.)
	Used	80 lb.	11mm (7/16 in.)	75 N·m (55 ft. lbs.)

2.5L engine belt tension chart

2.6L Engine BELTS-TENSION CHART and REMOVE/INSTALL-ADJUST

Accessory Drive Belt		Gauge	Deflection	Torque
Power Steering Pump	New	95 lb.	6mm (1/4 in.)	149 N·m (110 ft. lbs.)
	Used	80 lb.	9mm (3/8 in.)	102 N·m (75 ft. lbs.)
Alternator	New	115 lb.	4mm (3/16 in.)	—
	Used	80 lb.	6mm (1/4 in.)	—
Alternator/Air Conditioning Compressor	New	115 lb.	6mm (1/4 in.)	—
	Used	80 lb.	8mm (5/16 in.)	—
Water Pump	New	—	8mm (5/16 in.)	—
	Used	—	9mm (3/8 in.)	—

2.6L engine belt tension chart

3.0L Engine BELTS—TENSION CHART and REMOVE/INSTALL-ADJUST

Accessory Drive Belt		Gauge	Deflection
Air Conditioning Compressor	New	125 lb.	8mm (5/16 in.)
	Used	80 lb.	8mm (5/16 in.)
Alternator/Water Pump/ Power Steering Pump	New		
	Used	Dynamic Tensioner	

3.0L engine belt tension chart

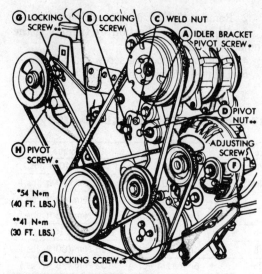

2.2L drive belt adjusting points

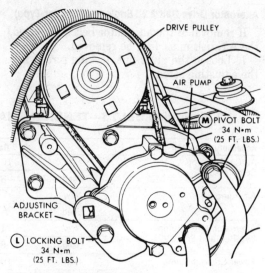

2.2L air pump belt adjustment

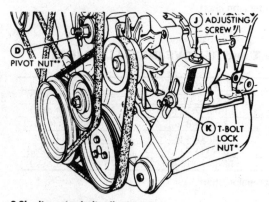

2.2L alternator belt adjustment

Alternator Belt 2.2L Engines (Bosch Type)

If removal of the alternator belt is required, the A/C belt must first be removed.

1. Loosen the pivot nut, locking nut, and adjusting screw.
2. Remove the belt and install replacement.
3. Adjust to specification by tightening the adjusting screw.
4. Tighten the locking nut to 25 ft. lbs.
5. Tighten the pivot nut to 30 ft. lbs.

Power Steering Belt 2.2L Engine

If removal of the power steering belt is required, the A/C and alternator belts must first be removed.

1. Loosen the locking screw, and pivot screw.
2. Remove the belt and install replacement.
3. Install a ½" breaker bar into the pump bracket slot, apply pressure with the breaker bar and adjust the belt to specification.
4. Tighten the locking screw first, then the pivot screw. Tighten to 40 ft. lbs.

Air Pump — 2.2L Engine

NOTE: *When servicing the air pump, use the square holes provided in the pulley to prevent camshaft rotation.*

1. Remove the nuts and bolts retaining the drive pulley cover.
2. Remove the locking bolt and pivot bolt from the pump bracket, and remove the pump.
3. Remove the belt and install replacement.
4. Position the pump, and install the locking bolt and pivot bolt finger tight.
5. Install a ½" breaker bar into the bracket assembly (block the drive pulley to prevent camshaft rotation), and adjust the belt to specification.
6. Tighten locking bolt and pivot bolt to 25 ft. lbs.

Air Conditioning Compressor — 2.5L Engine

1. Loosen the idler bracket pivot screw and the locking screws to replace, or adjust belt.
2. Remove the belt and install replacement.
3. Adjust the belt to specification by applying torque to weld nut on the idler bracket.
4. Tighten locking screw first, followed by the pivot screw. Tighten to 40 ft. lbs.

Alternator Belt 2.5L Engine

If replacement of the alternator belt is required, the A/C drive belt must first be removed.

1. Loosen the pivot nut, locking nut, and adjusting screw.
2. Remove the belt and install replacement.
3. Adjust the belt to specification by tightening the adjusting screw.
4. Tighten the locking nut to 25 ft. lbs.
5. Tighten the pivot nut to 30 ft. lbs.

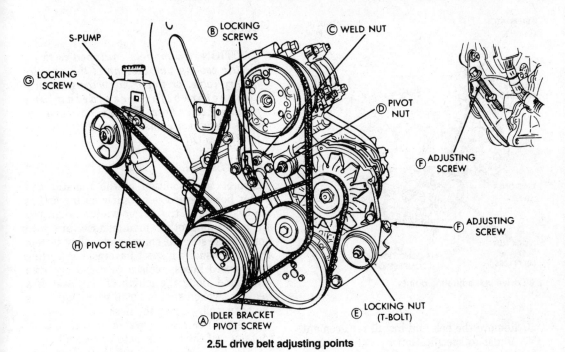

2.5L drive belt adjusting points

Power Steering Pump 2.5L Engines

If replacement of the power steering belt is required, the A/C and alternator belts must first be remove.

1. Loosen the locking screw and pivot screw to replace, or adjust the belt.

2. Remove the belt and install replacement.

3. Using a ½" breaker bar positioned in adjusting bracket slot, adjust the belt to specification.

4. Tighten the locking screw followed by the pivot screw. Tighten to 40 ft. lbs.

Alternator/Air Condition Compressor – 2.6L Engine

1. Loosen the locking screw, jam nut, and pivot nut.

2. Loosen the adjusting screw.

3. Remove the belt and install replacement.

4. Adjust the belt to specification by tightening the adjusting screw.

5. Tighten the locking screw followed by the pivot nut. Tighten to 195 in. lbs.

6. Tighten the jam nut to 250 in. lbs.

Power Steering Pump Belt 2.6L Engines

If replacement of the power steering belt is required, the alternator and A/C belt must first be remove.

1. Loosen the pivot screw, and the locking screw.

2. Remove the timing pickup.

3. Remove the belt and install replacement.

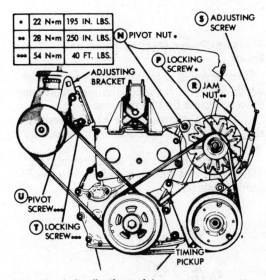

•	22 N•m	195 IN. LBS.
••	28 N•m	250 IN. LBS.
•••	54 N•m	40 FT. LBS.

2.6L drive belt adjusting points

4. Install a ½" breaker bar in the adjusting bracket slot, torque to specification.

5. Tighten the locking screw, followed by the pivot screw. Tighten to 40 ft. lbs.

6. Install the timing pick-up, and tighten to 160 in. lbs.

Air Conditioning Compressor Belt – 3.0L Engine

1. Loosen the locknut on the idler pulley.

2. Loosen the adjusting screw on the idler pulley.

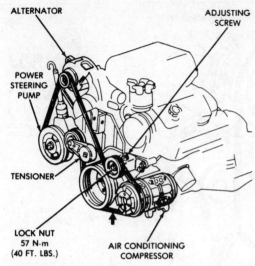

3.0L drive belt adjusting points

3. Remove the belt and install replacement.

4. Adjust to specification by tightening the adjusting screw.

5. Tighten the idler pulley locknut to 40 ft. lbs.

Alternator/Power Steering Pump Belt — 3.0L Engine

If replacement of the alternator/power steering drive belt is required, the air conditioner drive belt must first be removed.

1. Install a ½" breaker bar into the tensioner slot, and rotate counterclockwise to release belt tension.

2. Remove the belt and install replacement.

3. Proper belt tension is maintain by the dynamic tensioner.

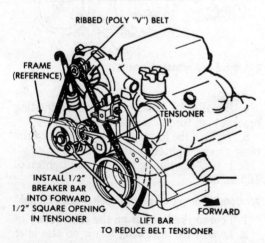

3.0L belt tensioner release

Hoses

CAUTION: *On models equipped with an electric cooling fan, disconnect the negative battery cable, or fan motor wiring harness connector before replacing any radiator/heater hose. The fan may come on, under certain circumstances, even though the ignition is Off.*

REPLACEMENT

Inspect the condition of the radiator and heater hoses periodically. Early spring and at the beginning of the fall or winter, when you are performing other maintenance, are good times. Make sure the engine and cooling system are cold. Visually inspect for cracking, rotting or collapsed hoses, replace as necessary. Run your hand along the length of the hose. If a weak or swollen spot is noted when squeezing the hose wall, replace the hose.

1. Drain the cooling system into a suitable container (if the coolant is to be reused).

CAUTION: *When draining the coolant, keep in mind that cats and dogs are attracted by the ethylene glycol antifreeze, and are quite likely to drink any that is left in an uncovered container or in puddles on the ground. This will prove fatal in sufficient quantity. Always drain the coolant into a sealable container. Coolant should be reused unless it is contaminated or several years old.*

2. Loosen the hose clamps at each end of the hose that requires replacement.

3. Twist, pull and slide the hose off the radiator, water pump, thermostat or heater connection.

4. Clean the hose mounting connections. Position the hose clamps on the new hose.

5. Coat the connection surfaces with a water resistant sealer and slide the hose into position. Make sure the hose clamps are located beyond the raised bead of the connector (if equipped) and centered in the clamping area of the connection.

6. Tighten the clamps to 20-30 in.lb. Do not overtighten.

7. Fill the cooling system.

8. Start the engine and allow it to reach normal operating temperature. Check for leaks.

Air Conditioning
GENERAL SERVICING PROCEDURES

The most important aspect of air conditioning service is the maintenance of pure and adequate charge of refrigerant in the system. A refrigeration system cannot function properly if a significant percentage of the charge is lost.

HOW TO SPOT WORN V-BELTS

V-Belts are vital to efficient engine operation—they drive the fan, water pump and other accessories. They require little maintenance (occasional tightening) but they will not last forever. Slipping or failure of the V-belt will lead to overheating. If your V-belt looks like any of these, it should be replaced.

Cracking or weathering

This belt has deep cracks, which cause it to flex. Too much flexing leads to heat build-up and premature failure. These cracks can be caused by using the belt on a pulley that is too small. Notched belts are available for small diameter pulleys.

Softening (grease and oil)

Oil and grease on a belt can cause the belt's rubber compounds to soften and separate from the reinforcing cords that hold the belt together. The belt will first slip, then finally fail altogether.

Glazing

Glazing is caused by a belt that is slipping. A slipping belt can cause a run-down battery, erratic power steering, overheating or poor accessory performance. The more the belt slips, the more glazing will be built up on the surface of the belt. The more the belt is glazed, the more it will slip. If the glazing is light, tighten the belt.

Worn cover

The cover of this belt is worn off and is peeling away. The reinforcing cords will begin to wear and the belt will shortly break. When the belt cover wears in spots or has a rough jagged appearance, check the pulley grooves for roughness.

Separation

This belt is on the verge of breaking and leaving you stranded. The layers of the belt are separating and the reinforcing cords are exposed. It's just a matter of time before it breaks completely.

Leaks are common because the severe vibration encountered in an automobile can easily cause a sufficient cracking or loosening of the air conditioning fittings. As a result, the extreme operating pressures of the system force refrigerant out.

The problem can be understood by considering what happens to the system as it is operated with a continuous leak. Because the expansion valve regulates the flow of refrigerant to the evaporator, the level of refrigerant there is fairly constant. The receiver/drier stores any excess of refrigerant, and so a loss will first appear there as a reduction in the level of liquid. As this level nears the bottom of the vessel, some refrigerant vapor bubbles will begin to appear in the stream of liquid supplied to the expansion valve. This vapor decreases the capacity of the expansion valve very little as the valve opens to compensate for its presence. As the quantity of liquid in the condenser decreases, the operating pressure will drop there and throughout the high side of the system. As the R-12 continues to be expelled, the pressure available to force the liquid through the expansion valve will continue to decrease, and, eventually, the valve's orifice will prove to be too much of a restriction for adequate flow even with the needle fully withdrawn.

At this point, low side pressure will start to drop, and severe reduction in cooling capacity, marked by freeze-up of the evaporator coil, will result. Eventually, the operating pressure of the evaporator will be lower than the pressure of the atmosphere surrounding it, and air will be drawn into the system wherever there are leaks in the low side.

Because all atmospheric air contains at least some moisture, water will enter the system and mix with the R-12 and the oil. Trace amounts of moisture will cause sludging of the oil, and corrosion of the system. Saturation and clogging of the filter/drier, and freezing of the expansion valve orifice will eventually result. As air fills the system to a greater and greater extend, it will interfere more and more with the normal flows of refrigerant and heat.

A list of general precautions that should be observed while doing this follows:

1. Keep all tools as clean and dry as possible.
2. Thoroughly purge the service gauges and hoses of air and moisture before connecting them to the system. Keep them capped when not in use.
3. Thoroughly clean any refrigerant fitting before disconnecting it, in order to minimize the entrance of dirt into the system.
4. Plan any operation that requires opening the system beforehand in order to minimize the length of time it will be exposed to open air. Cap or seal the open ends to minimize the entrance of foreign material.
5. When adding oil, pour it through an extremely clean and dry tube or funnel. Keep the oil capped whenever possible. Do not use oil that has not been kept tightly sealed.
6. Use only refrigerant 12. Purchase refrigerant intended for use in only automotive air conditioning system. Avoid the use of refrigerant 12 that may be packaged for another use, such as cleaning, or powering a horn, as it is impure.
7. Completely evacuate any system that has been opened to replace a component, other than when isolating the compressor, or that has leaked sufficiently to draw in moisture and air. This requires evacuating air and moisture with a good vacuum pump for at least one hour.

If a system has been open for a considerable length of time it may be advisable to evacuate the system for up to 12 hours (overnight).
8. Use a wrench on both halves of a fitting that is to be disconnected, so as to avoid placing torque on any of the refrigerant lines.

ADDITIONAL PREVENTIVE MAINTENANCE CHECKS

Antifreeze

In order to prevent heater core freeze-up during A/C operation, it is necessary to maintain permanent type antifreeze protection of +15°F (–9°C) or lower. A reading of –15°F (–26°C) is ideal since this protection also supplies sufficient corrosion inhibitors for the protection of the engine cooling system.

WARNING: *Do not use antifreeze longer than specified by the manufacturer.*

Radiator Cap

For efficient operation of an air conditioned van's cooling system, the radiator cap should have a holding pressure which meets manufacturer's specifications. A cap which fails to hold these pressure should be replaced.

Condenser

Any obstruction of or damage to the condenser configuration will restrict the air flow which is essential to its efficient operation. It is therefore, a good rule to keep this unit clean and in proper physical shape.

NOTE: *Bug screens are regarded as obstructions.*

Condensation Drain Tube

This single molded drain tube expels the condensation, which accumulates on the bottom of the evaporator housing, into the engine compartment.

HOW TO SPOT BAD HOSES

Both the upper and lower radiator hoses are called upon to perform difficult jobs in an inhospitable environment. They are subject to nearly 18 psi at under hood temperatures often over 280°F., and must circulate nearly 7500 gallons of coolant an hour—3 good reasons to have good hoses.

A good test for any hose is to feel it for soft or spongy spots. Frequently these will appear as swollen areas of the hose. The most likely cause is oil soaking. This hose could burst at any time, when hot or under pressure.

Swollen hose

Cracked hoses can usually be seen but feel the hoses to be sure they have not hardened; a prime cause of cracking. This hose has cracked down to the reinforcing cords and could split at any of the cracks.

Cracked hose

Weakened clamps frequently are the cause of hose and cooling system failure. The connection between the pipe and hose has deteriorated enough to allow coolant to escape when the engine is hot.

Frayed hose end (due to weak clamp)

Debris, rust and scale in the cooling system can cause the inside of a hose to weaken. This can usually be felt on the outside of the hose as soft or thinner areas.

Debris in cooling system

If this tube is obstructed, the air conditioning performance can be restricted and condensation buildup can spill over onto the vehicle's floor.

SAFETY PRECAUTIONS

Because of the importance of the necessary safety precautions that must be exercised when working with air conditioning systems and R-12 refrigerant, a recap of the safety precautions are outlined.

1. Avoid contact with a charged refrigeration system, even when working on another part of the air conditioning system or vehicle. If a heavy tool comes into contact with a section of copper tubing or a heat exchanger, it can easily cause the relatively soft material to rupture.

2. When it is necessary to apply force to a fitting which contains refrigerant, as when checking that all system couplings are securely tightened, use a wrench on both parts of the fitting involved, if possible. This will avoid putting torque on the refrigerant tubing. (It is advisable, when possible, to use tube or line wrenches when tightening these flare nut fittings.)

3. Do not attempt to discharge the system by merely loosening a fitting, or removing the service valve caps and cracking these valves. Precise control is possibly only when using the service gauges. Place a rag under the open end of the center charging hose while discharging the system to catch any drops of liquid that might escape. Wear protective gloves when connecting or disconnecting service gauge hoses.

4. Discharge the system only in a well ventilated area, as high concentrations of the gas can exclude oxygen and act as an anesthetic. When leak testing or soldering this is particularly important, as toxic gas is formed when R-12 contacts any flame.

5. Never start a system without first verifying that both service valves are backseated, if equipped, and that all fittings are throughout the system are snugly connected.

6. Avoid applying heat to any refrigerant line or storage vessel. Charging may be aided by using water heated to less than 125°F (52°C) to warm the refrigerant container. Never allow a refrigerant storage container to sit out in the sun, or near any other source of heat, such as a radiator.

7. Always wear goggles when working on a system to protect the eyes. If refrigerant contacts the eye, it is advisable in all cases to see a physician as soon as possible.

8. Frostbite from liquid refrigerant should be treated by first gradually warming the area with cool water, and then gently applying petroleum jelly. A physician should be consulted.

9. Always keep refrigerant can fittings capped when not in use. Avoid sudden shock to the can which might occur from dropping it, or from banging a heavy tool against it. Never carry a refrigerant can in the passenger compartment of a van.

10. Always completely discharge the system before painting the vehicle (if the paint is to be baked on), or before welding anywhere near the refrigerant lines.

TEST GAUGES

Most of the service work performed in air conditioning requires the use of a set of two gauges, one for the high (head) pressure side of the system, the other for the low (suction) side.

The low side gauge records both pressure and vacuum. Vacuum readings are calibrated from 0 to 30 inches Hg and the pressure graduations read from 0 to no less than 150 psi.

The high side gauge measures pressure from 0 to at least 300 psi.

With the gauge set you can perform the following procedures:

1. Test high and low side pressures.
2. Remove air, moisture, and contaminated refrigerant.
3. Purge the system of refrigerant.
4. Charge the system with refrigerant.

Gauge sets used on the older RV-2 compressors must be equipped with 3 gauges: 2 compound gauges (suction and inlet) and 1 discharge pressure gauge.

Gauge sets used on the newer C-171 compressor have 2 gauges: 1 compound gauge for suction and 1 discharge pressure gauge.

All gauge sets must have 3 hoses, with 1 being for center manifold outlet.

WARNING: *When connecting the hoses to the compressor service ports, the manifold gauge valves must be closed!*

The suction gauge valve is opened to provide a passage between the suction gauge and the center manifold outlet. The discharge gauge valve is opened to provide a passage between the discharge pressure gauge and the center manifold outlet.

INSPECTION

CAUTION: *The compressed refrigerant used in the air conditioning system expands into the atmosphere at a temperature of –21.7°F (–30°C) or lower. This will freeze any surface, including your eyes, that it contacts. In addition, the refrigerant decomposes into a poisonous gas in the presence of a flame. Do not open or disconnect any part of the air conditioning system.*

Sight Glass Check

You can safely make a few simple checks to determine if your air conditioning system needs service. The tests work best if the temperature is warm (about 70°F [21.1°C]).

NOTE: *If your vehicle is equipped with an aftermarket air conditioner, the following system check may not apply. You should contact the manufacturer of the unit for instructions on systems checks.*

1. Place the automatic transmission in Park or the manual transmission in Neutral. Set the parking brake.

2. Run the engine at a fast idle (about 1,500 rpm) either with the help of a friend or by temporarily readjusting the idle speed screw.

3. Set the controls for maximum cold with the blower on High.

4. Locate the sight glass in one of the system lines. Usually it is on the left alongside the top of the radiator.

5. If you see bubbles, the system must be recharged. Very likely there is a leak at some point.

6. If there are no bubbles, there is either no refrigerant at all or the system is fully charged. Feel the two hoses going to the belt driven compressor. If they are both at the same temperature, the system is empty and must be recharged.

7. If one hose (high pressure) is warm and the other (low pressure) is cold, the system may be all right. However, you are probably making these tests because you think there is something wrong, so proceed to the next step.

8. Have an assistant in the van turn the fan control on and off to operate the compressor clutch. Watch the sight glass.

9. If bubbles appear when the clutch is disengaged and disappear when it is engaged, the system is properly charged.

10. If the refrigerant takes more than 45 seconds to bubble when the clutch is disengaged, the system is overcharged. This usually causes poor cooling at low speeds.

WARNING: *If it is determined that the system has a leak, it should be corrected as soon as possible. Leaks may allow moisture to enter and cause a very expensive rust problem.*

Exercise the air conditioner for a few minutes, every two weeks or so, during the cold months. This avoids the possibility of the compressor seals drying out from lack of lubrication.

TESTING THE SYSTEM

1. Connect a gauge set.

2. Close (clockwise) both gauge set valves.

3. Park the van in the shade, at least 5 feet from any walls. Start the engine, set the parking brake, place the transmission in **N** and establish an idle of 1100–1300 rpm.

4. Run the air conditioning system for full cooling, in the **MAX** or **COLD** mode.

5. The low pressure gauge should read 5-20 psi; the high pressure gauge should indicate 120–180 psi.

WARNING: *These pressures are the norm for an ambient temperature of 70-80°F (21-27°C). Higher air temperatures along with high humidity will cause higher syustem pressures. At idle speed and an ambient temperature of 110°F (43°C), the high pressure reading can exceed 300 psi.*

Under these extreme conditions, you can keep the pressures down by directing a large electric floor fan through the condenser.

DISCHARGING THE SYSTEM

1. Remove the caps from the high and low pressure charging valves in the high and low pressure lines.

2. Turn both manifold gauge set hand valves to the fully closed (clockwise) position.

3. Connect the manifold gauge set.

4. If the van does not have a service access gauge port valve, connect the gauge set low pressure hose to the evaporator service access gauge port valve.

5. Place the end of the center hose away from you and the van, preferably into a container such as an old coffee can to catch the refrigerant oil.

6. Open the low pressure gauge valve slightly and allow the system pressure to bleed off.

7. Whe the system is just about empty, open the high pressure valve very slowly to avoid losing an excessive amount of refrigerant oil. Allow any remaining refrigerant to escape.

EVACUATING THE SYSTEM

NOTE: *This procedure requires the use of a vacuum pump.*

1. Connect the manifold gauge set.

2. Discharge the system.

3. Make sure that the low pressure gauge set hose is connected to the low pressure service gauge port on the top center of the accumulator/drier assembly and the high pressure hose connected to the high pressure service gauge port on the compressor discharge line.

4. Connect the center service hose to the inlet fitting of the vacuum pump.

5. Turn both gauge set valves to the wide open position.

6. Start the pump and note the low side gauge reading.

7. Operate the pump until the low pressure gauge reads 25-30 in.Hg. Continue running the vacuum pump for 10 minutes more. If you've replaced some component in the system, run the pump for an additional 20-30 minutes.

8. Leak test the system. Close both gauge set valves. Turn off the pump. The needle should remain stationary at the point at which the pump was turned off. If the needle drops to zero rapidly, there is a leak in the system which must be repaired.

LEAK TESTING

Some leak tests can be performed with a soapy water solution. There must be at least a ½ lb. charge in the system for a leak to be detected. The most extensive leak tests are performed with either a Halide flame type leak tester or the more preferable electronic leak tester.

In either case, the equipment is expensive, and, the use of a Halide detector can be **extremely** hazardous!

CHARGING THE SYSTEM

CAUTION: *NEVER OPEN THE HIGH PRESSURE SIDE WITH A CAN OF REFRIGERANT CONNECTED TO THE SYSTEM! OPENING THE HIGH PRESSURE SIDE WILL OVERPRESSURIZE THE CAN, CAUSING IT TO EXPLODE!*

1. Connect the gauge set.

2. Close (clockwise) both gauge set valves.

3. Connect the center hose to the refrigerant can opener valve.

4. Make sure the can opener valve is closed, that is, the needle is raised, and connect the valve to the can. Open the valve, puncturing the can with the needle.

5. Loosen the center hose fitting at the pressure gauge, allowing refrigerant to purge the hose of air. When the air is bled, tighten the fitting.

CAUTION: *IF THE LOW PRESSURE GAUGE SET HOSE IS NOT CONNECTED TO THE ACCUMULATOR/DRIER, KEEP THE CAN IN AN UPRIGHT POSITION!*

6. Start the engine and move the air conditioning controls to the low blower position.

7. Open the low side gauge set valve and the can valve.

8. Allow refrigerant to be drawn into the system. Adjust the valve so that charging pressure does not exceed 50 psi.

NOTE: *The low pressure (cycling) cut-out switch will prevent the compressor clutch from energizing until refrigerant is added to the system. If the clutch does not engage, replace the switch.*

9. When no more refrigerant is drawn into the system, start the engine and run it at about 1,300 rpm. Turn on the system and operate it at the full high position. The compressor will operate and pull refrigerant gas into the system.

NOTE: *To help speed the process, the can may be placed, upright, in a pan of warm water, not exceeding 125°F (52°C).*

10. If more than one can of refrigerant is needed, close the can valve and gauge set low side valve when the can is empty and connect a new can to the opener. Repeat the charging process until the sight glass indicates a full charge. The frost line on the outside of the can will indicate what portion of the can has been used.

CAUTION: *NEVER ALLOW THE HIGH PRESSURE SIDE READING TO EXCEED 240 psi.*

11. When the charging process has been completed, close the gauge set valve and can valve. Remove the jumper wire and reconnect the cycling clutch wire. Run the system for at least five minutes to allow it to normalize. Low pressure side reading should be 4-25 psi; high pressure reading should be 120-210 psi at an ambient temperature of 70-90°F (21-32°C).

12. Loosen both service hoses at the gauges to allow any refrigerant to escape. Remove the gauge set and install the dust caps on the service valves.

NOTE: *Multi-can dispensers are available which allow a simultaneous hook-up of up to four 1 lb. cans of R-12.*

Windshield Wipers

Wiper blades exposed to the weather over a period of time tend to lose their wiping effectiveness. Clean the wiping surface of the blade with a sponge and a mild solution of water and detergent. If the blades continue to smear, they should be replaced with either a new blade or refill.

BLADE REFILLS

1. Turn the wiper switch to the ON position. Turn the ignition switch ON. When the blades reach a convenient place on the windshield, turn the ignition switch to OFF, thus stopping the blades.

2. Lift the wiper arm to raise the blade from the windshield.

3. Insert a small blade type tool into the release slot of wiper blade and pry slightly upward.

4. Pinch lock on each end of blade and slide wiping element out of blade.

5. Install a new wiping element into blade. Make certain each release points are properly locked in position.

Troubleshooting Basic Air Conditioning Problems

Problem	Cause	Solution
There's little or no air coming from the vents (and you're sure it's on)	• The A/C fuse is blown • Broken or loose wires or connections • The on/off switch is defective	• Check and/or replace fuse • Check and/or repair connections • Replace switch
The air coming from the vents is not cool enough	• Windows and air vent wings open • The compressor belt is slipping • Heater is on • Condenser is clogged with debris • Refrigerant has escaped through a leak in the system • Receiver/drier is plugged	• Close windows and vent wings • Tighten or replace compressor belt • Shut heater off • Clean the condenser • Check system • Service system
The air has an odor	• Vacuum system is disrupted • Odor producing substances on the evaporator case • Condensation has collected in the bottom of the evaporator housing	• Have the system checked/repaired • Clean the evaporator case • Clean the evaporator housing drains
System is noisy or vibrating	• Compressor belt or mountings loose • Air in the system	• Tighten or replace belt; tighten mounting bolts • Have the system serviced

Sight glass condition
  Constant bubbles, foam or oil streaks
  Clear sight glass, but no cold air
  Clear sight glass, but air is cold
  Clouded with milky fluid
	
	• Undercharged system
	
	• No refrigerant at all
	• System is OK
	• Receiver drier is leaking dessicant
		
		• Charge the system
		
		• Check and charge the system
		
		• Have system checked

Large difference in temperature of lines	• System undercharged	• Charge and leak test the system
Compressor noise	• Broken valves • Overcharged • Incorrect oil level • Piston slap • Broken rings • Drive belt pulley bolts are loose	• Replace the valve plate • Discharge, evacuate and install the correct charge • Isolate the compressor and check the oil level. Correct as necessary. • Replace the compressor • Replace the compressor • Tighten with the correct torque specification
Excessive vibration	• Incorrect belt tension • Clutch loose • Overcharged • Pulley is misaligned	• Adjust the belt tension • Tighten the clutch • Discharge, evacuate and install the correct charge • Align the pulley
Condensation dripping in the passenger compartment	• Drain hose plugged or improperly positioned • Insulation removed or improperly installed	• Clean the drain hose and check for proper installation • Replace the insulation on the expansion valve and hoses
Frozen evaporator coil	• Faulty thermostat • Thermostat capillary tube improperly installed • Thermostat not adjusted properly	• Replace the thermostat • Install the capillary tube correctly • Adjust the thermostat
Low side low—high side low	• System refrigerant is low • Expansion valve is restricted	• Evacuate, leak test and charge the system • Replace the expansion valve
Low side high—high side low	• Internal leak in the compressor—worn	• Remove the compressor cylinder head and inspect the compressor. Replace the valve plate assembly if necessary. If the compressor pistons, rings or

Troubleshooting Basic Air Conditioning Problems (cont.)

Problem	Cause	Solution
Low side high—high side low (cont.)		cylinders are excessively worn or scored replace the compressor
	• Cylinder head gasket is leaking	• Install a replacement cylinder head gasket
	• Expansion valve is defective	• Replace the expansion valve
	• Drive belt slipping	• Adjust the belt tension
Low side high—high side high	• Condenser fins obstructed	• Clean the condenser fins
	• Air in the system	• Evacuate, leak test and charge the system
	• Expansion valve is defective	• Replace the expansion valve
	• Loose or worn fan belts	• Adjust or replace the belts as necessary
Low side low—high side high	• Expansion valve is defective	• Replace the expansion valve
	• Restriction in the refrigerant hose	• Check the hose for kinks—replace if necessary
	• Restriction in the receiver/drier	• Replace the receiver/drier
	• Restriction in the condenser	• Replace the condenser
Low side and high side normal (inadequate cooling)	• Air in the system	• Evacuate, leak test and charge the system
	• Moisture in the system	• Evacuate, leak test and charge the system

6. Install blade on wiper arm.

Most Anco® styles uses a release button that is pushed down to allow the refill to slide out of the yoke jaws. The new refill slides in and locks in place. Some Trico® refills are removed by locating where the metal backing strip of the refill is wider. Insert a small screwdriver blade between the frame and metal backing strip. Press down to release the refill from the retaining tab.

The Trico® style is unlocked at one end by squeezing 2 metal tabs, and the refill is slide out of the frame jaws. When the new refill is installed, the tabs will click into place, locking the refill.

The polycarbonate type is held in place by a locking lever that is pushed downward out of the groove in the arm to free the refill. When the new refill is installed, it will lock in place automatically.

The Tridon® refill has a plastic backing strip with a notch about an inch from the end. Hold the blade (frame) on a hard surface so that the frame is tightly bowed. Grip the tip of the backing strip and pull up while twisting conterckockwise. The backing strip will snap out of the retaining tab. Do this for the remaining tabs until the refill is free of the arm. The length of these refills is molded into the end and they should be replaced with identical types.

No matter which type of refill you use, be sure that all of the frame claws engage the refill. Before operating the wiper, be sure that no part of the metal frame is contacting the windshield.

Tires and Wheels

TIRE ROTATION

Tires installed on the front or rear of any vehicle are subjected to different loads, breaking, or steering functions. Because of these conditions, tires develop uneven wear patterns. Rotating the tires every 6000 miles or so will result in increased thread life. Use the correct pattern for tire rotation. Refer to Tire Rotation Patterns chart.

Most automotive experts are in agreement that radial tires are better all around performers, giving prolonged wear and better handling. An added benefit which you should consider when purchasing tires is that radials have less rolling resistance and can give up to a 10% increase in fuel economy over a bias-ply tire.

TIRE INFLATION

Check the air pressure in your vehicle's tires every few weeks. Make sure that the tires are cool. Air pressure increases with higher temperature, and will indicate false reading. A decal located on the glovebox door or side doorframe will tell you the proper tire pressure for the standard equipment tires.

NOTE: *Never exceed the maximum inflation pressure on the side of the tire. Also never mixed tires of different size or construction (Belted vs Bias-ply, or Radial vs Belted etc.).*

It pays to buy a tire pressure gauge to keep in your vehicle, since those of service stations are often inaccurate or broken. While you are checking the tire pressure, take a look at the

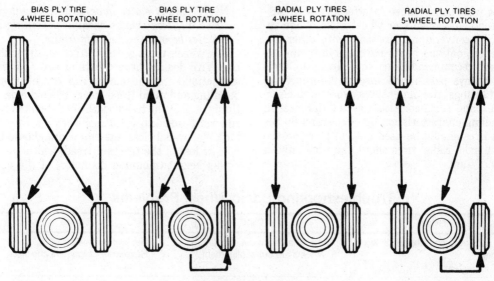

| BIAS PLY TIRE 4-WHEEL ROTATION | BIAS PLY TIRE 5-WHEEL ROTATION | RADIAL PLY TIRES 4-WHEEL ROTATION | RADIAL PLY TIRES 5-WHEEL ROTATION |

Tire rotation patterns

tread. The tread should be wearing evenly across the tire. Excessive wear in the center of the tread indicates overinflation. Excessive wear on the outer edges indicates underinflation. An irregular wear pattern is usually a sign of incorrect front wheel alignment or wheel balance.

A front end that is out of alignment will usually pull to one side when the steering wheel is released. Conditions which relate to front end alignment are associated by tire wear patterns. Tire treads being worn on one side more than the other, or wear on the tread edges may be noticeable. Front wheels which are incorrectly balance, is usually accompanied by high speed vibration.

TIRE ROTATION

It is recommended that you have the tires rotated and the balance checked every 6,000 miles. There is no way to give a tire rotation diagram for every combination of tires and vehicles, but the accompanying diagrams are a general rule to follow. Radial tires should not be cross-switched; they last longer if their direction of rotation is not changed. Truck tires and some high-performance tires sometimes have directional tread, indicated by arrows on the sidewalls; the arrow shows the direction of rotation. They will wear very rapidly if reversed. Studded snow tires will lose their studs if their direction of rotation is reversed.

NOTE: *Mark the wheel position or direction of rotation on radial tires or studded snow tires before removing them.*

If your van is equipped with tires having different load ratings on the front and the rear,

the tires should not be rotated front to rear. Rotating these tires could affect tire life (the tires with the lower rating will wear faster, and could become overloaded), and upset the handling of the van.

When installing the wheels on the vehicle, tighten the lug nuts in a criss-cross pattern. Lug nuts should be torqued to 85 ft. lbs.

TIRE USAGE

The tires on your van were selected to provide the best all around performance for normal operation when inflated as specified. Oversize tires will not increase the maximum carrying capacity of the vehicle, although they will provide an extra margin of tread life. Be sure to check overall height before using larger size

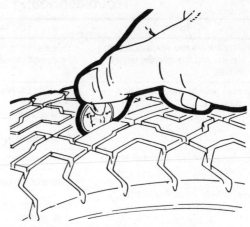

Tread depth can be roughly checked with a Lincoln penny. If the top of Lincoln's head is visible, replace the tires

tires which may cause interference with suspension components or wheel wells. When replacing conventional tire sizes with other tire size designations, be sure to check the manufacturer's recommendations. Interchangeability is not always possible because of differences in load ratings, tire dimensions, wheel well clearances, and rim size. Also due to differences in handling characteristics, 70 Series and 60 Series tires should be used only in pairs on the same axle; radial tires should be used only in sets of four.

NOTE: *Many states have vehicle height restrictions; some states prohibit the lifting of vehicles beyond their design limits.*

The wheels must be the correct width for the tire. Tire dealers have charts of tire and rim compatibility. A mismatch can cause sloppy handling and rapid tread wear. The old rule of thumb is that the tread width should match the rim width (inside bead to inside bead) within an inch. For radial tires, the rim width should be 80% or less of the tire (not tread) width.

The height (mounted diameter) of the new

Troubleshooting Basic Wheel Problems

Problem	Cause	Solution
The car's front end vibrates at high speed	• The wheels are out of balance • Wheels are out of alignment	• Have wheels balanced • Have wheel alignment checked/adjusted
Car pulls to either side	• Wheels are out of alignment • Unequal tire pressure • Different size tires or wheels	• Have wheel alignment checked/adjusted • Check/adjust tire pressure • Change tires or wheels to same size
The car's wheel(s) wobbles	• Loose wheel lug nuts • Wheels out of balance • Damaged wheel • Wheels are out of alignment • Worn or damaged ball joint • Excessive play in the steering linkage (usually due to worn parts) • Defective shock absorber	• Tighten wheel lug nuts • Have tires balanced • Raise car and spin the wheel. If the wheel is bent, it should be replaced • Have wheel alignment checked/adjusted • Check ball joints • Check steering linkage • Check shock absorbers
Tires wear unevenly or prematurely	• Incorrect wheel size • Wheels are out of balance • Wheels are out of alignment	• Check if wheel and tire size are compatible • Have wheels balanced • Have wheel alignment checked/adjusted

Troubleshooting Basic Tire Problems

Problem	Cause	Solution
The car's front end vibrates at high speeds and the steering wheel shakes	• Wheels out of balance • Front end needs aligning	• Have wheels balanced • Have front end alignment checked
The car pulls to one side while cruising	• Unequal tire pressure (car will usually pull to the low side) • Mismatched tires • Front end needs aligning	• Check/adjust tire pressure • Be sure tires are of the same type and size • Have front end alignment checked
Abnormal, excessive or uneven tire wear See "How to Read Tire Wear"	• Infrequent tire rotation • Improper tire pressure • Sudden stops/starts or high speed on curves	• Rotate tires more frequently to equalize wear • Check/adjust pressure • Correct driving habits
Tire squeals	• Improper tire pressure • Front end needs aligning	• Check/adjust tire pressure • Have front end alignment checked

tires can greatly change speedometer accuracy, engine speed at a given road speed, fuel mileage, acceleration, and ground clearance. Tire manufacturers furnish full measurement specifications. Speedometer drive gears are available for correction.

NOTE: *Dimensions of tires marked the same size may vary significantly, even among tires from the same manufacturer.*

The spare tire should be of the same size, construction and design as the tires on the vehicle. It's not a good idea to carry a spare of a different contstruction.

TIRE DESIGN

For maximum satisfaction, tires should be used in sets of five. Mixing or different types (radial, bias-belted, fiberglass belted) should be avoided. Conventional bias tires are constructed so that the cords run bead-to-bead at an angle. Alternate plies run at an opposite angle. This type of construction gives rigidity to both tread and sidewall. Bias-belted tires are similar in construction to conventional bias ply tires. Belts run at an angle and also at a 90° angle to the bead, as in the radial tire. Tread life is improved considerably over the conventional bias tire. The radial tire differs in construction, but instead of the carcass plies running at an angle of 90° to each other, they run at an angle of 90° to the bead. This gives the tread a great deal of rigidity and the sidewall a great deal of flexibility and accounts for the characteristic bulge associated with radial tires.

When radial tires are used, tire sizes and wheel diameters should be selected to maintain

Tire Size Comparison Chart

"Letter" sizes			Inch Sizes	Metric-inch Sizes		
"60 Series"	"70 Series"	"78 Series"	1965–77	"60 Series"	"70 Series"	"80 Series"
		Y78-12	5.50-12, 5.60-12	165/60-12	165/70-12	155-12
			6.00-12			
		W78-13	5.20-13	165/60-13	145/70-13	135-13
		Y78-13	5.60-13	175/60-13	155/70-13	145-13
			6.15-13	185/60-13	165/70-13	155-13, P155/80-13
A60-13	A70-13	A78-13	6.40-13	195/60-13	175/70-13	165-13
B60-13	B70-13	B78-13	6.70-13	205/60-13	185/70-13	175-13
			6.90-13			
C60-13	C70-13	C78-13	7.00-13	215/60-13	195/70-13	185-13
D60-13	D70-13	D78-13	7.25-13			
E60-13	E70-13	E78-13	7.75-13			195-13
			5.20-14	165/60-14	145/70-14	135-14
			5.60-14	175/60-14	155/70-14	145-14
			5.90-14			
A60-14	A70-14	A78-14	6.15-14	185/60-14	165/70-14	155-14
	B70-14	B78-14	6.45-14	195/60-14	175/70-14	165-14
	C70-14	C78-14	6.95-14	205/60-14	185/70-14	175-14
D60-14	D70-14	D78-14				
E60-14	E70-14	E78-14	7.35-14	215/60-14	195/70-14	185-14
F60-14	F70-14	F78-14, F83-14	7.75-14	225/60-14	200/70-14	195-14
G60-14	G70-14	G77-14, G78-14	8.25-14	235/60-14	205/70-14	205-14
H60-14	H70-14	H78-14	8.55-14	245/60-14	215/70-14	215-14
J60-14	J70-14	J78-14	8.85-14	255/60-14	225/70-14	225-14
L60-14	L70-14		9.15-14	265/60-14	235/70-14	
	A70-15	A78-15	5.60-15	185/60-15	165/70-15	155-15
B60-15	B70-15	B78-15	6.35-15	195/60-15	175/70-15	165-15
C60-15	C70-15	C78-15	6.85-15	205/60-15	185/70-15	175-15
	D70-15	D78-15				
E60-15	E70-15	E78-15	7.35-15	215/60-15	195/70-15	185-15
F60-15	F70-15	F78-15	7.75-15	225/60-15	205/70-15	195-15
G60-15	G70-15	G78-15	8.15-15/8.25-15	235/60-15	215/70-15	205-15
H60-15	H70-15	H78-15	8.45-15/8.55-15	245/60-15	225/70-15	215-15
J60-15	J70-15	J78-15	8.85-15/8.90-15	255/60-15	235/70-15	225-15
	K70-15		9.00-15	265/60-15	245/70-15	230-15
L60-15	L70-15	L78-15, L84-15	9.15-15			235-15
	M70-15	M78-15				255-15
		N78-15				

Note: Every size tire is not listed and many size comparisons are approximate, based on load ratings. Wider tires than those supplied new with the vehicle, should always be checked for clearance.

ground clearance and tire load capacity equivalent to the minimum specified tire. Radial tires should always be used in sets of five, but in an emergency, radial tires can be used with caution on the rear axle only. If this is done, both tires on the rear should be of radial design.

WARNING: *Radial tires should never be used on only the front axle!*

FLUIDS AND LUBRICANTS

Fuel Recommendations

Chrysler recommends that unleaded fuel only with a minimum octane rating of at least 87 be used in your vehicle, if equipped with a catalytic converter. The use of unleaded gasoline is required in order to meet all emission regulations, and provide excellent fuel economy.

Fuels of the same octane rating have varying anti-knock qualities. Thus, if your engine knocks or pings, try switching brands of gasoline before trying a more expansive higher octane fuel.

Your engine's fuel requirements can change with time, due to carbon buildup which changes the compression ratio. If switching brands or grades of gas doesn't work, check the ignition timing. If it is necessary to retard timing from specifications, don't change it more than about 4°. Retarded timing will reduce power output and fuel mileage and increase engine temperature.

Engine

OIL RECOMMENDATIONS

A high quality heavy-duty detergent oil having the proper viscosity for prevailing temperatures and an SF/CC service rating should be used in your vehicle. A high quality SF/CC rated oil should be used for heavy duty service or turbocharged equipped engines. The SF/CC and SF/CD rated oil contain sufficient chemical additives to provide maximum engine protection.

Pick an oil with the viscosity that matches the anticipated temperature of the region your vehicle will be operated in before the next oil change. A chart is provided to help you with your selection. Choose the oil viscosity for the lowest expected temperature and you will be assured of easy cold weather starting and sufficient engine protection.

OIL LEVEL CHECK

The engine oil level is checked with the dipstick which is located on the radiator side of the engine.

NOTE: *The oil should be checked before the engine is started or five minutes after the engine has shut off. This gives the oil time to drain back to the oil pan and prevents an inaccurate oil level reading.*

Remove the dipstick from the tube, wipe it clean, and insert it back into the tube. Remove it again and observe the oil level. It should be maintained within the full range on the dipstick.

NOTE: *Do not overfill the crankcase. This will cause oil aeration and loss of oil pressure.*

OIL AND FILTER CHANGE

The recommended mileage figures for oil and filter changes are 7,500 miles or 12 months whichever comes first, assuming normal driving conditions. If your vehicle is being used under dusty conditions, frequent trailer pulling, excessive idling, or stop and go driving, it is recommended to change the oil and filter at 3,000 miles.

NOTE: *Improper disposing of all lubricants (engine, trans., and differential), can result in environmental problems. Contact your local dealerships of service stations for advice on proper disposal.*

Always drain the oil after the engine has been

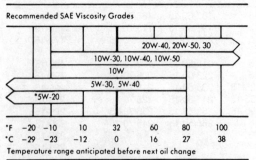

Recommended SAE Viscosity Grades

| | 20W-40, 20W-50, 30 |
| 10W-30, 10W-40, 10W-50 |
| 10W |
| 5W-30, 5W-40 |
| *5W-20 |

| °F | −20 | −10 | 10 | 32 | 60 | 80 | 100 |
| °C | −29 | −23 | −12 | 0 | 16 | 27 | 38 |

Temperature range anticipated before next oil change

*SAE 5W-20 Not recommended for sustained high speed vehicle operation.

Oil viscosity chart

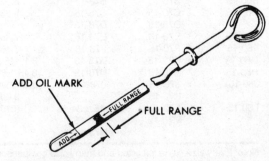

ADD OIL MARK
FULL RANGE

Oil dipstick

running long enough to bring it to operating temperature. Hot oil will flow easier and more contaminants will be removed along with the oil than if it were drained cold.

Chrysler recommends changing both the oil and filter during the first oil change and the filter every other oil change thereafter. For the small price of an oil filter, it's cheap insurance to replace the filter at every oil change. One of the larger filter manufacturers points out in its advertisements that not changing the filter leaves one quart of dirty oil in the engine. This claim is true and should be kept in mind when changing your oil.

1. Run the engine until it reaches normal operating temperature.

2. Jack up the front of the vehicle and support on jackstands, remove the shield if it will cause interference.

3. Slide a drain pan of at least 6 quarts capacity under the oil pan.

CAUTION: *The engine oil will be hot! Keep your arms, face and hands away from the oil as it drains out!*

4. Loosen the drain plug. It is located in the lowest point of the oil pan. Turn the plug out by hand. By keeping an inward pressure on the plug as you unscrew it, oil won't escape past the threads and you can remove it without being burned by hot oil.

5. Allow the oil to drain completely and then install the drain plug. Don't overtighten the plug, it will result in stripped threads.

6. Using a strap wrench, remove the oil filter. Keep in mind that it's holding about one quart of dirty, hot oil.

7. Empty the old filter into the drain pan and dispose of the filter.

8. Using a clean rag, wipe off the filter adapter on the engine block. Be sure that the rag doesn't leave any lint which could clog an oil passage.

9. Coat the rubber gasket on the filter with fresh oil. Spin it onto the engine by hand; when the gasket touches the adapter surface give it another 1/2-3/4 turn. No more, or you'll squash the gasket and it will leak.

10. Refill the engine with the correct amount of fresh oil. See the Capacities Chart.

11. Run the engine at idle for approximately one minute. Shut the engine off. Wait a few minutes and recheck oil level. Add oil, as necessary to bring the level up to **Fill**.

12. Shut the engine off and lower the vehicle.

CAUTION: *The EPA warns that prolonged contact with used engine oil may cause a number of skin disorders, including cancer! You should make every effort to minimize your exposure to used engine oil. Protective gloves should be worn when changing the oil. Wash your hands and any other exposed skin areas as soon as possible after exposure to used engine oil. Soap and water, or waterless hand cleaner should be used.*

Transaxle

FLUID RECOMMENDATION

Both the manual (4- or 5-speed) and the automatic transaxles use Dexron®II type automatic transmission fluid. Under normal operating conditions, periodic fluid change is not required. If the vehicle is operating under severe operating conditions change the fluid, or fluid and filter every 15,000 miles.

FLUID LEVEL CHECK

Manual Transaxle

1. The fluid level is checked by removing the fill plug on the end cover side of the transaxle.

2. The fluid level should be between the top of the fill hole and a point not more than $3/16''$ below the bottom of the fill hole.

3. Add Dexron®II type fluid as necessary. Secure the fill plug.

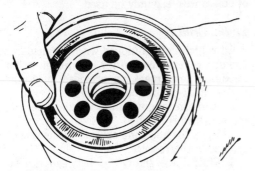

Lubricate the gasket on a new filter with clean engine oil

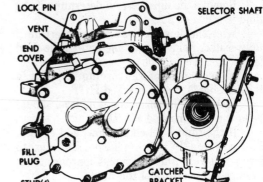

Manual transaxle filler plug location

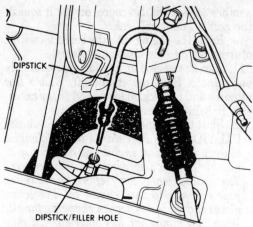

DIPSTICK

DIPSTICK/FILLER HOLE

Automatic transaxle dipstick location

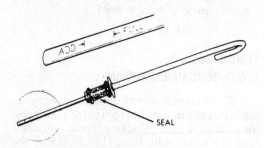

FULL

ADD

SEAL

Automatic transaxle dipstick markings

Automatic Transaxle

NOTE: *When checking the fluid level, the condition of the fluid should be observed. If severe darkening of the fluid and a strong odor are present, the fluid, filter and pan gasket (RTV sealant) should be changed and the bands readjusted.*

1. Make sure the vehicle is on level ground. The engine should be at normal operating temperatures, if possible.
2. Apply the parking brake, start the engine and move the gear selector through each position. Place the selector in the PARK position.
3. Remove the dipstick and determine if the fluid is warm or hot.
4. Wipe the dipstick clean and reinsert until fully seated. Remove and take note of the fluid level.
5. If the fluid is hot, the reading should be in the crosshatched area marked **HOT**.
6. If the fluid is warm, the fluid level should be in the area marked **WARM**.
7. If the fluid level checks low, add enough fluid (Dexron®II®) through the fill tube, to bring the level within the marks appropriate for average temperature of the fluid.
8. Insert the dipstick and recheck the level. Make sure the dipstick is fully seated to prevent

dirt from entering. Do not overfill the transaxle.

DRAIN AND REFILL

Manual Transaxle

1. Raise and support the front of the vehicle on jackstands.
2. Remove the undercarriage splash shield if it will interfere with fluid change.
3. Position a drain pan underneath the end of the transaxle and remove the differential end cover where the fill plug is located. Loosen the bolt slightly and pry the lower edge away so that the fluid will drain.
4. Remove the cover completely. Clean the gasket surfaces of the case and cover. Clean the magnet located on the cover.
5. Use an even $\frac{1}{16}''$ bead of RTV sealant to form a gasket on the cover and reinstall on the transaxle case.
6. Refill the transaxle with Dexron®II.

Automatic Transaxle

NOTE: *Band readjustment and filter replacement are recommended when the fluid is changed. Refer to Chapter 7 for required procedures.*

Differential

The transmission and differential share a common housing. Fluid check and change procedures are covered in the Transaxle Section. (Chapter 7).

Cooling System

FLUID RECOMMENDATION

A 50/50 mixture of water and ethylene glycol type antifreeze (containing Alguard or silicate type inhibitor) that is safe for use in aluminum components is recommended. The 50/50 mixture offers protection to $-34°F$. If addition cold weather protection is necessary a concentrate of 65% antifreeze may be used.

LEVEL CHECK

All vehicles are equipped with a transparent coolant reserve container. A minimum and maximum level mark are provided for a quick visual check of the coolant level.

1. Run the engine until normal operating temperature is reached.
2. Open the hood and observe the level of the coolant in the reserve.
3. Fluid level should be between the two lines. Add coolant, if necessary, through the fill cap of the reserve tank.

DRAIN AND REFILL

1. If the lower splash shield is in the way, remove it.

2. Place the heater control lever on the dash control to full on.

3. Place a drain pan under the radiator and open the drain cock. When the coolant reserve tank is drained completely, remove the radiator cap.

CAUTION: *When draining the coolant, keep in mind that cats and dogs are attracted by the ethylene glycol antifreeze, and are quite likely to drink any that is left in an uncovered container or in puddles on the ground. This will prove fatal in sufficient quantity. Always drain the coolant into a sealable container. Coolant should be reused unless it is contaminated or several years old.*

4. If your vehicle is equipped with the 2.2L engine, removal of the vacuum valve (located above the thermostat housing), is necessary to provide air displacement. If your vehicle is equipped with the 2.5L engine, removal of the drain/fill plug (located above the thermostat housing), is necessary to provide air displacement.

5. To remove the vacuum valve, disconnect the hose connector plug, and carefully unscrew the valve using the proper size wrench.

6. After draining the system, refill with water and run the engine until normal operating temperature is reached. (See the following refill procedures). Drain the system again, repeat procedure until the drained water runs clear.

7. Close the radiator draincock.

8. Fill the system with a 50/50 mixture of ethylene glycol type antifreeze.

9. When the coolant reaches the hole in the water box at thermostat housing (2.2L and 2.5L engines), install the vacuum valve or drain/fill plug to 20 N.m (15 ft. lbs.)

10. Continue filling system until full.

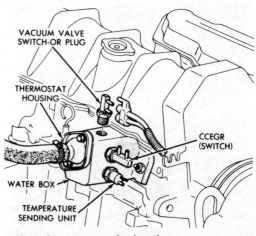

2.2L engine vacuum valve location

11. Install the radiator cap, start the engine, and run until normal operating temperature is reached. Fill the coolant reserve tank to **Max** mark. Stop engine and allowed to cool.

NOTE: *It may be necessary to warm up and cool down engine several times to remove trapped air. Recheck level in reserve tank, and adjust level if necessary.*

CHECK THE RADIATOR CAP

While you are checking the coolant level, check the radiator cap for a worn or cracked gasket. If the cap doesn't seal properly, fluid will be lost in the form of steam and the engine will overheat. Replace the cap with a new one, if necessary.

CLEAN RADIATOR OF DEBRIS

Periodically clean any debris—leaves, paper, insects, etc.—from the radiator fins. Pick the large pieces off by hand. The smaller pieces can be washed away with water pressure from a hose.

Carefully straighten any bent radiator fins with a pair of needle nose pliers. Be careful—

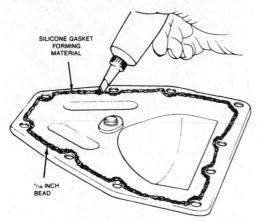

Form a silicone gasket as shown

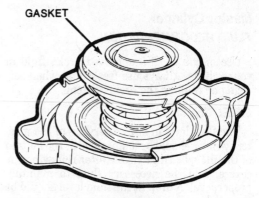

Check the radiator cap gasket

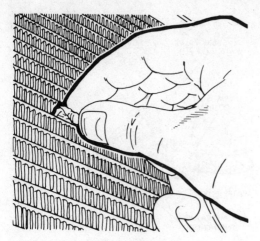

Remove debris from the radiator cooling fins

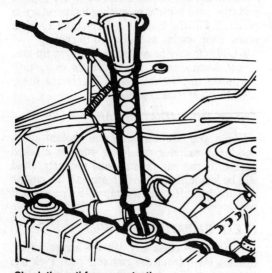

Check the anti-freeze protection

the fins are very soft! Don't wiggle the fins back and forth too much. Straighten them once and try not to move them again.

Master Cylinder

FLUID RECOMMENDATION

Use only a DOT 3 approved brake fluid in your vehicle. Always use fresh fluid when servicing or refilling the brake system.

LEVEL CHECK

The fluid level in both reservoirs of the master cylinder should be maintained at the bottom of the fill split rings visible after removing the covers. Add the necessary fluid to maintain proper level. A drop in the fluid level should be expected as the brake pads and shoes wear.

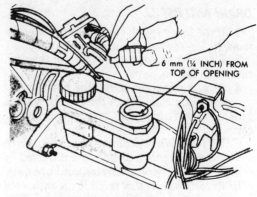

6 mm (¼ INCH) FROM TOP OF OPENING

Check master cylinder fluid level

However, if an unusual amount of fluid is required, check for system leaks.

Power Steering Pump

FLUID RECOMMENDATIONS

Power steering fluid such as Mopar Power Steering Fluid (Part Number 4318055) or equivalent should be used. Only petroleum fluids formulated for minimum effect on the rubber hoses should be added. Do not use automatic transmission fluid.

CAUTION: *Check the power steering fluid level with engine off, to avoid injury from moving parts.*

LEVEL CHECK

1. Wipe off the power steering pump reservoir cap with a cloth before removal.
2. A dipstick is built into the cover. Remove the reservoir cover cap and wipe the dipstick with a cloth.
3. Reinstall the dipstick and check the level indicated.
4. Add fluid as necessary, but do not overfill.

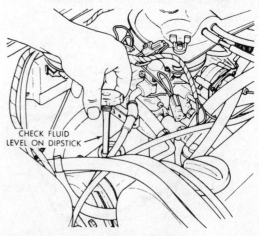

CHECK FLUID LEVEL ON DIPSTICK

Checking power steering fluid level

Steering Gear

NOTE: *The steering gear is lubricated and sealed at the factory, periodic lubrication is not necessary.*

Chassis Lubrication

All vehicles have two lower ball joints in the front suspension that are equipped with grease fittings as are the tie rod ends. Periodic lubrication (every 24,000 miles) using a hand grease gun and NLGI Grade 2, Multipurpose grease is required. Connect the grease gun to the fitting and pump until the boot seal on the tie rod ends or ball joints start to swell. Do not overfill until grease flows from under the boot edges.

Body Lubrication

The following body parts and mechanisms should be lubricated periodically at all pivot and sliding points. Use the lubricant specified;
Engine Oil:
- Door Hinges at pin and pivot contact area.
- Hinges
- Liftgate Hinges
- Sliding Door at center hinge pivot.

White Spray Lube:
- Hood Hinge cam and slide
- Lock cylinders
- Parking Brake Mechanisms
- Window Regulator: remove trim panel
- Liftgate Latches
- Liftgate Prop Pivots
- Ash Tray Slide

Multi-purpose Lubricant (Water Resistant):
- Door Latch, Lock control Linkage and Remote Control Mechanism (trim panel must be removed)
- Latch Plate and Bolt

Multi-purpose Grease, NLGI Grade 2:
- Sliding Door: lower, center and upper tracks. Open position striker spring.
- Fuel Tank Door

Rear Wheel Bearings

SERVICING

NOTE: *Sodium-based grease is not compatible with lithium-based grease. Read the package labels and be careful not to mix the two types. If there is any doubt as to the type of grease used, completely clean the old grease from the bearing and hub before replacing.*

Before handling the bearings, there are a few things that you should remember to do and not to do.

Remember to DO the following:
- Remove all outside dirt from the housing before exposing the bearing.

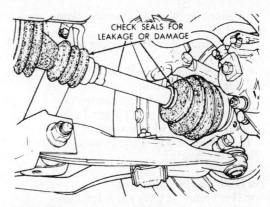

Inspect U-joint seals for leakage

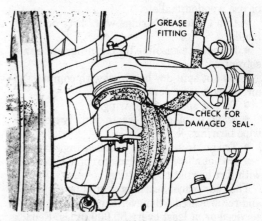

Check the tie-rod end ball joint seals

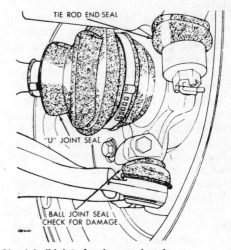

Check ball joints for damaged seals

- Treat a used bearing as gently as you would a new one.
- Work with clean tools in clean surroundings.
- Use clean, dry canvas gloves, or at least clean, dry hands.

- Clean solvents and flushing fluids are a must.
- Use clean paper when laying out the bearings to dry.
- Protect disassembled bearings from rust and dirt. Cover them up.
- Use clean rags to wipe bearings.
- Keep the bearings in oil-proof paper when they are to be stored or are not in use.
- Clean the inside of the housing before replacing the bearing.

Do NOT do the following:
- Don't work in dirty surroundings.
- Don't use dirty, chipped or damaged tools.
- Try not to work on wooden work benches or use wooden mallets.
- Don't handle bearings with dirty or moist hands.
- Do not use gasoline for cleaning; use a safe solvent.
- Do not spin-dry bearings with compressed air. They will be damaged.
- Do not spin dirty bearings.
- Avoid using cotton waste or dirty cloths to wipe bearings.
- Try not to scratch or nick bearing surfaces.
- Do not allow the bearing to come in contact with dirt or rust at any time.

The rear wheel bearings should be inspected and relubricated whenever the rear brakes are serviced or at least every 30,000 miles. Repack the bearings with high temperature multi-purpose grease.

Check the lubricant to see if it is contaminated. If it contains dirt or has a milky appearance indicating the presence of water, the bearings should be cleaned and repacked.

Clean the bearings in kerosene, mineral spirits or other suitable cleaning fluid. Do not dry them by spinning the bearings. Allow them to air dry.

1. Raise and support the vehicle with the rear wheels off the floor.
2. Remove the wheel grease cap, cotter pin, nut-lock and bearing adjusting nut.
3. Remove the thrust washer and bearing.
4. Remove the drum from the spindle.
5. Thoroughly clean the old lubricant from the bearings and hub cavity. Inspect the bearing rollers for pitting or other signs of wear. Light discoloration is normal.
6. Repack the bearings with high temperature multi-purpose EP grease and add a small amount of new grease to the hub cavity. Be sure to force the lubricant between all rollers in the bearing.
7. Install the drum on the spindle after coating the polished spindle surfaces with wheel bearing lubricant.

8. Install the outer bearing cone, thrust washer and adjusting nut.
9. Tighten the adjusting nut to 20-25 ft. lbs. while rotating the wheel.
10. Back off the adjusting nut to completely release the preload from the bearing.
11. Tighten the adjusting nut finger-tight.
12. Position the nut-lock with one pair of slots in line with the cotter pin hole. Install the cotter pin.
13. Clean and install the grease cap and wheel.
14. Lower the vehicle.

TOWING

The vehicle can be towed from either the front or rear. If the vehicle is towed from the front for an extended distance make sure the parking brake is completely released.

Manual transmission vehicles may be towed on the front wheels at speeds up to 30 mph, for a distance not to exceed 15 miles, provided the transmission is in neutral and the driveline has not been damaged. The steering wheel must be clamped in a straight ahead position.

WARNING: *Do not use the steering column lock to secure front wheel position for towing.*

Automatic transmission vehicles may be towed on the front wheels at speeds not to exceed 25 mph for a period of 15 miles.

WARNING: *If this requirement cannot be met the front wheels must be placed on a dolly.*

JACKING

The standard jack utilizes special receptacles located at the body sills. They accept the scissors jack supplied with the vehicle, for emergency road service only. The jack supplied with the vehicle should never be used for any service operation other then tire changing. Never get under the vehicle while it is supported by only a jack. Always block the wheels when changing tires.

The service operations in this book often require that one end or the other, or both, of the vehicle be raised and safely supported. The ideal method, of course, would be a hydraulic hoist. Since this is beyond both the resource and requirement of the do-it-yourselfer, a small hydraulic floor jack is recommended for certain procedures in this guide. Two sturdy jackstands should be acquired if you intend to work under the vehicle at any time. An alternate method of raising the vehicle would be drive-on ramps,

JUMP STARTING A DEAD BATTERY

The chemical reaction in a battery produces explosive hydrogen gas. This is the safe way to jump start a dead battery, reducing the chances of an accidental spark that could cause an explosion.

Jump Starting Precautions

1. Be sure both batteries are of the same voltage.
2. Be sure both batteries are of the same polarity (have the same grounded terminal).
3. Be sure the vehicles are not touching.
4. Be sure the vent cap holes are not obstructed.
5. Do not smoke or allow sparks around the battery.
6. In cold weather, check for frozen electrolyte in the battery.
7. Do not allow electrolyte on your skin or clothing.
8. Be sure the electrolyte is not frozen.

Jump Starting Procedure

1. Determine voltages of the two batteries; they must be the same.
2. Bring the starting vehicle close (they must not touch) so that the batteries can be reached easily.
3. Turn off all accessories and both engines. Put both cars in Neutral or Park and set the handbrake.
4. Cover the cell caps with a rag—do not cover terminals.
5. If the terminals on the run-down battery are heavily corroded, clean them.
6. Identify the positive and negative posts on both batteries and connect the cables in the order shown.
7. Start the engine of the starting vehicle and run it at fast idle. Try to start the car with the dead battery. Crank it for no more than 10 seconds at a time and let it cool off for 20 seconds in between tries.
8. If it doesn't start in 3 tries, there is something else wrong.
9. Disconnect the cables in the reverse order.
10. Replace the cell covers and dispose of the rags.

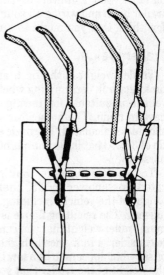

Side terminal batteries occasionally pose a problem when connecting jumper cables. There frequently isn't enough room to clamp the cables without touching sheet metal. Side terminal adaptors are available to alleviate this problem and should be removed after use.

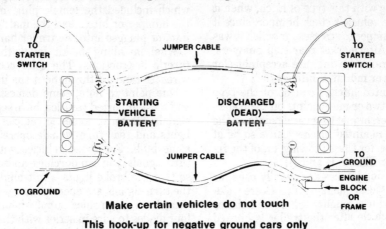

TO STARTER SWITCH

JUMPER CABLE

TO STARTER SWITCH

STARTING VEHICLE BATTERY

DISCHARGED (DEAD) BATTERY

TO GROUND

JUMPER CABLE

TO GROUND

ENGINE BLOCK OR FRAME

Make certain vehicles do not touch

This hook-up for negative ground cars only

Which are available commercially. Be sure to block the wheels when using ramps.

CAUTION: *Concrete blocks are not recommended for supporting the vehicle. They are likely to crumble if the load is not evenly distributed. Boxes and milk crates of any description must not be used to support the vehicle!*

TRAILER TOWING

Factory trailer towing packages are available on most vans. However, if you are installing a trailer hitch and wiring on your van, there are a few thing that you ought to know.

Trailer Weight

Trailer weight is the first, and most important, factor in determining whether or not your vehicle is suitable for towing the trailer you have in mind. The horsepower-to-weight ratio should be calculated. The basic standard is a ratio of 35:1. That is, 35 pounds of GVW for every horsepower.

To calculate this ratio, multiply you engine's rated horsepower by 35, then subtract the weight of the vehicle, including passengers and luggage. The resulting figure is the ideal maximum trailer weight that you can tow. One point to consider: a numerically higher axle ratio can offset what appears to be a low trailer weight. If the weight of the trailer that you have in mind is somewhat higher than the weight you just calculated, you might consider changing your rear axle ratio to compensate.

Hitch Weight

There are three kinds of hitches: bumper mounted, frame mounted, and load equalizing.

Bumper mounted hitches are those which attach solely to the vehicle's bumper. Many states prohibit towing with this type of hitch, when it attaches to the vehicle's stock bumper, since it subjects the bumper to stresses for which it was not designed. Aftermarket rear step bumpers, designed for trailer towing, are acceptable for use with bumper mounted hitches.

Frame mounted hitches can be of the type which bolts to two or more points on the frame, plus the bumper, or just to several points on the frame. Frame mounted hitches can also be of the tongue type, for Class I towing, or, of the receiver type, for Classes II and III.

Load equalizing hitches are usually used for large trailers. Most equalizing hitches are welded in place and use equalizing bars and chains to level the vehicle after the trailer is hooked up.

The bolt-on hitches are the most common, since they are relatively easy to install.

Check the gross weight rating of your trailer. Tongue weight is usually figured as 10% of gross trailer weight. Therefore, a trailer with a maximum gross weight of 2,000 lb. will have a maximum tongue weight of 200 lb. Class I trailers fall into this category. Class II trailers are those with a gross weight rating of 2,000-3,500 lb., while Class III trailers fall into the 3,500-6,000 lb. category. Class IV trailers are those over 6,000 lb. and are for use with fifth wheel trucks, only.

When you've determined the hitch that you'll need, follow the manufacturer's installation instructions, exactly, especially when it comes to fastener torques. The hitch will subjected to a lot of stress and good hitches come with hardened bolts. Never substitute an inferior bolt for a hardened bolt.

Wiring

Wiring the van for towing is fairly easy. There are a number of good wiring kits available and these should be used, rather than trying to design your own. All trailers will need brake lights and turn signals as well as tail lights and side marker lights. Most states require extra marker lights for overly wide trailers. Also, most states have recently required back-up lights for trailers, and most trailer manufacturers have been building trailers with back-up lights for several years.

Additionally, some Class I, most Class II and just about all Class III trailers will have electric brakes.

Add to this number an accessories wire, to operate trailer internal equipment or to charge the trailer's battery, and you can have as many as seven wires in the harness.

Determine the equipment on your trailer and buy the wiring kit necessary. The kit will contain all the wires needed, plus a plug adapter set which included the female plug, mounted on the bumper or hitch, and the male plug, wired into, or plugged into the trailer harness.

When installing the kit, follow the manufacturer's instructions. The color coding of the wires is standard throughout the industry.

One point to note, some domestic vehicles, and most imported vehicles, have separate turn signals. On most domestic vehicles, the brake lights and rear turn signals operate with the same bulb. For those vehicles with separate turn signals, you can purchase an isolation unit so that the brake lights won't blink whenever the turn signals are operated, or, you can go to your local electronics supply house and buy four diodes to wire in series with the brake and turn signal bulbs. Diodes will isolate the brake and turn signals. The choice is yours. The isolation units are simple and quick to install, but far more expensive than the diodes. The diodes, however, require more work to install properly, since they require the cutting of each bulb's wire and soldering in place of the diode.

One final point, the best kits are those with a spring loaded cover on the vehicle mounted socket. This cover prevents dirt and moisture from corroding the terminals. Never let the vehicle socket hang loosely. Always mount it securely to the bumper or hitch.

Cooling
ENGINE

One of the most common, if not THE most common, problem associated with trailer towing is engine overheating.

With factory installed trailer towing packages, a heavy duty cooling system is usually included. Heavy duty cooling systems are available as optional equipment on most vans, with or without a trailer package. If you have one of these extra-capacity systems, you shouldn't have any overheating problems.

If you have a standard cooling system, without an expansion tank, you'll definitely need to get an aftermarket expansion tank kit, preferably one with at least a 2 quart capacity. These kits are easily installed on the radiator's overflow hose, and come with a pressure cap designed for expansion tanks.

Another helpful accessory is a Flex Fan. These fan are large diameter units are designed to provide more airflow at low speeds, with blades that have deeply cupped surfaces. The blades then flex, or flatten out, at high speed, when less cooling air is needed. These fans are far lighter in weight than stock fans, requiring less horsepower to drive them. Also, they are far quieter than stock fans.

If you do decide to replace your stock fan with a flex fan, note that if your van has a fan clutch, a spacer between the flex fan and water pump hub will be needed.

Aftermarket engine oil coolers are helpful for prolonging engine oil life and reducing overall engine temperatures. Both of these factors increase engine life.

While not absolutely necessary in towing Class I and some Class II trailers, they are recommended for heavier Class II and all Class III towing.

Engine oil cooler systems consist of an adapter, screwed on in place of the oil filter, a remote filter mounting and a multi-tube, finned heat exchanger, which is mounted in front of the radiator or air conditioning condenser.

TRANSMISSION

An automatic transmission is usually recommended for trailer towing. Modern automatics have proven reliable and, of course, easy to operate, in trailer towing.

The increased load of a trailer, however, causes an increase in the temperature of the automatic transmission fluid. Heat is the worst enemy of an automatic transmission. As the temperature of the fluid increases, the life of the fluid decreases.

It is essential, therefore, that you install an automatic transmission cooler.

The cooler, which consists of a multi-tube, finned heat exchanger, is usually installed in front of the radiator or air conditioning compressor, and hooked inline with the transmission cooler tank inlet line. Follow the cooler manufacturer's installation instructions.

Select a cooler of at least adequate capacity, based upon the combined gross weights of the van and trailer.

Cooler manufacturers recommend that you use an aftermarket cooler in addition to, and not instead of, the present cooling tank in your van's radiator. If you do want to use it in place of the radiator cooling tank, get a cooler at least two sizes larger than normally necessary.

NOTE: *A transmission cooler can, sometimes, cause slow or harsh shifting in the transmission during cold weather, until the fluid has a chance to come up to normal operating temperature. Some coolers can be purchased with or retrofitted with a temperature bypass valve which will allow fluid flow through the cooler only when the fluid has reached operating temperature, or above.*

Lubrication and Maintenance Schedules

SCHEDULED MAINTENANCE FOR EMISSION CONTROL AND PROPER VEHICLE PERFORMANCE

Inspection and Service should also be performed any time a malfunction is observed or suspected. O = Except California Vehicles

Component	Service Interval	7.5 / 12	15 / 24	22.5 / 36	30 / 48	37.5 / 60	45 / 72	52.5 / 84	60 / 96	67.5 / 108	75 / 120	82.5 / 132	90 / 144	97.5 / 156	105 / 168	112.5 / 180	120 / 192
Change engine oil every 12 months	Or	O	O	O	O	O	O	O	O	O	O	O	O	O	O	O	O
Change engine oil filter every second oil change (1)	Or		X		X		X		O		O		O		O		O
Inspect & adjust drive belts tension; replace as necessary	At		X		X		O										
Replace spark plugs	At				X				O				O				
Replace engine air filter	At				X				O				O				
Replace oxygen sensor	At							O			O						
Replace EGR valve & tube & clean passages at 60 months	Or							O			O						
Replace PCV filter	At				X				O				O				
Replace PCV valve at 60 months	Or								O								
Replace vacuum operated emission components at 60 months	Or								O						O		
Inspect timing belt 3.0L only	At							O							O		
Adjust ignition timing if not to specifications	At								O								
Replace ignition cables, distributor cap & rotor	At								O								O
Flush & replace engine coolant at 36 months & 24 months or 30,000 miles (48 000 Km) thereafter	Or							O									
Replace alternator brushes	At										O						
Check engine coolant condition, coolant hoses & clamps every 12 months	At																

(1) Note: If mileage is less than 7,500 miles (12 000km) each 12 months, replace oil filter at each oil change.

GENERAL MAINTENANCE SERVICES FOR PROPER VEHICLE PERFORMANCE

General Maintenance	Service Intervals	Mileage in Thousands	7.5	15	22.5	30	37.5	45
		Kilometers in Thousands	12	24	36	48	60	72
Cooling System	Check & Service As Required Every 12 Months							
	Drain Flush, and Refill At 36 Months Or 52,500 Miles (84 000 Kilometers) And Every 24 Months Or 30,000 Miles (48 000 Kilometers) Thereafter							
Brake Hoses	Inspect For Deterioration And Leaks Whenever Brake System is Serviced And Every 7,500 Miles (12 000 km) Or 12 Months, Whichever Occurs First, For Non-turbocharged Vehicles and 7,500 Miles (12 000 km) or 6 Months, Whichever Occurs First, For Turbocharged Vehicles, Replace if Necessary.							
Brake Linings—Front	Inspect	At						X
Brake Linings—Rear	Inspect	At			X			X
Rear Wheel Bearings	Inspect	At			X			X
Tie Rod Ends and Steering Linkage	Lubricate Every 3 Years	Or				X		
Drive Shaft Boots	Inspect For Deterioration And Leaks Every Oil Change. Replace if Necessary	Or	X	X	X	X	X	X

SEVERE SERVICE MAINTENANCE*

	Service Intervals	Mileage in Thousands	3	6	9	12	15	18	21	24	27	30	33	36	39	42	45	48
		Kilometers In Thousands	4.8	9.6	14	19	24	29	34	38	43	48	53	58	62	67	72	77
Brake Linings (Front & Rear) and Rear Wheel Bearings	Inspect				X			X			X			X			X	
Constant Velocity Universal Joints	Inspect at every oil change																	
Engine Oil	Change every 3 months or		X	X	X	X	X	X	X	X	X	X	X	X	X	X	X	X
Engine Oil Filter	Change at every second oil change			X		X		X		X		X		X		X		X
Front Suspension Ball Joints	Inspect at every oil change																	
Transmission Fluid and Filter—Automatic	Change at (adjust bands at time of fluid and filter change)						X					X					X	
Steering Linkage Tie Rod Ends	Lubricate every 18 months or						X					X					X	
Engine Air Filter	Inspect and replace if required						X					X					X	

*Driving under any of the following operating conditions: Stop and go driving in dusty conditions, extensive idling, frequent short trips, operating at sustained high speeds during hot weather (above + 90°F, + 30°C)

Capacities

Year	No. Cylinder Displacement cu. in. (liter)	Engine Crankcase		Transmission (pts.)			Drive Axle (pts.)	Fuel Tank (gal.)	Cooling System (qts.)
		With Filter	Without Filter	4-Spd	5-Spd	Auto.			
1984	4-135 (2.2)	4	4	8	—	①	—	15 ②	8.5
	4-156 (2.6)	5	5	—	9	①	—	15 ②	9.5
1985	4-135 (2.2)	4	4	8	—	①	—	15 ②	8.5
	4-156 (2.6)	5	5	—	9	①	—	15 ②	9.5
1986	4-135 (2.2)	4	4	8	—	①	—	15 ②	8.5
	4-156 (2.6)	5	5	—	9	①	—	15 ②	9.5
1987	4-135 (2.2)	4	4	8	—	①	—	15 ②	8.5
	4-153 (2.5)	4	4	—	9	⑦	—	150	10.5
	4-156 (2.6)	5	5	—	9	①	—	15 ②	9.5
1988	4-153 (2.5)	4	4	—	9	⑦	—	150	8.5
	4-156 (2.6)	5	5	—	9	①	—	15 ②	9.5
	6-181 (3.0)	4	4	—	9	①	—	15 ②	10.5

① Except fleet: 18 pts
  Fleet: 19 pts
② Optional tank: 20 gal.

Engine Performance and Tune-Up

T2

TUNE-UP PROCEDURES

Neither tune-up nor troubleshooting can be considered independently since each has a direct relationship with the other.

It is advisable to follow a definite and thorough tune-up procedure. Tune-up consists of three separate steps: Analysis, (the process of determining whether normal wear is responsible for performance loss, and whether parts require replacement or service); Parts Replacement or Service; and Adjustment, (where engine adjustments are performed).

The manufacturer's recommended interval for tune-ups on non-catalyst vehicles is 15,000 miles. Models with a converter, every 30,000 miles. Models equipped with a 2.6L engine require a valve lash adjustment every 15,000 miles. this interval should be shortened if the vehicle is subjected to severe operating conditions such as trailer pulling or stop and start driving, or if starting and running problems are noticed. It is assumed that the routine mainte-

Gasoline Engine Tune-Up Specifications

Year	VIN	No. Cylinder Displacement cu. in. (liter)	Spark Plugs Type	Gap (in.)	Ignition Timing (deg.) MT	AT	Compression Pressure (psi)	Fuel Pump (psi)	Idle Speed (rpm) MT	AT	Valve Clearance (in.) In.	Ex.
1984	C	4-135 (2.2)	65PR	.035	12B	12B	130–150	4.5–6.0	850	900	Hyd.	Hyd.
	G	4-156 (2.6)	65PR	.041 ①		12B	149	4.5–6.0	—	800	Hyd.	Hyd.
1985	C	4-135 (2.2)	65PR	.035	12B	12B	130–150	4.5–6.0	850	900	Hyd.	Hyd.
	G	4-156 (2.6)	65PR	.041 ①	—	12B	149	4.5–6.0	—	800	Hyd.	Hyd.
1986	C	4-135 (2.2)	65PR	.035	12B	12B	130–150	4.5–6.0	800	900	Hyd.	Hyd.
	G	4-156 (2.6)	65PR	.041 ①	—	12B	149	4.5–6.0	—	800	Hyd.	Hyd.
1987	C	4-135 (2.2)	65PR	.035	12B	12B	130–150	4.5–6.0	800	900	Hyd.	Hyd.
	K	4-153 (2.5)	RN12YC	.035	12B	12B	100	14.5	850	850	Hyd.	Hyd.
	G	4-156 (2.6)	65PR	.041 ①	—	12B	149	4.5–6.0	—	800	Hyd.	Hyd.
1988	K	4-153 (2.5)	RN12YC	.035	12B	12B	100	14.5	850	850	Hyd.	Hyd.
	3	6-181 (3.0)	RN11YC4	.041	—	12B	178 ②	48	—	③	Hyd.	Hyd.

① Canada: .030
② At 250 rpm
③ 700 in Drive
   800 in Neutral
NOTE: If specifications differ from those on the underhood label. Use the label specifications.

Troubleshooting Engine Performance

Problem	Cause	Solution
Hard starting (engine cranks normally)	• Binding linkage, choke valve or choke piston	• Repair as necessary
	• Restricted choke vacuum diaphragm	• Clean passages
	• Improper fuel level	• Adjust float level
	• Dirty, worn or faulty needle valve and seat	• Repair as necessary
	• Float sticking	• Repair as necessary
	• Faulty fuel pump	• Replace fuel pump
	• Incorrect choke cover adjustment	• Adjust choke cover
	• Inadequate choke unloader adjustment	• Adjust choke unloader
	• Faulty ignition coil	• Test and replace as necessary
	• Improper spark plug gap	• Adjust gap
	• Incorrect ignition timing	• Adjust timing
	• Incorrect valve timing	• Check valve timing; repair as necessary
Rough idle or stalling	• Incorrect curb or fast idle speed	• Adjust curb or fast idle speed
	• Incorrect ignition timing	• Adjust timing to specification
	• Improper feedback system operation	• Refer to Chapter 4
	• Improper fast idle cam adjustment	• Adjust fast idle cam
	• Faulty EGR valve operation	• Test EGR system and replace as necessary
	• Faulty PCV valve air flow	• Test PCV valve and replace as necessary
	• Choke binding	• Locate and eliminate binding condition
	• Faulty TAC vacuum motor or valve	• Repair as necessary
	• Air leak into manifold vacuum	• Inspect manifold vacuum connections and repair as necessary
	• Improper fuel level	• Adjust fuel level
	• Faulty distributor rotor or cap	• Replace rotor or cap
	• Improperly seated valves	• Test cylinder compression, repair as necessary
	• Incorrect ignition wiring	• Inspect wiring and correct as necessary
	• Faulty ignition coil	• Test coil and replace as necessary
	• Restricted air vent or idle passages	• Clean passages
	• Restricted air cleaner	• Clean or replace air cleaner filler element
	• Faulty choke vacuum diaphragm	• Repair as necessary
Faulty low-speed operation	• Restricted idle transfer slots	• Clean transfer slots
	• Restricted idle air vents and passages	• Clean air vents and passages
	• Restricted air cleaner	• Clean or replace air cleaner filter element
	• Improper fuel level	• Adjust fuel level
	• Faulty spark plugs	• Clean or replace spark plugs
	• Dirty, corroded, or loose ignition secondary circuit wire connections	• Clean or tighten secondary circuit wire connections
	• Improper feedback system operation	• Refer to Chapter 4
	• Faulty ignition coil high voltage wire	• Replace ignition coil high voltage wire
	• Faulty distributor cap	• Replace cap
Faulty acceleration	• Improper accelerator pump stroke	• Adjust accelerator pump stroke
	• Incorrect ignition timing	• Adjust timing
	• Inoperative pump discharge check ball or needle	• Clean or replace as necessary
	• Worn or damaged pump diaphragm or piston	• Replace diaphragm or piston

Troubleshooting Engine Performance (cont.)

Problem	Cause	Solution
Faulty acceleration (cont.)	• Leaking carburetor main body cover gasket	• Replace gasket
	• Engine cold and choke set too lean	• Adjust choke cover
	• Improper metering rod adjustment (BBD Model carburetor)	• Adjust metering rod
	• Faulty spark plug(s)	• Clean or replace spark plug(s)
	• Improperly seated valves	• Test cylinder compression, repair as necessary
	• Faulty ignition coil	• Test coil and replace as necessary
	• Improper feedback system operation	• Refer to Chapter 4
Faulty high speed operation	• Incorrect ignition timing	• Adjust timing
	• Faulty distributor centrifugal advance mechanism	• Check centrifugal advance mechanism and repair as necessary
	• Faulty distributor vacuum advance mechanism	• Check vacuum advance mechanism and repair as necessary
	• Low fuel pump volume	• Replace fuel pump
	• Wrong spark plug air gap or wrong plug	• Adjust air gap or install correct plug
	• Faulty choke operation	• Adjust choke cover
	• Partially restricted exhaust manifold, exhaust pipe, catalytic converter, muffler, or tailpipe	• Eliminate restriction
	• Restricted vacuum passages	• Clean passages
	• Improper size or restricted main jet	• Clean or replace as necessary
	• Restricted air cleaner	• Clean or replace filter element as necessary
	• Faulty distributor rotor or cap	• Replace rotor or cap
	• Faulty ignition coil	• Test coil and replace as necessary
	• Improperly seated valve(s)	• Test cylinder compression, repair as necessary
	• Faulty valve spring(s)	• Inspect and test valve spring tension, replace as necessary
	• Incorrect valve timing	• Check valve timing and repair as necessary
	• Intake manifold restricted	• Remove restriction or replace manifold
	• Worn distributor shaft	• Replace shaft
	• Improper feedback system operation	• Refer to Chapter 4
Misfire at all speeds	• Faulty spark plug(s)	• Clean or replace spark plug(s)
	• Faulty spark plug wire(s)	• Replace as necessary
	• Faulty distributor cap or rotor	• Replace cap or rotor
	• Faulty ignition coil	• Test coil and replace as necessary
	• Primary ignition circuit shorted or open intermittently	• Troubleshoot primary circuit and repair as necessary
	• Improperly seated valve(s)	• Test cylinder compression, repair as necessary
	• Faulty hydraulic tappet(s)	• Clean or replace tappet(s)
	• Improper feedback system operation	• Refer to Chapter 4
	• Faulty valve spring(s)	• Inspect and test valve spring tension, repair as necessary
	• Worn camshaft lobes	• Replace camshaft
	• Air leak into manifold	• Check manifold vacuum and repair as necessary
	• Improper carburetor adjustment	• Adjust carburetor
	• Fuel pump volume or pressure low	• Replace fuel pump
	• Blown cylinder head gasket	• Replace gasket
	• Intake or exhaust manifold passage(s) restricted	• Pass chain through passage(s) and repair as necessary
	• Incorrect trigger wheel installed in distributor	• Install correct trigger wheel

Troubleshooting Engine Performance (cont.)

Problem	Cause	Solution
Power not up to normal	• Incorrect ignition timing	• Adjust timing
	• Faulty distributor rotor	• Replace rotor
	• Trigger wheel loose on shaft	• Reposition or replace trigger wheel
	• Incorrect spark plug gap	• Adjust gap
	• Faulty fuel pump	• Replace fuel pump
	• Incorrect valve timing	• Check valve timing and repair as necessary
	• Faulty ignition coil	• Test coil and replace as necessary
	• Faulty ignition wires	• Test wires and replace as necessary
	• Improperly seated valves	• Test cylinder compression and repair as necessary
	• Blown cylinder head gasket	• Replace gasket
	• Leaking piston rings	• Test compression and repair as necessary
	• Worn distributor shaft	• Replace shaft
	• Improper feedback system operation	• Refer to Chapter 4
Intake backfire	• Improper ignition timing	• Adjust timing
	• Faulty accelerator pump discharge	• Repair as necessary
	• Defective EGR CTO valve	• Replace EGR CTO valve
	• Defective TAC vacuum motor or valve	• Repair as necessary
	• Lean air/fuel mixture	• Check float level or manifold vacuum for air leak. Remove sediment from bowl
Exhaust backfire	• Air leak into manifold vacuum	• Check manifold vacuum and repair as necessary
	• Faulty air injection diverter valve	• Test diverter valve and replace as necessary
	• Exhaust leak	• Locate and eliminate leak
Ping or spark knock	• Incorrect ignition timing	• Adjust timing
	• Distributor centrifugal or vacuum advance malfunction	• Inspect advance mechanism and repair as necessary
	• Excessive combustion chamber deposits	• Remove with combustion chamber cleaner
	• Air leak into manifold vacuum	• Check manifold vacuum and repair as necessary
	• Excessively high compression	• Test compression and repair as necessary
	• Fuel octane rating excessively low	• Try alternate fuel source
	• Sharp edges in combustion chamber	• Grind smooth
	• EGR valve not functioning properly	• Test EGR system and replace as necessary
Surging (at cruising to top speeds)	• Low carburetor fuel level	• Adjust fuel level
	• Low fuel pump pressure or volume	• Replace fuel pump
	• Metering rod(s) not adjusted properly (BBD Model Carburetor)	• Adjust metering rod
	• Improper PCV valve air flow	• Test PCV valve and replace as necessary
	• Air leak into manifold vacuum	• Check manifold vacuum and repair as necessary
	• Incorrect spark advance	• Test and replace as necessary
	• Restricted main jet(s)	• Clean main jet(s)
	• Undersize main jet(s)	• Replace main jet(s)
	• Restricted air vents	• Clean air vents
	• Restricted fuel filter	• Replace fuel filter
	• Restricted air cleaner	• Clean or replace air cleaner filter element
	• EGR valve not functioning properly	• Test EGR system and replace as necessary
	• Improper feedback system operation	• Refer to Chapter 4

nance described in Chapter 1 has been kept up, as this will have an effect on the result of the tune-up. All the applicable tune-up steps should be followed, as each adjustment complements the effects of the other. If the tune-up (emission control) sticker in the engine compartment disagrees with the information presented in the Tune-up Specifications chart in this chapter, the sticker figures must be followed. The sticker information reflects running changes made by the manufacturer during production.

Troubleshooting is a logical sequence of procedures designed to locate a particular cause of trouble. While the apparent cause of trouble, in many cases, is worn or damaged parts, performance problems are less obvious. The first job is to locate the problem and cause. Once the problem has been isolated, repairs, removal or adjustment procedures can be performed.

It is advisable to read the entire chapter before beginning a tune-up, although those who are more familiar with tune-up procedures may wish to go directly to the instructions.

Spark Plugs

A typical spark plug consists of a metal shell surrounding a ceramic insulator. A metal electrode extends downward through the center of the insulator and protrudes a small distance. Located at the end of the plug and attached to the side of the outer metal shell is the side electrode. The side electrode bends in at a 90° angle so that its tip is even with, and parallel to, the tip of the center electrode. The distance between these two electrodes (measured in thousandths of an inch) is called the spark plug gap. The spark plug in no way produces a spark but merely provides a gap across which the current can arc. The coil produces anywhere from 20,000 to 40,000 volts which travels to the distributor where it is distributed through the spark plug wires to the spark plugs. The current passes along the center electrode and jumps the gap to the side electrode, and, in do doing, ignites the air/fuel mixture in the combustion chamber.

SPARK PLUG HEAT RANGE

Spark plug heat range is the ability of the plug to dissipate heat. The longer the insulator (or the farther it extends into the engine), the hotter the plug will operate; the shorter the insulator the cooler it will operate. A plug that absorbs little heat and remains too cool will quickly accumulate deposits of oil and carbon since it is not hot enough to burn them off. This leads to plug fouling and consequently to misfiring. A plug that absorbs too much heat will have no deposits, but, due to the excessive heat, the electrodes will burn away quickly and in some

instances, preignition may result. Preignition takes place when plug tips get so hot that they glow sufficiently to ignite the fuel/air mixture before the actual spark occurs. This early ignition will usually cause a pinging during low speeds and heavy loads.

The general rule of thumb for choosing the correct heat range when picking a spark plug is: if most of your driving is long distance, high speed travel, use a colder plug; if most of your driving is stop and go, use a hotter plug. Original equipment plugs are compromise plugs, but most people never have occasion to change their plugs from the factory-recommended heat range.

REMOVAL AND INSTALLATION

1. Before removing the spark plugs, number the plug wires so that the correct wire goes on the plug when replaced. This can be done with pieces of adhesive tape.

2. Next, clean the area around the plugs by blowing with compressed air. You can also loosen the plugs a few turns and crank the engine to blow the dirt away.

CAUTION: *Wear safety glasses to avoid possible eye injury due to flying dust particles.*

3. Disconnect the plugs wires by twisting and pulling on the rubber cap, not on the wire.

4. Remove each plug with a rubber insert spark plug socket. make sure that the socket is all the way down on the plug to prevent it from slipping and cracking the porcelain insulator.

5. After removing each plug, evaluate its condition. A spark plug's useful life is approximately 30,000 miles. Thus, it would make sense to replace a plug if it has been in service that long.

6. If the plugs are to be reused, file the center and side electrodes flat with a fine, flat point file. Heavy or baked on deposits can be carefully scraped off with a small knife blade, or the scraper tool of a combination spark plug tool. However, it is suggested that plugs be test and cleaned on a service station sandblasting machine. Check the gap between the electrodes with a round wire spark plug gapping gauge. Do

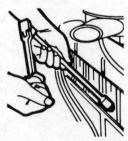

Remove the spark plugs with a ratchet and long extension

Check the spark plug gap with a wire feeler gauge

CABLE RESISTANCE CHART	
Minimum	**Maximum**
250 Ohms Per Inch	600 Ohms Per Inch
3000 Ohms Per Foot	7200 Ohms Per Foot

Plug cable resistance

not use a flat feeler gauge; it will give an inaccurate reading. If the gap is not as specified, use the bending tool on the spark plug gap gauge to bend the outside electrode. Be careful not to bend the electrode tool far or too often, because excessive bending may cause the electrode to break off and fall into the combustion chamber. This would require removing the cylinder head to reach the broken piece, and could also result in cylinder wall, piston ring, or valve damage.

7. Clean the threads of old plugs with a wire brush. Lubricate the threads with a drop of oil.

8. Screw the plugs in finger tight, and then tighten them with the spark plug socket to 26 ft. lbs. Be very careful not to overtighten them.

9. Reinstall the wires. If, by chance, you have forgotten to number the plug wires, refer to the Firing Order illustrations.

Spark Plug Wires

Check the spark plug wire connections at the coil, distributor cap towers, and at the spark plugs. Be sure they are fully seated, and the boot covers are not cracked or split. Clean the cables with a cloth and a non-flammable solvent. Check for brittle or cracked insulation, replace wires as necessary. If a wire is suspected of failure, test it with an ohmmeter. Test as follows:

1. Remove the plug wire from the spark plug. Twist the boot and pull. Never apply pressure to the wire itself.

2. Remove the distributor cap from the distributor with all wires attached.

NOTE: *Do not pull plugs wires from distributor cap, they must first be released from inside of cap.*

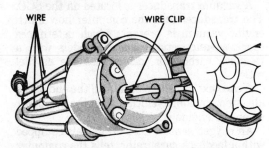

Removing the plug wires from the distributor cap

3. Connect the ohmmeter between the spark plug terminal, and the corresponding electrode inside the distributor cap. Resistance should be within limits of the cable resistance chart. If resistance is not within specs, remove the wire from the distributor cap and retest. If still not within specs, replace the wire.

4. Install the new wire into cap tower, then squeeze the wire nipple to release any trapped air between the cap tower and nipple.

5. Push firmly to properly seat wire electrode into cap.

6. Install plug end of wire onto plug until it snaps into place.

WARNING: *Do not allowed plug wires to contact exhaust manifold or any moving parts.*

FIRING ORDERS

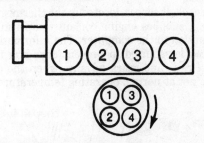

Engine firing order; 1-3-4-2, distributor rotation is clockwise

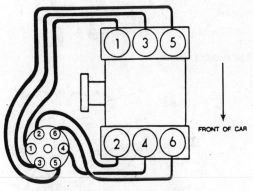

FRONT OF CAR

Chrysler Corp. 3.0L V6 engine
Firing order: 1-2-3-4-5-6
Distributor rotation: Counterclockwise
NOTE: The distributor cap contains current tracks. The firing order and cap terminal position will appear to disagree.

3.0L engine firing order

NOTE: *To avoid confusion, remove and tag the wires one at a time, for replacement.*

ELECTRONIC IGNITION

Electronic Ignition System 2.2L Engine

Models using the 2.2L engine are equipped with an Electronic Fuel Control System. This system consists of a Spark Control Computer (SCC), various engine sensors, and a specially calibrated carburetor.

The Spark Control Computer (SCC) is the heart of the entire engine control system. The SCC receives signals from the various sensors according to the different modes of engine operation and adjusts fuel and spark delivery accordingly.

The pick-up assembly, in the Hall Effect distributor, supplies the basic timing signal to the SCC. The computer, in turn, can determine from this signal, engine rpm and the precise instant when each piston is coming up on its compression stroke, or when the engine is in cranking mode.

The coolant sensor, located in the thermostat housing, supplies engine coolant temperature information to the computer. The information provided is required to prevent changing the air/fuel ratio and spark advance when the engine is not at normal operating temperature.

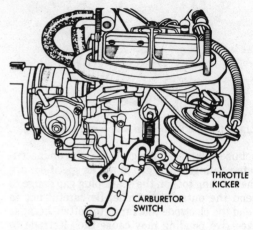

2.2L carburetor switch

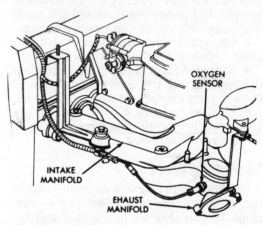

2.2L oxygen sensor

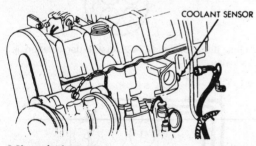

2.2L coolant sensor

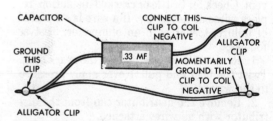

Special jumper wire construction for grounding coil

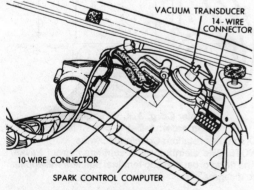

2.2L spark control vacuum transducer

A vacuum transducer is located on the SCC. The transducer tells the computer how much engine vacuum is present, which determines spark advance/retard and on models with a feedback carburetor, determines the air/fuel ratio.

A carburetor switch located on the end of the idle stop, on some vehicles, tells the computer when the engine is at idle.

An oxygen sensor, used on models equipped with a feedback carburetor, tells the computer how much oxygen is present in the exhaust gases. Since the oxygen level is proportional to a rich or lean mixture, the computer will adjust the air/fuel ratio to a level which will maintain the operating efficiency of the three-way catalyst system and the engine.

TEST PROCEDURES

NOTE: *An ignition coil test must first be performed before proceeding with these tests. Failure to perform coil test will result in incorrect diagnosis, and unnecessary parts replacement.*

1. Construct a special jumper wire, as shown in illustration.

2. Refer to troubleshooting procedures shown in the following charts.

Electronic Ignition System 2.6L Engine

The Electronic Ignition System (EIS) used on the 2.6L engine consists of the battery, ignition coil, IC igniter (electronic control unit) built

HALL EFFECT ELECTRONIC SPARK ADVANCE SYSTEM DIAGNOSIS

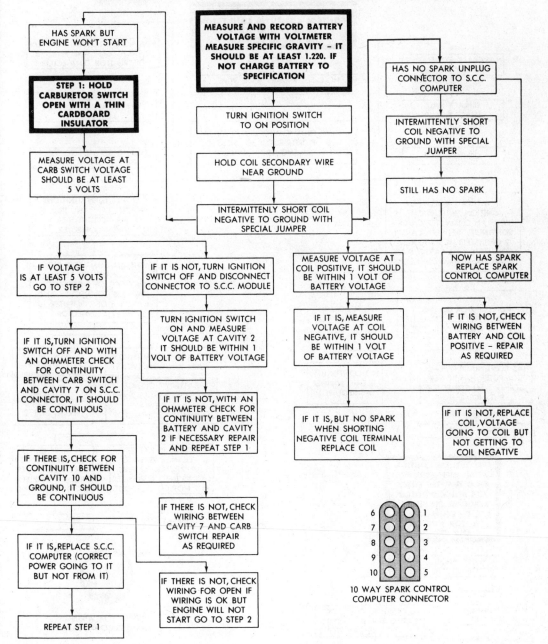

10 WAY SPARK CONTROL COMPUTER CONNECTOR

into the distributor, spark plugs and wiring. Primary current is switched by the IC igniter in response to timing signals produced by a magnetic pick-up in the distributor.

Components of the distributor consists of a power distributor section, signal generator, IC igniter, advance mechanism and drive section. The signal generator is a small magneto which produces signals for driving the IC igniter. The signal is produced in exact synchronism with the rotation of the distributor shaft, four times per rotation at equal intervals. The signal is used for maintaining correct ignition timing.

The distributor is equipped with both centrifugal and vacuum advance.

TEST PROCEDURES

WARNING: *Ignition coil test must first be performed before proceeding with this tests. Failure to perform coil test will result in incorrect diagnosis, and unnecessary parts replacement.*

HALL EFFECT ELECTRONIC SPARK ADVANCE SYSTEM DIAGNOSIS

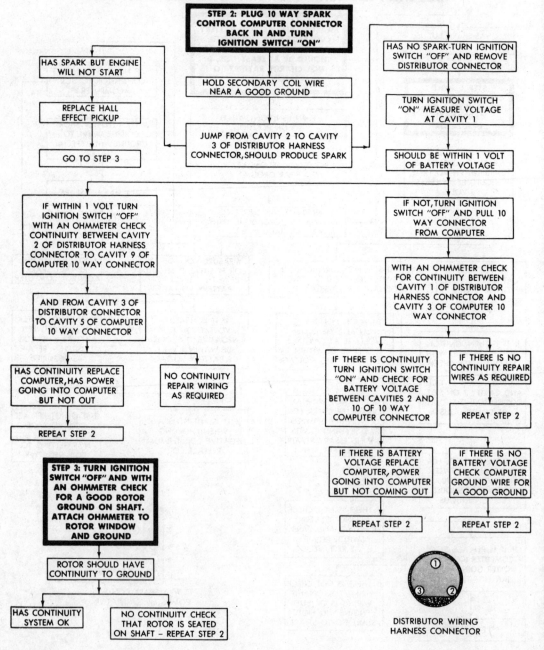

DISTRIBUTOR WIRING
HARNESS CONNECTOR

1. Remove the coil wire from the distributor cap. Hold the wire end about 3/8 inch away from a good engine ground point and have a helper crank the engine.

2. If a spark occurs, it must be constant and bright blue in color. If it is, continue to crank the engine while moving the wire further away from the engine ground point. If arcing at the coil tower occurs, replace the coil. If the spark is weak or there is no spark, proceed to Step 4.

3. If the spark is good, and there is no arcing at the coil, the ignition system is producing the necessary voltage. Make sure that the voltage is reaching the spark plugs. Check the distributor cap, rotor, plug wires and spark plugs. (See preceding paragraphs on cap and rotor inspection). If they are okay, check the fuel system and mechanical engine components.

4. Turn the ignition switch on and check the voltage at the negative (–) terminal of the coil. The voltage should be the same as battery voltage. If the voltage is 3 volts or less, the IC unit should be replaced. If no voltage is shown, check for an open circuit in the coil or wiring.

5. Connect a special jumper wire (see illustration), turn the key on and momentarily touch the negative (–) coil terminal while holding the coil wire ¼" away from a good engine ground point. A spark should be produced between the coil wire and ground.

6. If no spark was produced, check the voltage at the positive (+) coil terminal (have key on). The voltage should be at least 12 volts or battery voltage. If the required voltage is present, the coil is defective. Replace the coil. If the required voltage is not present, check the wiring and harness connections.

NOTE: *If the previous diagnostic procedures fail to correct a "No Start" condition, further ignition tests are necessary. (Refer to "CHILTON'S GUIDE TO ELECTRONIC ENGINE CONTROLS 1984-88 DOMESTIC CARS AND LIGHT TRUCKS MANUAL, Part No. 7768*

Electronic Ignition System 2.5L and 3.0L Engine

The 2.5L Turbo and 3.0L engines are equipped with a Single Module Engine Controller system (SMEC), which controls the entire ignition system. The SMEC has a built in microprocessor which continuously varies electronic spark timing based on inputs received from engine rpm, coolant temperature, exhaust oxygen content, and manifold vacuum.

During the crank-start operations the SMEC provides a preset amount of advanced timing to assure a quick efficient start. This preset value is determine basically by only three input factors, the coolant sensor, manifold vacuum, and engine rpm.

On 2.5L engines the SMEC receives its ignition signal from a hall effect pick-up located in the distributor.

On 3.0L engines the SMEC receives its ignition signal from an optical distributor. The timing member in the distributor is a thin disk, driven at half engine speed from the forward (left) bank camshaft.

TEST PROCEDURES

WARNING: *Ignition coil test must first be performed before proceeding with this tests. Failure to perform coil test will result in incorrect diagnosis, and unnecessary parts replacement.*

1. Conform that battery voltage (12.4 volts) is available for the ignition and cranking system.

2. Connect a voltmeter, positive lead to the ignition coil positive (+) terminal and negative lead to a good engine ground.

3. Crank the engine for 5 seconds while observing the voltmeter.

4. If the voltage remains at or near battery voltage during the entire 5 seconds, remove the 14-way connector from the SMEC, (key must be in off position). Check 14-way connector for any spread terminals.

5. Remove the coil (+) lead and connect a jumper wire between battery (+) and coil (+).

6. Using a special jumper, momentarily ground terminal #12 of the 14-way connector. A spark should be generated when the ground is removed.

7. If a spark is generated, replace the SMEC.

8. If no spark is notice, connect the special jumper to ground the coil (–) terminal directly.

9. If a spark is produced, repair open in wiring harness.

10. If no spark is notice, replace the ignition coil.

NOTE: *If the previous diagnostic procedures fail to correct a "No Start" condition, further ignition tests are necessary. (Refer to "CHILTON'S GUIDE TO ELECTRONIC ENGINE CONTROLS 1984-88 DOMESTIC CARS AND LIGHT TRUCKS MANUAL, Part No. 7768.*

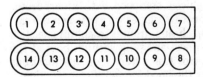

TERMINAL SIDE

14 way connector terminal identification

Ignition Timing

Basic timing should be checked at each tune-up in order to gain maximum engine performance. While timing isn't likely to change very much with electronic ignition system, it become a critical factor necessary to reduce engine emission and improve driveability.

A stroboscropic (dynamic) timing light must be used, because static lights are too inaccurate for emission controlled engines.

Some timing light have other features built into them, such as dwell meters or tachometers. These are nice, in that they reduce the tangle of wires under the hood when you're working, but may duplicate the functions of tools your already have. One worthwhile feature, which is becoming more of a necessity with higher voltage ignition systems, is an inductive pickup. The inductive pickup clamps around the No. 1 spark plug wire, sensing the surges of high voltage electricity as they are sent to the plug. The advantage is that no mechanical connection is inserted between the wire and the plug, which eliminates false signals to the timing light. A timing light with an inductive pickup should be used on electronic ignition systems

IGNITION TIMING ADJUSTMENT

CAUTION: *Always apply parking brake and block wheels before performing any engine running tests.*

2.2L And 2.6L Engines

1. With engine off, clean off the timing marks.

2. Mark the pulley or damper notch and the timing scale with white chalk or paint. If the timing notch on the damper or pulley is not visible, bump the engine around with the starter or turn the crankshaft with a wrench on the front pulley bolt to get it to an accessible position.

3. Connect a suitable inductive timing light to number one cylinder plug wire.

4. Connect a tachometer unit, Positive Lead to the negative terminal of the coil and the Negative Lead to a known good engine ground. Select the tachometer appropriate cylinder position.

5. Warm the engine to normal operating temperature. Open the throttle and release to make sure idle speed screw is against its stop, and not on fast idle.

6. On vehicles equipped with a carburetor switch, connect a jumper wire between the carburetor switch and ground to obtain specified rpm. Disconnect and plug vacuum hose at the Spark Control Computer. (See specifications decal under the hood for specific instructions).

7. Read engine rpm on the tachometer 1,000

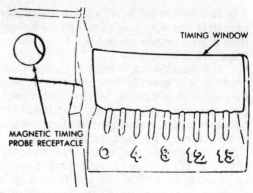

2.2L timing mark location

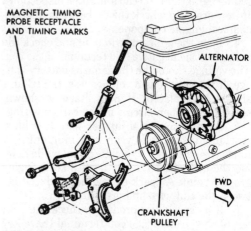

2.6L timing marks

rpm scale, and adjust curb idle to specification noted on the underhood label.

8. Aim the timing light toward timing indicator, and read degree marks. If flash occurs when timing mark is before specification, timing is advanced. If flash occurs when timing mark is after specification, timing is retarded.

NOTE: *Models equipped with the 2.2L engine have a notch on the torque converter or flywheel, with the numerical timing marks on the bell housing. Models equipped with the 2.6L engine have the timing marks on the front crankshaft pulley.*

9. If adjustment is necessary, loosen the distributor hold down screw. Turn the distributor slowly to specified value, and tighten hold down screw. Recheck timing and curb idle. If curb idle have change, readjust to specified value and reset ignition timing. Repeat curb idle setting, and ignition timing until both are within specification.

10. Disconnect timing light, and reconnect all vacuum hoses necessary.

11. Turn engine off and remove jumper wire, and tachometer.

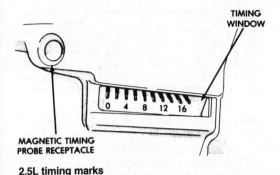

2.5L timing marks

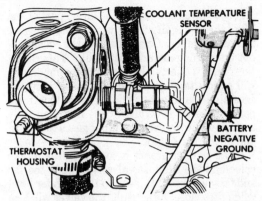

2.5L coolant sensor

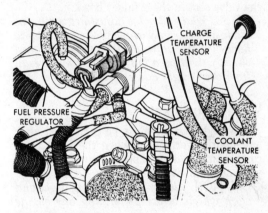

3.0L coolant sensor

3.0L timing marks

2.5L and 3.0L Engines

1. With the engine off, clean off the timing marks.

2. Mark the pulley or damper notch and the timing scale with white chalk or paint. If the timing notch on the damper or pulley is not visible, bump the engine around with the starter or turn the crankshaft with a wrench on the front pulley bolt to get it to an accessible position.

3. Connect a suitable inductive timing light to number one cylinder plug wire.

4. Connect a tachometer unit, positive lead to the negative terminal of the coil and the negative lead to a known good engine ground. Select the tachometer appropriate cylinder position.

5. Warm the engine to normal operating temperature.

6. With engine at normal operating temperature, disconnect coolant temperature sensor. Radiator fan and instrument panel check engine lamp should come on. (See specifications decal under the hood for specific instructions).

7. Read engine rpm on the tachometer 1,000 rpm scale, and adjust curb idle to specification noted on the underhood label.

8. Aim the timing light toward timing indicator, and read degree marks. If flash occurs when timing mark is before specification, timing is advanced. If flash occurs when timing mark is after specification, timing is retarded.

NOTE: *Models equipped with the 2.5L engine have the timing marks visible through a window on the transaxle housing. Models equipped with the 3.0L engine have the timing marks on the front crankshaft pulley.*

9. If adjustment is necessary, loosen the distributor holddown screw. Turn the distributor slowly to specified value, and tighten holddown screw. Recheck ignition timing.

10. Turn the engine off and removed the tachometer and timing light.

11. Connect the coolant temperature sensor.

NOTE: *Reconnecting the coolant temperature sensor will turn the check engine lamp off; however, a fault code will be stored in the SMEC. After 50 to 100 key on/off cycles the SMEC will cancel the fault code.*

VALVE LASH

Valve adjustment determines how far the valves enter the cylinder and how long they stay open and closed.

If the valve clearance is too large, part of the lift of the camshaft will be used in removing the excess clearance. Consequently, the valve will not be opening as far as it should. This condition has two effects: the valve train components will emit a tapping sound as they take up the excessive clearance and the engine will perform poorly because the valves does not open fully and allow the proper amount of gases to flow in and out of the engine.

If the valve clearance is too small, the intake valve and the exhaust valves will open too far and they will not fully seat on the cylinder head when they close. As a result, the valves will also become overheated and will warp, since they cannot transfer heat unless they are touching the valve seat in the cylinder head.

NOTE: *While all valve adjustments must be made as accurately as possible, it is better to have the valve adjustment slightly loose then slightly tight as a burned valve may result from overly tight adjustments.*

Valve Adjustment

Valve adjustment must be performed after any engine overhaul or when the valve train components emit a tapping sound requiring valve adjustment service.

CAUTION: *Always apply parking brake and block wheels before performing any engine running tests.*

2.2L, 2.5L and 3.0L Engines

The 2.2L, 2.5L and 3.0L engines use hydraulic lash adjusters. No periodic adjustment or checking is necessary.

2.6L Engine (With Jet Valves)

A jet valve is added on some models. The jet valve adjuster is located on the intake valve

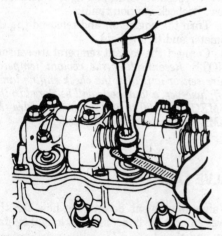

Adjusting the valve lash on 2.6L engine

Exhaust Valve Closing	Adjust
No. 1 Cylinder	No. 4 Cylinder Valves
No. 2 Cylinder	No. 3 Cylinder Valves
No. 3 Cylinder	No. 2 Cylinder Valves
No. 4 Cylinder	No. 1 Cylinder Valves

rocker arm and must be adjusted before the intake valve.

1. Start the engine and allow it to reach normal operating temperature.

2. Stop the engine and remove the air cleaner and its hoses. Remove any other cables, hoses, wires, etc., which are attached to the valve cover, and remove the valve cover.

3. Disconnect the high tension coil-to-distributor wire at the distributor, and allow it to contact a known good engine ground.

4. Retorque the cylinder head bolts.

5. Have a helper bump the ignition switch. Watch the rocker arms until piston No. 4 cylinder is at Top Dead Center (TDC) and adjust jet valves as follow.

6. Back out the intake valve adjusting screw two or three turns.

7. Loosen the locknut on the jet valve and back out jet valve adjusting screw.

8. Install a 0.15mm feeler gauge between the jet valve stem and the jet valve adjusting screw.

9. Turn in jet valve adjusting screw until it slightly makes contact with the jet valve stem. While holding jet valve adjusting screw in place tighten jet valve lock nut. Recheck clearance.

10. Complete the adjustment by adjusting intake and exhaust valve clearance on the same cylinder as jet valve you've finished. Refer to Valve Clearance Specification Chart.

2.6L Engine (Without Jet Valves)

1. Start the engine and allow it to reach normal operating temperature.

2. Stop the engine and remove the air cleaner and its hoses. Remove any other cables, hoses, wires, etc., which are attached to the valve cover, and remove the valve cover.

3. Disconnect the high tension coil-to-distributor wire at the distributor, and allow it to contact a known good engine ground.

4. Retorque cylinder head bolts.

5. Have a helper bump the ignition switch. Watch the rocker arms until piston is at Top Dead Center (TDC) of the compression stroke (both valves closed).

6. Loosen valve adjuster lock nut. Back out valve adjusting screw and install a feeler gauge between adjusting screw and valve stem.

7. Turn in valve adjusting screw until it slightly touches the feeler gauge. While holding the adjusting screw in place tighten adjusting

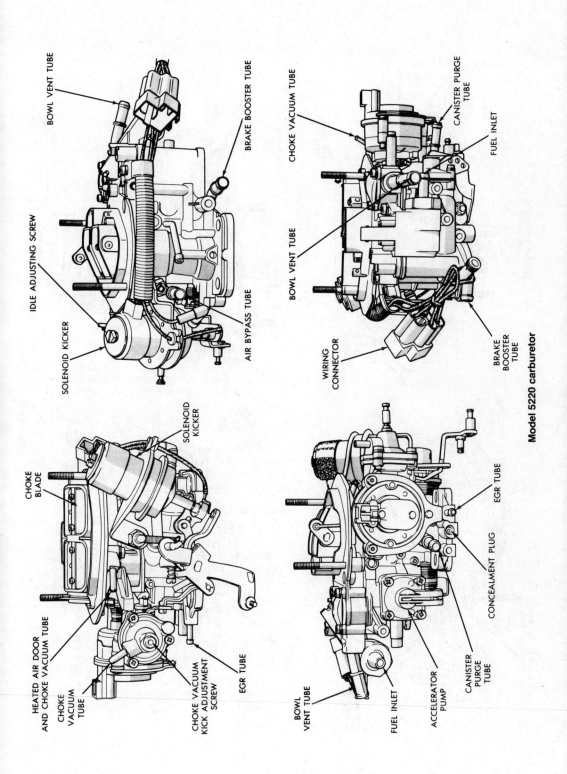

BOWL VENT TUBE

BRAKE BOOSTER TUBE

IDLE ADJUSTING SCREW

SOLENOID KICKER

AIR BYPASS TUBE

CHOKE VACUUM TUBE

CANISTER PURGE TUBE

FUEL INLET

BOWL VENT TUBE

WIRING CONNECTOR

BRAKE BOOSTER TUBE

CHOKE BLADE

SOLENOID KICKER

HEATED AIR DOOR AND CHOKE VACUUM TUBE

CHOKE VACUUM TUBE

CHOKE VACUUM KICK ADJUSTMENT SCREW

EGR TUBE

BOWL VENT TUBE

FUEL INLET

ACCELERATOR PUMP

CANISTER PURGE TUBE

CONCEALMENT PLUG

EGR TUBE

Model 5220 carburetor

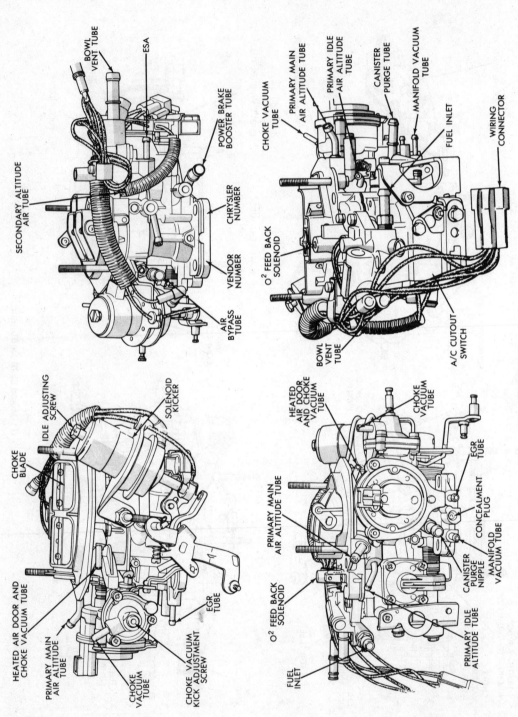

SECONDARY ALTITUDE AIR TUBE

BOWL VENT TUBE

ESA

POWER BRAKE BOOSTER TUBE

CHRYSLER NUMBER

VENDOR NUMBER

AIR BYPASS TUBE

CHOKE VACUUM TUBE

PRIMARY MAIN AIR ALTITUDE TUBE

PRIMARY IDLE AIR ALTITUDE TUBE

CANISTER PURGE TUBE

MANIFOLD VACUUM TUBE

FUEL INLET

WIRING CONNECTOR

O^2 FEED BACK SOLENOID

BOWL VENT TUBE

A/C CUTOUT SWITCH

CHOKE BLADE

IDLE ADJUSTING SCREW

SOLENOID KICKER

HEATED AIR DOOR AND CHOKE VACUUM TUBE

PRIMARY MAIN AIR ALTITUDE TUBE

CHOKE VACUUM TUBE

CHOKE VACUUM KICK ADJUSTMENT SCREW

EGR TUBE

HEATED AIR DOOR AND CHOKE VACUUM TUBE

CHOKE VACUUM TUBE

EGR TUBE

CONCEALMENT PLUG

MANIFOLD VACUUM TUBE

PRIMARY IDLE ALTITUDE TUBE

CANISTER PURGE NIPPLE

O^2 FEED BACK SOLENOID

PRIMARY MAIN AIR ALTITUDE TUBE

FUEL INLET

Model 6520 carburetor

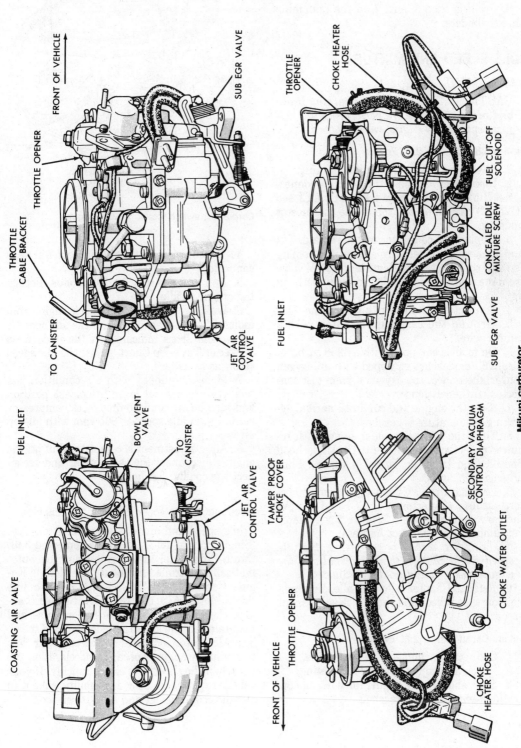

Mikuni carburetor

screw lock nut. Refer to Valve Clearance Specification Chart.

8. Perform Step 5 thru 7 on the remaining three cylinders.

IDLE SPEED AND MIXTURE

ADJUSTMENT

CAUTION: *Always apply the parking brake and block wheels before performing idle adjustment, or any engine running tests.*

Holley 5220/6520 — 2.2L Engine

1. Check and adjust the ignition timing.
2. Disconnect and plug the vacuum connector at the Coolant Vacuum Switch Cold Closed (CVSCC) located on the top of the thermostat housing.
3. Unplug the connector at the radiator fan and connect a jumper wire so that the cooling fan will run constantly. Remove the PCV valve from the engine and allow it to draw underhood air.
4. Connect a tachometer to the engine.
5. Ground the carburetor switch with a jumper wire.
6. On models equipped with a 6250 carburetor (6250 models are equipped with an oxygen sensor) disconnect the oxygen system test connector on the left fender shield.
7. Start the engine and run until normal operating temperature is reached.
8. Turn the idle adjustment screw until required rpm is reached. (Refer to the Underhood Specification Label or Tune-Up Chart). Shut off engine.
9. Reconnect the PCV valve, oxygen connector, vacuum connector (CVSCC) and remove the carb switch jumper. Remove the radiator fan jumper and reconnect harness.

NOTE: *After Step 9 is completed, the idle speed might change, this is normal and the engine speed should not be readjusted.*

10. Refer to Chapter 5 for fast idle, air condition idle speed check and choke kick adjustment procedures.

Mikuni Carburetor — 2.6L Engine

1. Connect a tachometer to the engine.
2. Check and adjust the ignition timing.
3. Start and run the engine until normal operating temperature is reached.

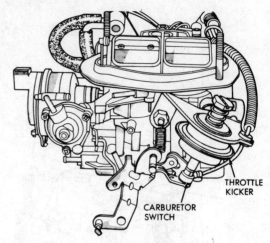

Carburetor switch location—2.2L engine

4. Disconnect the cooling fan harness connector.
5. Run at 2500 rpm for 10 seconds. Return the engine to idle.
6. Wait two minutes and check engine rpm indicated on the tachometer. If the idle speed is not within specs indicated on the underhood sticker or Tune-Up Chart, adjust the idle speed screw as necessary.
7. Models equipped with air condition, set temperature control lever to coldest position and turn on air conditioning. With compressor running, set idle speed to 900 rpm with idle up screw.
8. After adjustment is complete, shut off the engine, disconnect the tachometer and reconnect the cooling fan harness.

Electronic Fuel Injection 2.5L and 3.0L Engines

Idle speed and mixture adjustment on 2.5L (Single Point Fuel Injection System) and 3.0L (Multi-Point Fuel Injection System) are automatically controlled by the Single Module Engine Controller (SMEC). An Automatic Idle Speed Motor (AIS) controlled by the SMEC adjusts the air portion of the air/fuel mixture, and maintains engine idle to a predetermined speed. The AIS motor increases or decreases air flow to maintain engine speed, or deceleration die out when the throttle is closed quickly. If your vehicle experiences poor driveability, take it to an authorized dealer and have it serviced.

Engine and Engine Overhaul

3

UNDERSTANDING THE ENGINE ELECTRICAL SYSTEM

The engine electrical system can be broken down into three separate and distinct systems:
1. The starting system.
2. The charging system.
3. The ignition system.

BATTERY AND STARTING SYSTEM

Basic Operating Principles

The battery is the first link in the chain of mechanisms which work together to provide cranking of the automobile engine. In most modern cars, the battery is a lead/acid electro-chemical device consisting of six 2v subsections connected in series so the unit is capable of producing approximately 12v of electrical pressure. Each subsection, or cell, consists of a series of positive and negative plates held a short distance apart in a solution of sulfuric acid and water. The two types of plates are of dissimilar metals. This causes a chemical reaction to be set up, and it is this reaction which produces current flow from the battery when its positive and negative terminals are connected to an electrical appliance such as a lamp or motor. The continued transfer of electrons would eventually convert the sulfuric acid in the electrolyte to water, and make the two plates identical in chemical composition. As electrical energy is removed from the battery, its voltage output tends to drop. Thus, measuring battery voltage and battery electrolyte composition are two ways of checking the ability of the unit to supply power. During the starting of the engine, electrical energy is removed from the battery. However, if the charging circuit is in good condition and the operating conditions are normal, the power removed from the battery will be replaced by the generator (or alternator) which will force electrons back through the bat-

tery, reversing the normal flow, and restoring the battery to its original chemical state.

The battery and starting motor are linked by very heavy electrical cables designed to minimize resistance to the flow of current. Generally, the major power supply cable that leaves the battery goes directly to the starter, while other electrical system needs are supplied by a smaller cable. During starter operation, power flows from the battery to the starter and is grounded through the car's frame and the battery's negative ground strap.

The starting motor is a specially designed, direct current electric motor capable of producing a very great amount of power for its size. One thing that allows the motor to produce a great deal of power is its tremendous rotating speed. It drives the engine through a tiny pinion gear (attached to the starter's armature), which drives the very large flywheel ring gear at a greatly reduced speed. Another factor allowing it to produce so much power is that only intermittent operation is required of it. This, little allowance for air circulation is required, and the windings can be built into a very small space.

The starter solenoid is a magnetic device which employs the small current supplied by the starting switch circuit of the ignition switch. This magnetic action moves a plunger which mechanically engages the starter and electrically closes the heavy switch which connects it to the battery. The starting switch circuit consists of the starting switch contained within the ignition switch, a transmission neutral safety switch or clutch pedal switch, and the wiring necessary to connect these in series with the starter solenoid or relay.

A pinion, which is a small gear, is mounted to a one-way drive clutch. This clutch is splined to the starter armature shaft. When the ignition switch is moved to the **start** position, the solenoid plunger slides the pinion toward the flywheel ring gear via a collar and spring. If the teeth on the pinion and flywheel match properly, the pinion will engage the flywheel immediately. If the gear teeth butt one another, the spring will be compressed and will force the gears to mesh as soon as the starter turns far enough to allow them to do so. As the solenoid plunger reaches the end of its travel, it closes the contacts that connect the battery and starter and then the engine is cranked.

As soon as the engine starts, the flywheel ring gear begins turning fast enough to drive the pinion at an extremely high rate of speed. At this point, the one-way clutch begins allowing the pinion to spin faster than the starter shaft so that the starter will not operate at excessive speed. When the ignition switch is released from the starter position, the solenoid is de-energized, and a spring contained within the solenoid assembly pulls the gear out of mesh and interrupts the current flow to the starter.

Some starter employ a separate relay, mounted away from the starter, to switch the motor and solenoid current on and off. The relay thus replaces the solenoid electrical switch, buy does not eliminate the need for a solenoid mounted on the starter used to mechanically engage the starter drive gears. The relay is used to reduce the amount of current the starting switch must carry.

THE CHARGING SYSTEM

Basic Operating Principles

The automobile charging system provides electrical power for operation of the vehicle's ignition and starting systems and all the electrical accessories. The battery services as an electrical surge or storage tank, storing (in chemical form) the energy originally produced by the engine driven generator. The system also provides a means of regulating generator output to protect the battery from being overcharged and to avoid excessive voltage to the accessories.

The storage battery is a chemical device incorporating parallel lead plates in a tank containing a sulfuric acid/water solution. Adjacent plates are slightly dissimilar, and the chemical reaction of the two dissimilar plates produces electrical energy when the battery is connected to a load such as the starter motor. The chemical reaction is reversible, so that when the generator is producing a voltage (electrical pressure) greater than that produced by the battery, electricity is forced into the battery, and the battery is returned to its fully charged state.

The vehicle's generator is driven mechanically, through V-belts, by the engine crankshaft. It consists of two coils of fine wire, one stationary (the stator), and one movable (the rotor). The rotor may also be known as the armature, and consists of fine wire wrapped around an iron core which is mounted on a shaft. The electricity which flows through the two coils of wire (provided initially by the battery in some cases) creates an intense magnetic field around both rotor and stator, and the interaction between the two fields creates voltage, allowing the generator to power the accessories and charge the battery.

There are two types of generators: the earlier is the direct current (DC) type. The current produced by the DC generator is generated in the armature and carried off the spinning armature by stationary brushes contacting the commutator. The commutator is a series of smooth metal contact plates on the end of the armature. The commutator is a series of smooth metal contact plates on the end of the armature. The commutator plates, which are separated from one another by a very short gap, are connected to the armature circuits so that current will flow in one directions only in the wires carrying the generator output. The generator stator consists of two stationary coils of wire which draw some of the output current of the generator to form a powerful magnetic field and create the interaction of fields which generates the voltage. The generator field is wired in series with the regulator.

Newer automobiles use alternating current generators or alternators, because they are more efficient, can be rotated at higher speeds, and have fewer brush problems. In an alternator, the field rotates while all the current produced passes only through the stator winding. The brushes bear against continuous slip rings rather than a commutator. This causes the current produced to periodically reverse the direction of its flow. Diodes (electrical one-way switches) block the flow of current from traveling in the wrong direction. A series of diodes is wired together to permit the alternating flow of the stator to be converted to a pulsating, but unidirectional flow at the alternator output. The alternator's field is wired in series with the voltage regulator.

The regulator consists of several circuits. Each circuit has a core, or magnetic coil of wire, which operates a switch. Each switch is connected to ground through one or more resistors. The coil of wire responds directly to system voltage. When the voltage reaches the required level, the magnetic field created by the winding of wire closes the switch and inserts a resistance into the generator field circuit, thus reducing the output. The contacts of the switch cycle open and close many times each second to precisely control voltage.

While alternators are self-limiting as far as maximum current is concerned, DC generators employ a current regulating circuit which responds directly to the total amount of current flowing through the generator circuit rather than to the output voltage. The current regulator is similar to the voltage regulator except that all system current must flow through the energizing coil on its way to the various accessories.

ENGINE ELECTRICAL

Ignition Coil

TESTING

All Models

1. Remove the coil wire from the distributor cap. Hold the end of the wire about ¼″ away from a good engine ground point.
2. Have a helper crank the engine. Check for a spark between the coil wire end and the ground point.
3. If there is a spark, it must be constant and bright blue in color.
4. Continue to crank the engine. Slowly move the wire away from the ground point. If arching at the coil tower occurs, replace the coil.
5. If the spark is good and no arching at the coil tower occurs, the ignition system is producing the necessary high secondary voltage.
6. Check to make sure that the voltage is getting to the spark plugs. Inspect the distributor cap, rotor, spark plug wires and spark plugs.
7. If all of the components check okay, the ignition system is probably not the reason why the engine does not start.
8. Check the fuel system and engine mechanical items such as the timing belt.

Distributor Cap

REMOVAL AND INSTALLATION

1. Remove the splash shield retaining screws and the splash shield.

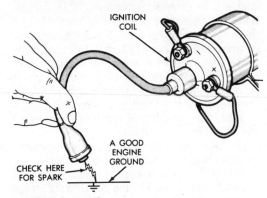

IGNITION COIL

CHECK HERE FOR SPARK

A GOOD ENGINE GROUND

Checking for spark

2. Loosen the distributor cap retaining screws.
3. Remove the distributor cap
4. Inspect the inside, of the cap, for spark flashover (burnt tracks on cap or terminals), center carbon button wear or cracking, and worn terminals. Replace the cap if any of these problems are present or suspected.

Light deposits on the terminals can be cleaned with a knife, heavy deposits or scaling will require cap replacement.

Wash the cap with a solution of warm water and mild detergent, scrub with a soft brush and dry with a clean soft cloth to remove dirt and grease.

5. If cap replacement is necessary, take notice of cap installed position in relationship to distributor assembly.
6. Number each plug wire so that the correct wire goes on the proper cap terminal when replaced. This can be done with pieces of adhesive tape.

NOTE: *Do not pull plugs wires from distributor cap, they must first be released from inside of cap.*

7. Position the replacement cap on the distributor assembly, and tighten the distributor cap retaining screws.
8. Push the wire terminals firmly to properly seat the wires into the cap.
9. Reinstall the splash shield.

Distributor Rotor

With the distributor cap removed, remove the rotor. Inspect the rotor for cracks, excessive wear or burn marks and sufficient spring tension of the spring to cap carbon button terminal. Clean light deposits, replace the rotor if scaled or burnt heavily. Clean the ground strap on the inner side of the shaft mount. Take care not to bend any of the shutter blades, if blades are bent replace the rotor.

Distributor

REMOVAL AND INSTALLATION

NOTE: *Although not absolutely necessary, it is probably easier (for reference reinstallation, especially if the engine is rotated after distributor removal) to bring the engine to No. 1 cylinder at TDC (top dead center) before removing the distributor.*

1. Disconnect the distributor lead wires, and vacuum hose as necessary.
2. Remove the distributor cap.
3. Rotate the engine crankshaft (in the direction of normal rotation) until No. 1 cylinder is at TDC on compression stroke. make a mark on the block where the rotor points for installation reference.

4. Remove the distributor holddown bolt.

5. Carefully lift the distributor from the engine. The shaft will rotate slightly as the distributor is removed.

6. If the engine was not disturbed while the distributor was out, lower the distributor into the engine, engaging the gears and making sure that the gasket is properly seated in the block. The rotor should line up with the mark made before removal.

7. Install the distributor cap.

8. Tighten the holddown bolt. Connect the wires and vacuum hose as necessary.

9. Check and, if necessary, adjust the ignition timing.

NOTE: *The following procedure is to be used if the engine was cranked with the distributor removed.*

10. If the engine has been cranked/turned while the distributor was removed, rotate the crankshaft until the number one piston is at TDC on the compression stroke. This will be indicated by the O mark on the flywheel (2.2L and 2.5L engines) aligned with the pointer on the clutch housing, or crank pulley (2.6L and 3.0L engines) aligned with the pointer on engine front cover.

11. Position the rotor just ahead of the No. 1 terminal of the cap and lower the distributor into the engine. With the distributor fully seat-

ed, the rotor should be directly under the No. 1 terminal.

12. Install the distributor cap.

13. Tighten the holddown bolt. Connect the wires and vacuum hose as necessary.

14. Check and, if necessary, adjust the ignition timing.

Alternator

The alternator charging system is a negative (−) ground system which consists of an alternator, a regulator, a charge indicator, a storage battery and wiring connecting the components, and fuse link wire.

The alternator is belt-driven from the engine. Energy is supplied from the alternator/regulator system to the rotating field through two brushes to two slip-rings. The slip-rings are mounted on the rotor shaft and are connected to the field coil. This energy supplied to the rotating field from the battery is called excitation current and is used to initially energize the field to begin the generation of electricity. Once the alternator starts to generate electricity, the excitation current comes from its own output rather than the battery.

The alternator produces power in the form of alternating current. The alternating current is rectified by 6 diodes into direct current. The direct current is used to charge the battery and power the rest of the electrical system.

When the ignition key is turned on, current flows from the battery, through the charging system indicator light on the instrument panel, to the voltage regulator, and to the alternator. Since the alternator is not producing any current, the alternator warning light comes on. When the engine is started, the alternator begins to produce current and turns the alternator light off. As the alternator turns and produces current, the current is divided in two ways: part to the battery to charge the battery and power the electrical components of the vehicle, and part is returned to the alternator to enable it to increase its output. In this situation, the alternator is receiving current from the battery and from itself. A voltage regulator is wired into the current supply to the alternator to prevent it from receiving too much current which would cause it to put out too much current. Conversely, if the voltage regulator does not allow the alternator to receive enough current, the battery will not be fully charged and will eventually go dead.

The battery is connected to the alternator at all times, whether the ignition key is turned on or not. If the battery were shorted to ground, the alternator would also be shorted. This would damage the alternator. To prevent this, a

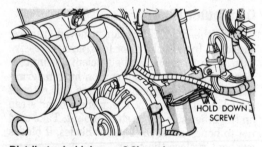

HOLD DOWN SCREW

Distributor hold down—2.2L engine

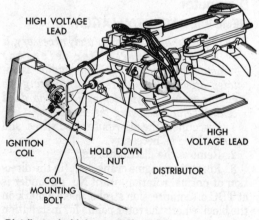

HIGH VOLTAGE LEAD

IGNITION COIL

HOLD DOWN NUT

COIL MOUNTING BOLT

HIGH VOLTAGE LEAD

DISTRIBUTOR

Distributor hold down—2.6L engine

fuse link is installed in the wiring between the battery and the alternator. If the battery is shorted, the fuse link is melted, protecting the alternator.

ALTERNATOR PRECAUTIONS

Some precautions should be taken when working on this, or any other, AC charging system.

1. Never switch battery polarity.

2. When installing a battery, always connect the grounded terminal first.

3. Never disconnect the battery while the engine is running.

4. If the molded connector is disconnected from the alternator, never ground the hot wire.

5. Never run the alternator with the main output cable disconnected.

6. Never electric weld around the truck without disconnecting the alternator.

7. Never apply any voltage in excess of battery voltage while testing.

8. Never jump a battery for starting purposes with more than 12v.

CHARGING SYSTEM TROUBLESHOOTING

There are many possible ways in which the charging system can malfunction. Often the source of a problem is difficult to diagnose, requiring special equipment and a good deal of experience. This is usually not the case, however, where the charging system fails completely and causes the dash board warning light to come on or the battery to become dead. To troubleshoot a complete system failure only two pieces of equipment are needed: a test light, to determine that current is reaching a certain point; and a current indicator (ammeter), to determine the direction of the current flow and its measurement in amps.

This test works under three assumptions:

1. The battery is known to be good and fully charged.

2. The alternator belt is in good condition and adjusted to the proper tension.

3. All connections in the system are clean and tight.

NOTE: *In order for the current indicator to give a valid reading, the car must be equipped with battery cables which are of the same gauge size and quality as original equipment battery cables.*

1. Turn off all electrical components on the car. Make sure the doors of the car are closed. If the car is equipped with a clock, disconnect the clock by removing the lead wire from the rear of the clock. Disconnect the positive battery cable from the battery and connect the ground wire on a test light to the disconnected positive battery cable. Touch the probe end of the test light to the positive battery post. The test light should not light. If the test light does light, there is a short or open circuit on the car.

2. Disconnect the voltage regulator wiring harness connector at the voltage regulator. Turn on the ignition key. Connect the wire on a test light to a good ground (engine bolt). Touch the probe end of a test light to the ignition wire connector into the voltage regulator wiring connector. This wire corresponds to the **I** terminal on the regulator. If the test light goes on, the charging system warning light circuit is complete. If the test light does not come on and the warning light on the instrument panel is on, either the resistor wire, which is parallel with the warning light, or the wiring to the voltage regulator, is defective. If the test light does not come on and the warning light is not on, either the bulb is defective or the power supply wire form the battery through the ignition switch to the bulb has an open circuit. Connect the wiring harness to the regulator.

3. Examine the fuse link wire in the wiring harness from the starter relay to the alternator. If the insulation on the wire is cracked or split, the fuse link may be melted. Connect a test light to the fuse link by attaching the ground wire on the test light to an engine bolt and touching the probe end of the light to the bottom of the fuse link wire where it splices into the alternator output wire. If the bulb in the test light does not light, the fuse link is melted.

4. Start the engine and place a current indicator on the positive battery cable. Turn off all electrical accessories and make sure the doors are closed. If the charging system is working properly, the gauge will show a draw of less than 5 amps. If the system is not working properly, the gauge will show a draw of more than 5 amps. A charge moves the needle toward the battery, a draw moves the needle away from the battery. Turn the engine off.

5. Disconnect the wiring harness from the voltage regulator at the regulator at the regulator connector. Connect a male spade terminal (solderless connector) to each end of a jumper wire. Insert one end of the wire into the wiring harness connector which corresponds to the **A** terminal on the regulator. Insert the other end of the wire into the wiring harness connector which corresponds to the **F** terminal on the regulator. Position the connector with the jumper wire installed so that it cannot contact any metal surface under the hood. Position a current indicator gauge on the positive battery cable. Have an assistant start the engine. Observe the reading on the current indicator. Have your assistant slowly raise the speed of the engine to about 2,000 rpm or until the current indicator needle stops moving, whichever comes first. Do

not run the engine for more than a short period of time in this condition. If the wiring harness connector or jumper wire becomes excessively hot during this test, turn off the engine and check for a grounded wire in the regulator wiring harness. If the current indicator shows a charge of about three amps less than the output of the alternator, the alternator is working properly. If the previous tests showed a draw, the voltage regulator is defective. If the gauge does not show the proper charging rate, the alternator is defective.

REMOVAL AND INSTALLATION
Chrysler Alternator
2.2L Engine

1. Disconnect the negative battery cable.
2. Disconnect the wiring and label for easy installation.
3. Remove the air conditioning compressor drive belt if equipped.
4. Loosen the alternator adjusting bracket bolt and adjusting bolt. Remove the alternator belt.
5. Remove the bracket bolt and the mounting bolt.
6. Remove the pivot bolt and nut.
7. Remove the alternator.
8. Position the alternator against the engine.
9. Install the pivot bolt and nut.
10. Install the mounting bracket bolts, and adjusting bolt.
11. Install drive belts and adjust to specification.
12. Tighten all the mounting bolts and nuts.
13. Connect all alternator terminals.
14. Connect the negative battery cable.

Bosch Alternator
2.2L Engine

1. Disconnect the negative battery cable.
2. Disconnect the wiring and label for easy installation.
3. Remove the air conditioning compressor drive belt.
4. Loosen the alternator adjusting bracket lock nut and adjusting screw. Remove the alternator belt.
5. Remove the bracket locknut and mounting bolt.
6. Remove the pivot bolt and nut.
7. Remove the alternator.
8. Position the alternator against the engine.
9. Install pivot bolt and nut.
10. Set the mounting bracket in place and install the bracket mounting bolt and locknut.
11. Install the drive belts and adjust to specification.
12. Tighten all the mounting bolts and nuts.

13. Connect all alternator terminals.
14. Connect the negative battery cable.

Bosch and Chrysler Alternators
2.5L Engine

1. Disconnect the negative battery cable.
2. Remove the drive belts.
3. Remove the adjusting bracket to engine mounting bolt.
4. Remove the adjusting locking bolt and nut, and remove the mounting bracket.
5. Position the alternator to gain access to the wiring.
6. Disconnect the wiring and label for easy installation.
7. Remove the pivot bolt, nut, and washers.
8. Remove the alternator assembly from the engine.
9. Position the alternator assembly against the engine.
10. Loosely install the pivot bolt, washers, and nut.
11. Install all wiring.
12. Position the mounting bracket and install engine mounting bolt.
13. Loosely install the adjusting locking bolt and nut.
14. Install the drive belts, and adjust to specification.
15. Tighten all mounting bolts and nuts.
16. Connect the negative battery cable.

Mitsubishi Alternator
2.6L Engine

1. Disconnect the negative battery cable.
2. Disconnect the wiring and label for easy installation.
3. Remove the adjusting strap mounting bolt.
4. Remove the drive belts.
5. Remove the support mounting bolt and nut.
6. Remove the alternator assembly.
7. Position the alternator assembly against the engine and install the support bolt.
8. Install the adjusting strap mounting bolt.
9. Install the alternator belts and adjust to specification.
10. Tighten all the support bolts and nuts.
11. Connect all alternator terminals.
12. Connect the negative battery cable.

Bosch and Nippondenso Alternator
3.0L Engine

1. Disconnect the negative battery cable.
2. Install a ½″ breaker bar in the tensioner slot. Rotate counterclockwise to release belt tension and remove poly-V belt.
3. Remove the alternator mounting bolts (2).
4. Remove the wiring and remove alternator.

5. To install, position the alternator and install wiring.

6. Set the alternator against the mounting bracket and install the mounting bolts.

7. Rotate the tensioner counterclockwise and install poly-V belt.

8. Connect the negative battery cable.

Regulator

REMOVAL AND INSTALLATION

Chrysler Alternator (Early Models)

1. Disconnect the negative battery cable.

2. Remove the electrical connection from voltage regulator assembly.

3. Remove the mounting bolts and remove the regulator.

4. This regulator is not adjustable and must be replaced as a unit if found to be defective.

5. Clean any dirt or corrosion from the regulator mounting surface, including mounting holes.

6. Install the replacement electronic voltage regulator.

7. Secured the mounting screws.

8. Connect the voltage regulator wiring connector. Connect the negative battery cable.

NOTE: *All Bosch, Nippondenso, Mitsubishi, and Chrysler (Late Models) alternators have an integral electronic voltage regulator. Voltage regulator replacement on these models requires removal and disassembly of the alternator.*

Starter

TEST PROCEDURES (ON VEHICLE)

NOTE: *The battery is the heart of the electrical system. If the battery is not up to specification it will not deliver the necessary amperage for proper starter operation.*

Starter Does Not Operate

CAUTION: *Before performing this test, disconnect the coil wire from the distributor cap center tower and secure to a good engine ground. This will prevent the engine from accidently starting.*

1. Connect a voltmeter across the battery terminals and conferm that battery voltage (12.4 volts) is available for the ignition and cranking system.

2. Turn the headlights on.

3. If the headlights do not operate. Check the battery cables for loose or corroded connection.

4. If the headlights glow normally, have a helper operate the ignition switch. Headlights should remained reasonably bright when ignition switch is operated. If the headlights dim considerably or go out when the ignition switch is operated, the problem is battery related.

5. If headlights remain bright when the ignition switch is operated. The problem is at the starter relay, wiring, or starter motor.

6. Connect a test light to the battery feed terminal of the starter relay. The test light should

Troubleshooting Basic Charging System Problems

Problem	Cause	Solution
Noisy alternator	• Loose mountings • Loose drive pulley • Worn bearings • Brush noise • Internal circuits shorted (High pitched whine)	• Tighten mounting bolts • Tighten pulley • Replace alternator • Replace alternator • Replace alternator
Squeal when starting engine or accelerating	• Glazed or loose belt	• Replace or adjust belt
Indicator light remains on or ammeter indicates discharge (engine running)	• Broken fan belt • Broken or disconnected wires • Internal alternator problems • Defective voltage regulator	• Install belt • Repair or connect wiring • Replace alternator • Replace voltage regulator
Car light bulbs continually burn out— battery needs water continually	• Alternator/regulator overcharging	• Replace voltage regulator/alternator
Car lights flare on acceleration	• Battery low • Internal alternator/regulator problems	• Charge or replace battery • Replace alternator/regulator
Low voltage output (alternator light flickers continually or ammeter needle wanders)	• Loose or worn belt • Dirty or corroded connections • Internal alternator/regulator problems	• Replace or adjust belt • Clean or replace connections • Replace alternator or regulator

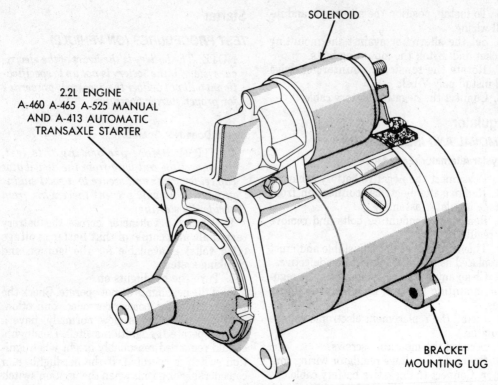

SOLENOID

2.2L ENGINE
A-460 A-465 A-525 MANUAL
AND A-413 AUTOMATIC
TRANSAXLE STARTER

BRACKET
MOUNTING LUG

Bosch direct drive starter motor

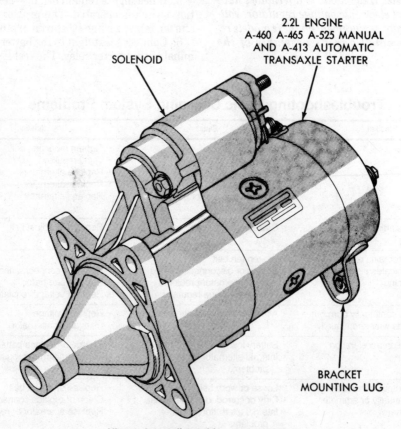

2.2L ENGINE
A-460 A-465 A-525 MANUAL
AND A-413 AUTOMATIC
TRANSAXLE STARTER

SOLENOID

BRACKET
MOUNTING LUG

Nippondenso direct drive starter motor

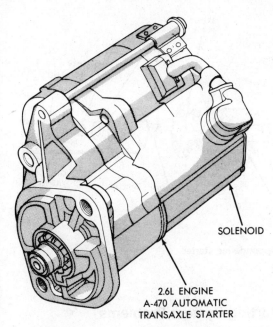

SOLENOID

2.6L ENGINE
A-470 AUTOMATIC
TRANSAXLE STARTER

Nippondenso reduction gear starter motor

go on. If the test light is off, check the battery feed wire to starter relay.

7. Connect the test light to the ignition switch terminal of starter relay and a known good engine ground. Have a helper operate the ignition switch. If the test light does not come on when the ignition switch is operated, check the wiring from the ignition switch to the relay. Test light should have came on.

8. Test light on.

9. Connect a heavy jumper wire, between the battery relay feed and the relay solenoid termi-

nal. If the starter motor operates replace the starter relay. If the motor does not operate, remove the starter for repairs.

REMOVAL AND INSTALLATION

1. Disconnect the negative battery cable.
2. Remove the heatshield and its clamps if so equipped.
3. On the 2.2L and 2.5L engine loosen the air pump tube at the exhaust manifold and move the tube bracket away from the starter.
4. Remove the electrical connections from the starter.
5. Remove the bolts attaching the starter to the flywheel housing and the rear bracket to the engine or transaxle.
6. Remove the starter.
7. Position the replacement starter against the mounting surface.
8. Install the mounting bolts.
9. Connect the starter wiring.
10. On 2.2L and 2.5L engines, position the air pump tube toward starter and connect tube bracket the to exhaust manifold.
11. Install the heatshield and clamp.
12. Connect the negative battery cable.

SOLENOID REPLACEMENT

1. Remove the starter as previously outlined.
2. Disconnect the field coil wire from the solenoid.
3. Remove the solenoid mounting screws.
4. Work the solenoid off of shift fork lever and remove the solenoid.
5. Install plunger on replacement solenoid.
6. Install plunger on shift fork lever.
7. Secure solenoid with mounting screws.

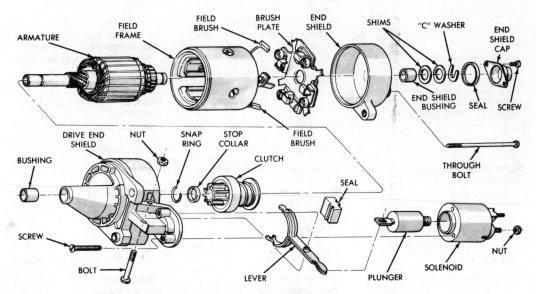

Exploded view of a Bosch starter

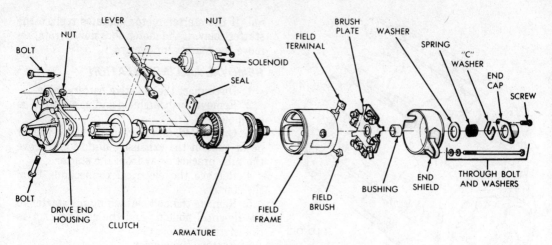

Exploded view of a Nippondenso starter

Troubleshooting Basic Starting System Problems

Problem	Cause	Solution
Starter motor rotates engine slowly	• Battery charge low or battery defective	• Charge or replace battery
	• Defective circuit between battery and starter motor	• Clean and tighten, or replace cables
	• Low load current	• Bench-test starter motor. Inspect for worn brushes and weak brush springs.
	• High load current	• Bench-test starter motor. Check engine for friction, drag or coolant in cylinders. Check ring gear-to-pinion gear clearance.
Starter motor will not rotate engine	• Battery charge low or battery defective	• Charge or replace battery
	• Faulty solenoid	• Check solenoid ground. Repair or replace as necessary.
	• Damage drive pinion gear or ring gear	• Replace damaged gear(s)
	• Starter motor engagement weak	• Bench-test starter motor
	• Starter motor rotates slowly with high load current	• Inspect drive yoke pull-down and point gap, check for worn end bushings, check ring gear clearance
	• Engine seized	• Repair engine
Starter motor drive will not engage (solenoid known to be good)	• Defective contact point assembly	• Repair or replace contact point assembly
	• Inadequate contact point assembly ground	• Repair connection at ground screw
	• Defective hold-in coil	• Replace field winding assembly
Starter motor drive will not disengage	• Starter motor loose on flywheel housing	• Tighten mounting bolts
	• Worn drive end busing	• Replace bushing
	• Damaged ring gear teeth	• Replace ring gear or driveplate
	• Drive yoke return spring broken or missing	• Replace spring
Starter motor drive disengages prematurely	• Weak drive assembly thrust spring	• Replace drive mechanism
	• Hold-in coil defective	• Replace field winding assembly
Low load current	• Worn brushes	• Replace brushes
	• Weak brush springs	• Replace springs

ENGINE MECHANICAL

Engine Overhaul Tips

Most engine overhaul procedures are fairly standard. In addition to specific parts replacement procedures and complete specifications for your individual engine, this chapter also is a guide to accept rebuilding procedures. Examples of standard rebuilding practice are shown and should be used along with specific details concerning your particular engine.

Competent and accurate machine shop services will ensure maximum performance, reliability and engine life.

In most instances it is more profitable for the do-it-yourself mechanic to remove, clean and inspect the component, buy the necessary parts and deliver these to a shop for actual machine work.

On the other hand, much of the rebuilding work (crankshaft, block, bearings, piston rods, and other components) is well within the scope of the do-it-yourself mechanic.

TOOLS

The tools required for an engine overhaul or parts replacement will depend on the depth of your involvement. With a few exceptions, they will be the tools found in a mechanic's tool kit (see Chapter 1). More in-depth work will require any or all of the following:
- A dial indicator (reading in thousandths) mounted on a universal base
- Micrometers and telescope gauges
- Jaw and screw-type pullers
- Scraper
- Valve spring compressor
- Ring groove cleaner
- Piston ring expander and compressor
- Ridge reamer
- Cylinder hone or glaze breaker
- Plastigage®
- Engine stand

The use of most of these tools is illustrated in this chapter. Many can be rented for a one-time use from a local parts jobber or tool supply house specializing in automotive work.

Occasionally, the use of special tools is called for. See the information on Special Tools and Safety Notice in the front of this book before substituting another tool.

INSPECTION TECHNIQUES

Procedures and specifications are given in this chapter for inspecting, cleaning and assessing the wear limits of most major components. Other procedures such as Magnaflux® and Zyglo® can be used to locate material flaws and stress cracks. Magnaflux® is a magnetic process applicable only to ferrous materials. The Zyglo® process coats the material with a fluorescent dye penetrant and can be used on any material Check for suspected surface cracks can be more readily made using spot check dye. The dye is sprayed onto the suspected area, wiped off and the area sprayed with a developer. Cracks will show up brightly.

OVERHAUL TIPS

Aluminum has become extremely popular for use in engines, due to its low weight. Observe the following precautions when handling aluminum parts:
- Never hot tank aluminum parts (the caustic hot tank solution will eat the aluminum.
- Remove all aluminum parts (identification tag, etc.) from engine parts prior to the tanking.
- Always coat threads lightly with engine oil or anti-seize compounds before installation, to prevent seizure.
- Never over-torque bolts or spark plugs especially in aluminum threads.

Stripped threads in any component can be repaired using any of several commercial repair kits (Heli-Coil®, Microdot®, Keenserts®, etc.).

When assembling the engine, any parts that will be frictional contact must be prelubed to provide lubrication at initial start-up. Any product specifically formulated for this purpose can be used, but engine oil is not recommended as a prelube.

When semi-permanent (locked, but removable) installation of bolts or nuts is desired, threads should be cleaned and coated with Loctite® or other similar, commercial nonhardening sealant.

REPAIRING DAMAGED THREADS

Several methods of repairing damaged threads are available. Heli-Coil® (shown here), Keenserts® and Microdot® are among the most widely used. All involve basically the same principle — drilling out stripped threads, tapping the hole and installing a prewound insert — making welding, plugging and oversize fasteners unnecessary.

Two types of thread repair inserts are usually supplied: a standard type for most Inch Coarse, Inch Fine, Metric Course and Metric Fine thread sizes and a spark lug type to fit most spark plug port sizes. Consult the individual manufacturer's catalog to determine exact applications. Typical thread repair kits will contain a selection of prewound threaded inserts, a tap (corresponding to the outside diameter threads of the insert) and an installation tool. Spark plug inserts usually differ because they require a tap equipped with pilot threads and a

Troubleshooting Engine Mechanical Problems

Problem	Cause	Solution
External oil leaks	• Fuel pump gasket broken or improperly seated	• Replace gasket
	• Cylinder head cover RTV sealant broken or improperly seated	• Replace sealant; inspect cylinder head cover sealant flange and cylinder head sealant surface for distortion and cracks
	• Oil filler cap leaking or missing	• Replace cap
	• Oil filter gasket broken or improperly seated	• Replace oil filter
	• Oil pan side gasket broken, improperly seated or opening in RTV sealant	• Replace gasket or repair opening in sealant; inspect oil pan gasket flange for distortion
	• Oil pan front oil seal broken or improperly seated	• Replace seal; inspect timing case cover and oil pan seal flange for distortion
	• Oil pan rear oil seal broken or improperly seated	• Replace seal; inspect oil pan rear oil seal flange; inspect rear main bearing cap for cracks, plugged oil return channels, or distortion in seal groove
	• Timing case cover oil seal broken or improperly seated	• Replace seal
	• Excess oil pressure because of restricted PCV valve	• Replace PCV valve
	• Oil pan drain plug loose or has stripped threads	• Repair as necessary and tighten
	• Rear oil gallery plug loose	• Use appropriate sealant on gallery plug and tighten
	• Rear camshaft plug loose or improperly seated	• Seat camshaft plug or replace and seal, as necessary
	• Distributor base gasket damaged	• Replace gasket
Excessive oil consumption	• Oil level too high	• Drain oil to specified level
	• Oil with wrong viscosity being used	• Replace with specified oil
	• PCV valve stuck closed	• Replace PCV valve
	• Valve stem oil deflectors (or seals) are damaged, missing, or incorrect type	• Replace valve stem oil deflectors
	• Valve stems or valve guides worn	• Measure stem-to-guide clearance and repair as necessary
	• Poorly fitted or missing valve cover baffles	• Replace valve cover
	• Piston rings broken or missing	• Replace broken or missing rings
	• Scuffed piston	• Replace piston
	• Incorrect piston ring gap	• Measure ring gap, repair as necessary
	• Piston rings sticking or excessively loose in grooves	• Measure ring side clearance, repair as necessary
	• Compression rings installed upside down	• Repair as necessary
	• Cylinder walls worn, scored, or glazed	• Repair as necessary
	• Piston ring gaps not properly staggered	• Repair as necessary
	• Excessive main or connecting rod bearing clearance	• Measure bearing clearance, repair as necessary
No oil pressure	• Low oil level	• Add oil to correct level
	• Oil pressure gauge, warning lamp or sending unit inaccurate	• Replace oil pressure gauge or warning lamp
	• Oil pump malfunction	• Replace oil pump
	• Oil pressure relief valve sticking	• Remove and inspect oil pressure relief valve assembly
	• Oil passages on pressure side of pump obstructed	• Inspect oil passages for obstruction

Troubleshooting Engine Mechanical Problems (cont.)

Problem	Cause	Solution
No oil pressure (cont.)	• Oil pickup screen or tube obstructed	• Inspect oil pickup for obstruction
	• Loose oil inlet tube	• Tighten or seal inlet tube
Low oil pressure	• Low oil level	• Add oil to correct level
	• Inaccurate gauge, warning lamp or sending unit	• Replace oil pressure gauge or warning lamp
	• Oil excessively thin because of dilution, poor quality, or improper grade	• Drain and refill crankcase with recommended oil
	• Excessive oil temperature	• Correct cause of overheating engine
	• Oil pressure relief spring weak or sticking	• Remove and inspect oil pressure relief valve assembly
	• Oil inlet tube and screen assembly has restriction or air leak	• Remove and inspect oil inlet tube and screen assembly. (Fill inlet tube with lacquer thinner to locate leaks.)
	• Excessive oil pump clearance	• Measure clearances
	• Excessive main, rod, or camshaft bearing clearance	• Measure bearing clearances, repair as necessary
High oil pressure	• Improper oil viscosity	• Drain and refill crankcase with correct viscosity oil
	• Oil pressure gauge or sending unit inaccurate	• Replace oil pressure gauge
	• Oil pressure relief valve sticking closed	• Remove and inspect oil pressure relief valve assembly
Main bearing noise	• Insufficient oil supply	• Inspect for low oil level and low oil pressure
	• Main bearing clearance excessive	• Measure main bearing clearance, repair as necessary
	• Bearing insert missing	• Replace missing insert
	• Crankshaft end play excessive	• Measure end play, repair as necessary
	• Improperly tightened main bearing cap bolts	• Tighten bolts with specified torque
	• Loose flywheel or drive plate	• Tighten flywheel or drive plate attaching bolts
	• Loose or damaged vibration damper	• Repair as necessary
Connecting rod bearing noise	• Insufficient oil supply	• Inspect for low oil level and low oil pressure
	• Carbon build-up on piston	• Remove carbon from piston crown
	• Bearing clearance excessive or bearing missing	• Measure clearance, repair as necessary
	• Crankshaft connecting rod journal out-of-round	• Measure journal dimensions, repair or replace as necessary
	• Misaligned connecting rod or cap	• Repair as necessary
	• Connecting rod bolts tightened improperly	• Tighten bolts with specified torque
Piston noise	• Piston-to-cylinder wall clearance excessive (scuffed piston)	• Measure clearance and examine piston
	• Cylinder walls excessively tapered or out-of-round	• Measure cylinder wall dimensions, rebore cylinder
	• Piston ring broken	• Replace all rings on piston
	• Loose or seized piston pin	• Measure piston-to-pin clearance, repair as necessary
	• Connecting rods misaligned	• Measure rod alignment, straighten or replace
	• Piston ring side clearance excessively loose or tight	• Measure ring side clearance, repair as necessary
	• Carbon build-up on piston is excessive	• Remove carbon from piston

Troubleshooting Engine Mechanical Problems (cont.)

Problem	Cause	Solution
Valve actuating component noise	• Insufficient oil supply	• Check for: (a) Low oil level (b) Low oil pressure (c) Plugged push rods (d) Wrong hydraulic tappets (e) Restricted oil gallery (f) Excessive tappet to bore clearance
	• Push rods worn or bent	• Replace worn or bent push rods
	• Rocker arms or pivots worn	• Replace worn rocker arms or pivots
	• Foreign objects or chips in hydraulic tappets	• Clean tappets
	• Excessive tappet leak-down	• Replace valve tappet
	• Tappet face worn	• Replace tappet; inspect corresponding cam lobe for wear
	• Broken or cocked valve springs	• Properly seat cocked springs; replace broken springs
	• Stem-to-guide clearance excessive	• Measure stem-to-guide clearance, repair as required
	• Valve bent	• Replace valve
	• Loose rocker arms	• Tighten bolts with specified torque
	• Valve seat runout excessive	• Regrind valve seat/valves
	• Missing valve lock	• Install valve lock
	• Push rod rubbing or contacting cylinder head	• Remove cylinder head and remove obstruction in head
	• Excessive engine oil (four-cylinder engine)	• Correct oil level

combined reamer/tap section. Most manufacturers also supply blister-packed thread repair inserts separately in addition to a master kit containing a variety of taps and inserts plus installation tools.

Before effecting a repair to a threaded hole, remove any snapped, broken or damaged bolts or studs. Penetrating oil can be used to free frozen threads; the offending item can be removed with locking pliers or with a screw or stud extractor. After the hole is clear, the thread can be repaired, as follows:

Checking Engine Compression

A noticeable lack of engine power, excessive oil consumption and/or poor fuel mileage measured over an extended period are all indicators of internal engine war. Worn piston rings, scored or worn cylinder bores, blown head gaskets, sticking or burnt valves and worn valve seats are all possible culprits here. A check of each cylinder's compression will help you locate the problems.

As mentioned in the Tools and Equipment section of Chapter 1, a screw-in type compression gauge is more accurate that the type you simply hold against the spark plug hole, although it takes slightly longer to use. It's worth it to obtain a more accurate reading. Follow the procedures below for gasoline and diesel engined trucks.

1. Warm up the engine to normal operating temperature.

2. Remove all spark plugs.

3. Disconnect the high tension lead from the ignition coil.

4. On fully open the throttle either by operating the carburetor throttle linkage by hand or by having an assistant floor the accelerator pedal.

5. Screw the compression gauge into the no.1 spark plug hole until the fitting is snug.

NOTE: *Be careful not to crossthread the plug hole. On aluminum cylinder heads use extra care, as the threads in these heads are easily ruined.*

6. Ask an assistant to depress the accelerator pedal fully on both carbureted and fuel injected trucks. Then, while you read the compression gauge, ask the assistant to crank the engine two or three times in short bursts using the ignition switch.

7. Read the compression gauge at the end of each series of cranks, and record the highest of these readings. Repeat this procedure for each of the engine's cylinders. Compare the highest reading of each cylinder to the compression pressure specification in the Tune-Up Specifi-

Troubleshooting the Cooling System

Problem	Cause	Solution
High temperature gauge indication— overheating	• Coolant level low	• Replenish coolant
	• Fan belt loose	• Adjust fan belt tension
	• Radiator hose(s) collapsed	• Replace hose(s)
	• Radiator airflow blocked	• Remove restriction (bug screen, fog lamps, etc.)
	• Faulty radiator cap	• Replace radiator cap
	• Ignition timing incorrect	• Adjust ignition timing
	• Idle speed low	• Adjust idle speed
	• Air trapped in cooling system	• Purge air
	• Heavy traffic driving	• Operate at fast idle in neutral intermittently to cool engine
	• Incorrect cooling system component(s) installed	• Install proper component(s)
	• Faulty thermostat	• Replace thermostat
	• Water pump shaft broken or impeller loose	• Replace water pump
	• Radiator tubes clogged	• Flush radiator
	• Cooling system clogged	• Flush system
	• Casting flash in cooling passages	• Repair or replace as necessary. Flash may be visible by removing cooling system components or removing core plugs.
	• Brakes dragging	• Repair brakes
	• Excessive engine friction	• Repair engine
	• Antifreeze concentration over 68%	• Lower antifreeze concentration percentage
	• Missing air seals	• Replace air seals
	• Faulty gauge or sending unit	• Repair or replace faulty component
	• Loss of coolant flow caused by leakage or foaming	• Repair or replace leaking component, replace coolant
	• Viscous fan drive failed	• Replace unit
Low temperature indication— undercooling	• Thermostat stuck open	• Replace thermostat
	• Faulty gauge or sending unit	• Repair or replace faulty component
Coolant loss—boilover	• Overfilled cooling system	• Reduce coolant level to proper specification
	• Quick shutdown after hard (hot) run	• Allow engine to run at fast idle prior to shutdown
	• Air in system resulting in occasional "burping" of coolant	• Purge system
	• Insufficient antifreeze allowing coolant boiling point to be too low	• Add antifreeze to raise boiling point
	• Antifreeze deteriorated because of age or contamination	• Replace coolant
	• Leaks due to loose hose clamps, loose nuts, bolts, drain plugs, faulty hoses, or defective radiator	• Pressure test system to locate source of leak(s) then repair as necessary
	• Faulty head gasket	• Replace head gasket
	• Cracked head, manifold, or block	• Replace as necessary
	• Faulty radiator cap	• Replace cap
Coolant entry into crankcase or cylinder(s)	• Faulty head gasket	• Replace head gasket
	• Crack in head, manifold or block	• Replace as necessary
Coolant recovery system inoperative	• Coolant level low	• Replenish coolant to FULL mark
	• Leak in system	• Pressure test to isolate leak and repair as necessary
	• Pressure cap not tight or seal missing, or leaking	• Repair as necessary
	• Pressure cap defective	• Replace cap
	• Overflow tube clogged or leaking	• Repair as necessary
	• Recovery bottle vent restricted	• Remove restriction

Troubleshooting the Cooling System (cont.)

Problem	Cause	Solution
Noise	• Fan contacting shroud	• Reposition shroud and inspect engine mounts
	• Loose water pump impeller	• Replace pump
	• Glazed fan belt	• Apply silicone or replace belt
	• Loose fan belt	• Adjust fan belt tension
	• Rough surface on drive pulley	• Replace pulley
	• Water pump bearing worn	• Remove belt to isolate. Replace pump.
	• Belt alignment	• Check pulley alignment. Repair as necessary.
No coolant flow through heater core	• Restricted return inlet in water pump	• Remove restriction
	• Heater hose collapsed or restricted	• Remove restriction or replace hose
	• Restricted heater core	• Remove restriction or replace core
	• Restricted outlet in thermostat housing	• Remove flash or restriction
	• Intake manifold bypass hole in cylinder head restricted	• Remove restriction
	• Faulty heater control valve	• Replace valve
	• Intake manifold coolant passage restricted	• Remove restriction or replace intake manifold

NOTE: *Immediately after shutdown, the engine enters a condition known as heat soak. This is caused by the cooling system being inoperative while engine temperature is still high. If coolant temperature rises above boiling point, expansion and pressure may push some coolant out of the radiator overflow tube. If this does not occur frequently it is considered normal.*

Troubleshooting the Serpentine Drive Belt

Problem	Cause	Solution
Tension sheeting fabric failure (woven fabric on outside circumference of belt has cracked or separated from body of belt)	• Grooved or backside idler pulley diameters are less than minimum recommended	• Replace pulley(s) not conforming to specification
	• Tension sheeting contacting (rubbing) stationary object	• Correct rubbing condition
	• Excessive heat causing woven fabric to age	• Replace belt
	• Tension sheeting splice has fractured	• Replace belt
Noise (objectional squeal, squeak, or rumble is heard or felt while drive belt is in operation)	• Belt slippage	• Adjust belt
	• Bearing noise	• Locate and repair
	• Belt misalignment	• Align belt/pulley(s)
	• Belt-to-pulley mismatch	• Install correct belt
	• Driven component inducing vibration	• Locate defective driven component and repair
	• System resonant frequency inducing vibration	• Vary belt tension within specifications. Replace belt.
Rib chunking (one or more ribs has separated from belt body)	• Foreign objects imbedded in pulley grooves	• Remove foreign objects from pulley grooves
	• Installation damage	• Replace belt
	• Drive loads in excess of design specifications	• Adjust belt tension
	• Insufficient internal belt adhesion	• Replace belt
Rib or belt wear (belt ribs contact bottom of pulley grooves)	• Pulley(s) misaligned	• Align pulley(s)
	• Mismatch of belt and pulley groove widths	• Replace belt
	• Abrasive environment	• Replace belt
	• Rusted pulley(s)	• Clean rust from pulley(s)
	• Sharp or jagged pulley groove tips	• Replace pulley
	• Rubber deteriorated	• Replace belt

Troubleshooting the Serpentine Drive Belt (cont.)

Problem	Cause	Solution
Longitudinal belt cracking (cracks between two ribs)	• Belt has mistracked from pulley groove • Pulley groove tip has worn away rubber-to-tensile member	• Replace belt • Replace belt
Belt slips	• Belt slipping because of insufficient tension • Belt or pulley subjected to substance (belt dressing, oil, ethylene glycol) that has reduced friction • Driven component bearing failure • Belt glazed and hardened from heat and excessive slippage	• Adjust tension • Replace belt and clean pulleys • Replace faulty component bearing • Replace belt
"Groove jumping" (belt does not maintain correct position on pulley, or turns over and/or runs off pulleys)	• Insufficient belt tension • Pulley(s) not within design tolerance • Foreign object(s) in grooves • Excessive belt speed • Pulley misalignment • Belt-to-pulley profile mismatched • Belt cordline is distorted	• Adjust belt tension • Replace pulley(s) • Remove foreign objects from grooves • Avoid excessive engine acceleration • Align pulley(s) • Install correct belt • Replace belt
Belt broken (Note: identify and correct problem before replacement belt is installed)	• Excessive tension • Tensile members damaged during belt installation • Belt turnover • Severe pulley misalignment • Bracket, pulley, or bearing failure	• Replace belt and adjust tension to specification • Replace belt • Replace belt • Align pulley(s) • Replace defective component and belt
Cord edge failure (tensile member exposed at edges of belt or separated from belt body)	• Excessive tension • Drive pulley misalignment • Belt contacting stationary object • Pulley irregularities • Improper pulley construction • Insufficient adhesion between tensile member and rubber matrix	• Adjust belt tension • Align pulley • Correct as necessary • Replace pulley • Replace pulley • Replace belt and adjust tension to specifications
Sporadic rib cracking (multiple cracks in belt ribs at random intervals)	• Ribbed pulley(s) diameter less than minimum specification • Backside bend flat pulley(s) diameter less than minimum • Excessive heat condition causing rubber to harden • Excessive belt thickness • Belt overcured • Excessive tension	• Replace pulley(s) • Replace pulley(s) • Correct heat condition as necessary • Replace belt • Replace belt • Adjust belt tension

cations chart in Chapter 2. The specs in this chart are maximum values.

A cylinder's compression pressure is usually acceptable if it is not less than 80% of maximum. The difference between each cylinder should be no more than 12-14 pounds.

8. If a cylinder is unusually low, pour a tablespoon of clean engine oil into the cylinder through the spark plug hole and repeat the compression test. If the compression comes up after adding the oil, it appears that the cylinder's piston rings or bore are damaged or worn. If the pressure remains low, the valves may not be seating properly (a valve job is needed), or the head gasket may be blown near that cylinder. If compression in any two adjacent cylinders is low, and if the addition of oil doesn't help the compression, there is leakage past the head gasket. Oil and coolant water in the combustion chamber can result from this problem. There

may be evidence of water droplets on the engine dipstick when a head gasket has blown.

Engine

REMOVAL AND INSTALLATION

Engine Removal and Installation procedures are similar on all models.

1. Disconnect the negative battery cable.
2. Scribe the hood hinge outlines on the hood, and remove the hood.
3. Drain the cooling system. Remove the radiator hoses from the radiator and engine connections.

CAUTION: *When draining the coolant, keep in mind that cats and dogs are attracted by the ethylene glycol antifreeze, and are quite likely to drink any that is left in an uncovered container or in puddles on the ground. This will prove fatal in sufficient quantity. Always drain the coolant into a sealable container. Coolant should be reused unless it is contaminated or several years old.*

4. Remove the radiator and fan assembly.
5. Remove the air conditioner compressor from the engine and mounting brackets and hoses connected. Position the assembly to the side and secure out of the way.
6. Remove the power steering pump from the engine with mounting brackets and hoses connected. Position the assembly to the side and secure out of the way.
7. Disconnect all electrical connectors at the alternator, carburetor, injection unit and engine.
8. Disconnect the fuel line from the gas tank at the fuel pump. Disconnect the heat hoses from the engine. Disconnect the accelerator cable at the carburetor.
9. Remove the alternator. Disconnect the clutch cable from the clutch lever, if equipped with a manual transaxle.

10. Remove the transaxle case lower cover.
11. Automatic transaxle, mark the flex plate to torque converter location.
12. Remove the bolts that mount the converter to the flexplate. Attach a small C-clamp to the front bottom of the converter housing to prevent the converter from falling off of the transaxle.
13. Disconnect the starter motor wiring and remove the starter motor.
14. Disconnect the exhaust pipe from the exhaust manifold.
15. Remove the right inner engine splash shield. Drain the engine oil and remove the oil filter. Disconnect the engine ground strap.

CAUTION: *The EPA warns that prolonged contact with used engine oil may cause a number of skin disorders, including cancer! You should make every effort to minimize your exposure to used engine oil. Protective gloves should be worn when changing the oil. Wash your hands and any other exposed skin areas as soon as possible after exposure to used engine oil. Soap and water, or waterless hand cleaner should be used.*

16. Attach hoist to the engine.
17. Support the transaxle. Apply slight upward pressure with the chain hoist and remove the through bolt from the right (timing case cover) engine mount.

NOTE: *If the complete engine mount is to be removed, mark the insulator position on the side rail to insure exact reinstallation location.*

18. Remove the transaxle to cylinder block mounting bolts.
19. Remove the front engine mount through bolt. Remove the manual transaxle anti-roll strut.

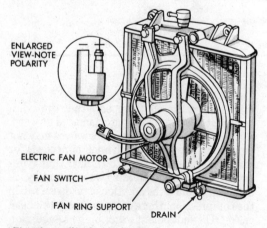

Electric cooling fan and motor

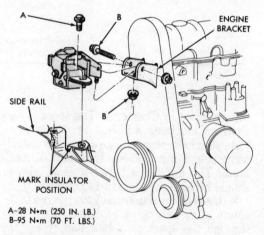

A–28 N•m (250 IN. LB.)
B–95 N•m (70 FT. LBS.)

Right side engine mount

General Engine Specifications

Year	VIN	No. Cylinder Displacement cu. in. (liter)	Fuel System Type	Net Horsepower @ rpm	Net Torque @ rpm (ft. lbs.)	Bore x Stroke (in.)	Com-pression Ratio	Oil Pressure @ 2000 rpm
1984	C	4-135 (2.2)	2 bbl	84 @ 4800	111 @ 2400	3.44 x 3.62	8.5:1	60–90
	G	4-156 (2.6)	2 bbl	92 @ 4500	131 @ 2500	3.59 x 3.86	8.2:1	56
1985	C	4-135 (2.2)	2 bbl	84 @ 4800	111 @ 2400	3.44 x 3.62	9.5:1	60–90
	G	4-156 (2.6)	2 bbl	92 @ 4500	131 @ 2500	3.59 x 3.86	8.7:1	56
1986	C	4-135 (2.2)	2 bbl	84 @ 4800	111 @ 2400	3.44 x 3.62	9.5:1	60–90
	G	4-156 (2.6)	2 bbl	92 @ 4500	131 @ 2500	3.59 x 3.86	8.7:1	56
1987	C	4-135 (2.2)	2 bbl	84 @ 4800	111 @ 2400	3.44 x 3.62	9.5:1	60–90
	K	4-153 (2.5)	EFI	96 @ 4400	170 @ 2800	3.59 x 2.99	8.0:1	35–65
	G	4-156 (2.6)	2 bbl	92 @ 4500	131 @ 2500	3.59 x 3.86	8.7:1	56
1988	K	4-153 (2.5)	EFI	96 @ 4400	133 @ 2800	3.45 x 4.09	8.0:1	35–65
	3	6-181 (3.0)	EFI	140 @ 4800	170 @ 2800	3.59 x 2.99	8.8:1	30–80

Valve Specifications

Year	VIN	No. Cylinder Displacement cu. in. (liter)	Seat Angle (deg.)	Face Angle (deg.)	Spring Test Pressure (lbs.)	Spring Installed Height (in.)	Stem-to-Guide Clearance (in.) Intake	Exhaust	Stem Diameter (in.) Intake	Exhaust
1984	C	4-135 (2.2)	45	45	175	1.65	.001–.003	.002–.004	.312–.313	.311–.312
	G	4-156 (2.6)	45	45	61	1.59	.0012–.0024	.0020–.0035	.315	.315
1985	C	4-135 (2.2)	45	45	175	1.65	.001–.003	.002–.004	.312–.313	.311–.312
	G	4-156 (2.6)	45	45	61	1.59	.0012–.0024	.0020–.0035	.315	.315
1986	C	4-135 (2.2)	45	45	175	1.65	.001–.003	.002–.004	.312–.313	.311–.312
	G	4-156 (2.6)	45	45	61	1.59	.0012–.0024	.0020–.0035	.315	.315
1987	C	4-135 (2.2)	45	45	165	2.39	.0009–.0026	.0030–.0035	.312–.313	.311–.312
	K	4-153 (2.5)	45	45	165	2.39	.0009–.0026	.0030–.0047	—	—
	G	4-156 (2.6)	45	45	61	1.59	.0012–.0024	.0020–.0035	.315	.315
1988	C	4-135 (2.2)	45	45	165	2.39	.0009–.0026	.0030–.0047	.312–.313	.311–.312
	K	4-153 (2.5)	45	45	165	2.39	.0009–.0026	.0030–.0047	—	—
	3	6-181 (3.0)	44	45	73	1.988	.001–.002	.0019–.0030	.313–.314	.3120–.3125

Piston and Ring Specifications

All measurements are given in inches.

Year	VIN	No. Cylinder Displacement cu. in. (liter)	Piston Clearance	Ring Gap			Ring Side Clearance		
				Top Compression	Bottom Compression	Oil Control	Top Compression	Bottom Compression	Oil Control
1984	C	4-135 (2.2)	.0005–.0015	.011–.012	.011–.021	.016–.055	.0016–.0028	.0008–.0020	.0008–.0020
	G	4-156 (2.6)	.0008–.0016	.010–.018	.010–.018	.0078–.0350	.0015–.0031	.0015–.0037	—
1985	C	4-135 (2.2)	.0005–.0015	.011–.012	.011–.021	.016–.055	.0016–.0028	.0008–.0020	.0008–.0020
	G	4-156 (2.6)	.0008–.0016	.010–.018	.010–.018	.0078–.0350	.0015–.0031	.0015–.0037	—
1986	C	4-135 (2.2)	.0005–.0015	.011–.012	.011–.021	.016–.055	.0016–.0028	.0008–.0020	.0008–.0020
	G	4-156 (2.6)	.0008–.0016	.010–.018	.010–.018	.0078–.0350	.0015–.0031	.0015–.0037	—
1987	C	4-135 (2.2)	.0005–.0015	.011–.012	.011–.021	.016–.055	.0016–.0028	.0008–.0020	.0008–.0020
	K	4-153 (2.5)	.0005–.0015	.011–.021	.011–.021	.015–.055	.0015–.0031	.0015–.0037	—
	G	4-156 (2.6)	.0008–.0016	.010–.018	.010–.018	.0078–.0350	.0015–.0031	.0015–.0037	—
1988	K	4-153 (2.5)	.0005–.0015	.011–.021	.011–.021	.015–.055	.0015–.0031	.0015–.0037	—
	3	6-181 (3.0)	.0008–.0015	.012–.018	.010–.016	.012–.035	.0020–.0035	.0008–.0020	—

Camshaft Specfications

Engine	Year	Journal Diameter					Bearing Oil Clearance	Camshaft End Play
		#1	#2	#3	#4	#5		
2.2L	'84–'87	1.375	1.375	1.375	1.375	1.375	.002–.004	.005–.013
2.5L	'87–'88	1.375	1.375	1.375	1.375	1.375	.002–.004	.005–.013
2.6L	'84–'86	—	—	—	—	—	.002–.004	.004–.008
3.0L	'87–'88	N/A	N/A	N/A	N/A	N/A	N/A	N/A

20. Remove the insulator through bolt from the inside wheel house mount, or remove the insulator bracket to transaxle mounting bolt.

21. Raise the engine slowly with the hoist (transaxle supported). Separate the engine and transaxle and remove the engine.

22. With the hoist attached to the engine. Lower the engine into engine compartment.

23. Align the converter to flex plate and the engine mounts. Install all mounting bolts loosely until all are in position, then tighten to 40 ft. lbs.

24. Install the engine to transaxle mounting bolts. Tighten to 70 ft. lbs.

25. Remove the engine hoist and transaxle support.

26. Secure the engine ground strap.

27. Install the inner splash shield.

28. Install the starter assembly.

29. Install the exhaust system.

30. Install the transaxle case lower cover. (Manual Transaxle)

31. Remove the C-clamp from the orque converter housing, (Automatic Transaxle).

Crankshaft and Connecting Rod Specifications
All measurements are given in inches

Year	VIN	No. Cylinder Displacement cu. in. (liter)	Crankshaft				Connecting Rod		
			Main Brg. Journal Dia.	Main Brg. Oil Clearance	Shaft End-play	Thrust on No.	Journal Diameter	Oil Clearance	Side Clearance
1984	C	4-135 (2.2)	2.3630–2.3630	.0003–.0031	.002–.007	3	1.9680–1.9690	.0008–.0034	.005–.013
	G	4-156 (2.6)	2.3622	.0008–.0028	.002–.007	3	2.0866	.0008–.0028	.004–.010
1985	C	4-135 (2.2)	2.3620–2.3630	.0003–.0031	.002–.007	3	1.9680–1.9690	.0008–.0034	.005–.013
	G	4-156 (2.6)	2.3622	.0008–.0028	.002–.007	3	2.0866	.0008–.0028	.004–.010
1986	C	4-135 (2.2)	2.3620–2.3630	.0003–.0031	.002–.007	3	1.9680–1.9690	.0008–.0034	.005–.013
	G	4-156 (2.6)	2.3622	.0008–.0028	.002–.007	3	2.0866	.0008–.0028	.004–.010
1987	C	4-135 (2.2)	2.3620–2.3630	.0003–.0031	.002–.007	3	1.9680–1.9690	.0008–.0034	.005–.013
	K	4-153 (2.5)	2.3620–2.3630	.0004–.0028	.002–.007	3	1.9680–1.9690	.0008–.0034 ②	.004–.005
	G	4.156 (2.6)	2.3622	.0008–.0028	.002–.007	3	2.0866	.0008–.0028	.004–.010
1988	K	4-153 (2.5)	2.3620–2.3630	.0004–.0028	.002–.007	3	1.9680–1.9690	.0008–.0034 ②	.004–.005
	3	6-181 (3.0)	2.3610–2.3632	.0006–.0020	.002–.010	3	1.968–1.969	.0006–.002	.016 max

32. Align flex plate and torque converter with mark previously made. (Automatic Transaxle).

33. Install the convertor to flex plate mounting screws. Tighten to (40 ft. lbs.).

34. Install the case lower cover. (Automatic Transaxle).

35. Connect the clutch cable. (Manual Transaxle)

36. Install the power steering pump.

37. Install the air conditioning compressor.

38. Install the alternator.

39. Connect all wiring.

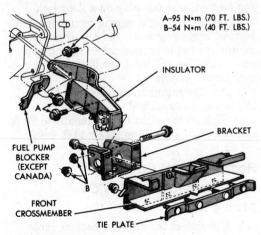

A–95 N•m (70 FT. LBS.)
B–54 N•m (40 FT. LBS.)

INSULATOR

FUEL PUMP BLOCKER (EXCEPT CANADA)

BRACKET

FRONT CROSSMEMBER

TIE PLATE

Front engine mount

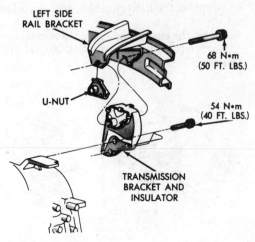

LEFT SIDE RAIL BRACKET

68 N•m (50 FT. LBS.)

U-NUT

54 N•m (40 FT. LBS.)

TRANSMISSION BRACKET AND INSULATOR

Left side engine mount

Torque Specifications
All readings in ft. lbs.

Year	VIN	No. Cylinder Displacement cu. in. (liter)	Cylinder Head Bolts	Main Bearing Bolts	Rod Bearing Bolts	Crankshaft Pulley Bolts	Flywheel Bolts	Manifold		Spark Plugs
								Intake	Exhaust	
1984	C	4-135 (2.2)	45 ①	30 ②	40 ②	50	65 ③	17	17	26
	G	4-156 (2.6)	69	58	34	87	④	12.5	12.5	18
1985	C	4-135 (2.2)	45 ①	30 ②	40 ②	50	65 ③	17	17	26
	G	4-156 (2.6)	69	58	34	87	④	12.5	12.5	18
1986	C	4-135 (2.2)	45 ①	30 ②	40 ②	50	65 ③	17	17	26
	G	4-156 (2.6)	69	58	34	87	④	12.5	12.5	18
1987	C	4-135 (2.2)	45 ①	30 ②	40 ②	50	65 ③	17	17	26
	G	4-156 (2.6)	69	58	34	87	④	12.5	12.5	18
1988	K	4-153 (2.5)	⑧	30 ②	40 ②	50	70	17	17	26
	3	6-181 (3.0)	70	60	38	110	70	⑥	⑦	20

① Tighten in four Steps:
  1st Step: 30 ft. lbs.
  2nd Step: 45 ft. lbs.
  3rd Step: 45 ft. lbs.
  4th Step: Turn the bolts 90° additional
② Plus 90° turn
③ Manual Transmission
④ With A–404 Transmission: 50 ft. lbs.
  With A–413 Transmission: 65 ft. lbs.
  With A–470 Transmission: 100 ft. lbs.

⑤ Tighten in four Steps:
  1st Step: 45 ft. lbs.
  2nd Step: 65 ft. lbs.
  3rd Step: 65 ft. lbs.
  4th Step: Turn the bolts 90° additional
⑥ Intake cross manifold: 174 inch lbs.
  Plenum screws: 130 inch lbs.
⑦ Exhaust manifold: 191 inch lbs.

40. Install the radiator, fan and shroud assembly.
41. Connect all cooling system hoses, accelerator cable and fuel lines.
42. Install the engine oil filter. Fill the crankcase to proper oil level.
43. Fill the cooling system.
44. Adjust linkages.
45. Install the air cleaner and hoses.
46. Install the hood.
47. Connect the battery cables, positive cable first.
48. Start the engine and run until normal operation temperature is indicated. Adjust the carburator.

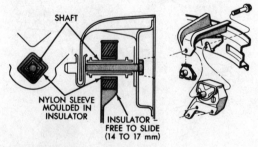

SHAFT
NYLON SLEEVE MOULDED IN INSULATOR
INSULATOR FREE TO SLIDE (14 TO 17 mm)

Left side mount movement

ENGINE/TRANSAXLE POSITIONING

The insulator on the frame rail (right side) and on the transmission bracket (left side) are adjustable to allow right/left drive train adjustment in relation to the driveshaft distress, front end damage or insulator replacement.

Adjustment

1. Remove the load on the engine mounts by carefully supporting the weight of the engine/transaxle assembly on a floor jack.
2. Loosen the right engine mount insulator vertical mounting bolts and the front engine mount bracket to crossmember mounting nuts and bolts. The left insulator is sleeved to provide lateral movement.
3. Pry the engine/transaxle assembly to the left or right as required.
4. Tighten the right engine mount to 20 ft. lbs. and front engine mount to 40 ft. lbs..

Rocker (Valve) Cover
REMOVAL AND INSTALLATION
2.2L Engine

1. Disconnect the negative battery cable.
2. Remove the air cleaner assembly. Remove

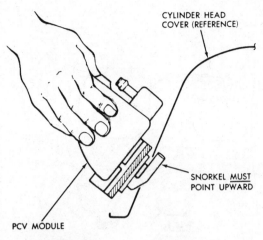

2.2L PCV module

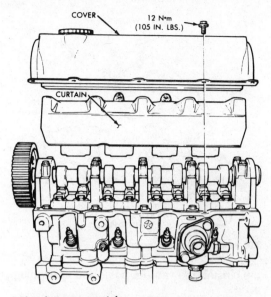

2.5L valve cover curtain

or relocate any hoses or cables that will interfere with rocker cover removal.

3. Depress the retaining clip that holds the PCV module in the rocker cover and turn the module conterclockwise to remove the module.

4. Remove the cover mounting bolts and the rocker cover from the cylinder head.

5. Clean the cover and head mounting surfaces. Install the PCV module in rocker cover. Turn clockwise to install.

NOTE: *With PCV module installed, snorkel mustpoint upward, toward top of valve cover. Snorkel should be free to rotate.*

6. Apply RTV sealant to the rocker cover mounting rail, or install a new cover gasket if provided.

7. Install the rocker cover and tighten to 105 in.lbs.

8. Install the vacuum hoses and spark plug wires.

9. Install the air cleaner assembly.

10. Connect the battery cable.

2.5L Engine

A curtain aiding air/oil separation is located beneath the rocker cover on the cylinder head. The curtain is retained by rubber bumpers.

1. Disconnect the negative battery cable.

2. Remove the air cleaner assembly.

3. Remove any vacuum hoses necessary and relocate spark plug wires.

4. Remove the cover screws and remove the cover.

5. Remove the air/oil separation curtain.

6. Clean the cylinder head, curtain and cover mating surfaces before installation.

7. Install a gasket on the valve cover while pushing the tabs through slots in cover.

8. Install the curtain (manifold side first) with cutouts over cam towers and against cylinder head. Press opposite side into position below the cylinder head rail.

9. Install the cover and tighten to 105 in.lbs..

10. Install the vacuum hoses and spark plug wires.

11. Install the air cleaner assembly.

12. Connect the battery cable.

2.6L Engine

1. Disconnect the negative battery cable.

2. Remove the air cleaner assembly. Remove or relocate any hoses or cables that will interfere with rocker cover removal.

3. Disconnect the hoses to the PCV tube.

4. Remove the cover mounting bolts and remove the rocker cover from the cylinder head. The water pump pully belt shield is attached at rear of rocker cover.

5. Clean the cover and head mounting surfaces.

6. Apply RTV sealant to the top of the rubber cam seal and install the rocker cover.

7. With rocker cover installed, apply RTV sealant to top of semi-circular packing.

8. Tighten screws to 55 in.lbs..

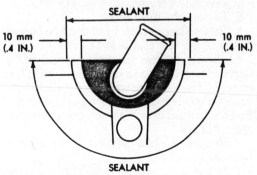

2.6L sealer application points

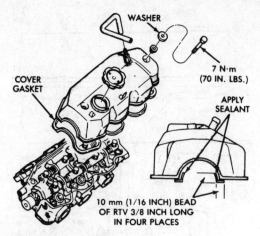

3.0L sealer application points

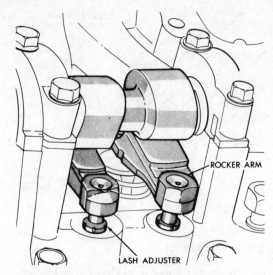

2.2L and 2.5L rocker arm and lash adjuster

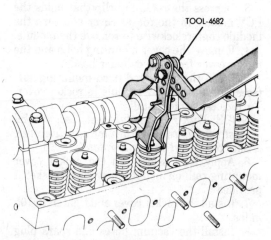

2.2L and 2.5L—compressing a valve spring

9. Install the vacuum hoses and spark plug wires.

10. Install the air cleaner assembly.

11. Connect the battery cable.

3.0L Engine

1. Disconnect the negative battery cable.

2. Remove the air cleaner assembly.

3. Remove any vacuum hoses necessary and relocate spark plug wires.

4. Remove the cover screws and remove cover.

5. Clean the cylinder head and cover mating surfaces before installation.

6. Install a new gasket. Apply RTV sealant to cover ends.

7. Install the cover and tighten to 68 in.lbs..

8. Install the vacuum hoses and spark plug wires.

9. Install the air cleaner assembly.

10. Connect the battery cable.

Rocker Arms and Shafts

REMOVAL AND INSTALLATION

2.2L and 2.5L Engines

1. Disconnect the negative battery cable.

2. Remove the valve cover.

3. Rotate the camshaft until the lobe base is on the rocker arm that is to be removed.

4. Slightly depress the valve spring using Chrysler tool-4682 or the equivalent. Slide the rocker off the lash adjuster and valve tip and remove. Label the rocker arms for position identification. Proceed to next rocker arm and repeat Steps 3 and 4.

5. Remove the lash adjuster if servicing is necessary.

6. If the lash adjuster was previously removed, partially fill with oil and install.

7. Rotate the camshaft until lobe base is in position with rocker arm. Slightly depress the valve spring using Chrysler tool 4682 or equivalent. Slide rocker arm in position.

NOTE: *When depressing the valve spring with Chrysler tool 4682, or the equivalent, the valve locks can become dislocated. Check and make sure both locks are fully seated in the valve grooves and retainer.*

8. Install the valve cover.

9. Connect the battery cable.

2.6L Engine

1. Disconnect the negative battery cable.

2. Remove the valve cover.

3. Loosen the camshaft bearing cap bolts. Do not remove bolts from bearing cap.

4. Remove the rocker arm, rocker shafts and bearing caps as an assembly.

5. Remove the bolts from the camshaft bear-

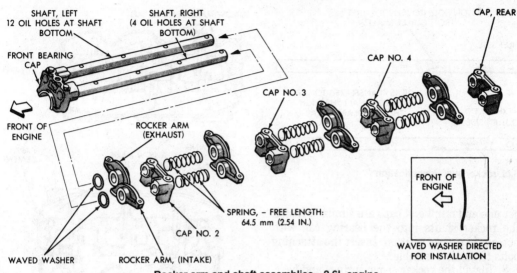

SHAFT, LEFT
12 OIL HOLES AT SHAFT
BOTTOM

SHAFT, RIGHT
(4 OIL HOLES AT SHAFT
BOTTOM)

CAP, REAR

FRONT BEARING
CAP

CAP NO. 4

CAP NO. 3

FRONT OF
ENGINE

ROCKER ARM
(EXHAUST)

FRONT OF
ENGINE

SPRING, – FREE LENGTH:
64.5 mm (2.54 IN.)

CAP NO. 2

WAVED WASHER DIRECTED
FOR INSTALLATION

WAVED WASHER

ROCKER ARM, (INTAKE)

Rocker arm and shaft assemblies—2.6L engine

ing caps and remove the rocker shafts, waved washers, rocker arms and springs. Keep all parts in order. Note the way the rocker shaft, rocker arms, bearing caps and springs are mounted. The rocker arm shaft on the Left side has 12 oil holes at shaft bottom, and the Right side shaft has 4 oil holes at shaft bottom.

6. Inspect the rocker arms mounting area and rockers for damage. Replace if worn or heavily damaged.

7. Position the camshaft bearing caps with arrows pointing toward the timing chain and in numerical order.

8. Insert both shafts into the front bearing cap and install bolts to hold shafts in postion.

9. Install the wave washers, rocker arms, bearing caps, and springs. Install bolts in the rear cap to retain assembly.

10. Place the assembly into position.

11. Tighten the camshaft bearing cap bolts in sequence to 10 N.m. (85 in.lbs.) as followed:

   a. No. 3 Cap
   b. No. 2 Cap
   c. No. 4 Cap
   d. Front Cap
   e. Rear Cap

12. Repeat Step 12 and increase torque to 175 in.lbs.

13. Install the distributor drive gear, timing chain/camshaft sprocket, and sprocket bolt. Torque sprocket bolt to 40 ft. lbs.

   NOTE: *After servicing the rocker shaft assembly, Jet Valve Clearance (if used) and Intake/Exhaust Valve Clearance must be performed.*

14. Install the water pump (upper shield) and valve cover.

15. Connect the battery cable.

3.0L Engine

1. Disconnect the negative battery cable.

2. Remove the valve cover.

3. Loosen the camshaft bearing cap bolts. Do not remove bolts from bearing cap.

4. Remove the rocker arm, rocker shafts and bearing caps as an assembly.

5. Remove the bolts from the camshaft bearing caps and remove the rocker shafts and arms. Keep all parts in order. Note the way the rocker shaft, rocker arms, bearing caps and springs are mounted. The rocker arm shaft on the Intake side has a 3mm diameter oil passage hole from the cylinder head. The Exhaust side does not have this oil passage.

6. Inspect the rocker arm mounting area and rocker for damage. Replace if worn or heavily damaged.

7. Identify number one bearing cap, (Num-

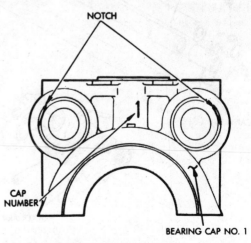

NOTCH

1

CAP
NUMBER

BEARING CAP NO. 1

3.0L number 1 camshaft bearing cap

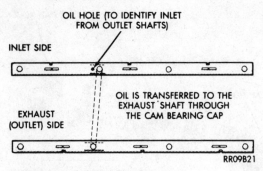

3.0L rocker shaft identification

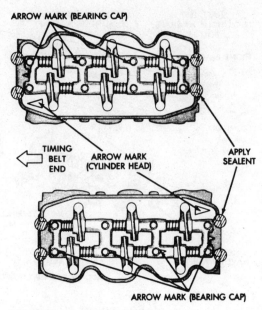

3.0L rocker assembly installation

ber one and number 4 caps are similar). Install the rocker shafts into the bearing cap with notches in proper position. Insert the attaching bolts to retain assemble.

8. Install the rocker arms, springs and bearing caps on shafts in numerical sequence.

9. Align the camshaft bearing caps with arrows (depending on cylinder bank).

10. Install the bolts in number 4 cap to retain assembly.

11. Apply sealant at bearing cap ends.

12. Install the rocker arm shaft assembly.

NOTE: *Make sure the arrow mark on the bearing caps and the arrow mark on the cylinder heads are in the same direction. The direction of arrow marks on the front and rear assmblies are opposite to each other.*

13. Tighten the bearing caps bolts to 85 in.lbs. in the following manner:

   a. No. 3 Cap
   b. No. 2 Cap
   c. No. 1 Cap
   d. No. 4 Cap

14. Repeat Step 13 increasing torque to 180 in.lbs.

15. Install the valve cover.

16. Connect the battery cable.

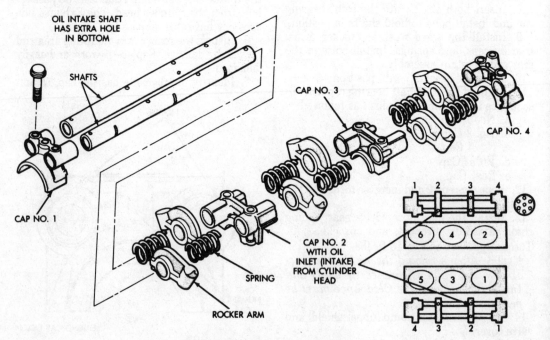

3.0L rocker arm and shaft asemblies

Thermostat

REMOVAL AND INSTALLATION

The thermostat is located in a water box at the side of the engine (facing grille) 2.2L and 2.5L engines. The thermostat on 2.6L and 3.0L engine is located in a water box at the timing belt end of the intake manifold.

1. Drain the cooling system to a level below the thermostat.

CAUTION: *When draining the coolant, keep in mind that cats and dogs are attracted by the ethylene glycol antifreeze, and are quite likely to drink any that is left in an uncovered container or in puddles on the ground. This will prove fatal in sufficient quantity. Always drain the coolant into a sealable container. Coolant should be reused unless it is contaminated or several years old.*

2. Remove the hoses from the thermostat housing.

3. Remove the thermostat housing.

4. Remove the thermostat and discard the gasket. Clean the gasket surfaces thoroughly.

5. Install a new gasket on water box housing 2.2L and 2.5L engines. Center the thermostat in the water box on gasket surface. Install the thermostat housing on gasket. Make sure thermostat sits in its recess of the housing. Tighten bolts to 15 ft. lbs. On 2.6L engine position gasket on water box. Center thermostat in water box and attached housing. Tighten bolts to 15 ft. lbs. On 3.0L engine position thermostat in water box pocket. Make sure thermostat flange in seated properly in flange groove of the water box. Position the new gasket on water box and install housing. Tighten bolts to 15 ft. lbs.

6. Connect the radiator hose to the thermostat housing. Tighten the hose clamp to 35 in.lbs.

7. Fill the cooling system.

Intake Manifold

REMOVAL AND INSTALLATION

2.6L Engine

1. Disconnect the negative battery cable.

2. Drain the cooling system and disconnect the hoses from the water pump to the intake manifold.

CAUTION: *When draining the coolant, keep in mind that cats and dogs are attracted by the ethylene glycol antifreeze, and are quite likely to drink any that is left in an uncovered container or in puddles on the ground. This will prove fatal in sufficient quantity. Always drain the coolant into a sealable container. Coolant should be reused unless it is contaminated or several years old.*

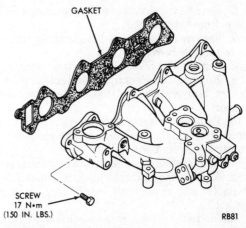

GASKET

SCREW
17 N•m
(150 IN. LBS.)

RB81

2.6L engine, intake manifold

3. Disconnect the carburetor air horn adapter and move to one side.

4. Disconnect the vacuum hoses and throttle link,age from the carburetor.

5. Disconnect the fuel inlet line at the fuel filter.

6. Remove the fuel filter and fuel pump and move to one side.

7. Remove the intake manifold retaining nuts and washers and remove the manifold.

8. Remove old gasket. Clean cylinder head and manifold gasket surface. Check for cracks or warpage. Install a new gasket on cylinder head.

9. Install manifold to cylinder head. Install washers and nuts. Refer to Torque Specification Chart.

10. Install the fuel pump and filter.

11. Install the carburator air horn.

12. Install the throttle control cable.

13. Install the cooling system hose from water pump to manifold.

14. Install the vacuum hoses.

15. Connect the negative battery cable.

3.0L Engine

1. Release fuel system pressure.

2. Disconnect the negative battery cable.

3. Drain the cooling system.

CAUTION: *When draining the coolant, keep in mind that cats and dogs are attracted by the ethylene glycol antifreeze, and are quite likely to drink any that is left in an uncovered container or in puddles on the ground. This will prove fatal in sufficient quantity. Always drain the coolant into a sealable container. Coolant should be reused unless it is contaminated or several years old.*

4. Remove the air cleaner.

5. Remove the throttle cable and transaxle kickdown cable.

6. Remove the electrical and vacuum connections from throttle body.

7. Remove the air intake hose from air cleaner to throttle body.

8. Remove the EGR tube to intake plenum.

9. Remove the electrical connection from charge temperature and coolant temperature sensor.

10. Remove thr vacuum connection from the pressure regulator and remove the air intake connection from the manifold.

11. Remove fuel hoses to fuel rail connection.

12. Remove the air intake plenum to manifold bolts (8) and remove air intake plenum and gasket.

WARNING: *Whenever the air intake plenum is removed, cover the intake manifold properly to avoid objects from entering cylinder head.*

13. Disconnect the fuel injector wiring harness from the engine wiring harness.

14. Remove the pressure regulator attaching bolts and remove pressure regulator from rail.

15. Remove the fuel rail attaching bolts and remove fuel rail.

16. Remove the radiator hose from thermostat housing and heater hose from pipe.

17. Remove the intake manifold attaching nuts and washers and remove intake manifold.

18. Clean the gasket material from cylinder head and manifold gasket surface. Check for cracks or damaged mounting surfaces.

19. Install a new gasket on the intake surface of the cylinder head and install the intake manifold.

20. Install the intake manifold washers and nuts. Tighten in sequence shown. Refer to Torque Specification Chart.

21. Clean the injectors and lubricate the injector O-rings with a drop of clean engine oil.

22. Place the tip of each injector into their ports. Push assembly into place until the injectors are seated in their ports.

23. Install rail attaching bolts and tighten to 115 in.lbs.

24. Install pressure regulator to rail. Install pressure regulator mounting bolts and tighten to 95 in.lbs.

25. Install fuel supply and return tube holddown bolt and vacuum crossover tube holddown bolt. Torque to 95 in.lbs.

26. Torque fuel pressure regulator hose clamps to 10 in.lbs.

27. Connect injector wiring harness to engine wiring harness.

28. Connect vacuum harness to fuel rail and pressure regulator.

29. Remove covering from intake manifold.

30. Position the intake manifold gasket, beaded side up, on the intake manifold.

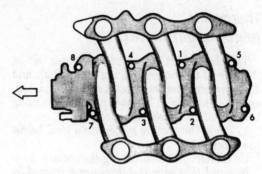

3.0L intake manifold torque sequence

31. Put the air intake plenum in place. Install attaching bolts and tighten in sequence to 115 in.lbs.

32. Connect the fuel line to fuel rail. Tighten clamps to 10 in.lbs.

33. Connect the vacuum hoses to intake plenum.

34. Connect the electrical connection to coolant temperature sensor and charge temperature sensor.

35. Connect the EGR tube flange to intake plenum and torque to 15 ft. lbs.

36. Connect the throttle body vacuum hoses and electrical connections.

37. Install the throttle cable and transaxle kickdown linkage.

38. Install the radiator and heater hose. Fill the cooling system.

39. Connect the negative battery cable.

Exhaust Manifold

REMOVAL AND INSTALLATION

2.6L Engine

1. Disconnect the negative battery cable.

2. Remove the air cleaner assembly.

3. Remove the belt from the power steering pump.

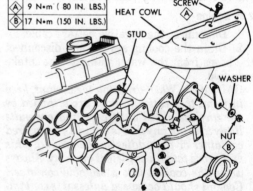

A	9 N·m (80 IN. LBS.)	
B	17 N·m (150 IN. LBS.)	

2.6L engine, exhaust manifold

4. Raise the vehicle and make sure it is supported safely.

5. Remove the exhaust pipe from the manifold.

6. Disconnect the air injection tube assembly from the exhaust manifold and lower the vehicle.

7. Remove the power steering pump assembly and move to one side.

8. Remove the heat cowl from the exhaust manifold.

9. Remove the exhaust manifold retaining nuts and remove the assembly from the vehicle.

10. Remove the carburetor air heater from the manifold.

11. Separate the exhaust manifold from the catalytic converter by removing the retaining screws.

12. Clean gasket material from cylinder head and exhaust manifold gasket surfaces. Check mating surfaces for cracks or distortion.

13. Install a new gasket between the exhaust manifold an catalytic converter. Install mounting screws and tighten to 32 N.m (24 ft. lbs.).

14. Install the carburetor air heater on manifold and tighten to 80 in.lbs.

15. Lightly coat the new exhaust manifold gasket with sealant (P/N 3419115) or equivalent on cylinder head side.

16. Install the exhaust manifold and mounting nuts. Refer to Torque Specification Chart.

17. Install the heat cowl to manifold and tighten screws to 80 in.lbs.

18. Install the air cleaner support bracket.

19. Install the power steering pump assembly.

20. Install the air injection tube assembly to air pump.

21. Raise the vehicle and install air injection tube assembly to exhaust manifold.

22. Install the exhaust pipe to manifold.

23. Lower the vehicle and install power steering belt.

24. Fill the cooling system.

25. Install the air cleaner assembly.

26. Connect the negative battery cable.

3.0L Engine

1. Disconnect the negative battery cable.

2. Raise vehicle and support properly.

3. Disconnect the exhaust pipe from rear (cowl side) exhaust manifold at articulated joint.

4. Remove the EGR tube from the rear manifold and disconnect oxygen sensor lead.

5. Remove the attaching bolts from crossover pipe to manifold.

6. Remove the attaching nuts which retained manifold to cylinder head and remove manifold.

7. Lower the vehicle and remove bolt securing front heat shield to front exhaust manifold.

8. Remove the bolts retaining crossover pipe to front exhaust manifold and nuts retaining manifold to cylinder head. Remove manifold assembly.

9. Clean all gasket material from cylinder the head and exhaust manifold gasket surfaces. Check mating surfaces for cracks or distortion.

10. Install the new gasket with the numbers 1-3-5 stamped on the top on the rear bank. The gasket with the numbers 2-4-6 must be installed on the front bank (radiator side).

11. Install rear exhaust manifold and tighten attaching nuts to 15 ft. lbs.

12. Install exhaust pipe to manifold and tighten shoulder bolts to 20 ft. lbs.

13. Install crossover pipe to manifold and tighten bolts to 69 N.m (51 ft. lbs.).

14. Install oxygen sensor lead and EGR tube.

15. Install front exhaust manifold and attach exhaust crossover.

16. Install front manifold heat shield and tighten bolts to 10 ft. lbs.

17. Connect the negative battery cable.

Combination Manifold
REMOVAL AND INSTALLATION
2.2L and 2.5L Engines

1. Disconnect the battery negative cable.

2. Drain the cooling system.

CAUTION: *When draining the coolant, keep in mind that cats and dogs are attracted by the ethylene glycol antifreeze, and are quite likely to drink any that is left in an uncovered container or in puddles on the ground. This will prove fatal in sufficient quantity. Always drain the coolant into a sealable container. Coolant should be reused unless it is contaminated or several years old.*

3. Remove the air cleaner, disconnect all

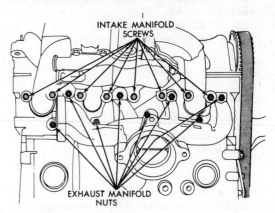

2.2L and 2.5L—combination manifold

vaccum lines, electrical wiring and fuel lines from carburator and intake manifold.

4. Remove the throttle linkage.

5. Remove the water hoses from water crossover.

6. Raise the vehicle and remove exhaust pipe from manifold.

7. Remove power steering pump and set aside.

8. Remove intake manifold support bracket and EGR tube.

9. On Canadian cars romove (4) air injection tube bolts and injection tube assembly.

10. Remove the intake manifold retaining screws.

11. Lower vehicle and remove the intake manifold.

12. Remove exhaust manifold retaining nuts and remove exhaust manifold.

13. Clean gasket surface of both manifold and cylinder block surface.

14. Install a new gasket on exhaust and intake manifold. Coat manifold with Sealer (P/N 3419115) or equivalent on manifold side.

15. Position the exhaust manifold against cylinder block and install nuts. Tighten nuts from center while alternating outward in both direction. See Torque Specification Chart.

16. Position the intake manifold against cylinder head.

17. From beneath the vehicle tighten intake manifold screws. Start at the center while alternating outward in both direction. See Torque Specification Chart.

18. Install the exhaust pipe to exhaust manifold.

19. On Canadian cars install air injection tube assembly.

20. Install the intake manifold support bracket and EGR tube.

21. Install the power steering pump assembly and power steering belt.

22. Install the water hoses to water crossover.

23. Install the fuel lines, vacuum lines, and electrical wiring.

24. Fill the cooling system.

25. Connect the negative battery cable.

Radiator

REMOVAL AND INSTALLATION

1. Disconnect the negative battery cable.

2. Drain the cooling system.

CAUTION: *When draining the coolant, keep in mind that cats and dogs are attracted by the ethylene glycol antifreeze, and are quite likely to drink any that is left in an uncovered container or in puddles on the ground. This will prove fatal in sufficient quantity. Always drain the coolant into a sealable container. Coolant should be reused unless it is contaminated or several years old.*

3. Remove the upper and lower hoses and coolant recovery tank tube to filler neck.

4. Disconnect the wiring harness from fan motor.

5. Remove the upper mounting bolts from fan assembly.

6. Lift fan assembly from bottom ring retaining clip.

7. Remove the radiator upper mounting bolts and carefully lift radiator from engine compartment.

8. Carefully slide the radiator into place while aligning radiator with holes in radiator support seat.

9. Install the upper radiator mounting bolts and tighten to 105 in.lbs.

10. Install the lower radiator hose and tighten to 35 in.lbs.

11. Carefully install the fan assembly while aligning lower fan support into retaining clip.

12. Attach washers and nuts to upper fan support.

13. Connect the fan electrical connector.

14. Install the upper radiator hose and tighten clamp to 35 in.lbs.

15. Fill the cooling system.

Automatic Transmission Oil Cooler

REMOVAL AND INSTALLATION

The transmission oil cooler used on these models are externally mounted ahead of the radiator. This is considered an oil-to-air type system.

1. Remove the electrical cooling fan assembly and remove radiator. Refer to Radiator Removal procedures.

2. Loosen the clamps retaining the hoses from the transmisssion cooler lines.

3. Place an oil drain pan under the hoses and remove hoses from the cooler assembly.

4. Remove (2) screws retaining the cooler assembly to support and remove cooler assebly.

5. If reusing the cooler assembly, reverse flush the cooler.

6. Position the cooler assembly against its support.

7. Install the cooler mounting bolts and tighten to 35 in.lbs.

8. Install hoses from the cooler lines to cooler assembly and tighten clamps to 16 in.lbs.

9. Install the radiator and cooling fan assembly. Refer to Radiator procedures previously outlined.

Water Pump

REMOVAL AND INSTALLATION

2.2L and 2.5L Engine

1. Disconnect the negative battery cable.
2. Remove the drive belts.
3. Drain the cooling system.

CAUTION: *When draining the coolant, keep in mind that cats and dogs are attracted by the ethylene glycol antifreeze, and are quite likely to drink any that is left in an uncovered container or in puddles on the ground. This will prove fatal in sufficient quantity. Always drain the coolant into a sealable container. Coolant should be reused unless it is contaminated or several years old.*

4. Remove the upper radiator hose.
5. Without discharging the system, remove the air conditioning compressor from the engine brackets and set to one side.
6. Remove the alternator and move to one side.
7. Disconnect the lower radiator hose and heater hose.
8. Remove (3) upper screws and (1) lower screw retaining water pump to the engine and remove pump assembly.
9. Position the replacement pump against the engine and install mounting screws. Tighten the (3) upper screws to 20 ft. lbs. and lower screw to 50 ft. lbs.
10. Install heater hose and lower radiator hose. Tighten clamps to 16 in.lbs.
11. Install air conditioning compressor and alternator.
12. Install the drive belts and adjust to specification. Refer to specifications in Chapter 1.
13. Fill the cooling system. Refer to Drain/Refill procedure in Chapter 1.
14. Connect the negative battery cable.

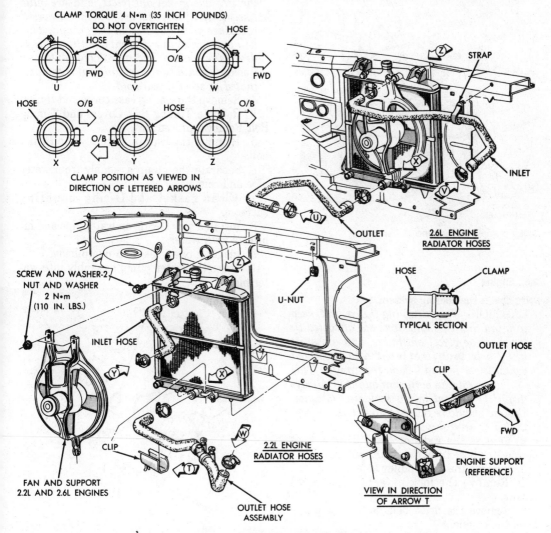

Radiator removal and installation

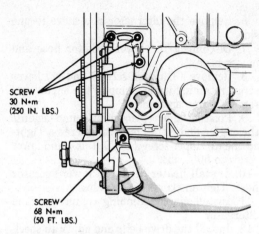

SCREW
30 N•m
(250 IN. LBS.)

SCREW
68 N•m
(50 FT. LBS.)

2.2L and 2.5L—water pump

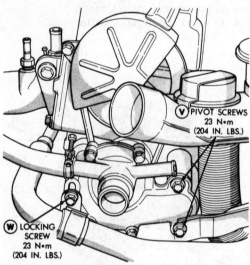

V PIVOT SCREWS
23 N•m
(204 IN. LBS.)

W LOCKING
SCREW
23 N•m
(204 IN. LBS.)

Water pump—2.6L engine

2.6L Engine

1. Drain the cooling system.
CAUTION: *When draining the coolant, keep in mind that cats and dogs are attracted by the ethylene glycol antifreeze, and are quite likely to drink any that is left in an uncovered container or in puddles on the ground. This will prove fatal in sufficient quantity. Always drain the coolant into a sealable container. Coolant should be reused unless it is contaminated or several years old.*
2. Remove the radiator hose, by-pass hose and heater hose from the water pump.
3. Remove the drive pulley shield.
4. Remove the locking screw and pivot screws.
5. Remove the drive belt and water pump from the engine.
6. Install a new O-ring gasket in O-ring groove of pump body assembly to cylinder block.
7. Position the water pump assembly against the engine and install pivot screws and locking screw finger tight.
8. Install the water pump drive belt and adjust to specification. New belt 8mm deflection, used belt 9mm deflection.
9. Install drive belt pully cover.
10. Install the radiator hose, by-pass hose and heater hose.
11. Fill the cooling system. Refer to Drain/Refill procedures in Chapter 1.

3.0L Engine

1. Disconnect the negative battery cable.
2. Remove the drive belts.
3. Drain the cooling system.
CAUTION: *When draining the coolant, keep in mind that cats and dogs are attracted by the ethylene glycol antifreeze, and are quite likely to drink any that is left in an uncovered container or in puddles on the ground. This will prove fatal in sufficient quantity. Always drain the coolant into a sealable container. Coolant should be reused unless it is contaminated or several years old.*
4. Remove the timing case cover and timing belt. Refer to Timing Belt Covers and Timing Belt Removal procedures.
5. Remove the pump assembly mounting bolts.
6. Separate the pump assembly from water pipe and remove.
7. Clean gasket and O-ring mounting surfaces.
8. Install a new O-ring on water pipe and lubricate with water.
9. Install a new gasket on pump body.
10. Press the water pump assembly into water pipe.

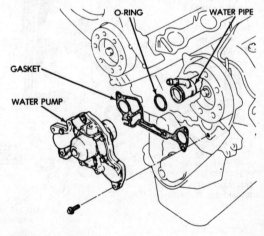

O-RING   WATER PIPE

GASKET

WATER PUMP

3.0L water pump

11. Install pump mounting bolts and tighten to 27 N.m (20 ft. lbs.).

12. Install timing belt and cover. Refer to Timing Belt procedures.

13. Install drive belts. Refer to specification in Chapter 1.

14. Fill the cooling system. Refer to Drain/Refill procedures in Chapter 1.

Cylinder Head

REMOVAL

2.2L and 2.5L Engines

The following procedures are performed with engine in vehicle.

WARNING: *Do not perform this operation on a warm engine. Do not attempt to slide the cylinder head off of the block. Lift head straight up and off of the engine block.*

1. Disconnect the negative battery cable.

2. Drain the cooling system. Refer to Cooling System procedures in Chapter 1.

CAUTION: *When draining the coolant, keep in mind that cats and dogs are attracted by the ethylene glycol antifreeze, and are quite likely to drink any that is left in an uncovered container or in puddles on the ground. This will prove fatal in sufficient quantity. Always drain the coolant into a sealable container. Coolant should be reused unless it is contaminated or several years old.*

3. Remove the air cleaner assembly. Mark the various hoses for installation identification.

4. Disconnect all lines, hoses, wiring harnesses, etc. from the manifold, carburetor and cylinder head.

5. Remove accessory drive belts.

6. Remove the air pump pulley and remove air pump assembly 2.2L engine.

7. Remove the air conditioning compressor and mounting brackets.

8. Remove power steering pump and brackets.

9. Remove the intake and exhaust manifolds. Refer to Combination Manifold Removal procedures previously outlined.

10. Remove the valve cover.

11. Remove the upper half of the timing case (front cover).

NOTE: *Removal of the cylinder head requires removal of the camshaft sprocket. To maintain proper engine timing the timing belt is left indexed on the sprocket with the assembly suspended under light tension. Maintain adequate tension on the sprocket and belt assembly to prevent the belt from disengaging the crankshaft or intermediate shaft sprockets. If timing is lost, refer to Engine Timing Procedures.*

12. Disconnect the dipstick tube from ther-

mostat housing. Carefully rotate bracket from stud.

13. Remove the cylinder head bolts in sequence for the outer ends to the center.

14. Remove the cylinder head. =

CLEANING AND INSPECTION

1. Turn the cylinder head over so that the mounting surface is facing up and support evenly on wooden blocks.

2. Use a scraper and remove all of the gasket material and carbon stuck to the head mounting surface and engine block. Mount a wire carbon removal brush in an electric drill and clean away the carbon on the valve heads and head combustion chambers.

NOTE: *When scraping or decarbonizing the cylinder head, take care not to damage or nick the gasket mounting surface or combustion chamber.*

3. Clean cylinder head oil passages.

4. After cleaning check cylinder head for cracks or damage.

5. Check cylinder head flatness. Flatness must be within 0.1mm.

INSTALLATION

1. Install a new cylinder head gasket.

2. Set cylinder head assembly in place.

3. Install all bolts finger tight. Tighten bolts in sequence.

4. Install the dipstick tube at thermostat housing.

5. With adequate tension on timing belt and sprocket assembly position sprocket on camshaft. Install sprocket bolt and torque to 88 N.m (65 ft. lbs.).

6. Install the engine timimg cover upper half.

7. Install the valve cover.

8. Install the combination manifold assembly. Refer to Combination Manifold Procedures.

9. Install thepower steering brackets and pump.

10. Install the air conditioning compressor brackets and compressor.

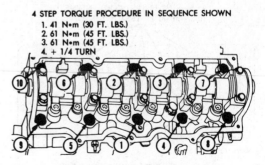

4 STEP TORQUE PROCEDURE IN SEQUENCE SHOWN
1. 41 N•m (30 FT. LBS.)
2. 61 N•m (45 FT. LBS.)
3. 61 N•m (45 FT. LBS.)
4. + 1/4 TURN

Torque sequence—2.2L & 2.5L cylinder head

11. Install the air pump and air pump pully 2.2L engine.

12. Install the accessory drive belts.

13. Connect all vaccum hoses and wiring.

14. Fill the cooling system.

15. Connect the negative battery cable.

REMOVAL

2.6L Engine

1. Disconnect the battery and drain the cooling system.

CAUTION: *When draining the coolant, keep in mind that cats and dogs are attracted by the ethylene glycol antifreeze, and are quite likely to drink any that is left in an uncovered container or in puddles on the ground. This will prove fatal in sufficient quantity. Always drain the coolant into a sealable container. Coolant should be reused unless it is contaminated or several years old.*

2. Remove the air cleaner assembly.

3. Disconnect the upper radiator hose and heater hose.

4. Disconnect the vacuum hoses and electrical wiring.

5. Separate the carburetor linkage.

6. Remove carburetor-to-valve cover bracket.

7. Disconnect the spark plug wires after marking them for reinstallation. Remove the distributor.

8. Remove the fuel line and fuel pump. Plug the line leading to the gas tank to prevent fuel leakage.

9. Remove the engine valve cover.

10. Remove the water pump belt and pully.

11. Rotate crankshaft until number 1 piston is at the top of its compression stroke (both valves closed).

12. Draw a mark on the timing chain in line with the timing mark on the camshaft sprocket.

13. Remove the camshaft sprocket bolt, sprocket and distributor drive gear. Maintain adequate tension on the sprocket and chain assembly to prevent the chain from disengaging the crankshaft sprocket.

14. Raise the vehicle and disconnect air feeder hoses.

15. Remove the power steering pump and set aside.

16. Remove the dipstick tube and engine ground wire.

17. Remove the exhaust manifold shield.

18. Separate the exhaust manifold from converter.

19. Remove the cylinder head bolts in sequence shown. Head bolts should be loosened in sequence to prevent head warpage.

20. Remove the cylinder head.

CLEANING AND INSPECTION

1. Turn the cylinder head over so that the mounting surface is facing up and support evenly on wooden blocks.

2. Use a scraper and remove all of the gasket material and carbon stuck to the head mounting surface and engine block. Mount a wire carbon removal brush in an electric drill and clean away the carbon on the valve heads and head combustion chambers.

NOTE: *When scraping or decarbonizing the cylinder head, take care not to damage or nick the gasket mounting surface or combustion chamber.*

3. Clean cylinder head oil passages.

4. After cleaning check cylinder head for cracks or damage.

5. Check cylinder head flatness. Standard dimension: Less than 0.05mm. Service limit: 0.1mm.

INSTALLATION

1. Install a new cylinder head gasket. Install the cylinder head assembly.

2. Install the cylinder head bolts and torque bolts No. 1 thru 10 in sequence shown. Refer to Torque Specification Chart. Torque cylinder head to chain case cover bolts (2) to 13 ft. lbs.

3. From beneath the vehicle connect the converter to exhaust manifold.

4. Connect the air feeder hoses.

5. Install the exhaust manifold shield.

6. Install the power steering pump.

7. Install the dipstick tube and engine ground wire.

8. Install the camshaft sprocket and chain assembly with marks previously made. Install the distributor drive gear and sprocket bolt, tighten sprocket bolt to 54 N.m. (40 ft. lbs.).

9. Install the water pump pully and belt. Refer to Water Pump service procedures.

10. Install the engine valve cover.

11. Install the fuel pump and fuel line.

12. Install the distributor and connect spark plug wires.

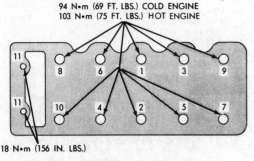

94 N•m (69 FT. LBS.) COLD ENGINE
103 N•m (75 FT. LBS.) HOT ENGINE

18 N•m (156 IN. LBS.)

Torque sequence for 2.6L cylinder head

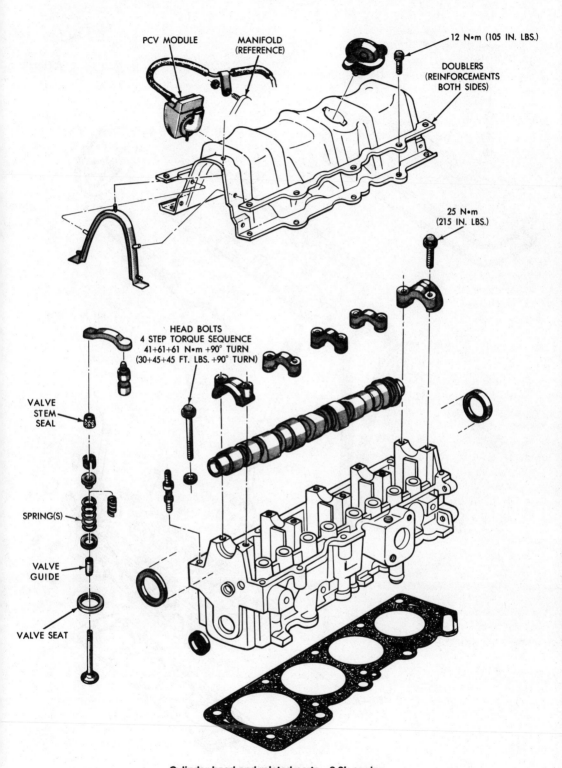

PCV MODULE

MANIFOLD (REFERENCE)

12 N•m (105 IN. LBS.)

DOUBLERS (REINFORCEMENTS BOTH SIDES)

25 N•m (215 IN. LBS.)

HEAD BOLTS
4 STEP TORQUE SEQUENCE
41+61+61 N•m +90° TURN
(30+45+45 FT. LBS. +90° TURN)

VALVE STEM SEAL

SPRING(S)

VALVE GUIDE

VALVE SEAT

Cylinder head and related parts—2.2L engine

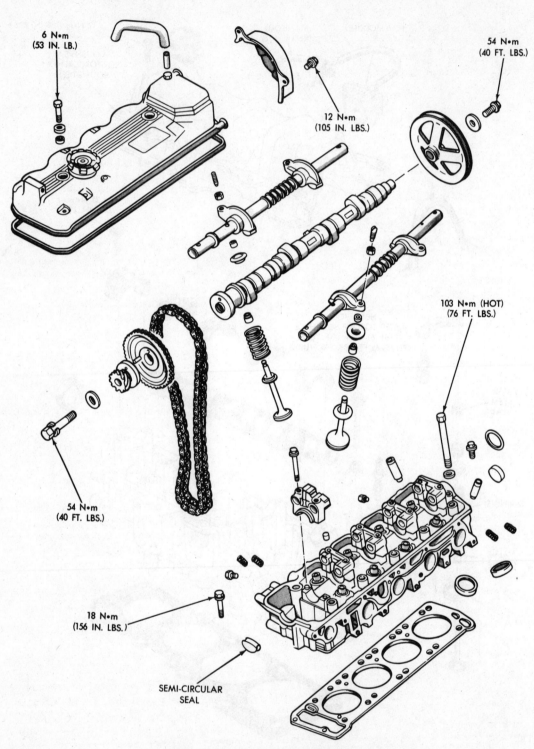

6 N•m
(53 IN. LB.)

54 N•m
(40 FT. LBS.)

12 N•m
(105 IN. LBS.)

103 N•m (HOT)
(76 FT. LBS.)

54 N•m
(40 FT. LBS.)

18 N•m
(156 IN. LBS.)

SEMI-CIRCULAR
SEAL

Cylinder head and related parts—2.6L engine

13. Install the carburetor-to-valve cover bracket.

14. Install the carburetor linkage.

15. Install the vacuum hoses and electrical wiring.

16. Install the upper radiator hose and heater hose.

17. Install the air cleaner.

18. Connect battery cable and refill cooling system.

REMOVAL

3.0L Engine

1. Disconnect the negative battery cable.
2. Remove the accessory drive belts.
3. Remove the air cleaner assembly.
4. Remove the timing belt covers and timing belt.
5. Remove the rocker arm covers.
6. Remove the intake manifold. Refer to Intake Manifold Removal procedures.
7. Remove the exhaust manifold from cylinder heads. Refer to Exhaust Manifold Removal procedures.
8. Remove the cylinder head bolts in sequence working from the outer edges toward the center. Use a 10 mm Allen Hex to remove the bolts, remove cylinder head.

CLEANING AND INSPECTION

1. Turn the cylinder head over so that the mounting surface is facing up and support evenly on wooden blocks.
2. Use a scraper and remove all of the gasket material and carbon stuck to the head mounting surface and engine block. Mount a wire carbon removal brush in an electric drill and clean away the carbon on the valve heads and head combustion chambers.

NOTE: *When scraping or decarbonizing the*

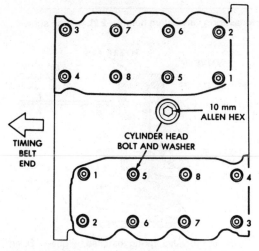

3.0L cylinder head bolt loosening sequence

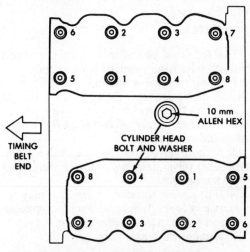

3.0L cylinder head bolt tightening sequence

cylinder head, take care not to damage or nick the gasket mounting surface or combustion chamber.

3. Clean cylinder head oil passages.
4. After cleaning check cylinder head for cracks or damage.
5. Check cylinder head flatness. Standard dimension: Less than 0.5mm. Service limit: 0.2mm.

INSTALLATION

1. Position a new head gasket on cylinder head over dowel pins.
2. Set cylinder head in place on dowel pins.
3. Install cylinder head bolts with washers and tighten gradually working in two or three steps according to sequence shown. Refer to Torque Specification Chart.
4. Install the exhaust manifold. Refer to Exhaust Manifold Installation procedures.
5. Install the intake manifold. Refer to Intake Manifold Installation procedures.
6. Install the rocker arm covers. See Rocker Cover Installation procedures.
7. Install the timing belt and timing belt covers.
8. Install the accessory drive belts.
9. Install the air cleaner assembly.
10. Connect battery negative cable.

CYLINDER HEAD RESURFACING

If the cylinder head is warped, resurfacing by a automotive machine shop will be required. After cleaning the gasket surface, place a straight-edge across the mounting surface of the head, diagonally from one end to the other. Using a feeler gauge , determine the clearance at the center and alone the length between the head and straight-edge. Refer to Cylinder Head Inspection for the appropriate engine specifications.

Valves

REMOVAL

The following procedures to be performed with cylinder head removed from engine.

1. Compress valve springs using Tool C-3422A or equivalent. Do not mix removed parts. Place the parts from each valve in a separate container, numbered and identified for the valve and cylinder.

2. Remove valve retaining locks, valve spring retainers, valve stem seal, valve springs and valve spring seats.

NOTE: *Before removing valve assembly remove any burrs from valve stem lock grooves to prevent damage to valve guides.*

3. Remove valve assembly.

INSPECTION

1. Clean valves thoroughly.

2. Check valve stem tip for pitting or depression.

3. Check for ridge wear on valve stem area.

4. Inspect valve (with Prussian blue) for even contact between valve face and cylinder head valve seat.

5. Gently remove valve stem seals with a pliers or screwdriver by prying side-to-side. Do not reused old seals.

6. Remove carbon and varnish deposits from inside of valve guides of cylinder head with a suitable guide cleaner.

7. Use an electric drill and soft rotary wire brush to clean the intake and exhaust valve ports, combustion chamber and valve seats. In some cases, the carbon build-up will have to be chipped away. Use a blunt pointed drift for carbon chipping, be careful around valve seat areas.

NOTE: *When using a wire brush to clean carbon on the valve ports, valves, etc., be sure the deposits are actually removed, rather then burnished.*

8. Wash and clean all valve spring, locks, retainers etc., in safe solvent. Remember to keep parts from each valve separate.

NOTE: *If valve guide replacement is necessary, or valve or seat refacing is necessary, the job must be handled by a qualified machine shop.*

If a valve seat is damaged, burnt or loose, the seat may be resurfaced or replaced as necessary. The automotive machine shop can handle the job for you.

CHECKING VALVE SPRINGS

Place the valve spring on a flat surface next to a carpenters square. Measure the height of the spring, and rotate the spring against the edge of the square to measure distortion. If the spring height varies (by comparison) by more than $\frac{1}{16}$" or if the distortion exceeds $\frac{1}{16}$", replace the spring.

Have the valve springs tested for spring pressure at the installed and compressed (installed height minus valve lift) height using a valve spring tester. Springs should be within one pound, plug or minus each other. Replace springs as necessary.

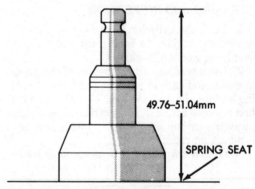

Measuring valve stem height—2.2L engine shown

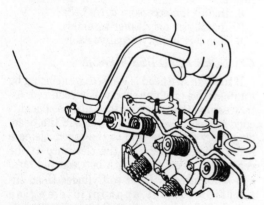

Removing the valve springs

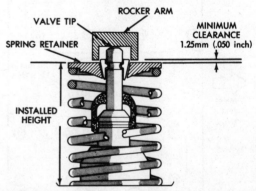

Checking the valve spring installed height—2.2L engine shown

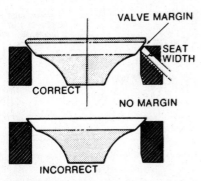

Valve seat width and centering

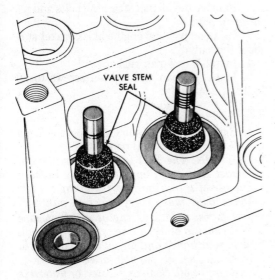

Valve stem oil seals—2.2L engine shown

INSTALLATION

1. Coat valve stems with lubrication oil and install in cylinder head.

2. Install a new valve stem seal on the valve. The valve stem seal should be install firmly and squarely over the valve guide. The lower edge of the seal should rest on the valve guide boss.

3. Install the valve spring seat, valve spring, and retainer.

4. Using Tool C-3422A or equivalent compress valve spring only enough to install retainer locks. Install retainer locks and make certain locks are in their correct location before removing valve compressor.

5. Repeat step 1 thru 4 on remaining valves.

Oil Pan

REMOVAL AND INSTALLATION

2.2L Engine

1. Raise and safely support the vehicle on jackstands. Drain the oil pan.

CAUTION: *The EPA warns that prolonged*

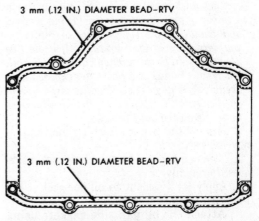

2.2L oil pan RTV sealer application

contact with used engine oil may cause a number of skin disorders, including cancer! You should make every effort to minimize your exposure to used engine oil. Protective gloves should be worn when changing the oil. Wash your hands and any other exposed skin areas as soon as possible after exposure to used engine oil. Soap and water, or waterless hand cleaner should be used.

2. Remove the oil pan attaching bolts and remove oil pan.

3. Clean the oil pan and engine block gasket surfaces thoroughly.

4. Apply RTV sealant to oil pan side rails.

5. Install new oil pan seals and install oil pan. Torque the pan screws to 15 ft. lbs.

6. Refill the crankcase, start the engine and check for leaks.

2.5L Engine

1. Raise and safely support the vehicle on jackstands. Drain the oil pan.

CAUTION: *The EPA warns that prolonged*

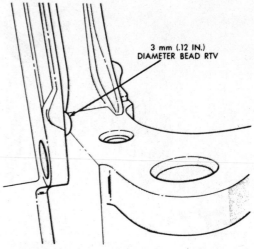

RTV application on front and rear oil pan seals

contact with used engine oil may cause a number of skin disorders, including cancer! You should make every effort to minimize your exposure to used engine oil. Protective gloves should be worn when changing the oil. Wash your hands and any other exposed skin areas as soon as possible after exposure to used engine oil. Soap and water, or waterless hand cleaner should be used.

2. Remove the oil pan attaching bolts and remove oil pan.

3. Clean oil pan and engine block gasket surfaces thoroughly.

4. Apply RTV sealant to oil pan rail at the front seal retainer parting line.

5. Attach the oil pan side gaskets using heavy grease or RTV to hold the gasket in place.

6. Install the new oil pan seals and apply RTV sealant to the ends of the seals at junction where seals and gasket meets.

7. Install oil pan and tighten M8 screws to 15 ft. lbs., and M6 screws to 105 in.lbs.

2.6L Engine

1. Raise and safely support the vehicle on jackstands. Drain the oil pan.

CAUTION: *The EPA warns that prolonged contact with used engine oil may cause a number of skin disorders, including cancer! You should make every effort to minimize your exposure to used engine oil. Protective gloves should be worn when changing the oil. Wash your hands and any other exposed skin areas as soon as possible after exposure to*

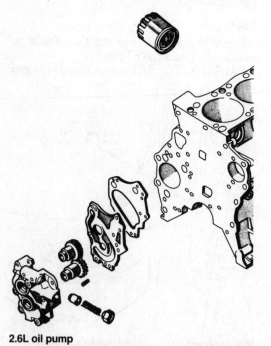

2.6L oil pump

3mm DIAMETER OF RTV

SEALANT MUST NOT BE FORCED OUT FROM THIS FLANGE AREA

3.0L oil pan RTV sealer application

used engine oil. Soap and water, or waterless hand cleaner should be used.

2. Remove the oil pan attaching bolts and remove oil pan.

3. Clean oil pan and engine block gasket surfaces thoroughly.

4. Install a new pan gasket.

5. Install oil pan and tighten screws to 60 in.lbs.

3.0L Engine

1. Raise and safely support the vehicle on jackstands. Drain the oil pan.

CAUTION: *The EPA warns that prolonged contact with used engine oil may cause a number of skin disorders, including cancer! You should make every effort to minimize your exposure to used engine oil. Protective gloves should be worn when changing the oil. Wash your hands and any other exposed skin areas as soon as possible after exposure to used engine oil. Soap and water, or waterless hand cleaner should be used.*

2. Remove the oil pan attaching bolts and remove oil pan.

3. Clean oil pan and engine block gasket surfaces thoroughly.

4. Apply RTV sealant to oil pan.

5. Install oil pan to engine and tighten screws in sequence, working from the center toward the ends, to 50 in.lbs.

Oil Pump

REMOVAL AND INSTALLATION

2.2L and 2.5L Engine

1. Raise and safely support the vehicle.

2. Drain the oil and remove engine oil pan. See Oil Pan Removal.

CAUTION: *The EPA warns that prolonged contact with used engine oil may cause a number of skin disorders, including cancer! You should make every effort to minimize your exposure to used engine oil. Protective gloves should be worn when changing the oil. Wash your hands and any other exposed skin areas as soon as possible after exposure to*

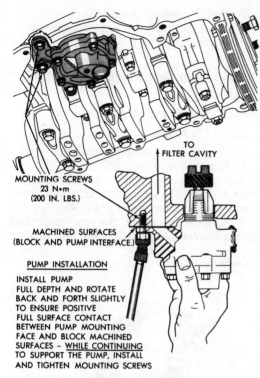

MOUNTING SCREWS
23 N•m
(200 IN. LBS.)

TO
FILTER CAVITY

MACHINED SURFACES
(BLOCK AND PUMP INTERFACE.)

PUMP INSTALLATION

INSTALL PUMP
FULL DEPTH AND ROTATE
BACK AND FORTH SLIGHTLY
TO ENSURE POSITIVE
FULL SURFACE CONTACT
BETWEEN PUMP MOUNTING
FACE AND BLOCK MACHINED
SURFACES – WHILE CONTINUING
TO SUPPORT THE PUMP, INSTALL
AND TIGHTEN MOUNTING SCREWS

2.2L and 2.5L—oil pump installation

used engine oil. Soap and water, or waterless hand cleaner should be used.

3. Remove the pump mounting bolts.

4. Pull the pump down and out of the engine.

5. Prime, by filling pump with fresh oil. Check crankshaft/intermediate shaft timing and oil pump drive alignment. Adjust if necessary.

6. Install pump and rotate back and forth slightly to ensure full surface contact of pump and block.

7. While holding pump in fully seated position, install pump mounting bolts. Torque to 15 ft. lbs.

8. Install engine oil pan. Refer to Oil Pan Installation procedures.

9. Refill crankcase, start engine.

10. Check engine oil pressure.

2.6L Engine

1. Remove accessory drive belts.

2. Remove the timing chain case cover. Refer to Timing Chain Case Cover Removal procedures.

3. Remove the silent shaft chain assembly and timing chain assembly. Refer to Timing Chain Removal procedures.

4. Remove the silent shaft bolt (bolt directly above the silent chain sprocket).

5. Remove the oil pump bolts and pull the pump housing straight forward. Remove the gaskets and the oil pump backing plate.

6. Clean gasket from mounting surfaces.

7. Install new gaskets/seals, align mating marks of the oil pump gears, refill the pump with oil, and install the pump assembly.

8. Install oil pump silent shaft sprocket and sprocket bolt. Tighten sprocket bolt to 34 N.m (25 ft. lbs.).

9. Install timing chain and silent shaft chain assembly. Refer to Timing Chain Installation procedures.

10. Install timing chain case cover. Refer to Timing Chain Case Cover Installation procedures.

11. Install accessory drive belts.

12. Reconnect battery negative cable.

13. Start engine and check engine oil pressure.

3.0L Engine

The oil pump assembly used on this engine is mounted at the front of the crankshaft. The oil pump also retains the crankshaft front oil seal.

1. Remove accessory drive belts.

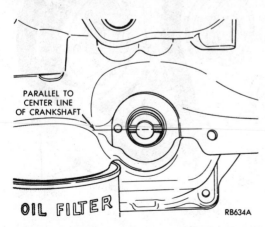

PARALLEL TO
CENTER LINE
OF CRANKSHAFT

OIL FILTER

RB634A

Oil pump shaft alignment—2.2L engine

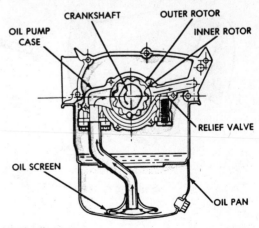

CRANKSHAFT   OUTER ROTOR

OIL PUMP
CASE

INNER ROTOR

RELIEF VALVE

OIL SCREEN

OIL PAN

3.0L oil pump

2. Remove the timing belt cover and timing belt. Refer to Timing Belt Removal procedures.

3. Remove the crankshaft sprocket.

4. Remove the oil pump mounting bolts (5), and remove oil pump assembly. Mark mounting bolts for proper installation during reassembly.

5. Clean the oil pump and engine block gasket surfaces thoroughly.

6. Position a new gasket on pump assembly and install on cylinder block. Make sure correct length bolts are in proper locations and torque all bolts to 10 ft. lbs.

7. Install the crankshaft sprocket and timing belt. Recheck engine timimg marks. Refer to Timing Belt Installation procedures.

8. Install the timing belt covers . Refer to Timing Belt Cover Installation procedures.

9. Install accessory drive belts.

10. Refill the crankcase and start the engine.

11. Check engine oil pressure.

Timing Gear/Belt/Chain Cover and Seal

REMOVAL AND INSTALLATION

2.2L and 2.5L Engine

1. Remove the accessory drive belts.

2. Remove the alternator.

3. Remove the air condition compressor belt idler bracket and disconnect air conditioning compressor and locate out of the way.

4. Remove the power steering pump lock screw. Remove the pivot bolt and nut. Remove

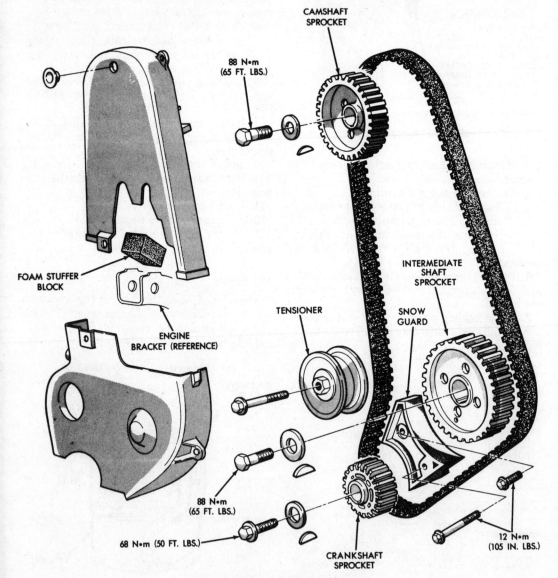

2.2L and 2.5L—timing belt and cover

Description	Flaw conditions
1. Hardened back surface rubber	Back surface glossy. Non-elastic and so hard that even if a finger nail is forced into it, no mark is produced.
2. Cracked back surface rubber	
3. Cracked or exfoliated canvas	
4. Badly worn teeth (initial stage)	Canvas on load side tooth flank worn (Fluffy canvas fibers, rubber gone and color changed to white, and unclear canvas texture)
5. Badly worn teeth (last stage)	Canvas on load side tooth flank worn down and rubber exposed (tooth width reduced)
6. Cracked tooth bottom	
7. Missing tooth	
8. Side of belt badly worn	
9. Side of belt cracked	

Note: Normal belt should have clear-cut sides as if cut by a sharp knife.

Checking timing belt wear

the power steering pump and mounting bracket. The hoses need not be disconnected, locate the pump out of the way.

5. Loosen and remove the water pump pulley mounting screws and remove the pulley.

6. Support the vehicle on jackstands and remove the right inner splash shield.

7. Remove the crankshaft pulley.

8. Remove the nuts at upper portion of timing cover and screws from lower protion and remove both halves of cover.

9. Install the cover. Secure the upper section to cylinder head with nuts and lower section to cylinder block with screws.

10. Install the crankshaft pulley and tighten the bolt to 20 ft. lbs., lower vehicle.

11. Install the water pump pulley and tighten screws to 105 in.lbs.

12. Install the power steering pump assembly.

13. Install the air conditioning compressor assembly.

14. Install the alternator assembly.

15. Install the accessory drive belts.

2.6L Engine

1. Disconnect the negative battery cable.

2. Remove the air cleaner assembly.

3. Remove the accessory drive belts.

4. Remove the alternator mounting bolts and remove alternator.

5. Remove the power steering mounting bolts and set power steering pump aside.

6. Remove the air condition compressor mounting bolts and set compressor aside.

7. Support the vehicle on jackstands and remove right inner splash shield.

8. Drain the engine oil.

CAUTION: *The EPA warns that prolonged contact with used engine oil may cause a number of skin disorders, including cancer! You should make every effort to minimize your exposure to used engine oil. Protective gloves should be worn when changing the oil. Wash your hands and any other exposed skin areas as soon as possible after exposure to used engine oil. Soap and water, or waterless hand cleaner should be used.*

9. Remove the crankshaft pulley.

10. Lower the vehicle and place a jack under the engine with a piece of wood between jack and lifting point.

11. Raise the jack until contact is made with the engine. Relieve pressure by jacking slightly and remove the center bolt from the right engine mount. Remove right engine mount.

12. Remove the engine oil dipstick.

13. Remove the engine valve cover. Refer to Rocker Cover Removal procedures.

14. Remove the front (2) cylinder head to tim-

ing chain cover bolts. DO NOT LOOSEN ANY OTHER CYLINDER HEAD BOLTS.

15. Remove the oil pan retaining bolts and lower the oil pan.

16. Remove the screws holding the timing indicator and engine mounting plate.

17. Remove the bolts holding the timing chain case cover and remove cover.

18. Clean and inspect chain case cover for crack or other damage.

19. Position a new timing chain case cover gasket on case cover. Trim as required to assure fit at top and bottom.

20. Coat the cover gasket with sealant (P/N 3419115) or equivaltent. Install chain case cover and tighten mounting bolts to 13 ft. lbs.

21. Install the (2) front cylinder head to timing chain case cover mounting bolts and tighten to 13 ft. lbs.

22. Install the engine oil pan tighten screws to 53 in.lbs.

23. Install the engine mounting plate and timing indicator.

24. Install the crankshaft pulley.

25. Install the right engine mount, lower engine and install right engine mount center bolt.

26. Install the engine valve cover. Refer to Rocker Cover Installation procedures.

27. Install the engine oil dipstick.

28. Install the air conditioner compressor.

29. Install the power steering pump.

30. Install the alternator.

31. Install the accessory drive belts.

32. Fill the engine crankcase with recommended engine oil.

33. Install the air cleaner assembly.

34. Connect the negative battery cable.

3.0L Engine

1. Disconnect the negative battery cable.

2. Remove the accessory drive belts.

3. Remove the air conditioner compressor mounting bracket bolts and lay compressor aside.

4. Remove the air conditioner mounting bracket and adjustable drive belt tensioner from engine.

5. Remove the steering pump/alternator belt tensioner mounting bolt and remove belt tensioner.

6. Remove the power steering pump mounting bracket bolts, rear support lock nut and set power steering pump aside.

7. Raise the vehicle and support on jackstands.

8. Remove the right inner splash shield.

9. Remove the crankshaft drive pulley bolt, drive pullly and torsional damper.

10. Lower the vehicle and place a floor jack

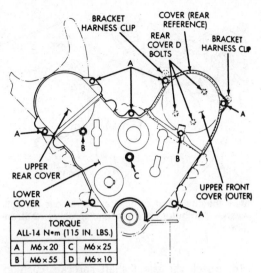

3.0L front timing covers

TORQUE ALL-14 N•m (115 IN. LBS.)			
A	M6 × 20	C	M6 × 25
B	M6 × 55	D	M6 × 10

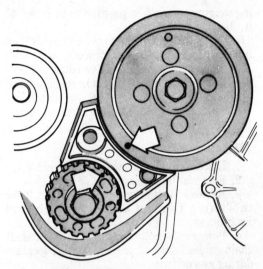

2.2L and 2.5L crankshaft and intermediate shaft timing mark alignment

Camshaft sprocket timing alignment

under the engine. Separate engine mount insulator from engine mount bracket.

11. Raise the engine slightly and remove engine mount bracket.

12. Remove the timing belt covers.

13. Install the timing belt covers and tighten all screws to 10 ft. lbs.

14. Raise the engine slightly and install engine mount bracket.

15. Install the engine mount insulator into engine mount bracket.

16. Install the torsional damper, drive pulley and drive pulley bolt. Torque bolt to 110 N.m (150 ft. lbs.). Install the right inner splash shield.

17. Install the power steering mounting bracket and install the power steering pump.

18. Install the steering pump/alternator belt tensioner.

19. Install the air conditioner adjustable drive belt tensioner and mounting bracket.

20. Install the air conditioner compressor.

21. Install the accessory drive belts.

22. Connect the negative battery cable.

Timing Belt and/or Chain
REMOVAL AND INSTALLATION
2.2L and 2.5L Engine

1. Remove the accessory drive belts.

2. Remove the timing belt cover. Refer to Timing Belt Cover Removal procedures.

3. Loosen the timing belt tensioner screw, rotate the hex nut, and remove timing belt.

4. Turn the crankshaft and intermediate shaft until markings on both sprockets are aligned.

5. Rotate the camshaft so that the arrows on the hub are in line with No. 1 camshaft cap to cylinder head line. Small hole must be in vertical center line.

6. Install the timing belt over the drive sprockets and adjust.

7. Tighten the tensioner by turning the the tensioner hex to the right. Tension should be correct when the belt can be twisted 90 degrees with the thumb and forefinger, midway between the camshaft and intermediate sprocket.

8. Turn the engine clockwise from TDC two revolutions with crankshaft bolt. Check the timing marks for correct alignment.

WARNING: *Do not used the camshaft or intermediate shaft to rotate the engine. Also, do not allow oil or solvent to contact timing belt as they will deteriate the belt and cause slipping.*

9. Tighten lock nut on tensioner while hold-

ing weighted wrench in position to 61 N.m. (45 ft. lbs.).

10. Install the timing belt cover. Refer to Timing Belt Cover Installation procedures.

11. Install the accessory drive belts.

NOTE: *With timing belt cover installed and number one cylinder at TDC, the small hole in the cam sprocket should be centered in timing belt cover hole.*

2.6L Engine

1. Disconnect the negative battery cable.

2. Remove the accessory drive belts.

3. Remove the timing chain case cover. Refer to Timing Chain Case Cover Removal Procedures.

4. Remove the bolts securing the silent shaft chain guides. Mark all parts for proper location during assembly.

5. Remove the sprocket bolts, silent shaft drive chain, crankshaft/silent sprocket, silent shaft sprockets and spacer.

6. Remove the camshaft sprocket bolt and washer.

7. Remove the distributor drive gear.

8. Remove the camshaft sprocket holder and timing chain guides.

9. Depress the tensioner and remove the timing chain and camshaft sprocket.

10. Remove the crankshaft sprocket.

11. Remove the tensioner shoe, washer and spring.

12. Clean and inspect all parts.

13. Check the tensioner shoe for wear or damage and tensioner spring for deterioration. Spring free length 65.7mm.

14. Check the chain cover for damage or cracks.

15. Check the silent shaft and camshaft chain guides for damage or excessive wear.

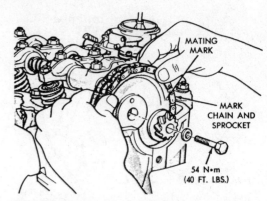

Mark the chain and sprockets and remove the bolt, washer distributor drive gear and sprocket—2.6L engine

16. Check the silent shaft sprocket cushion ring for free and smooth rotation and ring guides for damage.

17. Check the silent chain and timing chain for excessive play, wear or damage links.

18. Check all sprockets for wear or damage teeth.

19. Rotate the camshaft until the dowel pin is at vertical center line with cylinder.

20. Install the timing chain sprocket holders.

21. Rotate the crankshaft until No. 1 piston is at Top Dead Center (TDC) of its compression stroke.

22. Install the timing chain tensioner spring, washer and shoe on oil pump body.

23. Assemble the timing chain on the camshaft and crankshaft sprockets.

NOTE: *The mating mark on the camshaft*

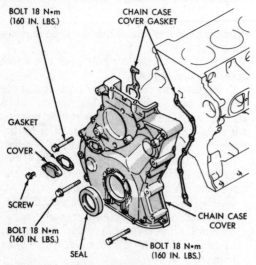

Timing case cover—2.6L engine

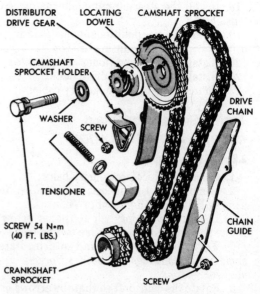

Timing chain components—2.6L engine

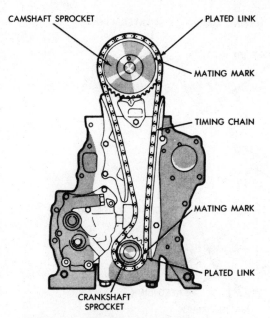

Timing chain installation—2.6L engine

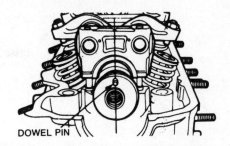

Dowel pin set at 12 o'clock—2.6L engine

and crankshaft sprocket teeth must line up with plated links on timing chain.

24. While holding the sprockets and chain as an assembly, install the crankshaft sprocket to

keyway of crankshaft and camshaft sprocket to dowel pin of camshaft.

25. Install the distributor drive gear, camshaft sprocket bolt and washer, and torque bolt to 54 N.m (40 ft. lbs.).

26. Install the silent shaft chain drive sprocket on crankshaft.

27. Assemble the silent shaft chain to oil pump sprocket and to silent shaft sprocket.

NOTE: *The timing marks on the sprockets teeth must line up with plated links on of silent shaft chain.*

28. While holding the parts as an assembly, align the crankshaft sprocket plated link with the punch mark on the sprocket. With the chain installed on crankshaft sprocket, install the oil

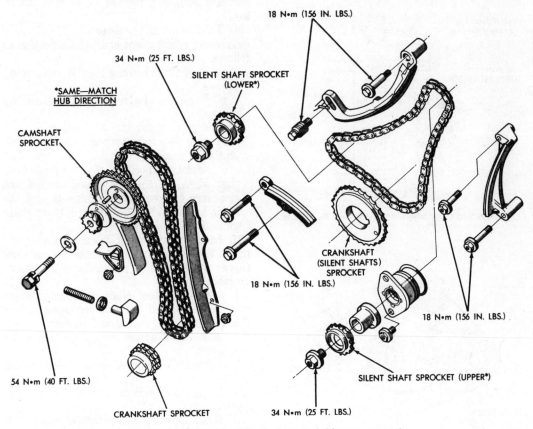

2.6L engine timing/silent shaft chain and drive components

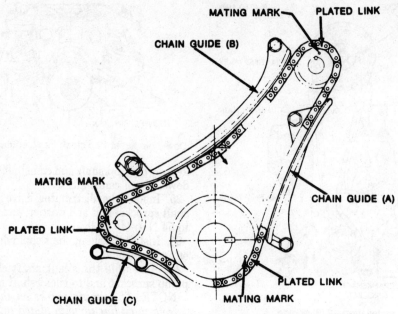

Timing mark alignment for silent shaft timing chain installation—2.6L engine

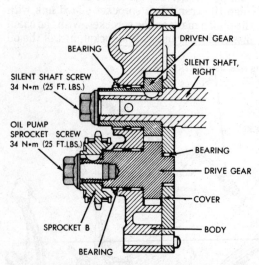

Oil pump and silent shaft installation—2.6L engine

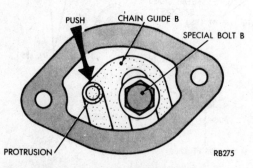

Silent shaft chain adjustment—2.6L engine

pump sprocket and silent chain sprocket on their resspective shafts.

29. Install the oil pump and silent shaft sprocket bolts and tighten to 34 N.m (25 ft. lbs.).

30. Loosely install the three silent shaft chain guides and adjust silent shaft chain tension as follows.

    a. Tighten chain guide **A** mounting screws.

    b. Tighten chain guide **C** mounting screws.

    c. Slightly rotate the oil pump and silent shaft sprockets to remove any slack in the silent shaft chain.

    d. Adjust the position of chain guide **B** so that when the chain is pulled inward, the clearance between chain guide **B** and the chain links will be 1.0-3.5mm. Tighten chain guide **B** mounting screws.

31. Install a new timing case cover gasket and install timing case cover. Refer to Timing Case Cover Installation procedures outlined previously.

If necessary silent shaft chain adjustment may be performed without removing timing chain case cover. Proceed as followed:

1. Remove the access cover from the timing case cover.

2. Through the access hole loosen special bolt **B**

3. Using your finger only push on boss to apply tension.

4. While applying tension tighten special bolt **B** to 13 ft. lbs.

5. Install access cover to timing chain case cover.

3.0L Engine

NOTE: *The timing belt can be inspected by removing the upper (front outer) timing cover.*

1. Disconnect the negative battery cable.
2. Remove the accessory drive belts.
3. Remove the timing belt covers. Refer to Timing Belt Cover Removal Procedures.
4. Identify the timing belt running direction to avoid reversal during installation.
5. Loosen timing belt tensioner bolt and remove timing belt.
6. Remove the crankshaft sprocket flange.
7. Rotate the crankshaft sprocket until timing mark on crankshaft sprocket is lined up with the oil pump timing mark at 1 o'clock position.
8. Rotate the (inner) camshaft sprocket until mark on (inner) camshaft sprocket is lined up with the timing mark on alternator bracket.
9. Rotate the (outer) camshaft sprocket (radiator side) until mark on the sprocket is lined up with the timing mark on the timing belt inner cover. Refer to timing belt illustration.
10. Install the timing belt on the crankshaft sprocket while maintaining pressure on the tensioner side.
11. Position the timing belt over the camshaft sprocket (radiator side). Next, position the belt under the water pump pulley, then over the (inner) sprocket and finally over the tensioner.

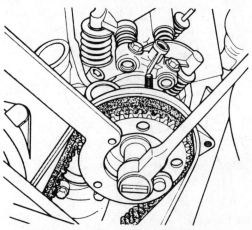

Secure sprocket when removing/installing nut

12. Apply rotating force in the opposite direction to the camshaft sprocket (radiator side) to create tension on the timing belt tension side.
13. Rotate the crankshaft in a clockwise direction and recheck engine timing marks.
14. Install the crankshaft sprocket flange.
15. Loosen the tensioner bolt and allow tensioner spring to tension the belt.
16. Again rotate the crankshaft in a clockwise direction (2) full turns. Recheck the engine timing. Tighten the tensioner bolt to 31 N.m (23 ft. lbs.).
17. Install the timing covers.
18. Install the accessory drive belts.
19. Connect battery negative cable.

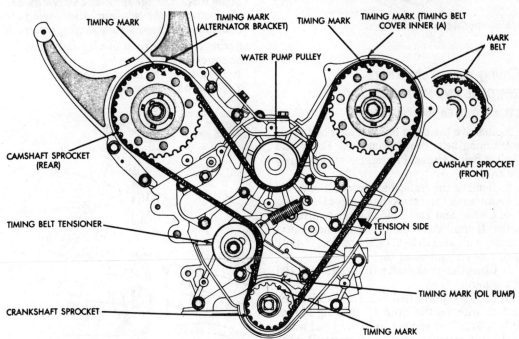

3.0L sprocket timing for belt installation

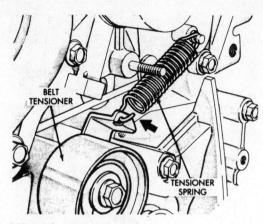

3.0L tensioner

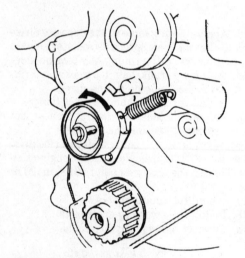

3.0L positioning the tensioner

Timing Sprockets/Gears
REMOVAL AND INSTALLATION
2.2L and 2.5L Engines

1. Remove the drive belts, timing belt cover and timing belt. See Timing Belt Cover and Timing Belt Removal Procedures as previously outlined.
2. Remove the crankshaft sprocket bolt.
3. Remove the crankshaft sprocket using Tool C-4685 and Tool L-4524 or an equivalent puller. If crankshaft seal removal is necessary, remove with Tool C-4679 (2.2L) or Tool C-4991 (2.5L), or an equivalent tool.
4. Clean the crankshaft seal surface with 400 grit paper.
5. Lightly coat the seal (Steel case seal) outer surface with Loctite Stud N' Bearing Mount (P/N 4057987) or equivalent. A soap and water solution is recommended to lubricate (Rubber Coated Case Seal) outer surface.

6. Lightly lubricate the seal lip with engine oil.
7. Install seal with Tool No. C-4680 (2.2L) or Tool No. C-4992 (2.5L).
8. Install the sprocket and install sprocket bolt.
9. Remove and install the camshaft and intermediate shaft sprockets with Tool C-4687 and Tool C-4687-1 in similar fashion.
10. Install the timing belt and and timing belt cover. See Timing Belt and Timing Belt Cover Installation Procedures as previously outlined.
11. Install the accessory drive belts.

2.6L Engine

Refer to Timing Chain Case Cover Removal procedures.

3.0L Engine

Refer to Timing Case Cover Removal procedures.

Camshaft and Bearings
REMOVAL
2.2L and 2.5L Engines

The following procedures are performed with engine in vehicle.

NOTE: *Removal of the camshaft requires removal of the camshaft sprocket. To maintain proper engine timing the timing belt is left indexed on the sprocket with the assembly suspended under light tension. Maintain adequate tension on the sprocket and belt assembly to prevent the belt from disengaging the crankshaft or intermediate shaft sprockets. If timing is lost, refer to Timing Belt Installation procedures.*

1. Disconnect the negative battery.
2. Remove the drive belts.

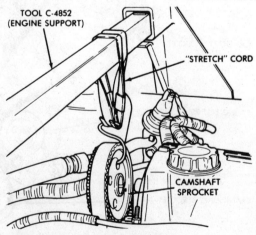

Suspending the sprocket and belt

3. Remove the air pump pulley bolts and remove air pump pulley (2.2L engine).

4. Remove the timimg case cover upper half.

5. Remove the valve cover.

6. Remove the camshaft sprocket bolt.

7. Remove the camshaft sprocket and suspend with the timing belt.

8. Loosen the cam bearing cap mounting bolts slightly. With a soft mallet bump camshaft at the rear to break free the bearing caps.

9. Remove the camshaft bearing cap bolts and remove caps.

10. Carefully remove the camshaft without cocking to prevent damage to cam. Remove the rocker arms and mark for installation in the same position.

INSPECTION

1. Check for camshaft lobe wear as follows:

(a) With a micrometer take a first reading in an unworn area at the edge of the lobe. Record this reading.

(b) Take a second reading in the worn area where rocker arm contacts the lobe.

(c) Subtract the second reading from the first. The difference is camshaft lobe wear. Lobe wear should not exceed 0.5mm.

2. Inspect the camshaft journal caps and cylinder head journals for wear, scoring or oversize markings.

3. Oversize components are identify as follows:

Cylinder Head: Top of bearing caps painted GREEN and **O/SJ** stamped rearward of oil gallery plug on air pump end of head.

Camshaft: Barrel of camshaft painted GREEN and **O/SJ** stamped on air pump end of shaft.

4. Check the cap oil holes for blockage. Clear as necessary.

INSTALLATION

1. Lubricate the camshaft and set in place.

2. Position the camshaft bearing caps in proper sequence. Cap No. 1 at timing belt and Cap No. 5 at transmission end. No. 1, 2, 3, 4 must point toward the timing belt end.

2.2L and 2.5L camshaft bearing caps

3. Apply anaerobic form-in-place gasket to No. 1 and No. 5 bearing caps.

4. Install the camshaft caps tighten to 18 ft. lbs. Caps must be installed before camshaft seals are installed.

Check camshaft end play as Follows:

a. Mount a dial indicator on cylinder head.

b. Using a suitable tool, move camshaft as far rearward as possible.

c. Zero the dial indicator. Move the camshaft forward as far as possible and read dial indicator. End Play Travel: 2.2L engine 0.15mm maximum; 2.5L engine 0.13-0.33mm.

5. Install the camshaft oil seals.

6. Install the camshaft sprocket. Rotate camshaft to align camshaft with sprocket.

7. Install the camshaft sprocket bolt. Tighten to 88 N.m (65 ft. lbs.).

8. Install the rocker arms. Refer to Rocker Arms Installation procedure.

9. Install the timing case cover upper half.

10. Install the valve cover. Refer to Valve Cover Installation procedures.

11. Install the air pump pulley and air pump belt (2.2L engine).

12. Install the drive belts.

13. Connect the negative battery cable.

REMOVAL

2.6L Engine

1. Disconnect the negative battery cable.

2. Remove the air cleaner assembly.

3. Remove the rocker cover. Refer to Rocker Cover Removal procedures.

4. Remove the water pump belt and pulley.

5. Rotate the crankshaft until number 1 piston is at the top of its compression stroke (both valves closed).

6. Record the position of mating mark on camshaft sprocket and plated link on timing chain.

7. Remove the camshaft sprocket bolt, washer and distributor drive gear.

8. Remove the timing chain and camshaft sprocket assembly and lay aside.

9. Remove the rocker arms/shafts assembly. Refer to Rocker Arms/Shaft Removal procedures.

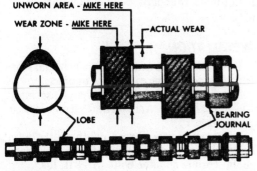

UNWORN AREA - **MIKE HERE**

WEAR ZONE - **MIKE HERE**

ACTUAL WEAR

LOBE

BEARING JOURNAL

Checking camshaft lobe wear

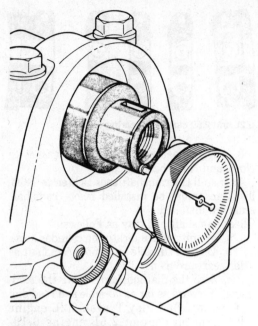

Measuring camshaft end play

10. Carefully remove camshaft without cocking to prevent damage to cam.

INSPECTION

1. Check camshaft lobe wear as follows:

a. With a micrometer take a first reading in an unworn area at the edge of the lobe. Record this reading.

b. Take a second reading in the worn area where rocker arm contacts the lobe.

c. Subtract the second reading from the first. The difference is camshaft lobe wear. Lobe wear should not exceed 0.5mm.

2. Inspect camshaft journal caps and cylinder head journals for wear, scoring or damage.

3. Check cap oil holes and cylinder head oil holes for blockage. Unclog if necessary.

INSTALLATION

1. Lubricate the camshaft and set in place.

2. Install the rocker arms/shafts assembly. Refer to Rocker Arms/Shaft Installation procedures.

3. With the rocker arms/shafts assembly and bearing caps torqued down, rotate the camshaft so that dowel hole is on vertical centerline of cylinder head.

4. Install the timing chain and camshaft sprocket assembly. Make sure mating mark on camshaft sprocket and plated link on timing chain are lined up.

5. Install the distributor drive gear, washer and camshaft sprocket bolt tighten to 54 N.m (40 ft. lbs.).

6. Install the water pump pulley and belt.

NOTE: *After servicing rocker shaft assembly, Jet Valve Clearance (if used) and Intake/Exhaust Valve Clearance adjustment must be performed. See Valve Adjusting Procedure.*

7. Install the valve cover. Refer to Rocker Cover Installation procedures.

8. Install the air cleaner assembly.

9. Connect the negative battery cable.

REMOVAL

3.0L Engine

1. Disconnect the negative battery cable.

2. Remove the accessory drive belts.

3. Remove the distributor assembly.

4. Remove the timing belt covers. Refer to Timing Belt Cover Removal Procedures.

5. Loosen the timing belt tensioner bolt and remove the timing belt from the camshaft sprockets.

6. Remove the camshaft sprocket bolts and remove the camshaft sprockets (front and rear).

7. Remove the valve covers. Refer to Rocker Cover Removal procedures.

8. Remove the distributor drive adaptor assembly from right camshaft.

9. Remove the rocker arms/shafts assembly. Refer to Rocker Arms/Shafts Removal procedures.

10. Remove the camshafts (front and rear) from cylinder head.

INSPECTION

1. Inspect the camshaft bearing journals for wear or damage.

2. Inspect the cylinder head and check oil return holes.

3. Check the tooth surface of the distributor drive gear teeth of the right camshaft for wear or damage.

4. Check both camshaft surfaces for wear or damage.

5. Remove the distributor drive adaptor seal.

6. Check camshaft lobe height and replace if out of limit. Standard value is 41.00mm. Wear limit is 40.50mm.

INSTALLATION

1. Lubricate the camshaft journals and lobes with engine oil. Set camshafts in place.

2. Install the rocker arms/shafts assembly. Refer to Rocker Arms/Shafts Installation procedures.

3. Install a new O-ring on the distributor drive adaptor and install adaptor on right camshaft. Torque adaptor bolts to 11 ft. lbs.).

4. Install a new distributor drive adaptor

seal using seal installer MD998713 or equivalent.

5. Install end seal plug into adaptor using tool MB998306 or equivalent.

6. Install camshaft sprockets (front and rear).

7. Check valve timing and install timing belt. Refer to Timing Belt Installation procedures.

8. Install the distributor assembly. Refer to Distributor Installation procedures in this Chapter.

9. Install the timing covers. Refer to Timing Cover Installation procedures.

10. Install the accessory drive belts.

11. Connect the negative battery cable.

Auxiliary (Idler) Shaft
REMOVAL AND INSTALLATION
2.2L and 2.5L Engines

The following procedures to be performed with engine removed from vehicle.

1. Remove the distributor assembly.

2. Remove the fuel pump.

3. Remove timing case cover, and timing belt.

4. Remove the intermediate shaft sprocket. See Sprocket Removal Procedures.

5. Remove the intermediate shaft retainer screws and remove retainer.

6. Remove the intermediate shaft and inspect journals and bushing.

7. When installing the shaft, lubricate the fuel pump eccentric and distributor drive gear. Install the intermediate shaft.

8. Inspect the shaft seal in retainer. Replace if necessary.

9. Lightly lubricate the seal lip with engine oil.

10. Install the intermediate shaft retainer assembly and retainer screws. Tighten screws to 105 in.lbs. On 2.5L engine apply anaerobic (Form-in-Place) gasket material to retainer sealing surface before installing.

11. Install the intermediate shaft sprocket.

12. Check engine timing. See Engine Timing Check Procedures.

13. Install the timing belt and adjust.

14. Install the timing belt cover.

15. Install the fuel pump.

16. Install the distributor. See Distributor Installation Procedures.

Balance Shafts

The 2.5L engine is equipped with two balance shafts located in a housing attached to the lower crankcase. These shafts are driven by a chain and two gears from the crankshaft at two times crankshaft speed. This conterbalance certain engine reciprocating masses.

REMOVAL

1. Remove the engine from vehicle.

2. Remove the timing case cover, timing belt and sprockets.

3. Remove the engine oil pan.

4. Remove the front crankshaft seal retainer.

5. Remove the balance shafts chain cover.

6. Remove the chain guide and tensioner.

7. Remove the balance shafts sprocket retaining screws and crankshaft chain sprocket torx screws. Remove the chain and sprocket assembly.

8. Remove the balance shafts carrier front gear cover retaining double ended stud. Remove the cover and balance shafts gears.

9. Remove the carrier rear cover and balance shafts.

10. To separate the carrier, remove (6) crankcase to carrier attaching bolts and remove carrier.

11. Take notice of all parts to avoid interchanging.

INSTALLATION

1. Install both shafts into carrier the assembly from rear of carrier.

2. Install the rear cover.

3. Install the balance shafts drive and driven gears to shafts.

4. Position the carrier assembly on crankcase and tighten (6) bolts to 54 N.m. (40 ft. lbs.).

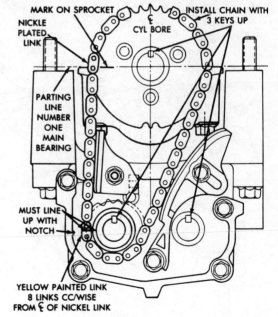

MARK ON SPROCKET
NICKLE PLATED LINK
CYL BORE
INSTALL CHAIN WITH 3 KEYS UP
PARTING LINE NUMBER ONE MAIN BEARING
MUST LINE UP WITH NOTCH
YELLOW PAINTED LINK
8 LINKS CC/WISE
FROM ℄ OF NICKEL LINK

2.5L balance shaft timing

5. Crankshaft to Balance Shaft Timing must be established. Rotate both balance shafts until the keyways are in the Up position.

6. Install the short hub drive gear on balance shaft driving shaft.

7. Install the long hub gear on the driven shaft.

8. With both gears on the balance shafts and keyways Up, the timing marks should be meshed.

9. Align the balance shaft carrier cover with the carrier housing dowel pin and install double ended stud. Tighten to 105 in.lbs.

10. Install the crankshaft sprocket and tighten sprocket torx screw to 11 ft. lbs.

11. Turn the crankshaft until number one cylinder is at TDC. The timing marks on the chain sprocket should line up with the parting line on the left side of number one main bearing cap.

12. Install the chain over the crankshaft sprocket so the nickel plated link of the chain is over the timing mark on the crankshaft sprocket.

13. Install the balance shaft sprocket into the timing chain so that the timing mark on the

FASTNER TORQUE			
LETTER	N·m	IN. LBS.	FT. LBS.
A	12	105	–
B	28	250	–
C	54	–	40
★D	★41	–	★30
E	95	–	70
F	(PLUG - LOCTITE 277)		
G	15	130	–

★SPECIFIED TORQUE
PLUS 1/4 TURN

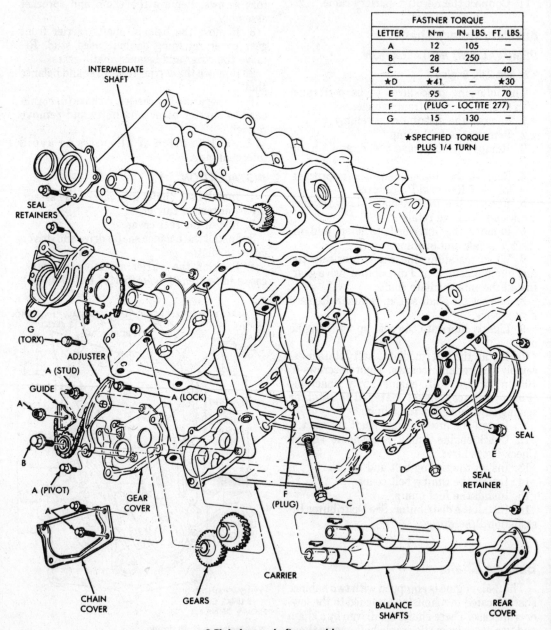

2.5L balance shaft assembly

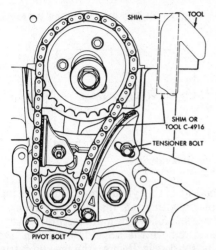

2.5L balance shaft chain tensioner adjustment

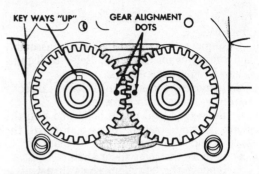

2.5L balance shaft gear timing

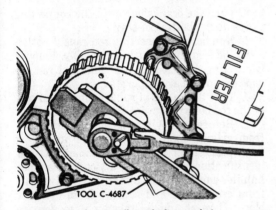

Removing the intermediate shaft sprocket

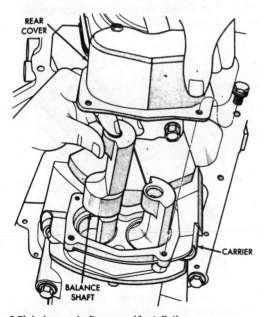

2.5L balance shaft removal/installation

sprocket (yellow dot) mates with the yellow painted link on the chain.

14. With the balance shaft keyway in 12 o'clock position slide the balance shaft sprocket on the nose of the balance shaft. The balance shaft may have to be pushed in slightly to allow for clearance.

NOTE: *The timing mark on the sprocket, the painted link, and the arrow on the side ot the gear cover should line up if the balance shafts are timed correctly.*

15. Install the balance shaft bolt and tighten to 21 ft. lbs. Placed a wooden block between the crankcase and crankshaft counterbalance to prevent crankshaft from turning.

16. Proper balance shaft Timing Chain Tension must be established.

17. Place a shim 1.0mm thick by 70mm long between the chain and tensioner.

18. Apply firm hand pressure behind the adjustment slot and tighten adjustment bolt first, followed by the pivot screw to 105 in.lbs. Remove the shim.

19. Install the chain guide making sure the tab on the guide fits into slot on the gear cover. Install nut/washer and tighten to 105 in.lbs.

20. Install the chain cover and tighten screws to 105 in.lbs.

21. Apply a 1.5mm diameter bead of RTV gasket material to retainer sealing surface. Install retainer assembly.

22. Install the crankshaft sprocket and timing belt. See Timing Belt Adjustment and Engine Timing Procedures.

23. Install the timing cover.

Silent Shafts

The 2.6L engine uses two countershafts (silent shafts) in the cylinder block to reduce engine noise and vibration.

REMOVAL

The following procedures to be performed with engine removed from vehicle.

1. Remove the timing chain case cover. Refer

to Timing Chain Case Cover Removal procedures.

2. Remove the silent shaft chain assembly and timing chain assembly. Refer to Timing Chain Removal procedures.

3. Remove the silent shaft bolt (bolt directly above the silent chain sprocket).

4. Remove the oil pump bolts and pull the pump housing straight forward. Remove the gaskets and the oil pump backing plate.

5. Remove the right silent shaft.

6. Remove the left silent shaft thrust plate by screwing two 8mm screws into tapped holes in thrust plate. Remove left silent shaft.

SILENT SHAFT CLEARANCE

1. Outer diameter to outer bearing clearance: 0.02-0.06mm.

2. Inner diameter to inner bearing clearance: 0.05-0.09mm.

INSTALLATION

1. Install both silent shafts into cylinder block. Be careful not to damage inner bearings.

2. Install the left silent shaft thrust plate on the left silent shaft using a new O-ring.

3. Install the oil pump. Refer to Oil Pump Installation procedures.

4. Install the timing chain and silent chain assembly. Refer to Timing Chain Installation procedures.

5. Install the timing chain case cover. See Timing Chain Case Cover Installation procedures.

Pistons and Connecting Rods

REMOVAL

The following procedures are performed with the engine removed from vehicle.

1. Remove the engine from the vehicle. Refer to Engine Removal procedures.

2. Remove the timing case cover, timing belt or chain and sprockets.

3. Remove the intake manifold.

4. Remove the cylinder head from engine.

5. Remove the engine oil pan.

6. Remove the oil pump.

7. Remove the balance shaft carrier (2.5L engine).

NOTE; *Because the top piston ring does not travel to the very top of the cylinder bore, a ridge is built up between the end of the travel and the top of the cylinder walls. Pushing the piston and connecting rod assembly past the ridge is difficult and may cause damage to the piston. If new rings are installed and the ridge has not been removed, ring breakage and piston damage can occur.*

Turn the crankshaft to position the piston at

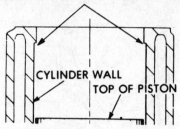

Cylinder bore ridge

the bottom of the cylinder bore. Cover the top of the piston with a rag. Install a ridge reamer in the bore and follow the manufacturer's instructions to remove the ridge. Use caution, avoid cutting too deeply. Remove the rag and cuttings from the top of the piston. Remove the ridge from all cylinders.

8. Turn the crankshaft until the connecting d is at the bottom of travel.

9. Number all connecting rod caps if not already labeled to aid during assembly. Remove connecting rod bearing cap nuts and remove caps. Keep all parts separated.

10. Take two pieces of rubber tubing and cover the rod bolts to prevent cylinder wall scoring.

11. Before removing the piston assembly from cylinder bore scribe a mark indicating front position, or take notice of manufacturer identification mark. Using a wooden hammer handle, carefully tap piston assembly away from crankshaft and remove from cylinder block. Care should be taken not to damage crankshaft connecting rod journals or threads on connecting rod cap bolts.

12. Remove all the pistons from cylinder block in similar fashion.

Use lengths of vacuum hose or rubber tubing to protect the crankshaft journal and cylinder walls during piston and rod removal and installation

NOTE: *It is not necessary to remove the crankshaft from cylinder block for piston service. If crankshaft service is necessary refer to Crankshaft Removal procedures.*

CLEANING AND INSPECTION

1. Use a piston ring expander and remove the rings from the piston.

2. Clean the ring grooves using an appropriate cleaning tool, exercise care to avoid cutting too deeply.

3. Clean all varnish and carbon from the piston with a safe solvent. Do not use a wire brush or caustic solution on the pistons.

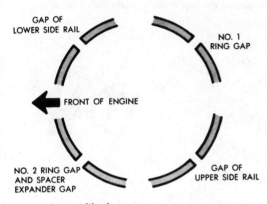

Piston ring positioning

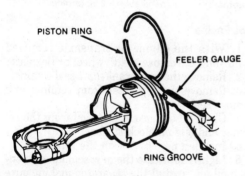

Check the piston ring side clearance

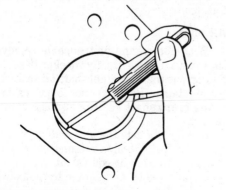

Check the piston ring end gap

4. Inspect the pistons for scuffing, scoring, cracks, pitting or excessive ring groove wear. If wear is evident, the piston must be replaced.

5. Have the piston and connecting rod assembly checked by a machine shop for correct alignment, piston pin wear and piston diameter. If the piston has collapsed it will have to be replaced or knurled to restore original diameter. Connecting rod bushing replacement, piston pin fitting and piston changing can be handled by the machine shop.

6. Check the cylinder bore diameter and cylinder bore for wear using a telescope gauge at three different levels. Cylinder bore out of round: 0.05mm maximum. Cylinder bore taper: 0.13mm maximum. Refer to General Engine Specification Chart for cylinder bore specification.

7. Check piston dimensions. Measure approximately 2mm above the bottom of the piston skirt and across the thrust face. Refer to Piston and Ring Specificaion Chart for piston diameter.

8. After recording cylinder bore measurement and piston diameter, subtract the low reading. The difference is Piston to Cylinder Wall Clearance: 0.02-0.04mm.

9. Check piston ring gap using a piston to position the ring at least 16mm from the bottom of cylinder bore. Measure clearance using a feeler gauge. Refer to Piston and Rings Specification Chart.

10. Check the piston ring to piston ring groove clearance using a feeler gauge.

11. Check the ring groove by rolling the new piston ring around the groove to check for burrs or carbon deposits. If any are found, remove with a fine file.

12. If all clearances and measurements are within specifications, honing or glaze breaking the cylinder bore is all that is required.

INSTALLATION

1. Start with the oil ring expander in the lower oil ring groove.

2. Install one oil rail at bottom of the oil ring expander and the other at top. The oil rails must be spaced 180 degrees apart from each other.

3. Using the ring expander install the intermediate piston ring.

4. Install the upper piston ring using the ring expander.

NOTE: *Generally marks on the upper and intermediate piston rings must point toward the crown of piston. Consult the illustration with piston ring set instruction sheet for ring positioning.*

5. Install a ring compressor and insert the piston and rod assembly into the engine with

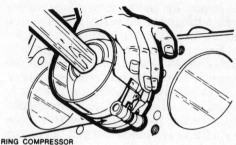

RING COMPRESSOR
Piston installation

mark previously made or labeled mark on piston head toward timing chain end of cylinder block.

6. Rotate the crankshaft so that the connecting rod journal is on center of cylinder bore. Install a new connecting rod bearing in connecting rod and cap. Check the connecting rod bearing oil clearnace using Plastigage. Follow the manufacturer procedures. Refer to Crankshaft and Connecting Rod Specification Chart.

7. Tighten the connecting rod cap nuts to specification. Refer to Torque Specification Chart.

8. Install the remaining piston and rod assemblies.

9. Using a feeler gauge, check connecting rod side clearance.

10. On 2.5L engine install the balance shaft carrier. Refer to Balance Shaft Installation procedures.

11. Install the oil pump and pick-up.

12. Install the cylinder head.

13. Install the intake manifold.

14. Install the timing chain or belt and sprockets. Refer to Engine Timing procedures.

15. Install the timing case cover.

16. Install the engine oil pan. Refer to Oil Pan Installation procedures.

Rear Main Seal

REMOVAL AND INSTALLATION

2.2L and 2.5L Engines

1. With the engine or transaxle removed from vehicle, remove the flywheel or flexplate.

2. Pry out rear crankshaft oil seal from seal retainer. Be carefull not to nick of damage crankshaft sealing surface or seal retainer.

3. Place Tool C-4681 or equivalent on the crankshaft.

4. Lubricate outer diameter with Locite Stud N' Bearing Mount (PN. 4057987) or equivalent.

5. Lightly lubricate the seal lip with engine oil and tap in place with a plastic hammer.

6. Install the flywheel/flexplate and tighten bolts to 95 N.m. (70 ft. lbs.).

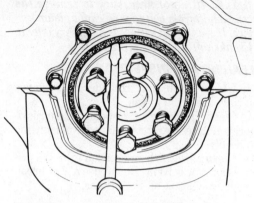

Removing the rear main oil seal—2.2L engine

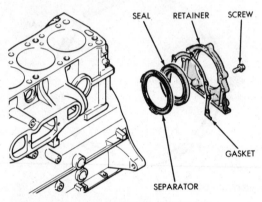

Rear main oil seal installation—2.6L engine

2.6L Engine

1. With the engine or transaxle removed from vehicle, remove the flywheel or flexplate.

2. Remove the rear crankshaft seal retainer.

3. Remove the separater from retainer and remove seal.

4. Clean all old gasket material from the retainer and engine block surface.

5. Install a new gasket on the retainer.

6. Lightly lubricate the new seal lip with engine oil and install the separator making sure the oil hole is at the bottom of separator.

7. Install flywheel tighten bolts to 95 N.m. (70 ft. lbs.).

3.0L Engine

1. With the engine or transaxle removed from vehicle, remove the flywheel or flexplate.

2. Pry out the rear crankshaft oil seal from the seal retainer. Be careful not to nick or damage the crankshaft sealing surface or seal retainer.

3. Lightly lubricate the new seal lip with engine oil and install seal in retainer housing using Tool MD998718 or equivalent.

4. Install flywheel and tighten the bolts to 95 N.m. (70 ft. lbs.).

Crankshaft and Main Bearings

Although, crankshaft service can be performed without removing the engine from the vehicle, it is far easier to work on the engine after it has been removed from the vehicle.

REMOVAL

1. Remove the engine from vehicle. Refer to Engine Removal procedures.
2. Remove the timing case cover, timing belt or chain and sprockets.
3. Remove the flywheel.
4. Remove the engine oil pan.
5. Remove the front crankshaft seal retainer if used. On 3.0L engine the front crankshaft seal is located in the oil pump assembly.
6. Remove the oil pump assembly 3.0L engine.
7. On 2.5L engines, remove the balance shaft carrier assembly. See Balance Shafts Removal Procedures.
8. Remove the rear crankshaft oil seal retainer bolts and remove retainer.
9. Before removing the crankshaft check Crankshaft End Play. as follows:
   a. Position a screwdriver between a main bearing cap and crankshaft. Move the crankshaft all the way to the rear of its travel.
   b. Position a feeler gauge between the thrust bearing and crankshaft machined surface to determine end play. Refer to Crankshaft and Connecting Rod Specification Chart.

Use the following procedure if only crank-

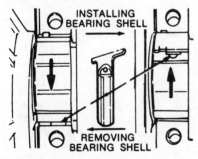

Remove the upper main bearing insert using a roll-out pin

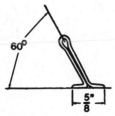

Home made rollout pin

shaft removal is necessary. If other engine repairs are being perform complete engine disassembly will be required.

10. Number all connecting rod caps if not already labeled to aid during assembly. Remove the connecting rod bearing caps nuts and remove caps.
11. Take two pieces of rubber tubing and cover the rod bolts to prevent crankshaft scoring.
12. Tap the piston assembly lightly away from crankshaft. Care should be taken not to damage crankshaft connecting rod journals or threads on connecting rod cap bolts.
13. Remove the main bearing cap bolts and remove caps. Remove crankshaft.

CLEANING AND INSPECTION

1. Inspect the main and connecting rod bearings replace if necessary.
2. Clean the crankshaft oil passages. Check the crankshaft main journals and connecting rod journals for wear or damage.

INSTALLATION

1. Install the main bearing shells with the lubrication groove in the cylinder block. Make certain the oil holes are in alignment, and bearing tabs seat in block.
2. Install the thrust bearing in journal No.3.
3. Oil the bearings and journals and install crankshaft.
4. Install the lower main bearing shells (without oil grooves) in lower bearing caps.
5. Check the main or connecting bearing oil clearance as followed:
   a. Wipe oil from bearing shells.
   b. Cut a piece of Plastigage to the same length as width of the bearing and place it in parallel with the journal.
   c. Install the bearing cap and torque to specification.
   NOTE: *Do not rotate crankshaft or the Plastigage will be smeared.*
   d. Carefully remove the bearing cap and measure the width of the plastigage at the widest part using the scale printed on the Plastigage package. Refer to Crankshaft and Connecting Rod Specification Chart.
6. Install all main bearing caps with arrows toward the timing chain end of cylinder block. Dip bolts in engine oil and install bolts finger tight then alternately torque each bolt. Refer to Torque Specificaion Chart.
7. Position theconnecting rods with new bearing shells against crankshaft. Install lower caps.
8. Before installing the nuts oil the threads. Install the nut on each bolt finger tight, then alternately torque each nut to specification. Refer to Torque Specificaion Chart.

9. On 2.5L engine install balance shaft carrier assembly. Refer to Balance Shaft Installation Procedures.

10. Install the front and rear crankshaft oil seal retainer assembly. Apply a 1.5mm diameter bead of RTV gasket material to retainers sealing surface.

11. Install the timing sprockets, timing belt and timing case cover. Refer to procedures previously outlined.

12. Install the engine oil pan. Refer to Oil Pan Installation procedures.

13. Install the flywheel. Refer to Torque Specifications.

EXHAUST SYSTEM

Safety Precautions

For a number of reasons, exhaust system work can be the most dangerous type of work you can do on your car. Always observe the following precautions:

• Support the car extra securely. Not only will you often be working directly under it, but you'll frequently be using a lot of force, say, heavy hammer blows, to dislodge rusted parts. This can cause a car that's improperly supported to shift and possibly fall.

• Wear goggles. Exhaust system parts are always rusty. Metal chips can be dislodged, even when you're only turning rusted bolts. Attempting to pry pipes apart with a chisel makes the chips fly even more frequently.

• If you're using a cutting torch, keep it a great distance from either the fuel tank or lines. Stop what you're doing and feel the temperature of the fuel bearing pipes on the tank frequently. Even slight heat can expand and/or vaporize fuel, resulting in accumulated vapor, or even a liquid leak, near your torch.

• Watch where your hammer blows fall and make sure you hit squarely. You could easily tap a brake or fuel line when you hit an exhaust system part with a glancing blow. Inspect all lines and hoses in the area where you've been working.

CAUTION: *Be very careful when working on or near the catalytic converter. External temperatures can reach 1,500°F (816°C) and more, causing severe burns. Removal or installation should be performed only on a cold exhaust system.*

Special Tools

A number of special exhaust system tools can be rented from auto supply houses or local stores that rent special equipment. A common one is a tail pipe expander, designed to enable you to join pipes of identical diameter.

It may also be quite helpful to use solvents designed to loosen rusted bolts or flanges. Soaking rusted parts the night before you do the job can speed the work of freeing rusted parts con-

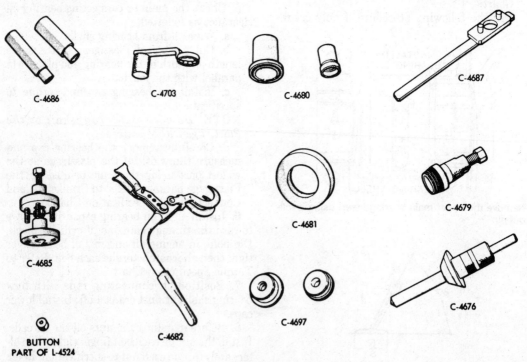

C-4686   C-4703   C-4680   C-4687

C-4685   C-4681   C-4679

C-4697   C-4676

C-4682

BUTTON
PART OF L-4524

Special tools

siderably. Remember that these solvents are often flammable. Apply only to parts after they are cool!

Exhaust (Converter/Resonator) Pipe

REMOVAL AND INSTALLATION

1. Raise the vehicle and properly support on jackstands.

CAUTION: *Be very careful when working on or near the catalytic converter! External temperatures can reach 1,500°F (816°C) and more, causing severe burns! Removal or installation should be performed only on a cold exhaust system.*

2. Apply penetrating oil to clamp bolts, nuts and connecting points of system to be remove.

3. Remove the nuts and clamp assembly from exhaust pipe to muffler connecting point.

4. Remove the shoulder bolts, springs and nuts attaching exhaust pipe to exhaust manifold.

5. Remove the exhaust pipe/converter assembly from muffler.

6. Clean the exhaust manifold to exhaust pipe/converter assembly gasket mating surfaces and the end of muffler with a wire brush.

7. Install the exhaust pipe/converter assembly or resonator into muffler. Make certain the key on the converter or resonator pipe bottomed in slot of muffler.

8. Install a new gasket on the exhaust pipe and position exhaust pipe into exhaust manifold. Install springs, shoulder bolts and nuts. Tighten nuts to 21 ft. lbs.

9. Align parts and install a new clamp assembly at exhaust pipe and muffler connecting point tighten clamps nuts to 23 ft. lbs.

Tailpipe

REMOVAL AND INSTALLATION

1. Raise the vehicle and properly support on jackstands.

2. Apply penetrating oil to clamp bolts, nuts and connecting points of system to be remove.

3. Remove the support saddle type clamp assembly from the tail pipe to muffler connecting point.

4. Remove the U-nut and shoulder bolts from tail pipe mid-point and rear tail pipe bracket.

5. When removing the tail pipe, raise the rear of vehicle enough to provide clearance between pipe and rear axle parts.

6. Remove the tailpipe from muffler.

7. Clean the muffler mating surface with a wire brush.

8. Replace broken or worn insulators, supports or attaching parts.

9. Loosely assemble the tail pipe to muffler, mid-point support and tail pipe bracket. Make certain slot in tail pipe is keyed with key in muffler.

10. Align parts and install support saddle type clamp tighten nuts to 28 ft. lbs.

Muffler

REMOVAL AND INSTALLATION

1. Raise the vehicle and properly support on jackstands.

2. Apply penetrating oil to clamp bolts, nuts and connecting points of system to be remove.

3. Disconnect the tail pipe from the muffler assembly. Refer to Tail Pipe Removal procedures.

4. Remove nuts and clamp from exhaust pipe and muffler connection and remove the muffler.

5. Clean the exhaust pipe and tail pipe mating surfaces with a wire brush.

6. Replace broken or worn insulators, supports or attaching parts.

7. Loosely assemble the muffler to exhaust pipe and tail pipe. Make certain keys are bottomed in slots of muffler and pipes.

8. Align parts and install support saddle type clamp between tail pipe and muffler connecting point. Tighten nuts to 28 ft. lbs.

9. Install clamp assembly and nuts at exhaust pipe and muffler connecting point and tighten to 25 ft. lbs.

Emission Controls

EMISSION CONTROLS

Vehicle Emission Control Information Label

All vehicles discribed in this Repair and Tune-Up Guide are equipped with a Vehicle Emission Control Information Label (VECI). The VECI label is located in the engine compartment and is permanently attached. No attempt should be made to remove the VECI label. The VECI label contains specific information for the vehicle to which it is attached. If the specifications on the VECI label differ from the information contain in this manual, those shown on the label should be followed.

Crankcase Ventilation System

The Positive Crankcase Ventilation System is described, and servicing procedures are detailed in Chapter 1.

Evaporative Emission Controls

The Evaporative Emission Control System prevents gasoline vapor emissions from the fuel tank and carburetor from entering the atmosphere.

Evaporating fuel from the gas tank or carburetor passes through vent hoses and tubes to a charcoal canister where they are temporarily stored until they can be drawn into the intake manifold and burned when the engine is running.

CHARCOAL CANISTER

The charcoal canister is a sealed, maintenance free unit which stores fuel vapors from the fuel tank and carbureter bowl. Although all carburetor bowls are vented internally, some models do not required venting to the canister. In cases where the carburetor is not vented to the canister, the bowl vent port on the canister will be capped. If the canister becomes dam-

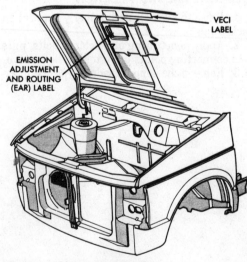

1984–86 underhood label location   1987–88 underhood label location

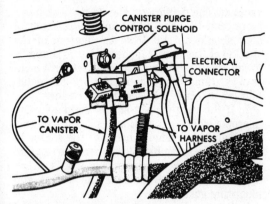

Typical canister purge solenoid

aged, replacement with a new unit is required. The hoses connecting the canister are of fuel resistant construction. Use only fuel resistant hoses if replacement is necessary.

DAMPING CANISTER

Some models are equipped with a damping canister that is connected in series with the charcoal canister. The damping canister cushions the effect of a sudden release of fuel rich vapors when the purge valve is signaled to open. The rich vapors are held momentarily and then gradually fed into the intake manifold to be burned.

CANISTER PURGE SOLENOID

2.5L and 3.0L engines are equipped with a canister purge solenoid which is connected in series with the charcoal canister. The canister purge solenoid is electrically operated by the Single Module Engine Controller (SMEC) which grounds the solenoid if engine temperature is below 66°C. This prevents vacuum from reaching the charcoal canister. When the engine reaches operating temperature the SMEC de-energizes the solenoid and allows purge vapors from the canister to pass through the throttle body.

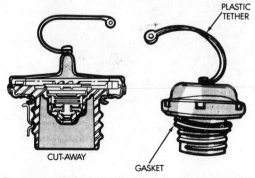

Pressure vacuum gas filler cap

GAS TANK FILLER CAP

The fuel tank is covered and sealed with a specially engineered pressure/vacuum relief gas cap. The built-in relief valve is a safety feature, and allows pressure to be relieved without separating the cap from the filler tube eliminating excessive tank pressure. If a replacement cap is required, a similar cap must be installed in order for the system to remain effective.

NOTE: *Always remove the gas tank cap to release pressure whenever the fuel system requires servicing.*

BOWL VENT VALVE

The bowl vent valve (carburetor equipped models) is connected to the carburetor fuel bowl, the charcoal canister, and the air pump discharge. When the engine is not running and no air pump pressure is applied, a direct connection between the carburetor and canister exists. When the engine is running, air pump pressure closes the connection between the canister and the fuel bowl. When the engine is shut off, air pressure in the valve bleeds down and the fuel bowl is allow to vent vapors into the canister.

Exhaust Emission Controls
HEATED INLET AIR SYSTEM

All engines (except 3.0L Multi-point fuel injection system) are equipped with a vacuum device located in the air cleaner air intake. A small door is operated by a vacuum diaphragm and a thermostatic spring. When the outside air temperature is below a specified level, the door will block off air entering from outside the air cleaner snorkel, and allow heated air channelled from the exhaust manifold area to enter the air cleaner assembly. With the engine warmed up and running the thermostatic spring allows the heat control door to draw outside air through the air cleaner snorkel.

SERVICE PROCEDURES

NOTE: *A malfunction in the heated air system will affect driveability and the emissions output of the vehicle.*

2.2L Engine

1. Verify all vacuum hoses and the flexible heat pipe between the air cleaner and heat stove are properly attached and in good condition.

2. On a cold engine with an ambient temperature less than 19°C (65°F) the heat door valve plate in the snorkel should be in the up position (Heat On).

3. With the engine running at normal oper-

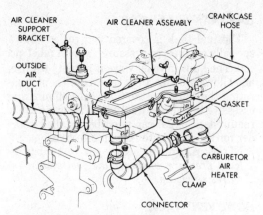

Heated air intake system on 2.2L engine

ating temperature, the heat door should be in the down position (Heat Off).

4. If the heat door valve plate does not respond to hot and cold temperatures, the door diaphram or the sensor may need replacing.

5. To test the diaphram, remove the air cleaner from the engine and allow it to cool down to 19°C (65°F).

6. Connect a hand operated vacuum pump to the vacuum diaphragm and apply 20 inches of

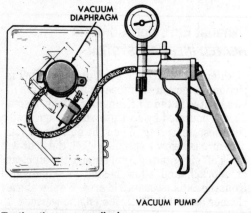

Testing the vacuum diaphram

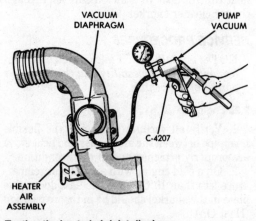

Testing the heated air inlet diaphram

vacuum. The diaphragm should not leak down more than 10 inches in 5 minutes. The control door should not lift from the bottom of the snorkel at less than 2 inches of vacuum and be in the full up position with no more than 4 inches of vacuum. If the vacuum test proves the diaphragm defective, replace the air cleaner.

7. If the vacuum test shows the diaphragm in proper working condition, replace the sensor.

8. Label the vacuum hoses at the sensor to aid during reassemble. Disconnect the vacuum hoses, remove the retaining clips with a screwdriver and discard. Remove the sensor and mounting gasket.

9. Position the new gasket on the sensor and install sensor. Support the sensor on the outer diameter, and install the retaining clips.

10. Reconnect vacuum hoses.

2.5L Engine

1. Verify all vacuum hoses and the flexible heat pipe between the air cleaner and heat stove are properly attached and in good condition.

2. On a cold engine with an ambient temperature less than 46°C (115°F) the heat door valave plate in the snorkel should be in the up position (Heat On).

3. With the engine running at normal operating temperature, the heat door should be in the down position (Heat Off).

4. If the heat door valve plate does not respond to hot and cold temperatures, the door diaphram or the sensor may need replacing.

5. To test the diaphram, remove the air cleaner from the engine and allow it to cool down to 46°C (115°F).

6. Connect a hand operated vacuum pump to the sensor and apply 20 inches of vacuum. The door valve should be in the up position (Heat On).

7. If the door does not raise to "Heat On" po-

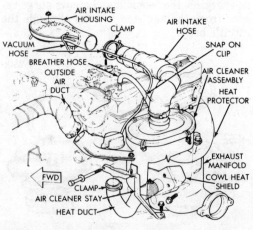

Heated air intake system on 2.6L engine

sition, test the vacuum diaphragm for proper operation.

8. Apply 20 inches of vacuum with a hand operated vacuum pump to the vacuum diaphragm. The diaphragm should not leak down more than 10 inches in 5 minutes. The control door should not lift from the bottom of the snorkel at less than 2 inches of vacuum and be in the full up position with no more than 4 inches of vacuum. If the vacuum test proves the diaphragm defective, replace the air cleaner.

9. If the vacuum test shows the diaphragm in proper working condition, replace the sensor.

10. Label the vacuum hoses at the sensor to aid during assembly. Disconnect the vacuum hoses, remove the retaining clips with a screwdriver and discard. Remove the sensor and mounting gasket.

11. Position the new gasket on the sensor and install sensor. Support the sensor on the outer diameter, and install the retaining clips.

12. Connect the vacuum hoses.

2.6L Engine

1. Verify all vacuum hoses and the flexible heat pipe between the air cleaner and heat stove are properly attached and in good condition.

2. On a cold engine with an ambient temperature less than 30°C (84°F) the heat door valave plate in the snorkel should be in the up position (Heat On).

3. With the engine running at normal operating temperature, the heat door should be in the down position (Heat Off).

4. If the heat door valve plate does not respond to hot and cold temperatures, the door diaphram or the sensor may need replacing.

5. To test the diaphram, remove the air cleaner from the engine and allow it to cool down to 30°C (84°F).

6. Connect a hand operated vacuum pump to the sensor and apply 15 inches of vacuum. The valve should be in the up position (Heat On).

7. If the door does not raise to Heat On position, test the vacuum motor for proper operation.

8. Apply 10 inches of vacuum to the vacuum motor with a hand operated vacuum pump, if the valve does not remain in the full up position replace the air cleaner body assembly.

9. If the door perform adequately with vacuum applied to the motor, replace the sensor.

Exhaust Gas Recirculation (EGR) System

The EGR system reduces the oxides of nitrogen in the engine exhaust. The reduction of NOx is accomplished by allowing a predetermined amount of the hot exhaust gas to recirculate and dilute the incoming fuel and air mixture. This dilution reduces peak flame temperature during combustion.

SERVICE

2.2L Engine

The components of the EGR system on the 2.2L engine are; a Coolant Controlled Exhaust Gas Recirculation/Coolant Vacuum Switch Cold Closed (CVSCC) unit mounted in the thermostat housing, an EGR valve, and a EGR tube.

The CVSCC prevents vacuum from being supplied to the EGR system or other systems until the coolant temperature reaches a certain level. When a certain temperature is reached the CVSCC opens and vacuum is supplied as necessary.

To assure proper operation test the system as follows:

1. Inspect all passages and moving parts for free movement.

2. Inspect all hoses. If any are hardened, cracked or have faulty connection, replacement is necessary.

3. Allow the engine to reach normal operating temperature. Locate the EGR valve at the end of the intake manifold. Allow the engine to idle for about a minute, then abruptly accelerate to about 2000 rpm, but not over 3000 rpm. Visible movement of the EGR valve stem should be noticed. Movement of the stem indicates the the valve is operation normally. If no movement is noticed. Remove the EGR valve and inspect it for deposits and wear.

4. If deposits around the poppet and seat are more than a film, apply some heat control solvent to the area to help soften the deposits. Apply vacuum to the valve with a hand operated vacuum pump. When the valve opens, scrap away the deposits from the poppet and seat. If the valve poppet does not open when vacuum is applied, replace the valve. If the stem or seat is worn replace the valve.

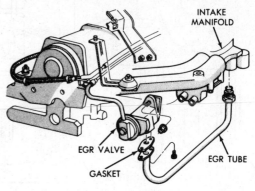

EGR system on the 2.2L engine

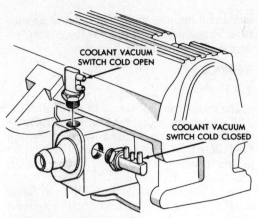

Coolant vacuum switch

5. If the EGR valve is functioning properly, check the CVSCC.

6. Check condition of vacuum hoses at the CVSCC and properly routed (see vacuum hose underhood sticker).

7. Check engine coolant level.

8. Disconnect the vacuum hoses and remove the valve from the thermostat housing. Place the valve in an ice bath below 4.4°C (40°F) so that the threaded portion is covered. Attach a vacuum pump to the lower connection on the valve (the one connected to the vacuum hose showing a yellow stripe). Apply 10 inches of vacuum. Pressure should drop no more than one inch in one minute. If the vacuum drops more, replace the CVSCC.

2.6L Engine

With this system exhaust gases are partially recirculated from an exhaust port in the cylin-

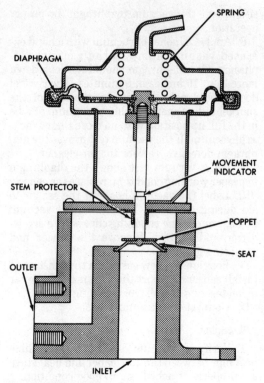

Typical EGR valve

der head into a port at the intake manifold below the carburetor. EGR flow is controlled by thermo valves, and a combination of a Dual EGR valve and Sub EGR valve.

The dual EGR valve consists of a primary and secondary valve which are controlled by a different carburetor vacuums in response to the

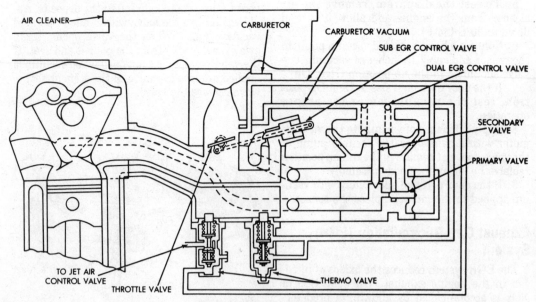

EGR system on the 2.6L engine

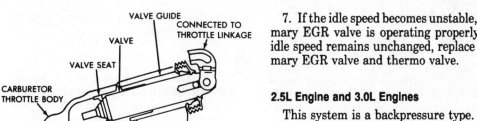

Typical sub EGR valve

throttle opening. EGR flow is halted at idle and wide open throttle operation. The primary valve controls the EGR flow at narrow throttle openings, while the secondary valve allows flow into the intake mixture at wider throttle openings. Vacuum to the dual EGR valve is controlled by thermo valves.

A carburetor mounted Sub EGR valve is directly opened and closed by the throttle linkage in order to closely modulate the EGR flow controlled by the EGR control valve, in response to the throttle opening.

Two thermo valves connected to the EGR system, sense coolant temperature changes and open and close accordingly to control the vacuum flow to the EGR system.

Test the system as follows:

1. Check the vacuum hose for good condition and proper routing (see vacuum hose underhood sticker).

2. Engine must be cold. Cold start the engine and allow to idle.

3. Check to make sure that the fast idle does not cause the secondary EGR valve to operate. If the secondary EGR valve operates at cold start fast idle, replace the secondary EGR valve thermo valve.

4. Run the engine until the operating temperature exceeds 65°C (149°F). The secondary EGR valve should now be in operation. If if it does not operate, inspect the EGR valve or thermo valve.

5. Disconnect the green stripped vacuum hose from the carburetor. Connect a hand vacuum pump to the hose and apply 6 inches of vacuum while opening the sub EGR valve by hand. If the idle speed becomes unstable, the secondary valve is operating properly. If the idle speed remains the same, replace the secondary EGR valve and thermo valve.

6. Connect the green stripped hose to the carburetor. Disconnect the yellow stripped hose from the carburetor and connect it to the hand vacuum pump. Hold the sub EGR valve opened and apply 6 inches of vacuum.

7. If the idle speed becomes unstable, the primary EGR valve is operating properly. If the idle speed remains unchanged, replace the primary EGR valve and thermo valve.

2.5L Engine and 3.0L Engines

This system is a backpressure type. A backpressure transducer monitors the amount of exhaust gas backpressure and in response increase or decrease the strength of the vacuum signal to the EGR valve. The 2.5L engine uses an EGR tube mounted to the exhaust manifold which supply EGR gases to the EGR valve. 3.0L engine uses an exhaust mounted EGR valve which supply EGR gases to the intake manifold.

California vehicles with EGR have an onboard diagnostic system and a solenoid in series with the vacuum line to the EGR valve. The engine controller monitors EGR system performance and energized or de-energized the solenoid base on engine/driving conditions. If the system malfunction the engine controller will turn on the Check Engine light and a fault code will be stored in the diagnostic system.

Test the system as follows:

1. Inspect all passages and moving parts for free movement.

2. Inspect all hoses. If any are hardened, cracked or have faulty connection, replacement is necessary.

3. Warm the engine to normal operating temperature. Allow the engine to idle for about a minute, then abruptly accelerate to about 2000 rpm, but not over 3000 rpm. Visible movement of the groove on EGR valve stem should be noticed. Movement of the stem indicates the the valve is operation normally. If no movement is noticed.

4. Disconnect the vacuum hoses from the EGR vacuum transducer, and attach a hand operated vacuum pump. Raise the engine to 2000 rpm and apply 10 inches of vacuum, while checking valve movement. If no valve movement occurs, replace the valve/transducer assembly.

NOTE: *If the back-pressure EGR valve does not function satisfactory. Replace the entire Valve/Transducer assembly. No attempt should be made to clean the valve.*

5. If movement occurs, check the diaphragm for leaks. Valve should remain open at least 30 seconds.

6. If the valve is functioning satisfactory, remove the throttle body and inspect port in throttle bore and associated passages. Apply some heat control solvent to the area to help soften any deposit.

7. Install the throttle body and recheck EGR operation.

Air Injection System

2.2L engines are equipped with an air injection system. This system is designed to supply a controlled amount of air to the exhaust gases, through exhaust ports, aiding in the oxidation of the gases and reduction of carbon monoxide and hydrocarbons to an appreciable level.

During engine warm-up air is injected into the base of the exhaust manifold. After the engine warms up, the air flow is switched (by a Coolant Vacuum Switch Cold Open or by a vacuuum solenoid) to the 3-way catalyst where it further aids in the reduction of carbon monoxide and hydrocarbons in the exhaust system.

The system consists of a belt driven air pump, hoses, a switch/relief valve and a check valve to prevent the components within the system from high temperature exhaust gases.

NOTE: *No repairs are possible on any of the air injection system components. All replacement parts must be service as a unit.*

Coolant Vacuum Switch Cold Open

1. Locate the switch on the thermostat housing.
2. Label the hoses before removing. Remove hoses.
3. Remove the vacuum switch from housing.
4. Install a new vacuum switch and connect the vacuum hoses. (See underhood vacuum hose routing label).

Air Pump

NOTE: *The air injection system is not completely noiseless. Do not assume the air pump is defective because it squeals. If the system creates excessive noise, remove the drive belt and operate the engine. If the noise ceases, check all hoses connection for proper tightening. Replace pump if necessary.*

1. Remove all hoses and vacuum lines from the air pump and diverter valve or switch/relief valve (depending on how equipped).
2. Remove the air pump drive pully shield.
3. Remove the air pump pivot bolt and remove air pump belt.
4. Remove the remaining mounting bolts and remove pump.
5. Remove the diverter valve or switch/relief valve from pump.
6. Clean all gasket material from valve and pump mounting surface.
7. Install the diverter valve or switch/relief valve using a new gasket, to the new pump.
8. Install the pump on the engine and loosely install pivot bolt.
9. Install drive belt and tighten pivot bolt.
10. Install air pump drive pully shield.
11. Install all hoses and vacuum lines.

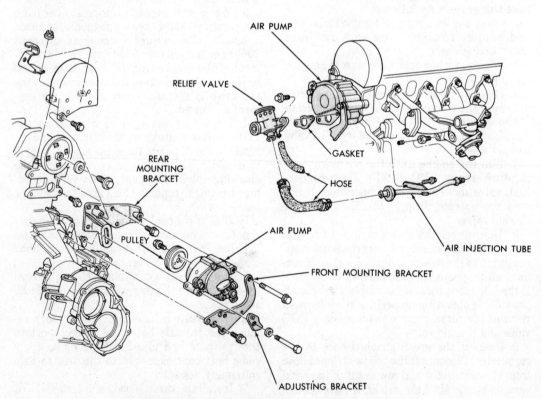

Air injection system on the 2.2L engine—Federal/Canadian shown

Switch/Relief Valve

If vacuum is apply to the valve and air injection is not upstream, or if air injection is in both upstream and downstream, the valve is faulty and must be replaced.

1. Remove all air hoses and vacuum hoses.
2. Remove the valve to pump mounting bolts, and remove valve.
3. Clean all gasket material from mounting surfaces.
4. Install the new valve to the pump with a new gasket.
5. Secure the valve with mounting bolts, tighten bolts to 14N.m (125 in.lbs.).
6. Reinstall all air hoses and vacuum hoses.

Relief Valve

The purpose of this valve is to control air pump pressure during high engine speeds. If the pump discharge pressure exceeds 9 PSI the valve will open and vent the excess pressure to the atmosphere.

1. Remove the air hoses from the valve.
2. Remove the valve mounting screws and remove valve.
3. Clean all gasket material from mounting surfaces.
4. Install a new gasket on valve and secure with mounting screws.
5. Reconnect air hoses.

Check Valve

The check valve is located in the injection tube which lead to the exhaust manifold and converter assembly. The valve has a one-way diaphragm to protect the pump and hoses from high exhaust system pressure if the belt or pump failed.

Remove the air hose from check valve inlet tube. If exhaust gas escapes from the inlet tube, the valve have failed and must be replaced.

1. Loosen clamp and remove inlet hose from the valve.
2. Remove the tube nut retaining the tube to the exhaust manifold or catalyst.
3. Loosen the starter motor mounting bolt and remove injection tube from engine.
4. Remove the catalyst injection tube mounting screws from catalyst flange and remove injection tube.
5. Position the injection tube to catalyst flange and secured with mounting screws.
6. Install the injection tube into fitting in exhaust manifold and bracket at starter motor.
7. Connect hoses to the check valve.

Pulse Air Feeder System

2.6L engines use a pulse air feeder system to promote oxidation of exhaust emissions in the rear catalytic converter. The system consists of a main reed valve and sub-reed valve. The main reed valve is controlled by a diaphragm which is activated by pressure pulses from the crankcase. The sub-reed valve is activated by pulsation in the exhaust system between the front and rear converters.

1. Remove the air duct from the right side of the radiator.
2. Remove the carburetor protector shield.
3. Remove the engine oil dipstick and tube.
4. Remove the pulse air feeder mounting bolts.
5. Raise and support the front of the vehicle on jackstands. Disconnect the pulse air feeder hoses and remove the feeder.

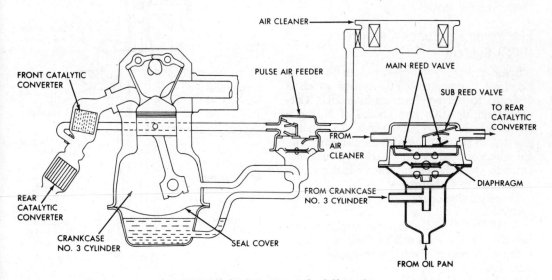

Pulse air feed system on the 2.6L engine

6. Install hoses on pulse air feeder.

7. Lower the vehicle and tighten feeder mounting bolts.

8. Check O-ring on lower end of the dipstick tube. Replace if damaged.

9. Install carburetor protector shield.

10. Install the air deflector on radiator.

Dual Air Aspirator System

2.6L engines use an air aspirator system which aids in reducing carbon monoxide (CO) and hydrocarbon emissions. The system uses pulsating exhaust pressure to draw fresh air from the air cleaner assembly. Failure of the aspirator valve will result in excess noise.

SYSTEM TEST

1. Check the aspirator tube/exhaust manifold assembly joint and hoses. If aspirator tube/exhaust manifold joint is leaking, retighten to 68 N.m (50 ft.lbs.). If hoses are harden, replace as necessary.

2. Disconnect the inlet hose from aspirator valve.

3. With engine at idle, the negative (vacuum) exhaust pulses should be felt at the valve inlet.

4. If hot exhaust gases escaped from the aspirator inlet, replace the valve.

REMOVAL AND INSTALLATION

1. Remove the air inlet hose from aspirator valve.

2. Remove screws from aspirator bracket, and remove tube assembly from engine.

3. Install tube and tighten nuts to 54 N.m (40 ft.lbs.).

4. Install tube bracket assembly and torque to 28 N.m (250 in.lbs.).

5. Connect the air hose to valve and air cleaner nipple, install clamps.

Electronic Feedback Carburetor (EFC) System

Some models are equipped with an Electronic Feedback Carburetor (EFC) System which is designed to convert Hydrocarbons(HC), Carbon Monoxide (CO) and Oxides of Nitrogen (NOx) into harmless substances. An exhaust gas oxygen sensor generates an electronic signal which is used by the Spark Control Computer to precisely control the air-fuel mixture ratio to the carburetor.

There are two operating modes in the EFC system:

1. OPEN LOOP-During cold engine operation the air-fuel ratio will be fixed to a richer mixture programmed into the computer by the manufacture.

2. CLOSED LOOP-The computer varries the air-fuel ratio based on information supplied by the oxygen sensor.

Oxygen Sensor

The oxygen sensor is a galvanic battery which produces electrical voltage after being heated by exhaust gases. The sensor monitors the oxygen content in the exhaust stream, convert it to an electrical voltage and transmit this voltage to the Spark Control Computer.

WARNING: *Use care when working around the oxygen sensor as the exhaust manifold may be extremely hot. The sensor must be removed using Tool C-4907.*

When the sensor is removed, the exhaust manifold threads must be cleaned with an 18mm x 1.5 x 6E tap.

If the sensor is to be reinstalled, the sensor threads must be coated with an anti-seize compound such as Loctite 771-64 or equivalent. New sensors are coated with compound on the threads and no additional compound is required. The sensor should be torque to 27 N.m (20 ft.lbs.).

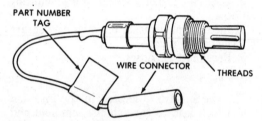

Typical oxygen sensor

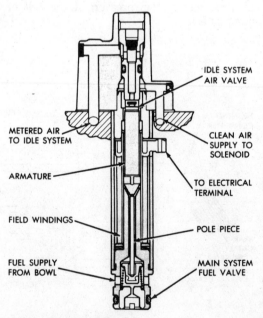

Oxygen feedback solenoid

Oxygen Feedback Solenoid

In addition to the oxygen sensor, EFC uses an Oxygen Feedback Solenoid. It purpose is to regulate the fuel-air ratio of the feedback carburetor, along with a conventional fixed main metering jet, in response to the electrical signal generated by the Spark Control Computer.

With the feedback solenoid de-energized, the main metering orifice is fully uncovered and the richest condition exists within the carburetor.

With the feedback solenoid energized, the solenoid push rod seals the main metering orifice. This position offers the leanest condition within the carburetor.

Electric Choke Assembly

The electric choke system is a heater and switch assembly sealed within the choke housing. When the engine is running and the engine oil pressure is 2.7 kPa (4 psi) or aboved, the contacts in the oil pressure switch closes and feed current to the automatic choke system to open the choke and keep it open.

NOTE: *The choke assembly must never be immersed in fluid as damage to the internal switch and heater assembly will result.*

TESTING

1. Disconnect the electrical lead from choke heater assembly.
2. Connect direct battery voltage to choke heater connection.
3. The choke valve should reach the open position within five minutes.

WARNING: *Operation of any type should be avoided if there is a lost of choke power. This condition cause a very rich mixture to burn and result in abnormally high exhaust system temperatures, which may cause damage to the catalyst or other underbody parts of the vehicle.*

Emission Vacuum Hose Diagrams

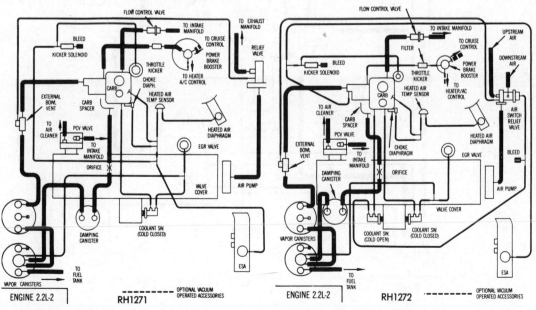

Federal 2.2L vacuum hose routing

California 2.2L vacuum hose routing

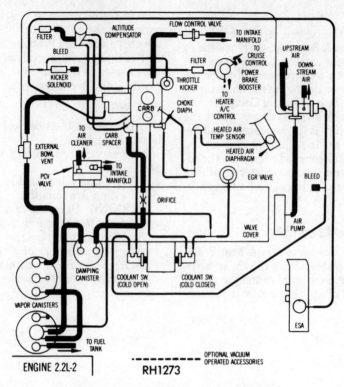

Federal high altitude 2.2L vacuum hose routing

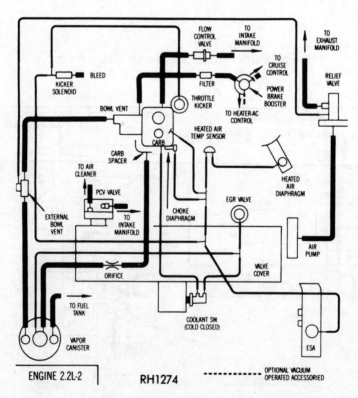

Canadian 2.2L vacuum hose routing

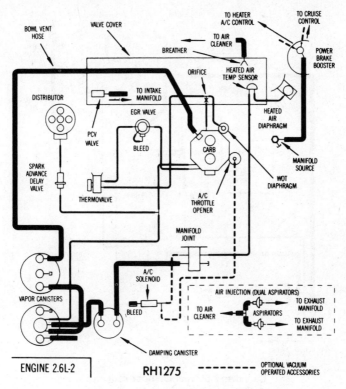

Federal 2.6L vacuum hose routing

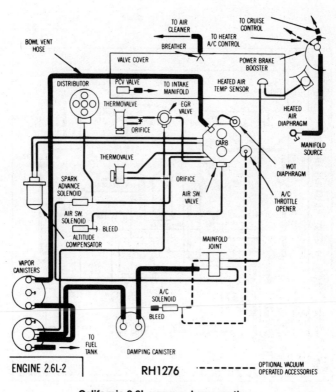

California 2.6L vacuum hose routing

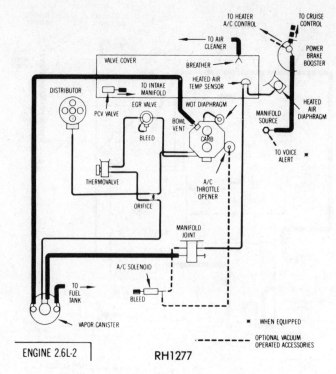

Canadian 2.6L vacuum hose routing

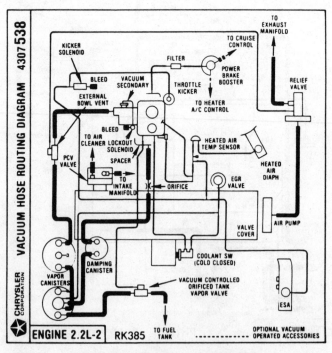

1985 Federal 2.2L vacuum hose routing

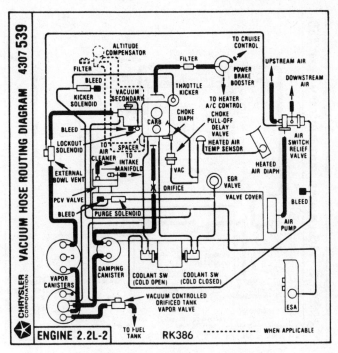

1985 Calif. 2.2L vacuum hose routing

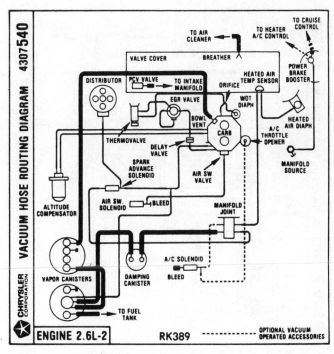

1985 Altitude vacuum hose routing

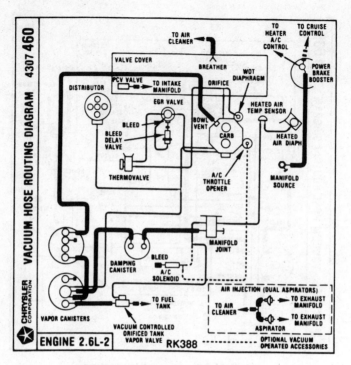

1985 Federal 2.6L vacuum hose routing

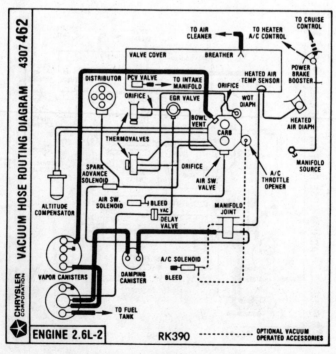

1985 Calif. 2.6L vacuum hose routing

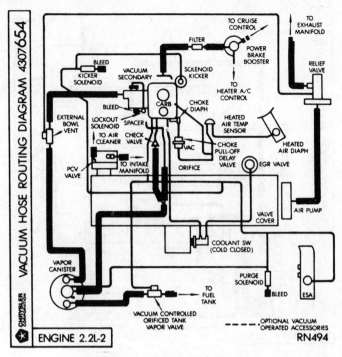

1986 Federal 2.2L vacuum hose routing

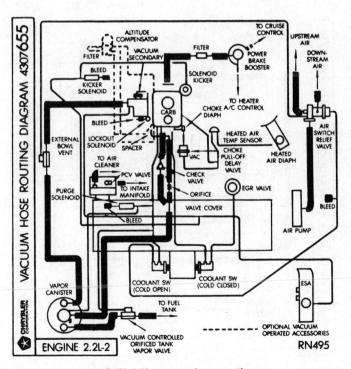

1986 Calif. 2.2L vacuum hose routing

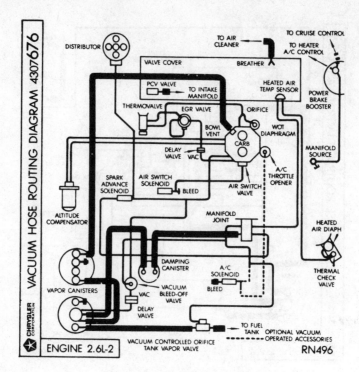

1986 Altitude vacuum hose routing

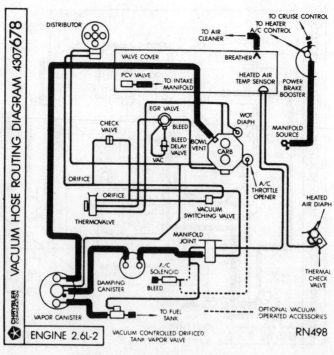

1986 Federal 2.6L vacuum hose routing

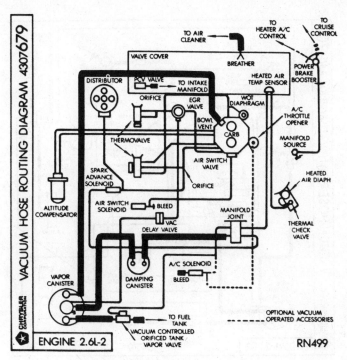

1986 Calif. 2.6L vacuum hose routing

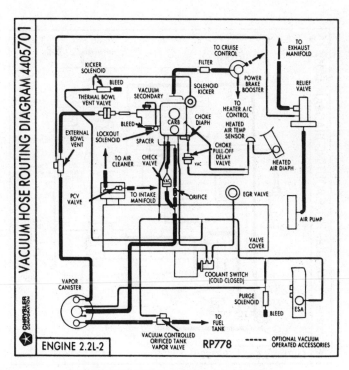

1987 Federal 2.2L vacuum hose routing

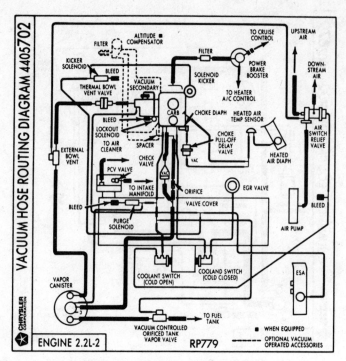

1987 Calif. 2.2L vacuum hose routing

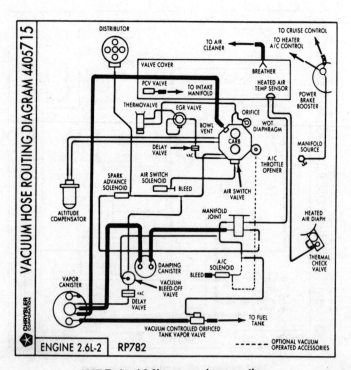

1987 Federal 2.6L vacuum hose routing

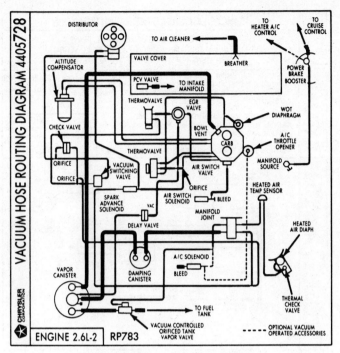

1987 Calif. 2.6L vacuum hose routing

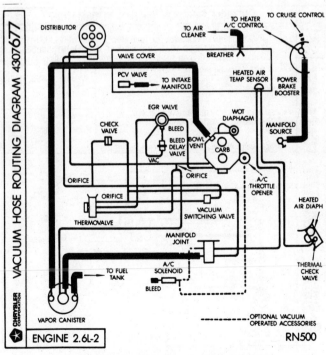

1987 Canadian 2.6L vacuum hose routing

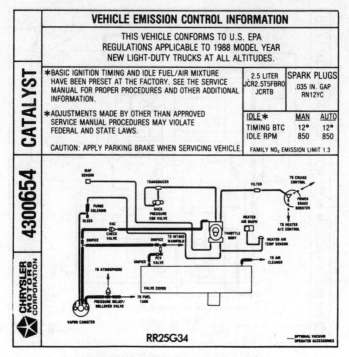

1988 Fed. and Alt. 2.5L vacuum hose routing

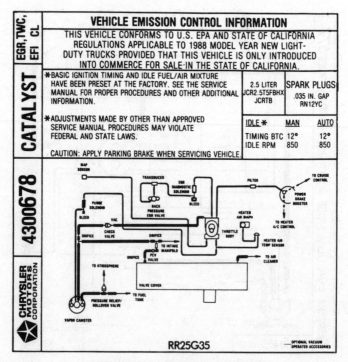

1988 Calif. 2.5L vacuum hose routing

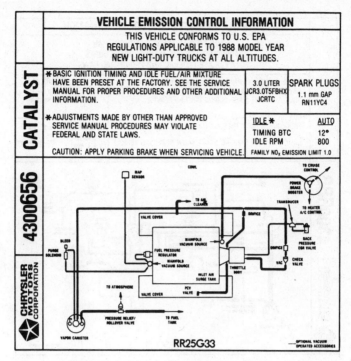

1988 Fed. and Alt. 3.0L vacuum hose routing

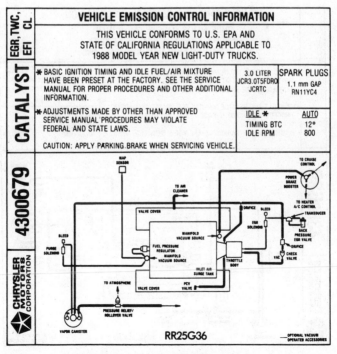

1988 Calif. 3.0L vacuum hose routing

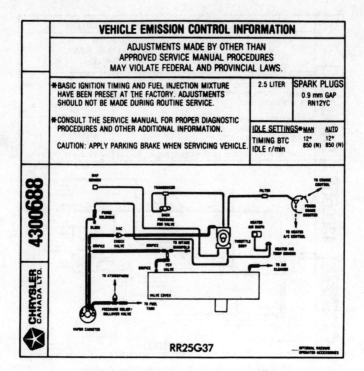

1988 Canadian 2.5L vacuum hose routing

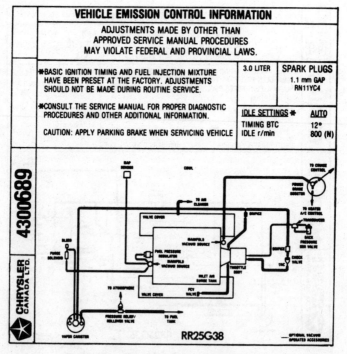

1988 Canadian 3.0L vacuum hose routing

Fuel System

5

CARBURETED FUEL SYSTEM

Mechanical Fuel Pump

The 2.2L and 2.6L engine use a mechanical type fuel pump located on the side of the engine. The fuel pump is driven by an eccentric cam which is cast on the accessory drive shaft.

REMOVAL AND INSTALLATION

CAUTION: *Don't smoke when working around gasoline, cleaning solvent or other flammable substances.*
1. Remove the oil filter.

2. Disconnect the fuel lines from the pump.
3. Plug the lines to prevent fuel leakage.
4. Remove the fuel pump blocker strut from front engine mount to blocker assembly.
5. Remove the fuel pump mounting bolts.
6. Clean all gasket material from engine block mounting surface and spacer block.
7. Assemble the new gaskets and spacer block to fuel pump.
8. Install the fuel pump mounting bolts in pump mounting flange.
9. Position the pump assembly on engine block and torque bolts alternately to 250 in. lbs.

Troubleshooting Basic Fuel System Problems

Problem	Cause	Solution
Engine cranks, but won't start (or is hard to start) when cold	• Empty fuel tank • Incorrect starting procedure • Defective fuel pump • No fuel in carburetor • Clogged fuel filter • Engine flooded • Defective choke	• Check for fuel in tank • Follow correct procedure • Check pump output • Check for fuel in the carburetor • Replace fuel filter • Wait 15 minutes; try again • Check choke plate
Engine cranks, but is hard to start (or does not start) when hot— (presence of fuel is assumed)	• Defective choke	• Check choke plate
Rough idle or engine runs rough	• Dirt or moisture in fuel • Clogged air filter • Faulty fuel pump	• Replace fuel filter • Replace air filter • Check fuel pump output
Engine stalls or hesitates on acceleration	• Dirt or moisture in the fuel • Dirty carburetor • Defective fuel pump • Incorrect float level, defective accelerator pump	• Replace fuel filter • Clean the carburetor • Check fuel pump output • Check carburetor
Poor gas mileage	• Clogged air filter • Dirty carburetor • Defective choke, faulty carburetor adjustment	• Replace air filter • Clean carburetor • Check carburetor
Engine is flooded (won't start accompanied by smell of raw fuel)	• Improperly adjusted choke or carburetor	• Wait 15 minutes and try again, without pumping gas pedal • If it won't start, check carburetor

10. Connect the fuel lines to the pump.

11. Position the fuel pump blocker strut on blocker assembly and front engine mount. Tighten assembly.

12. Install the oil filter. Check and adjust oil level.

13. Start the engine and check fuel fittings for leaks.

TESTING

Volume Test

The fuel pump should supply 1 qt. of fuel in 1 minute or less at idle.

Pressure Test

1. Insert a T-fitting in the fuel line at the carburetor.

CAUTION: *Never smoke when working around gasoline! Avoid all sources of sparks or ignition. Gasoline vapors are EXTREMELY volatile!*

2. Connect a six inch piece of hose between the T-fitting and a pressure gauge. A longer piece of hose will result in an inaccurate reading.

3. Disconnect the inlet line to the carburetor at the fuel pump and vent the pump. Failure to vent the pump will result in low pressure reading. Reconnect the fuel line.

4. Connect a tachometer to the engine. Start the engine and allow to idle. The pressure gauge should show a constant 4½-6 psi reading. When the engine is turned off, the pressure should slowly drop to zero. An instant drop to zero indicates a leaky diaphragm or weak spring. If pressure is too high, the main spring is too strong or the air vent is plugged.

5. Proceed with vacuum test.

Vacuum Test

1. Remove the inlet and outlet fuel lines from the pump.

CAUTION: *Never smoke when working around gasoline! Avoid all sources of sparks or ignition. Gasoline vapors are EXTREMELY volatile!*

2. Plug the fuel line to the carburetor to prevent fuel leakage.

3. Connect a vacuum gauge to the fuel pump inlet fitting.

4. Using the starter motor, turn the engine over several times and observe the vacuum gauge. The fuel pump should develop a minimum of 11 inches of vacuum.

5. If the vacuum readings are below specification, replace the pump.

Carburetor

ADJUSTMENTS

Holley Carburetors

Idle Speed/Solenoid Kicker Check

2.2L air conditioned vehicles are equipped with a solenoid kicker.

1. Start engine and run until operating temperature is reached.

2. Turn air conditioning switch on and set temperature control lever to the coldest position.

3. Notice the kicker solenoid for in and out movement as the compressor cycles on and off. If no movement occurred, check the kicker system for vacuum leaks. Check the operation of the vacuum solenoid. If no problems are found, replace the kicker.

4. If the kicker solenoid functions properly, turn off the air conditioning switch and shut engine off.

Solenoid Kicker Adjustment

1. Check ignition timing and adjust if necessary.

2. Disconnect and plug vacuum connector at the CVSCC.

3. Unplug connector at cooling fan and jumper harness so fan will run continuously.

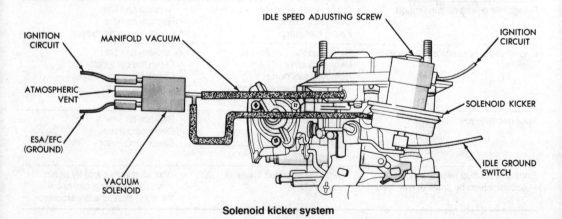

Solenoid kicker system

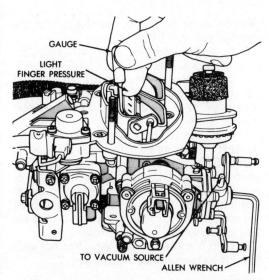

Choke vacuum kick adjustment on 2.2L carburetors

4. Remove the PCV valve and allow it to draw underhood air.

5. Connect a tachometer to the engine.

6. Ground the carburetor switch with a jumper wire.

7. Disconnect the oxygen system test lead located on the left fender shield on vehicles equipped with 6520 carburetors.

8. Start the engine and run until normal operating temperature is reached.

9. Adjust idle speed screw to specification given in underhood label.

10. Reconnect PCV valve, oxygen connector and CVSCC vacuum connector.

11. Remove the jumper from carburetor switch.

12. Remove the jumper from radiator fan and reconnect harness.

NOTE: *After Steps 10, 11 and 12 are completed, the idle speed may change slightly. This is normal and engine speed should not be readjusted.*

Fast Idle

Before adjusting fast idle, check and adjust ignition timing. Refer to Ignition Timing procedures in Chapter 2.

1. Disconnect the electrical harness at the radiator fan and install a jumper wire so the fan will run continuously.

2. Remove the PCV valve and allow it to draw underhood air.

3. Disconnect and plug the vacuum connector at the CVSCC.

4. Install a tachometer.

5. Jumper the carburetor switch.

6. Disconnect oxygen system test connector located on the left fender shield by shock tower.

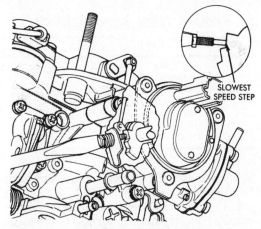

Fast idle adjustment on 2.2L carburetors

7. Start engine and allow to reach normal operating temperature.

8. Open throttle slightly and place adjustment screw on the lowest step of fast idle cam.

9. Adjust the fast idle screw to specification shown on underhood VECI label. Return engine to idle and repeat Step 8, readjust if necessary.

10. Stop engine, remove jumper wire from radiator fan harness and reconnect connector.

11. Reinstall PCV valve.

12. Reconnect oxygen system test connector, and vacuum connector at CVSCC.

Choke Vacuum Kick

1. Open the carburetor throttle and hold choke valve in closed position. While maintaining choke valve in closed position, release the throttle. Fast idle system should now be trapped at closed choke condition.

2. Disconnect carburetor vaccum source at carburetor.

3. Using light finger pressure, close choke valve to the smallest opening possible without disturbing linkage system.

4. Using the proper size drill or guage, insert between choke valve and air horn wall at prima-

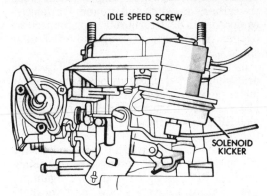

A/C kicker adjustment on 2.2L carburetors

Vacuum Kick Specifications

Carb Number	Setting
4288460	.07 in.
4288461	.07 in.
4288262	.07 in.
4288263	.07 in.
4288456	.08 in.
4288458	.08 in.
4288459	.08 in.

ry throttle end of carburetor. Refer to Choke Vacuum Kick Specification Chart.

5. Using an allen head screw in center of diaphragm housing, adjust by turning clockwise or counterclockwise to obtain correct setting.

6. Reconnect vacuum hose to carburetor vacuum source.

Mixture Adjustment (Propane Assisted)

NOTE: *The following procedures require the use of a propane cylinder, vacuum hose and a special control valve to provide proper enrichment. Any adjustments made other than those in the following procedures, may violate Federal and State Laws.*

1. Remove the concealment plug. Refer to Steps 18 through 20 under carburetor disassembling procedure.

2. Set the parking brake and place the transaxle in netural position. Turn off all accessories. Start engine and allow to idle on second highest step of fast idle cam until normal operating temperature is reached. Return engine to idle.

3. Disconnect vacuum connector at CVSCC and plug. Disconnect the vacuum hose to the heated air door sensor at the three way connector, and in its place, install the supply hose from the propane bottle.

4. Unplug the radiator fan connector and jumper harness so the fan will run continuously. Remove PCV valve and allow it to draw underhood air. Connect a jumper wire between the carburetor switch and ground. On vehicles equipped with 6520 carburetors, disconnect the oxygen test lead located on the left fender shield.

5. With the air cleaner installed. Open the propane main valve. Slowly open the propane metering valve until maximum engine RPM idle is reached. If too much propane is added engine RPM will decrease. Adjust metering valve for the highest engine RPM.

6. With the propane still flowing, adjust the idle speed screw on top of the solenoid to obtain specified RPM on underhood label. Again adjust the propane metering valve to get the highest engine RPM. If the maximum RPM

changes, readjust the idle speed screw to the specified propane RPM.

7. Shut off the propane main valve and allow the engine to stablize. With the air cleaner still in place, slowly adjust the mixture screws to obtain the specified set RPM. Pause for a few seconds after each adjustment to allow engine speed to stablized.

8. Again turn on the propane main valve and adjust the metering valve to obtain the highest engine RPM. If the maximum speed differs more than 25 RPM, repeat Steps 5 through 8.

9. Shut off both valves on propane cylinder. Disconnect the propane vacuum supply hose and connect the vacuum hose to the heated air door sensor at the three way connector.

10. Install concealment plug. Proceed with fast idle adjustment starting at Step 7.

Anti-Dieseling Adjustment

NOTE: *Always check and adjust ignition timing before any idle speed adjustment is performed.*

1. Warm engine to normal operating temperature. Place transaxle in neutral position and set parking brake.

2. Turn off all accessories. Jumper wire between carburetor switch and ground.

3. Remove the RED wire from the 6-Way connector (carburetor side).

4. Adjust the throttle stop speed screw to obtain 700 rpm.

5. Reconnect RED wire and remove jumper from carburetor switch.

Idle RPM
Mikuni Carburetor

1. Check and adjust ignition timing.

2. Set the parking brake and place transaxle in neutral. Turn off all accessories.

3. Disconnect the radiator fan.

4. Connect a tachometer to the engine.

5. Start engine and run until operating temperature is reached.

6. Disconnect cooling fan. Run engine at 2500 RPM for 10 seconds and return to idle.

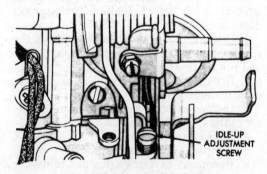

IDLE-UP ADJUSTMENT SCREW

Idle-up adjustment on the Mikuni carburetor

7. Wait 2 minutes and record RPM. If RPM differs from VECI underhood specification label, turn idle speed adjusting screw until specification is obtained.

8. On air condition models, set the temperature lever to the coldest position and turn air conditioning switch on. With the air condition running, set the engine speed to 900 RPM using the idle-up adjustment screw.

9. Shut engine off. Connect the cooling fan and remove tachometer.

Fast Idle
Mikuni Carburetor

1. Connect a tachometer to the engine. Check and adjust ignition timing.

2. Set the parking brake and place transaxle in neutral. Turn off all accessories.

3. Start engine and run until operating temperature is reached.

4. Disconnect radiator fan. Remove and plug vacuum advance hose at distributor.

5. Open the throttle slightly and install Tool 4812-2C on cam follower pin.

6. Release throttle lever and adjust fast idle adjusting screw to specification shown on VECI underhood label.

7. Remove tool and shut engine off. Reconnect fan, unplug and reconnect vacuum hose, and remove tachometer.

Idle Mixture (Propane Assist)
Mikuni Carburetor

NOTE: *The following procedures require the use of a propane cylinder, vacuum hose and a special control valve to provide proper enrichment. Any adjustments made other than those in the following procedures, may violate Federal and State Laws.*

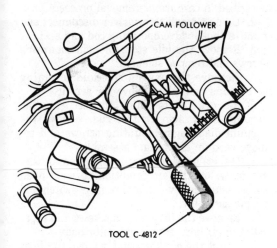

Installing tool C4812 on the Mikuni carburetor

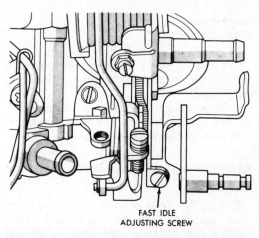

FAST IDLE
ADJUSTING SCREW

Fast idle adjustment on the Mikuni carburetor

1. Remove concealment plug. Refer to Concealment Plug Removal procedure. Check and adjust ignition timing.

2. Set the parking brake and place transaxle in neutral. Turn off all accessories.

3. Disconnect the cooling fan.

4. Connect a tachometer to the engine.

5. Start engine and run until operating temperature is reached.

6. Disconnect cooling fan. Run engine at 2500 RPM for 10 seconds and return to idle. Allow engine to idle for 2 minutes.

7. Remove the air cleaner fresh air duct. Place the propane bottle in a safe location and in an upright position. Insert the propane supply hose approximately 4 inches into the air cleaner snorkel.

8. Open the propane bottle main valve. Slowly open the metering valve until the highest engine RPM is reached. If too much propane is added, the engine RPM will decrease. Fine Tune the propane metering valve to obtain the highest engine RPM.

9. With the propane still flowing, adjust the idle speed screw to the specified RPM shown on VECI underhood label. Again Fine Tune the propane metering valve to get the highest engine RPM. If the RPM increases, readjust the idle speed screw to specification.

10. Shut off the propane main valve and allow the engine speed to stabilize. Slowly adjust the carburetor mixture screws to obtain the specified idle RPM. Pause between each adjustment to allow engine speed to stabilize.

11. Again turn on the propane main valve, Fine Tune the metering valve to get the highest engine RPM. If the RPM changes, repeat Step 8 through 10.

12. Shut off the propane main valve and metering valve. Remove the propane supply hose. Install the air cleaner fresh air duct. Install the concealment plug and impact plate.

Concealment Plug Removal
Mikuni Carburetor

1. Remove the impact plate, if used.
2. Remove the vacuum connector from high altitude compensator (HAC) fitting on carburetor, if used.
3. With an eight inch long ¼" diameter drill bit, drill out concealment plug at location show.
4. Remove concealment plug.

REMOVAL AND INSTALLATION

2.2L Engine

CAUTION: *Never remove a carburetor from an engine that has just been road tested. Allow the engine to cool down to prevent accidental fuel ignition or personal injury.*
1. Disconnect the negative battery cable.
2. Remove the air cleaner.
3. Remove the fuel tank filler cap to relieve fuel system pressure.
4. Disconnect all carburetor electrical wiring.
CAUTION: *Never smoke when working around gasoline! Avoid all sources of sparks or ignition. Gasoline vapors are EXTREMELY volatile!*
5. Disconnect the carburetor inlet line and block off line to prevent fuel leakage.
6. Disconnect the throttle linkage. Label and remove all vacuum hoses.
7. Remove the carburetor mounting nuts and remove carburetor.
8. Inspect the mating surfaces of the carburetor and isolator for nicks, burrs, dirt or other damage. It is not necessary to disturb the isolator to intake manifold mounting screws, unless the isolator is damage.
9. Carefully install carburetor on engine. Install nuts evenly and torque to 200 in. lbs. Make certain throttle plates and choke plate opens and closes properly when operated.
10. Connect the throttle linkage and fuel inlet line.
11. Connect the vacuum hoses.
12. Connect the negative battery cable.
13. Install the air cleaner and adjust the carburetor.

2.6L Engine

CAUTION: *Never remove a carburetor from an engine that has just been road tested. Allow the engine to cool down to prevent accidental fuel ignition or personal injury.*
1. Disconnect the negative battery cable.
2. Remove the air cleaner.
3. Remove the fuel tank filler cap.to relieve fuel system pressure.
4. Disconnect the carburetor protector and all carburetor electrical wiring.

5. Drain the cooling system. Label and remove the vacuum hoses and coolant hoses at carburetor.
CAUTION: *When draining the coolant, keep in mind that cats and dogs are attracted by the ethylene glycol antifreeze, and are quite likely to drink any that is left in an uncovered container or in puddles on the ground. This will prove fatal in sufficient quantity. Always drain the coolant into a sealable container. Coolant should be reused unless it is contaminated or several years old.*
6. Disconnect the carburetor inlet line and block off line to prevent fuel leakage.
CAUTION: *Never smoke when working around gasoline! Avoid all sources of sparks or ignition. Gasoline vapors are EXTREMELY volatile!*
7. Disconnect the throttle linkage.
8. Remove the carburetor mounting bolts and nuts and remove carburetor.
9. Inspect the mating surfaces of the carburetor and intake manifold for nicks, burrs, dirt or other damage.
10. Install a new gasket on intake manifold.
11. Carefully install the carburetor on the engine. Install mounting bolts and nuts. Tighten evenly and torque to 150 in. lbs. Make certain throttle plates and choke plate opens and closes properly when operated.
12. Connect the throttle linkage, fuel line and electrical connectors.
13. Install and tighten carburetor protector.
14. Fill the cooling system.
15. Connect the negative battery cable.
16. Install the air cleaner and adjust the carburetor.

OVERHAUL

Holley Model 5220/6520

1. Remove the carburetor from the engine as described in carburetor removal proceedure.
2. Using a small screwdriver disconnect and remove choke valve operating rod and seal.
3. Remove the idle stop solenoid mounting screws and remove solenoid.
4. Remove the oxygen solenoid retaining screws and carefully remove the sensor.
5. Remove the retaining clip securing the vacuum diaphragm control rod, remove the vacuum diaphragm mounting screws and remove vacuum diaphragm assembly.
6. Make a mark for proper alignment during assembly, on the air conditioning wide open throttle cut-out switch, and remove switch and wiring assembly.
7. Remove the (5) air horn screws and separate the air horn from carburetor body.
8. Invert the air horn and remove the float pin, float and inlet needle.

9. Remove the fuel inlet needle and seat.

10. Notice the size and position of the secondary main metering jets, and remove jets.

11. Notice the size and position of the primary main metering jets, and remove jets.

12. Using a small screwdriver remove the secondary high speed bleed and secondary main well tube. Note the size and position so it can be reinstalled in its proper location.

13. Remove the primary high speed bleed and primary main well tube. Note the size and position so it can be reinstalled in its proper location.

14. Remove the pump discharge nozzle retaining screw, nozzle and gasket. Invert the carburetor and remove the pump discharge weight ball and checkball. (Both are the same size).

15. Remove the accelerator pump cover retaining screws, cover, pump diaphragm and spring.

16. Remove the choke diaphragm retaining screws and remove cover and spring.

17. Rotate the choke shaft and lever assembly counterclockwise. Rotate choke diaphragm assembly clockwise and remove from housing. Remove end of lower screw from housing. If the choke diaphragm need replacement, the diaphragm cover must also be replaced.

18. To remove concealment plug, center punch at a point ¼" from the end of the mixture screw housing.

19. Drill through the outer housing with a ³⁄₁₆" drill bit.

20. Pry out the concealment plug and save for reinstallation.

21. Remove the idle mixture screws from carburetor body.

CLEANING AND INSPECTION

Efficient carburetion depends greatly on careful cleaning and inspection during overhaul, since dirt, gum, water, or varnish in or on the carburetor parts are often responsible for poor performance. There are many commercial carburetor cleaning solvent which can give satisfactory results.

NOTE: *Avoid placing any seals, O-rings, float, choke and vacuum diaphragm in cleaning solvent. Such components can be damage if immerse in cleaning solvent. Clean the external surfaces of these parts with a clean lint free cloth or brush.*

Soak carburetor parts in cleaning solvent, but do not leave parts in solvent no longer than necessary to loosen deposits. Remove parts and rinse with clean hot water. Blow out all passages and jets with compressed air. Blow dry all parts.

Inspect the following:

1. Check the float needle and seat for wear. If wear is found, needle/seat assembly.

2. Check the float pin for wear and the float for damage. Replace if necessary.

3. Check the throttle and choke shaft bores for wear or an out-of-round condition. Damage or wear to the throttle arm, shaft, or shaft bore will often require replacement of the throttle body. These parts require a close tolerance fit. Wear on these parts may allow air leakage, which could affect starting and idling.

4. Inspect the idle mixture adjusting needles for burrs or grooves, Any such condition requires replacement of the needle, since you will not be able to obtain a satisfactory idle.

5. Check the bowl cover for warped surfaces with a straightedge.

ASSEMBLY

1. Install the choke shaft, while rotating counterclockwise. Install the diaphragm with a clockwise motion. Position spring and cover over diaphragm, and install retaining screws. Be certain fast idle link has been properly installed.

2. Install the accelerator pump spring, diaphragm cover and screws.

CAUTION: *Never smoke when working around gasoline! Avoid all sources of sparks or ignition. Gasoline vapors are EXTREMELY volatile!*

3. Install the accelerator pump discharge check ball in discharge passage. Check the accelerator pump and seat operation before complete reassembling as follows:

a. Fill the fuel bowl with clean fuel.

b. Hold the discharge check ball down with a small brass rod and operate the pump plunger by hand. If the check ball and seat is leaking, no resistance will be felt when the plunger is operated. If the valve is leaking, use the old ball and carefully stake the ball using a suitable drift punch. Avoid damaging the bore containing the pump weight.

c. After staking the old ball, remove and replace with the new ball. Recheck for leaks.

4. Install a new gasket, discharge nozzle and nozzle retaining screw.

5. Install the primary main well tube and primary high speed bleed.

6. Install the secondary main well tube and secondary high speed bleed.

7. Install the primary main metering (smaller size number) jet.

8. Install the secondary main metering (larger size number) jet.

9. Install the needle and seat assembly with a new gasket.

10. Invert the air horn and install float, inlet

needle and float lever pin. Reset "dry float setting" and "float drop." Refer to carburetor adjustment procedures.

11. Install a new gasket on air horn, and install choke rod seal and choke rod.

12. Carefully position the air horn on carburetor body.

13. Install a new retainer on choke shaft lever and fast idle cam pickup lever and connect choke rod.

14. Install air horn retaining screws and torque to 30 in. lbs.

15. Install idle stop solenoid, and reinstall anti-rattle spring.

16. Install the air conditioning wide open throttle cut-out switch and aligned with mark previously made. The switch must be position so that the air conditioning clutch circuit is open 10 before wide open throttle position.

17. Install the oxygen solenoid gasket on air horn. Install new O-ring seal on oxygen solenoid. Coat the new O-ring seal with petroleum jelly and install solenoid in carburetor body. Tighten solenoid mounting screws and secure wiring and clamps.

18. Install the vacuum solenoid.

19. Install the vacuum control valve.

Float Setting

1. Invert the air horn. With gasket remove, insert a 12.2mm gauge or drill between air horn and float.

2. To obtain proper dry float level bend adjusting tang with a small screwdriver.

Float Drop

1. With the air horn upright, check float drop with a depth gauge.

2. To obtain proper float drop adjustment, hold float assembly securely with one hand. Using a small screwdriver, carefully bend adjusting tang to obtain a float drop of 47.6mm.

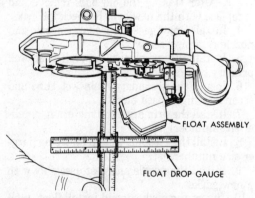

Measuring float drop on 2.2L carburetors

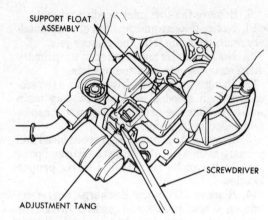

Float drop adjustment on 2.2L carburetors

Mikuni Carburetor

2.6L engines are equipped with a downdraft type two barrel carburetor, which can be identified with its black resin compound main body. The automatic choke is a thermowax type which is controlled by engine coolant temperature.

This carburetor also features a diaphragm type accelerator pump, bowl vent, fuel cut-off solenoid, air switching valve (ASV), sub-EGR valve, coasting air valve (CAV), jet air control valve (JACV) and a high altitude compensation (HAC) system. (California Only).

OVERHAUL

1. Grind head from screws of choke cover. Gently tap the remaining screw portions using a hammer and a pointed punch in a counterclockwise direction until screws are removed.

2. Take notice of the painted punch mark and scribed lines on choke pinion plate. During reassembly, these marks must be alinged.

3. Remove the E-clip from the throttle opener link. Remove the throttle opener mounting screws and set aside.

4. Remove the ground wire from the fuel cut-off solenoid, remove solenoid mounting screws, and remove solenoid.

5. Remove the throttle return spring and damper spring.

6. Remove the choke unloader E-clip from its link and remove choke unloader.

7. Remove vacuum hose and link from vacuum chamber. Remove vacuum chamber mounting screws and remove vacuum chamber.

8. Remove accelerator rod link from throttle lever.

9. Remove the air horn mounting screws (6) and carefully separate air horn from carburetor body.

10. Slide out float pivot pin and remove float assembly. Remove air horn gasket.

11. Unscrew needle/seat retainer, remove needle/seat, O-ring and screen.

12. Remove the primary and secondary venturi and O-rings. Mark both venturi for proper location during reassembly.

13. Remove primary and secondary main jets. Mark both jets for proper location during reassembly.

14. Remove primary and secondary pedastals and gaskets.

15. Remove bowl vent solenoid mounting screws, solenoid, bowl vent assembly, seal and gasket.

16. Remove the coasting air valve (CAV) mounting screws and remove valve assembly from air horn. (California and Altitude Models).

17. Remove enrichment valve mounting screws and remove enrichment valve assembly.

18. Remove air switching valve (ASV) mounting screws and remove air switching valve assembly from air horn.

19. Remove the primary and secondary pilot jet set screw and lock. Remove pilot jet set assembly.

20. Remove primary and secondary air bleed jets from top of air horn. Mark both jets for proper location during reassembly.

21. Invert the air horn, carefully drop out and note pump weight, check ball and hex nut.

22. Remove accelerator pump mounting screws and remove pump cover, diaphragm, spring, pump body and gasket.

23. Remove jet air control valve mounting screws and remove J.A.C.V. cover, spring, retainer and diaphragm seal.

24. Remove E-clip from sub-EGR lever. The sub-EGR valve is under pressure by a steel ball and spring. Care should be used when removing lever to prevent accidental lost of spring or ball. Carefully slide the pin from lever and sub-EGR valve. Remove the steel ball, spring, sub-EGR valve and boot seal.

CLEANING AND INSPECTION

Efficient carburetion depends greatly on careful cleaning and inspection during overhaul, since dirt, gum, water, or varnish in or on the carburetor parts are often responsible for poor performance. There are many commercial carburetor cleaning solvents which can give satisfactory results.

NOTE: *Avoid placing any seals, O-rings, float, choke and vacuum diaphragm in cleaning solvent. Such components can be damage if immerse in cleaning solvent. Clean the external surfaces of these parts with a clean lint free cloth or brush.*

Soak carburetor parts in cleaning solvent, but do not leave parts in solvent longer than necessary to loosen deposits. Remove parts and rinse with clean hot water. Blow out all passages and jets with compressed air. Blow dry all parts.

Inspect the following:

1. Check the float needle and seat for wear. If wear is found, needle/seat assembly.

2. Check the float pin for wear and the float for damage. Replace if necessary.

3. Check the throttle and choke shaft bores for wear or an out-of-round condition. Damage or wear to the throttle arm, shaft, or shaft bore will often require replacement of the throttle body. These parts require a close tolerance fit. Wear on these parts may allow air leakage, which could affect starting and idling.

4. Inspect the idle mixture adjusting needles for burrs or grooves, Any such condition requires replacement of the needle, since you will not be able to obtain a satisfactory idle.

5. Check the bowl cover for warped surfaces with a straightedge.

ASSEMBLY

1. Install the sub-EGR valve to throttle valve and check for proper operation.

2. Assemble the jet air control valve to throttle body and secure with mounting screws.

3. Assemble the accelerator pump to throttle body and secure with mounting screws.

4. Install the primary and secondary air bleed jets. The secondary air bleed jet has the largest number.

5. Position new O-ring seals on primary and secondary pilot jet side. Slide assembly into place and install lock and screw.

6. Assemble the air switching valve to air horn and secure with mounting screws.

7. Assemble the enrichment valve to air horn.

8. Assemble the coasting air valve to air horn.

9. Position a new O-ring and gasket on bowl vent assembly and install on air horn.

10. Position a new gasket on air horn and install primary and secondary pedastals.

11. Install primary and secondary main jets in their pedastals. The secondary main jet has the largest number.

12. Position new O-rings on both primary and secondary venturi. Install primary and secondary venturi and retainers.

13. Position a new O-ring on needle seat. Install a new screen on needle seat. Install shim and needle seat into air horn. Install retainer and screw.

14. Position the float on air horn and install float pivot pin. Refer to Float Level Adjustment procedure.

15. Position a new gasket on throttle body.

Install main body to throttle and install nut, check ball and weight in main body.

16. Position a new gasket on main body and carefully assemble air horn to main body.

17. Install vacuum hoses to air horn.

18. Connect accelerator rod link to throttle lever.

19. Install vacuum chamber to air horn. Connect vaccum hose and secondary throttle lever link.

20. Connect choke unloader link and install E-clip.

21. Position a new O-ring on fuel cut-off solenoid. Install the solenoid to main body and connect ground wire.

22. Install throttle opener to air horn. Connect throttle opener link and install E-clip.

23. Replace tamper-proof choke cover screws. Align the punch mark with the painted mark on gear.

24. Install the choke cover and peen over screws. Tighten the remaining screw using a pointed punch and a small hammer.

25. Install the choke water hose and clamp.

Float Level

1. Remove air horn from carburetor main body.

2. Remove air horn gasket and invert air horn.

3. Using a gauge measure the distance from bottom of float to air horn surface. The distance should be 20mm ± 1mm. If distance is not within specification, the shim under the needle and seat must be changed. Shim pack MD606952 or equivalent has three shims: 0.3mm, 0.4mm, or 0.5mm. Adding or removing one shim will change the float level three its thickness.

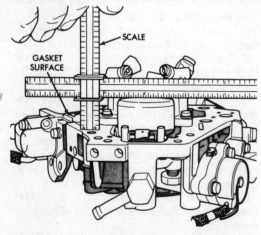

Measuring float level on the Mikuni carburetor

GASOLINE FUEL INJECTION SYSTEM

NOTE: *This book contains testing and service procedures for your fuel injection system. More comprehensive testing and diagnosis procedures may be found in Chilton's Guide To Fuel Injection And Feedback Carburetor Book, Part Number 7488, available at your local retailer.*

Electric Fuel Pump

The fuel pump used on vehicles with Single Point Fuel Injection (2.5L) and Multi-Point Fuel Injection System (3.0L), is an immersible pump with a permanent electric motor. Voltage to the pump is supplied through the Auto Shutdown Relay. The fuel pump also contains a check valve, located near the pump outlet. The purpose of the check valve is to restrict fuel movement in either direction, thereby maintaining fuel system pressure when the pump is not operational.

FUEL SYSTEM PRESSURE RELEASE PROCEDURE

1. Remove gas tank cap to release tank pressure.

CAUTION: *Never smoke when working around gasoline! Avoid all sources of sparks or ignition. Gasoline vapors are EXTREMELY volatile!*

2. Disconnect injector wiring harness.

3. Jumper one injector terminal to a known good engine ground.

4. Jumper the other injector terminal and touch battery positive for no more than 10 seconds.

5. Remove jumper wires.

FUEL PUMP TESTING

2.5L TBI and 3.0L MPFI

1. Release the fuel system pressure. Refer to fuel system pressure release procedure in this section.

CAUTION: *Never smoke when working around gasoline! Avoid all sources of sparks or ignition. Gasoline vapors are EXTREMELY volatile!*

2. Disconnect and carefully remove the $\frac{5}{16}''$ fuel supply hose from the engine fuel line assembly. Install fuel system testers C-3292 and C-4749 or equivalent, between fuel hose and fuel line assembly.

3. Remove harness connector from the Auto Shutdown Relay. Apply 12 volts to terminal number 3 (harness side) of Auto Shutdown Re-

CHILTON'S
FUEL ECONOMY & TUNE-UP TIPS

Tune-up • Spark Plug Diagnosis • Emission Controls

Fuel System • Cooling System • Tires and Wheels

General Maintenance

CHILTON'S FUEL ECONOMY & TUNE-UP TIPS

Fuel economy is important to everyone, no matter what kind of vehicle you drive. The maintenance-minded motorist can save both money and fuel using these tips and the periodic maintenance and tune-up procedures in this Repair and Tune-Up Guide.

There are more than 130,000,000 cars and trucks registered for private use in the United States. Each travels an average of 10-12,000 miles per year, and, and in total they consume close to 70 billion gallons of fuel each year. This represents nearly ⅔ of the oil imported by the United States each year. The Federal government's goal is to reduce consumption 10% by 1985. A variety of methods are either already in use or under serious consideration, and they all affect you driving and the cars you will drive. In addition to "down-sizing", the auto industry is using or investigating the use of electronic fuel delivery, electronic engine controls and alternative engines for use in smaller and lighter vehicles, among other alternatives to meet the federally mandated Corporate Average Fuel Economy (CAFE) of 27.5 mpg by 1985. The government, for its part, is considering rationing, mandatory driving curtailments and tax increases on motor vehicle fuel in an effort to reduce consumption. The government's goal of a 10% reduction could be realized — and further government regulation avoided — if every private vehicle could use just 1 less gallon of fuel per week.

How Much Can You Save?

Tests have proven that almost anyone can make at least a 10% reduction in fuel consumption through regular maintenance and tune-ups. When a major manufacturer of spark plugs sur-

TUNE-UP

1. Check the cylinder compression to be sure the engine will really benefit from a tune-up and that it is capable of producing good fuel economy. A tune-up will be wasted on an engine in poor mechanical condition.

2. Replace spark plugs regularly. New spark plugs alone can increase fuel economy 3%.

3. Be sure the spark plugs are the correct type (heat range) for your vehicle. See the Tune-Up Specifications.

Heat range refers to the spark plug's ability to conduct heat away from the firing end. It must conduct the heat away in an even pattern to avoid becoming a source of pre-ignition, yet it must also operate hot enough to burn off conductive deposits that could cause misfiring.

The heat range is usually indicated by a number on the spark plug, part of the manufacturer's designation for each individual spark plug. The numbers in bold-face indicate the heat range in each manufacturer's identification system.

Periodically, check the spark plugs to be sure they are firing efficiently. They are excellent indicators of the internal condition of your engine.

Manufacturer	Typical Designation
AC	R **45** TS
Bosch (old)	WA **145** T30
Bosch (new)	HR **8** Y
Champion	RBL **15** Y
Fram/Autolite	4**15**
Mopar	P-**62** PR
Motorcraft	BRF-**42**
NGK	BP **5** ES-15
Nippondenso	W **16** EP
Prestolite	14GR **5** 2A

On AC, Bosch (new), Champion, Fram/Autolite, Mopar, Motorcraft and Prestolite, a higher number indicates a hotter plug. On Bosch (old), NGK and Nippondenso, a higher number indicates a colder plug.

4. Make sure the spark plugs are properly gapped. See the Tune-Up Specifications in this book.

5. Be sure the spark plugs are firing efficiently. The illustrations on the next 2 pages show you how to "read" the firing end of the spark plug.

6. Check the ignition timing and set it to specifications. Tests show that almost all cars have incorrect ignition timing by more than 2°.

veyed over 6,000 cars nationwide, they found that a tune-up, on cars that needed one, increased fuel economy over 11%. Replacing worn plugs alone, accounted for a 3% increase. The same test also revealed that 8 out of every 10 vehicles will have some maintenance deficiency that will directly affect fuel economy, emissions or performance. Most of this mileage-robbing neglect could be prevented with regular maintenance.

Modern engines require that all of the functioning systems operate properly for maximum efficiency. A malfunction anywhere wastes fuel. You can keep your vehicle running as efficiently and economically as possible, by being aware of your vehicle's operating and performance characteristics. If your vehicle suddenly develops performance or fuel economy problems it could be due to one or more of the following:

PROBLEM	POSSIBLE CAUSE
Engine Idles Rough	Ignition timing, idle mixture, vacuum leak or something amiss in the emission control system.
Hesitates on Acceleration	Dirty carburetor or fuel filter, improper accelerator pump setting, ignition timing or fouled spark plugs.
Starts Hard or Fails to Start	Worn spark plugs, improperly set automatic choke, ice (or water) in fuel system.
Stalls Frequently	Automatic choke improperly adjusted and possible dirty air filter or fuel filter.
Performs Sluggishly	Worn spark plugs, dirty fuel or air filter, ignition timing or automatic choke out of adjustment.

Check spark plug wires on conventional point type ignition for cracks by bending them in a loop around your finger.

Be sure that spark plug wires leading to adjacent cylinders do not run too close together. (Photo courtesy Champion Spark Plug Co.)

7. If your vehicle does not have electronic ignition, check the points, rotor and cap as specified.

8. Check the spark plug wires (used with conventional point-type ignitions) for cracks and burned or broken insulation by bending them in a loop around your finger. Cracked wires decrease fuel efficiency by failing to deliver full voltage to the spark plugs. One misfiring spark plug can cost you as much as 2 mpg.

9. Check the routing of the plug wires. Misfiring can be the result of spark plug leads to adjacent cylinders running parallel to each other and too close together. One wire tends to pick up voltage from the other causing it to fire "out of time".

10. Check all electrical and ignition circuits for voltage drop and resistance.

11. Check the distributor mechanical and/or vacuum advance mechanisms for proper functioning. The vacuum advance can be checked by twisting the distributor plate in the opposite direction of rotation. It should spring back when released.

12. Check and adjust the valve clearance on engines with mechanical lifters. The clearance should be slightly loose rather than too tight.

SPARK PLUG DIAGNOSIS

Normal

APPEARANCE: This plug is typical of one operating normally. The insulator nose varies from a light tan to grayish color with slight electrode wear. The presence of slight deposits is normal on used plugs and will have no adverse effect on engine performance. The spark plug heat range is correct for the engine and the engine is running normally.

CAUSE: Properly running engine.

RECOMMENDATION: Before reinstalling this plug, the electrodes should be cleaned and filed square. Set the gap to specifications. If the plug has been in service for more than 10-12,000 miles, the entire set should probably be replaced with a fresh set of the same heat range.

Oil Deposits

APPEARANCE: The firing end of the plug is covered with a wet, oily coating.

CAUSE: The problem is poor oil control. On high mileage engines, oil is leaking past the rings or valve guides into the combustion chamber. A common cause is also a plugged PCV valve, and a ruptured fuel pump diaphragm can also cause this condition. Oil fouled plugs such as these are often found in new or recently overhauled engines, before normal oil control is achieved, and can be cleaned and reinstalled.

RECOMMENDATION: A hotter spark plug may temporarily relieve the problem, but the engine is probably in need of work.

Incorrect Heat Range

APPEARANCE: The effects of high temperature on a spark plug are indicated by clean white, often blistered insulator. This can also be accompanied by excessive wear of the electrode, and the absence of deposits.

CAUSE: Check for the correct spark plug heat range. A plug which is too hot for the engine can result in overheating. A car operated mostly at high speeds can require a colder plug. Also check ignition timing, cooling system level, fuel mixture and leaking intake manifold.

RECOMMENDATION: If all ignition and engine adjustments are known to be correct, and no other malfunction exists, install spark plugs one heat range colder.

Photos Courtesy Fram Corporation

Carbon Deposits

APPEARANCE: Carbon fouling is easily identified by the presence of dry, soft, black, sooty deposits.

CAUSE: Changing the heat range can often lead to carbon fouling, as can prolonged slow, stop-and-start driving. If the heat range is correct, carbon fouling can be attributed to a rich fuel mixture, sticking choke, clogged air cleaner, worn breaker points, retarded timing or low compression. If only one or two plugs are carbon fouled, check for corroded or cracked wires on the affected plugs. Also look for cracks in the distributor cap between the towers of affected cylinders.

RECOMMENDATION: After the problem is corrected, these plugs can be cleaned and reinstalled if not worn severely.

MMT Fouled

APPEARANCE: Spark plugs fouled by MMT (Methycyclopentadienyl Maganese Tricarbonyl) have reddish, rusty appearance on the insulator and side electrode.

CAUSE: MMT is an anti-knock additive in gasoline used to replace lead. During the combustion process, the MMT leaves a reddish deposit on the insulator and side electrode.

RECOMMENDATION: No engine malfunction is indicated and the deposits will not affect plug performance any more than lead deposits (see Ash Deposits). MMT fouled plugs can be cleaned, regapped and reinstalled.

High Speed Glazing

APPEARANCE: Glazing appears as shiny coating on the plug, either yellow or tan in color.

CAUSE: During hard, fast acceleration, plug temperatures rise suddenly. Deposits from normal combustion have no chance to fluff-off; instead, they melt on the insulator forming an electrically conductive coating which causes misfiring.

RECOMMENDATION: Glazed plugs are not easily cleaned. They should be replaced with a fresh set of plugs of the correct heat range. If the condition recurs, using plugs with a heat range one step colder may cure the problem.

Ash (Lead) Deposits

APPEARANCE: Ash deposits are characterized by light brown or white colored deposits crusted on the side or center electrodes. In some cases it may give the plug a rusty appearance.

CAUSE: Ash deposits are normally derived from oil or fuel additives burned during normal combustion. Normally they are harmless, though excessive amounts can cause misfiring. If deposits are excessive in short mileage, the valve guides may be worn.

RECOMMENDATION: Ash-fouled plugs can be cleaned, gapped and reinstalled.

Detonation

APPEARANCE: Detonation is usually characterized by a broken plug insulator.

CAUSE: A portion of the fuel charge will begin to burn spontaneously, from the increased heat following ignition. The explosion that results applies extreme pressure to engine components, frequently damaging spark plugs and pistons.

Detonation can result by over-advanced ignition timing, inferior gasoline (low octane) lean air/fuel mixture, poor carburetion, engine lugging or an increase in compression ratio due to combustion chamber deposits or engine modification.

RECOMMENDATION: Replace the plugs after correcting the problem.

Photos Courtesy Champion Spark Plug Co.

EMISSION CONTROLS

13. Be aware of the general condition of the emission control system. It contributes to reduced pollution and should be serviced regularly to maintain efficient engine operation.

14. Check all vacuum lines for dried, cracked or brittle conditions. Something as simple as a leaking vacuum hose can cause poor performance and loss of economy.

15. Avoid tampering with the emission control system. Attempting to improve fuel econ-

FUEL SYSTEM

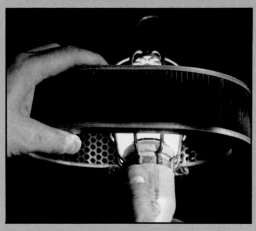

Check the air filter with a light behind it. If you can see light through the filter it can be reused.

Extremely clogged filters should be discarded and replaced with a new one.

18. Replace the air filter regularly. A dirty air filter richens the air/fuel mixture and can increase fuel consumption as much as 10%. Tests show that ⅓ of all vehicles have air filters in need of replacement.

19. Replace the fuel filter at least as often as recommended.

20. Set the idle speed and carburetor mixture to specifications.

21. Check the automatic choke. A sticking or malfunctioning choke wastes gas.

22. During the summer months, adjust the automatic choke for a leaner mixture which will produce faster engine warm-ups.

COOLING SYSTEM

29. Be sure all accessory drive belts are in good condition. Check for cracks or wear.

30. Adjust all accessory drive belts to proper tension.

31. Check all hoses for swollen areas, worn spots, or loose clamps.

32. Check coolant level in the radiator or expansion tank.

33. Be sure the thermostat is operating properly. A stuck thermostat delays engine warm-up and a cold engine uses nearly twice as much fuel as a warm engine.

34. Drain and replace the engine coolant at least as often as recommended. Rust and scale

TIRES & WHEELS

38. Check the tire pressure often with a pencil type gauge. Tests by a major tire manufacturer show that 90% of all vehicles have at least 1 tire improperly inflated. Better mileage can be achieved by over-inflating tires, but never exceed the maximum inflation pressure on the side of the tire.

39. If possible, install radial tires. Radial tires deliver as much as ½ mpg more than bias belted tires.

40. Avoid installing super-wide tires. They only create extra rolling resistance and decrease fuel mileage. Stick to the manufacturer's recommendations.

41. Have the wheels properly balanced.

omy by tampering with emission controls is more likely to worsen fuel economy than improve it. Emission control changes on modern engines are not readily reversible.

16. Clean (or replace) the EGR valve and lines as recommended.

17. Be sure that all vacuum lines and hoses are reconnected properly after working under the hood. An unconnected or misrouted vacuum line can wreak havoc with engine performance.

---

23. Check for fuel leaks at the carburetor, fuel pump, fuel lines and fuel tank. Be sure all lines and connections are tight.

24. Periodically check the tightness of the carburetor and intake manifold attaching nuts and bolts. These are a common place for vacuum leaks to occur.

25. Clean the carburetor periodically and lubricate the linkage.

26. The condition of the tailpipe can be an excellent indicator of proper engine combustion. After a long drive at highway speeds, the inside of the tailpipe should be a light grey in color. Black or soot on the insides indicates an overly rich mixture.

27. Check the fuel pump pressure. The fuel pump may be supplying more fuel than the engine needs.

28. Use the proper grade of gasoline for your engine. Don't try to compensate for knocking or "pinging" by advancing the ignition timing. This practice will only increase plug temperature and the chances of detonation or pre-ignition with relatively little performance gain.

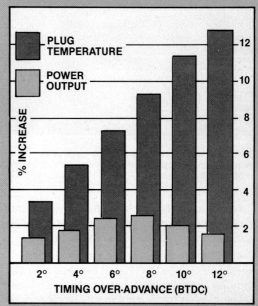

Increasing ignition timing past the specified setting results in a drastic increase in spark plug temperature with increased chance of detonation or preignition. Performance increase is considerably less. (Photo courtesy Champion Spark Plug Co.)

---

that form in the engine should be flushed out to allow the engine to operate at peak efficiency.

35. Clean the radiator of debris that can decrease cooling efficiency.

36. Install a flex-type or electric cooling fan, if you don't have a clutch type fan. Flex fans use curved plastic blades to push more air at low speeds when more cooling is needed; at high speeds the blades flatten out for less resistance. Electric fans only run when the engine temperature reaches a predetermined level.

37. Check the radiator cap for a worn or cracked gasket. If the cap does not seal properly, the cooling system will not function properly.

---

42. Be sure the front end is correctly aligned. A misaligned front end actually has wheels going in differed directions. The increased drag can reduce fuel economy by .3 mpg.

43. Correctly adjust the wheel bearings. Wheel bearings that are adjusted too tight increase rolling resistance.

Check tire pressures regularly with a reliable pocket type gauge. Be sure to check the pressure on a cold tire.

GENERAL MAINTENANCE

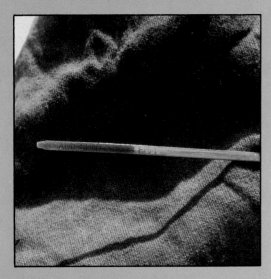

Check the fluid levels (particularly engine oil) on a regular basis. Be sure to check the oil for grit, water or other contamination.

A vacuum gauge is another excellent indicator of internal engine condition and can also be installed in the dash as a mileage indicator.

44. Periodically check the fluid levels in the engine, power steering pump, master cylinder, automatic transmission and drive axle.

45. Change the oil at the recommended interval and change the filter at every oil change. Dirty oil is thick and causes extra friction between moving parts, cutting efficiency and increasing wear. A worn engine requires more frequent tune-ups and gets progressively worse fuel economy. In general, use the lightest viscosity oil for the driving conditions you will encounter.

46. Use the recommended viscosity fluids in the transmission and axle.

47. Be sure the battery is fully charged for fast starts. A slow starting engine wastes fuel.

48. Be sure battery terminals are clean and tight.

49. Check the battery electrolyte level and add distilled water if necessary.

50. Check the exhaust system for crushed pipes, blockages and leaks.

51. Adjust the brakes. Dragging brakes or brakes that are not releasing create increased drag on the engine.

52. Install a vacuum gauge or miles-per-gallon gauge. These gauges visually indicate engine vacuum in the intake manifold. High vacuum = good mileage and low vacuum = poorer mileage. The gauge can also be an excellent indicator of internal engine conditions.

53. Be sure the clutch is properly adjusted. A slipping clutch wastes fuel.

54. Check and periodically lubricate the heat control valve in the exhaust manifold. A sticking or inoperative valve prevents engine warm-up and wastes gas.

55. Keep accurate records to check fuel economy over a period of time. A sudden drop in fuel economy may signal a need for tune-up or other maintenance.

3. Remove accelerator cable and transaxle kickdown linkage.

4. Remove harness connector from throttle position sensor (TPS), and automatic idle speed (AIS) motor.

5. Label and remove vacuum hoses necessary.

6. Remove throttle body mounting nuts and remove throttle body and gasket.

7. Install throttle body using a new gasket on air intake plenum. Secure with mounting nuts.

8. Reconnect vacuum hoses, TPS and ASI electrical connectors.

9. Reconnect accelerator cable and transaxle linkage.

10. Install air cleaner to throttle body hose and tighten clamps.

11. Reconnect battery negative cable.

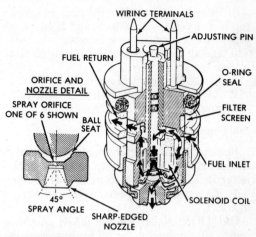

SPFI fuel injector

Fuel Injectors

The fuel injector used on 2.5L (TBI System) engine, is an electric solenoid controlled by the Single Module Engine Controller (SMEC). Based on various sensor inputs, the SMEC determines when and how long the fuel injector should operate. Fuel is supplied to the injector at a regulated pressure of 14.5 psi. Unused fuel is directed to the fuel tank through the fuel return line.

3.0L (MPFI) system uses six fuel injectors retained in a fuel rail by lock rings. Each injector is an electrical solenoid controlled by the Single Module Engine Controller (SMEC). Based on various sensor inputs, the SMEC determines when and how long the fuel injectors should operate. Fuel is supplied to the injectors at a regulated pressure of 48 psi. Unused fuel is redirected to the fuel tank through the fuel return line.

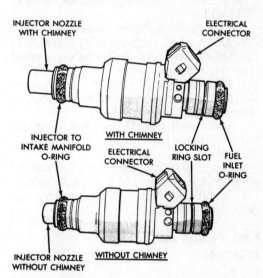

MPFI fuel injectors

REMOVAL

2.5L Engine

1. Remove the air cleaner assembly.

2. Perform fuel system pressure release procedure. Refer to fuel system pressure release procedure in this section.

CAUTION: *Never smoke when working around gasoline! Avoid all sources of sparks or ignition. Gasoline vapors are EXTREMELY volatile!*

3. Disconnect the negative battery cable.

4. Remove the torx screw securing the injector cap. Using two screwdrivers in cap slots, remove the injector cap.

5. Position a small screwdriver in hole of injector front area and pry fuel injector from the pod.

6. If necessary, remove the lower injector O-ring from the pod.

7. Place a new lower O-ring on injector as-

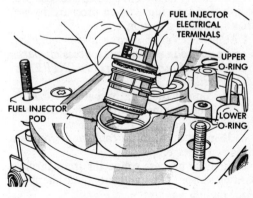

SPFI injector servicing

sembly and a new O-ring on cap. The upper injector O-ring would already be installed.

8. Install the fuel injector cap on fuel injector. Position the locating notch in fuel injector cap and locating lobe of fuel injector.

9. Place the injector into the pod and aligned cap and injector with attachment holes. Push down on cap to ensure a good seal.

10. Install the torx screw and torque to 34-45 in. lbs.

11. Install the pressure regulator.

12. Reconnect the battery negative cable.

13. Reinstall the air cleaner assembly.

3.0L Engine

Removal of the injectors requires removal of the fuel injector rail assembly. Refer to Fuel Injector Rail Removal procedure in this section.

1. Disconnect injector harness from injectors.

CAUTION: *Never smoke when working around gasoline! Avoid all sources of sparks or ignition. Gasoline vapors are EXTREMELY volatile!*

2. Invert fuel injector rail assembly.

3. Remove lock rings securing injectors to fuel rail receiver cups. Pull injectors upward from receiver cups.

4. If injectors are to be reused, place a protective cap on injector nozzle to prevent dirt or other damage.

5. Lubricate the new O-ring of each injectors with a clean drop of engine oil prior to installation.

6. Assemble each injectors into fuel rail receiver cups. Be careful not to damage O-rings.

7. Install lock ring between receiver cup ridge and injector slot.

Fuel Injector Rail

REMOVAL

3.0L Engine

1. Perform fuel system pressure release procedure. Refer to fuel system pressure release procedure in this section.

CAUTION: *Never smoke when working around gasoline! Avoid all sources of sparks or ignition. Gasoline vapors are EXTREMELY volatile!*

2. Disconnect the negative battery cable.

3. Loosen clamps securing air cleaner to throttle body hose and remove hose.

4. Remove the throttle cable and transaxle kickdown linkage.

5. Remove harness connector from throttle position sensor (TPS), and automatic idle speed (AIS) motor.

6. Label and remove vacuum hoses from throttle body. Remove PCV and brake booster hoses from air intake plenum.

7. Remove EGR tube to intake plenum.

8. Remove electrical connection from charge temperature and coolant temperature sensor.

9. Remove vacuum connection from pres-

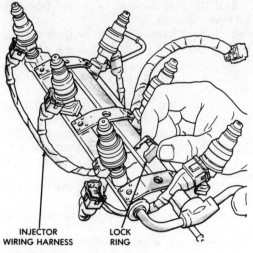

INJECTOR
WIRING HARNESS

LOCK
RING

MPFI fuel injectors and fuel rail

sure regulator and air intake connection from manifold.

10. Remove fuel hoses to fuel rail connection.

11. Remove air intake plenum to manifold bolts (8) and remove air intake plenum and gaskets.

WARNING: *Whenever air intake plenum is remove, cover intake manifold properly to avoid objects from entering cylinder head.*

12. Disconnect fuel injector wiring harness from engine wiring harness.

13. Remove pressure regulator attaching bolts and remove pressure regulator from rail.

14. Remove fuel rail attaching bolts and remove fuel rail.

INSTALLATION

1. Make certain injector are properly seated in receiver cup with lock rings in place and injector discharge holes are clean.

2. Lubricate injector O-rings with a clean drop of engine oil.

3. Install injector rail assembly making sure each injector seats in their respective ports. Torque fuel rail attaching bolts to 115 in. lbs.

4. Lubricate pressure regulator O-ring with a drop of clean engine oil and install regulator to fuel rail. Torque nuts to 77 in. lbs.

5. Install hold down bolts on fuel supply and return tube, and vacuum crossover tube.

6. Install and torque pressure regulator hose clamps to 10 in. lbs.

7. Reconnect injector wiring harness.

8. Reconnect vacuum hoses to fuel pressure regulator and fuel rail.

9. Set the air intake plenum gasket in place with beaded sealer in the **up** position.

10. Install air intake plenum and tighten (8) attaching screws to 115 in. lbs.

11. Reconnect fuel line to fuel rail and tighten clamps to 10 in. lbs.

12. Reconnect EGR tube to intake plenum and torque nuts to 200 in. lbs.

13. Reconnect electrical wiring to charge temperature sensor, coolant temperature sensor, TPS and AIS motor.

14. Reconnect vacuum connection to throttle body and air intake plenum.

15. Install accelerator cable and transaxle kickdown cable.

16. Install air cleaner to throttle body hose and tighten clamps.

17. Reconnect battery negative cable.

Fuel Pressure Regulator

REMOVAL AND INSTALLATION

2.5L Engine

1. Remove air cleaner assembly.

2. Release fuel system pressure. Refer to fuel system pressure release procedure in this section.

CAUTION: *Never smoke when working around gasoline! Avoid all sources of sparks or ignition. Gasoline vapors are EXTREMELY volatile!*

3. Disconnect battery negative cable.

4. Remove (3) retaining screws and remove pressure regulator assembly. Always cover inlet chamber when pressure regulator is removed, to prevent fuel contamination.

5. Place a new gasket on pressure regulator, and carefully install a new seal.

6. Position pressure regulator on throttle body and push into place. Install retaining screws and torque to 40 in. lbs.

7. Reconnect battery negative cable. Start engine and check for leaks.

8. Install air cleaner assembly.

3.0L Engine

Refer to Fuel Injector Rail Removal and Installation procedure in this section.

Fuel Tank

REMOVAL

1. Release the fuel system pressure. Refer to fuel system pressure release procedure in this section.

CAUTION: *Never smoke when working around gasoline! Avoid all sources of sparks or ignition. Gasoline vapors are EXTREMELY volatile!*

2. Disconnect battery negative cable.

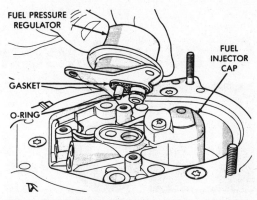

SPFI fuel pressure regulator

3. Raise the vehicle and support properly.

4. Remove drain tube rubber cap on left rail and connect a siphon hose to drain tube. Drain fuel into a safe gasoline container.

5. Remove screws supporting filler tube to inner and outer quarter panel.

6. Disconnect wiring and lines from the tank.

7. Position a transmission jack to support the fuel tank and remove the bolts from fuel tank straps.

8. Lower tank slightly, and carefully work filler tube from tank.

9. Lower tank, disconnect vapor separator rollover valve hose and remove the fuel tank and insulator pad from vehicle.

INSTALLATION

1. Support the fuel tank with a transmission jack. Connect the vapor separator rollover valve hose and position insulator pad on fuel tank.

NOTE: *Be certain vapor vent hose is clipped to the tank and not pinch between tank and floor pan during installation.*

2. Raise tank into position and carefully work filler tube into tank.

3. Install straps and tighten bolts to 54.2 N.m (40 ft.lbs.). Remove transmission jack.

4. Connect lines, drain tube cap and wiring connector, use new hose clamps.

5. Install and tighten filler tube to inner and outer quarter panel. On some models be sure to install the gasket between the filler tube and the inner quarter panel, before installing the mounting screws.

6. Replace cap on drain tube using a new hose clamp.

7. Fill the fuel tank, install the cap, connect battery cable and check operation.

Chassis Electrical

UNDERSTANDING AND TROUBLESHOOTING ELECTRICAL SYSTEMS

With the rate at which both import and domestic manufacturers are incorporating electronic control systems into their production lines, it won't be long before every new vehicle is equipped with one or more on-board computer, like the EEC-IV unit installed on the truck. These electronic components (with no moving parts) should theoretically last the life of the vehicle, provided nothing external happens to damage the circuits or memory chips.

While it is true that electronic components should never wear out, in the real world malfunctions do occur. It is also true that any computer-based system is extremely sensitive to electrical voltages and cannot tolerate careless or haphazard testing or service procedures. An inexperienced individual can literally do major damage looking for a minor problem by using the wrong kind of test equipment or connecting test leads or connectors with the ignition switch ON. When selecting test equipment, make sure the manufacturers instructions state that the tester is compatible with whatever type of electronic control system is being serviced. Read all instructions carefully and double check all test points before installing probes or making any test connections.

The following section outlines basic diagnosis techniques for dealing with computerized automotive control systems. Along with a general explanation of the various types of test equipment available to aid in servicing modern electronic automotive systems, basic repair techniques for wiring harnesses and connectors is given. Read the basic information before attempting any repairs or testing on any computerized system, to provide the background of information necessary to avoid the most common and obvious mistakes that can cost both time and money. Although the replacement and testing procedures are simple in themselves, the systems are not, and unless one has a thorough understanding of all components and their function within a particular computerized control system, the logical test sequence these systems demand cannot be followed. Minor malfunctions can make a big difference, so it is important to know how each component affects the operation of the overall electronic system to find the ultimate cause of a problem without replacing good components unnecessarily. It is not enough to use the correct test equipment; the test equipment must be used correctly.

Safety Precautions

CAUTION: *Whenever working on or around any computer based microprocessor control system, always observe these general precautions to prevent the possibility of personal injury or damage to electronic components.*

• Never install or remove battery cables with the key ON or the engine running. Jumper cables should be connected with the key OFF to avoid power surges that can damage electronic control units. Engines equipped with computer controlled systems should avoid both giving and getting jump starts due to the possibility of serious damage to components from arcing in the engine compartment when connections are made with the ignition ON.

• Always remove the battery cables before charging the battery. Never use a high output charger on an installed battery or attempt to use any type of "hot shot" (24 volt) starting aid.

• Exercise care when inserting test probes into connectors to insure good connections without damaging the connector or spreading the pins. Always probe connectors from the rear (wire) side, NOT the pin side, to avoid accidental shorting of terminals during test procedures.

• Never remove or attach wiring harness connectors with the ignition switch ON, especially to an electronic control unit.

• Do not drop any components during service procedures and never apply 12 volts directly to any component (like a solenoid or relay) unless instructed specifically to do so. Some component electrical windings are designed to safely handle only 4 or 5 volts and can be destroyed in seconds if 12 volts are applied directly to the connector.

• Remove the electronic control unit if the vehicle is to be placed in an environment where temperatures exceed approximately 176°F (80°C), such as a paint spray booth or when arc or gas welding near the control unit location in the car.

ORGANIZED TROUBLESHOOTING

When diagnosing a specific problem, organized troubleshooting is a must. The complexity of a modern automobile demands that you approach any problem in a logical, organized manner. There are certain troubleshooting techniques that are standard:

1. Establish when the problem occurs. Does the problem appear only under certain conditions? Were there any noises, odors, or other unusual symptoms?

2. Isolate the problem area. To do this, make some simple tests and observations; then eliminate the systems that are working properly. Check for obvious problems such as broken wires, dirty connections or split or disconnected vacuum hoses. Always check the obvious before assuming something complicated is the cause.

3. Test for problems systematically to determine the cause once the problem area is isolated. Are all the components functioning properly? Is there power going to electrical switches and motors? Is there vacuum at vacuum switches and/or actuators? Is there a mechanical problem such as bent linkage or loose mounting screws? Doing careful, systematic checks will often turn up most causes on the first inspection without wasting time checking components that have little or no relationship to the problem.

4. Test all repairs after the work is done to make sure that the problem is fixed. Some causes can be traced to more than one component, so a careful verification of repair work is important to pick up additional malfunctions that may cause a problem to reappear or a different problem to arise. A blown fuse, for example, is a simple problem that may require more than another fuse to repair. If you don't look for a problem that caused a fuse to blow, for example, a shorted wire may go undetected.

Experience has shown that most problems tend to be the result of a fairly simple and obvious cause, such as loose or corroded connectors or air leaks in the intake system; making careful inspection of components during testing essential to quick and accurate troubleshooting. Special, hand held computerized testers designed specifically for diagnosing the EEC-IV system are available from a variety of aftermarket sources, as well as from the vehicle manufacturer, but care should be taken that any test equipment being used is designed to diagnose that particular computer controlled system accurately without damaging the control unit (ECU) or components being tested.

NOTE: *Pinpointing the exact cause of trouble in an electrical system can sometimes only be accomplished by the use of special test equipment. The following describes commonly used test equipment and explains how to put it to best use in diagnosis. In addition to the information covered below, the manufacturer's instructions booklet provided with the tester should be read and clearly understood before attempting any test procedures.*

TEST EQUIPMENT

Jumper Wires

Jumper wires are simple, yet extremely valuable, pieces of test equipment. Jumper wires are merely wires that are used to bypass sections of a circuit. The simplest type of jumper wire is merely a length of multistrand wire with an alligator clip at each end. Jumper wires are usually fabricated from lengths of standard automotive wire and whatever type of connector (alligator clip, spade connector or pin connector) that is required for the particular vehicle being tested. The well equipped tool box will have several different styles of jumper wires in several different lengths. Some jumper wires are made with three or more terminals coming from a common splice for special purpose testing. In cramped, hard-to-reach areas it is advisable to have insulated boots over the jumper wire terminals in order to prevent accidental grounding, sparks, and possible fire, especially when testing fuel system components.

Jumper wires are used primarily to locate open electrical circuits, on either the ground (-) side of the circuit or on the hot (+) side. If an electrical component fails to operate, connect the jumper wire between the component and a good ground. If the component operates only with the jumper installed, the ground circuit is open. If the ground circuit is good, but the component does not operate, the circuit between the power feed and component is open. You can sometimes connect the jumper wire directly from the battery to the hot terminal of the component, but first make sure the component uses 12 volts in operation. Some electrical components, such as fuel injectors, are designed to operate on about 4 volts and running 12 volts directly to the injector terminals can burn out the wiring. By inserting an inline fuseholder between a set of test leads, a fused jumper wire can be used for bypassing open circuits. Use a 5 amp fuse to provide protection against voltage spikes. When in doubt, use a voltmeter to check the voltage input to the component and measure how much voltage is being applied normally. By moving the jumper wire successively back from the lamp toward the power source, you can isolate the area of the circuit where the open is located. When the component stops functioning, or the power is cut off, the open is in the segment of wire between the jumper and the point previously tested.

CAUTION: *Never use jumpers made from wire that is of lighter gauge than used in the circuit under test. If the jumper wire is of too small gauge, it may overheat and possibly melt. Never use jumpers to bypass high resistance loads (such as motors) in a circuit. Bypassing resistances, in effect, creates a short circuit which may, in turn, cause damage and fire. Never use a jumper for anything other than temporary bypassing of components in a circuit.*

12 Volt Test Light

The 12 volt test light is used to check circuits and components while electrical current is flowing through them. It is used for voltage and ground tests. Twelve volt test lights come in different styles but all have three main parts; a ground clip, a probe, and a light. The most commonly used 12 volt test lights have pick-type probes. To use a 12 volt test light, connect the ground clip to a good ground and probe wherever necessary with the pick. The pick should be sharp so that it can penetrate wire insulation to make contact with the wire, without making a large hole in the insulation. The wrap-around light is handy in hard to reach areas or where it is difficult to support a wire to push a probe pick into it. To use the wrap around light, hook the wire to probed with the hook and pull the trigger. A small pick will be forced through the wire insulation into the wire core.

CAUTION: *Do not use a test light to probe electronic ignition spark plug or coil wires. Never use a pick-type test light to probe wiring on computer controlled systems unless specifically instructed to do so. Any wire insulation that is pierced by the test light probe*

should be taped and sealed with silicone after testing.

Like the jumper wire, the 12 volt test light is used to isolate opens in circuits. But, whereas the jumper wire is used to bypass the open to operate the load, the 12 volt test light is used to locate the presence of voltage in a circuit. If the test light glows, you know that there is power up to that point; if the 12 volt test light does not glow when its probe is inserted into the wire or connector, you know that there is an open circuit (no power). Move the test light in successive steps back toward the power source until the light in the handle does glow. When it does glow, the open is between the probe and point previously probed.

NOTE: *The test light does not detect that 12 volts (or any particular amount of voltage) is present; it only detects that some voltage is present. It is advisable before using the test light to touch its terminals across the battery posts to make sure the light is operating properly.*

Self-Powered Test Light

The self-powered test light usually contains a 1.5 volt penlight battery. One type of self-powered test light is similar in design to the 12 volt test light. This type has both the battery and the light in the handle and pick-type probe tip. The second type has the light toward the open tip, so that the light illuminates the contact point. The self-powered test light is dual purpose piece of test equipment. It can be used to test for either open or short circuits when power is isolated from the circuit (continuity test). A powered test light should not be used on any computer controlled system or component unless specifically instructed to do so. Many engine sensors can be destroyed by even this small amount of voltage applied directly to the terminals.

Open Circuit Testing

To use the self-powered test light to check for open circuits, first isolate the circuit from the vehicle's 12 volt power source by disconnecting the battery or wiring harness connector. Connect the test light ground clip to a good ground and probe sections of the circuit sequentially with the test light. (start from either end of the circuit). If the light is out, the open is between the probe and the circuit ground. If the light is on, the open is between the probe and end of the circuit toward the power source.

Short Circuit Testing

By isolating the circuit both from power and from ground, and using a self-powered test light, you can check for shorts to ground in the circuit. Isolate the circuit from power and ground. Connect the test light ground clip to a good ground and probe any easy-to-reach test point in the circuit. If the light comes on, there is a short somewhere in the circuit. To isolate the short, probe a test point at either end of the isolated circuit (the light should be on). Leave the test light probe connected and open connectors, switches, remove parts, etc., sequentially, until the light goes out. When the light goes out, the short is between the last circuit component opened and the previous circuit opened.

NOTE: *The 1.5 volt battery in the test light does not provide much current. A weak battery may not provide enough power to illuminate the test light even when a complete circuit is made (especially if there are high resistances in the circuit). Always make sure that the test battery is strong. To check the battery, briefly touch the ground clip to the probe; if the light glows brightly the battery is strong enough for testing. Never use a self-powered test light to perform checks for opens or shorts when power is applied to the electrical system under test. The 12 volt vehicle power will quickly burn out the 1.5 volt light bulb in the test light.*

Voltmeter

A voltmeter is used to measure voltage at any point in a circuit, or to measure the voltage drop across any part of a circuit. It can also be used to check continuity in a wire or circuit by indicating current flow from one end to the other. Voltmeters usually have various scales on the meter dial and a selector switch to allow the selection of different voltages. The voltmeter has a positive and a negative lead. To avoid damage to the meter, always connect the negative lead to the negative (-) side of circuit (to ground or nearest the ground side of the circuit) and connect the positive lead to the positive (+) side of the circuit (to the power source or the nearest power source). Note that the negative voltmeter lead will always be black and that the positive voltmeter will always be some color other than black (usually red). Depending on how the voltmeter is connected into the circuit, it has several uses.

A voltmeter can be connected either in parallel or in series with a circuit and it has a very high resistance to current flow. When connected in parallel, only a small amount of current will flow through the voltmeter current path; the rest will flow through the normal circuit current path and the circuit will work normally. When the voltmeter is connected in series with a circuit, only a small amount of current can flow through the circuit. The circuit will not

work properly, but the voltmeter reading will show if the circuit is complete or not.

Available Voltage Measurement

Set the voltmeter selector switch to the 20V position and connect the meter negative lead to the negative post of the battery. Connect the positive meter lead to the positive post of the battery and turn the ignition switch ON to provide a load. Read the voltage on the meter or digital display. A well charged battery should register over 12 volts. If the meter reads below 11.5 volts, the battery power may be insufficient to operate the electrical system properly. This test determines voltage available from the battery and should be the first step in any electrical trouble diagnosis procedure. Many electrical problems, especially on computer controlled systems, can be caused by a low state of charge in the battery. Excessive corrosion at the battery cable terminals can cause a poor contact that will prevent proper charging and full battery current flow.

Normal battery voltage is 12 volts when fully charged. When the battery is supplying current to one or more circuits it is said to be "under load". When everything is off the electrical system is under a "no-load" condition. A fully charged battery may show about 12.5 volts at no load; will drop to 12 volts under medium load; and will drop even lower under heavy load. If the battery is partially discharged the voltage decrease under heavy load may be excessive, even though the battery shows 12 volts or more at no load. When allowed to discharge further, the battery's available voltage under load will decrease more severely. For this reason, it is important that the battery be fully charged during all testing procedures to avoid errors in diagnosis and incorrect test results.

Voltage Drop

When current flows through a resistance, the voltage beyond the resistance is reduced (the larger the current, the greater the reduction in voltage). When no current is flowing, there is no voltage drop because there is no current flow. All points in the circuit which are connected to the power source are at the same voltage as the power source. The total voltage drop always equals the total source voltage. In a long circuit with many connectors, a series of small, unwanted voltage drops due to corrosion at the connectors can add up to a total loss of voltage which impairs the operation of the normal loads in the circuit.

INDIRECT COMPUTATION OF VOLTAGE DROPS

1. Set the voltmeter selector switch to the 20 volt position.

2. Connect the meter negative lead to a good ground.

3. Probe all resistances in the circuit with the positive meter lead.

4. Operate the circuit in all modes and observe the voltage readings.

DIRECT MEASUREMENT OF VOLTAGE DROPS

1. Set the voltmeter switch to the 20 volt position.

2. Connect the voltmeter negative lead to the ground side of the resistance load to be measured.

3. Connect the positive lead to the positive side of the resistance or load to be measured.

4. Read the voltage drop directly on the 20 volt scale.

Too high a voltage indicates too high a resistance. If, for example, a blower motor runs too slowly, you can determine if there is too high a resistance in the resistor pack. By taking voltage drop readings in all parts of the circuit, you can isolate the problem. Too low a voltage drop indicates too low a resistance. If, for example, a blower motor runs too fast in the MED and/or LOW position, the problem can be isolated in the resistor pack by taking voltage drop readings in all parts of the circuit to locate a possibly shorted resistor. The maximum allowable voltage drop under load is critical, especially if there is more than one high resistance problem in a circuit because all voltage drops are cumulative. A small drop is normal due to the resistance of the conductors.

HIGH RESISTANCE TESTING

1. Set the voltmeter selector switch to the 4 volt position.

2. Connect the voltmeter positive lead to the positive post of the battery.

3. Turn on the headlights and heater blower to provide a load.

4. Probe various points in the circuit with the negative voltmeter lead.

5. Read the voltage drop on the 4 volt scale. Some average maximum allowable voltage drops are:

FUSE PANEL — 7 volts
IGNITION SWITCH — 5volts
HEADLIGHT SWITCH — 7 volts
IGNITION COIL (+) — 5 volts
ANY OTHER LOAD — 1.3 volts
NOTE: *Voltage drops are all measured while a load is operating; without current flow, there will be no voltage drop.*

Ohmmeter

The ohmmeter is designed to read resistance (ohms) in a circuit or component. Although there are several different styles of ohmmeters,

all will usually have a selector switch which permits the measurement of different ranges of resistance (usually the selector switch allows the multiplication of the meter reading by 10, 100, 1000, and 10,000). A calibration knob allows the meter to be set at zero for accurate measurement. Since all ohmmeters are powered by an internal battery (usually 9 volts), the ohmmeter can be used as a self-powered test light. When the ohmmeter is connected, current from the ohmmeter flows through the circuit or component being tested. Since the ohmmeter's internal resistance and voltage are known values, the amount of current flow through the meter depends on the resistance of the circuit or component being tested.

The ohmmeter can be used to perform continuity test for opens or shorts (either by observation of the meter needle or as a self-powered test light), and to read actual resistance in a circuit. It should be noted that the ohmmeter is used to check the resistance of a component or wire while there is no voltage applied to the circuit. Current flow from an outside voltage source (such as the vehicle battery) can damage the ohmmeter, so the circuit or component should be isolated from the vehicle electrical system before any testing is done. Since the ohmmeter uses its own voltage source, either lead can be connected to any test point.

NOTE: *When checking diodes or other solid state components, the ohmmeter leads can only be connected one way in order to measure current flow in a single direction. Make sure the positive (+) and negative (-) terminal connections are as described in the test procedures to verify the one-way diode operation.*

In using the meter for making continuity checks, do not be concerned with the actual resistance readings. Zero resistance, or any resistance readings, indicate continuity in the circuit. Infinite resistance indicates an open in the circuit. A high resistance reading where there should be none indicates a problem in the circuit. Checks for short circuits are made in the same manner as checks for open circuits except that the circuit must be isolated from both power and normal ground. Infinite resistance indicates no continuity to ground, while zero resistance indicates a dead short to ground.

RESISTANCE MEASUREMENT

The batteries in an ohmmeter will weaken with age and temperature, so the ohmmeter must be calibrated or "zeroed" before taking measurements. To zero the meter, place the selector switch in its lowest range and touch the two ohmmeter leads together. Turn the calibration knob until the meter needle is exactly on zero.

NOTE: *All analog (needle) type ohmmeters must be zeroed before use, but some digital ohmmeter models are automatically calibrated when the switch is turned on. Self-calibrating digital ohmmeters do not have an adjusting knob, but its a good idea to check for a zero readout before use by touching the leads together. All computer controlled systems require the use of a digital ohmmeter with at least 10 meagohms impedance for testing. Before any test procedures are attempted, make sure the ohmmeter used is compatible with the electrical system or damage to the onboard computer could result.*

To measure resistance, first isolate the circuit from the vehicle power source by disconnecting the battery cables or the harness connector. Make sure the key is OFF when disconnecting any components or the battery. Where necessary, also isolate at least one side of the circuit to be checked to avoid reading parallel resistances. Parallel circuit resistances will always give a lower reading than the actual resistance of either of the branches. When measuring the resistance of parallel circuits, the total resistance will always be lower than the smallest resistance in the circuit. Connect the meter leads to both sides of the circuit (wire or component) and read the actual measured ohms on the meter scale. Make sure the selector switch is set to the proper ohm scale for the circuit being tested to avoid misreading the ohmmeter test value.

CAUTION: *Never use an ohmmeter with power applied to the circuit. Like the self-powered test light, the ohmmeter is designed to operate on its own power supply. The normal 12 volt automotive electrical system current could damage the meter.*

Ammeters

An ammeter measures the amount of current flowing through a circuit in units called amperes or amps. Amperes are units of electron flow which indicate how fast the electrons are flowing through the circuit. Since Ohms Law dictates that current flow in a circuit is equal to the circuit voltage divided by the total circuit resistance, increasing voltage also increases the current level (amps). Likewise, any decrease in resistance will increase the amount of amps in a circuit. At normal operating voltage, most circuits have a characteristic amount of amperes, called "current draw" which can be measured using an ammeter. By referring to a specified current draw rating, measuring the amperes, and comparing the two values, one can determine what is happening within the circuit to aid

in diagnosis. An open circuit, for example, will not allow any current to flow so the ammeter reading will be zero. More current flows through a heavily loaded circuit or when the charging system is operating.

An ammeter is always connected in series with the circuit being tested. All of the current that normally flows through the circuit must also flow through the ammeter; if there is any other path for the current to follow, the ammeter reading will not be accurate. The ammeter itself has very little resistance to current flow and therefore will not affect the circuit, but it will measure current draw only when the circuit is closed and electricity is flowing. Excessive current draw can blow fuses and drain the battery, while a reduced current draw can cause motors to run slowly, lights to dim and other components to not operate properly. The ammeter can help diagnose these conditions by locating the cause of the high or low reading.

Multimeters

Different combinations of test meters can be built into a single unit designed for specific tests. Some of the more common combination test devices are known as Volt/Amp testers, Tach/Dwell meters, or Digital Multimeters. The Volt/Amp tester is used for charging system, starting system or battery tests and consists of a voltmeter, an ammeter and a variable resistance carbon pile. The voltmeter will usually have at least two ranges for use with 6, 12 and 24 volt systems. The ammeter also has more than one range for testing various levels of battery loads and starter current draw and the carbon pile can be adjusted to offer different amounts of resistance. The Volt/Amp tester has heavy leads to carry large amounts of current and many later models have an inductive ammeter pickup that clamps around the wire to simplify test connections. On some models, the ammeter also has a zero-center scale to allow testing of charging and starting systems without switching leads or polarity. A digital multimeter is a voltmeter, ammeter and ohmmeter combined in an instrument which gives a digital readout. These are often used when testing solid state circuits because of their high input impedance (usually 10 megohms or more).

The tach/dwell meter combines a tachometer and a dwell (cam angle) meter and is a specialized kind of voltmeter. The tachometer scale is marked to show engine speed in rpm and the dwell scale is marked to show degrees of distributor shaft rotation. In most electronic ignition systems, dwell is determined by the control unit, but the dwell meter can also be used to check the duty cycle (operation) of some electronic engine control systems. Some tach/dwell meters are powered by an internal battery, while others take their power from the car battery in use. The battery powered testers usually require calibration much like an ohmmeter before testing.

Special Test Equipment

A variety of diagnostic tools are available to help troubleshoot and repair computerized engine control systems. The most sophisticated of these devices are the console type engine analyzers that usually occupy a garage service bay, but there are several types of aftermarket electronic testers available that will allow quick circuit tests of the engine control system by plugging directly into a special connector located in the engine compartment or under the dashboard. Several tool and equipment manufacturers offer simple, hand held testers that measure various circuit voltage levels on command to check all system components for proper operation. Although these testers usually cost about $300-$500, consider that the average computer control unit (or ECM) can cost just as much and the money saved by not replacing perfectly good sensors or components in an attempt to correct a problem could justify the purchase price of a special diagnostic tester the first time it's used.

These computerized testers can allow quick and easy test measurements while the engine is operating or while the car is being driven. In addition, the on-board computer memory can be read to access any stored trouble codes; in effect allowing the computer to tell you where it hurts and aid trouble diagnosis by pinpointing exactly which circuit or component is malfunctioning. In the same manner, repairs can be tested to make sure the problem has been corrected. The biggest advantage these special testers have is their relatively easy hookups that minimize or eliminate the chances of making the wrong connections and getting false voltage readings or damaging the computer accidentally.

NOTE: *It should be remembered that these testers check voltage levels in circuits; they don't detect mechanical problems or failed components if the circuit voltage falls within the preprogrammed limits stored in the tester PROM unit. Also, most of the hand held testes are designed to work only on one or two systems made by a specific manufacturer.*

A variety of aftermarket testers are available to help diagnose different computerized control systems. Owatonna Tool Company (OTC), for example, markets a device called the OTC Monitor which plugs directly into the assembly line diagnostic link (ALDL). The OTC tester makes diagnosis a simple matter of pressing the correct buttons and, by changing the internal PROM or inserting a different diagnosis cartridge, it will work on any model from full size to subcompact, over a wide range of years. An adapter is supplied with the tester to allow connection to all types of ALDL links, regardless of the number of pin terminals used. By inserting an updated PROM into the OTC tester, it can be easily updated to diagnose any new modifications of computerized control systems.

Wiring Harnesses

The average automobile contains about ½ mile of wiring, with hundreds of individual connections. To protect the many wires from damage and to keep them from becoming a confusing tangle, they are organized into bundles, enclosed in plastic or taped together and called wire harnesses. Different wiring harnesses serve different parts of the vehicle. Individual wires are color coded to help trace them through a harness where sections are hidden from view.

A loose or corroded connection or a replacement wire that is too small for the circuit will add extra resistance and an additional voltage drop to the circuit. A ten percent voltage drop can result in slow or erratic motor operation, for example, even though the circuit is complete. Automotive wiring or circuit conductors can be in any one of three forms:

1. Single strand wire
2. Multistrand wire
3. Printed circuitry

Single strand wire has a solid metal core and is usually used inside such components as alternators, motors, relays and other devices. Multistrand wire has a core made of many small strands of wire twisted together into a single conductor. Most of the wiring in an automotive electrical system is made up of multistrand wire, either as a single conductor or grouped together in a harness. All wiring is color coded on the insulator, either as a solid color or as a colored wire with an identification stripe. A printed circuit is a thin film of copper or other conductor that is printed on an insulator backing. Occasionally, a printed circuit is sandwiched between two sheets of plastic for more protection and flexibility. A complete printed circuit, consisting of conductors, insulating material and connectors for lamps or other components is called a printed circuit board. Printed circuitry is used in place of individual wires or harnesses in places where space is limited, such as behind instrument panels.

Wire Gauge

Since computer controlled automotive electrical systems are very sensitive to changes in resistance, the selection of properly sized wires is critical when systems are repaired. The wire gauge number is an expression of the cross section area of the conductor. The most common system for expressing wire size is the American Wire Gauge (AWG) system.

Wire cross section area is measured in circular mils. A mil is $\frac{1}{1000}''$ (0.001″); a circular mil is the area of a circle one mil in diameter. For example, a conductor ¼″ in diameter is 0.250 in. or 250 mils. The circular mil cross section area of the wire is 250 squared (250^2) or 62,500 circular mils. Imported car models usually use metric wire gauge designations, which is simply the cross section area of the conductor in square millimeters (mm^2).

Gauge numbers are assigned to conductors of various cross section areas. As gauge number increases, area decreases and the conductor becomes smaller. A 5 gauge conductor is smaller than a 1 gauge conductor and a 10 gauge is smaller than a 5 gauge. As the cross section area of a conductor decreases, resistance increases and so does the gauge number. A conductor with a higher gauge number will carry less current than a conductor with a lower gauge number.

NOTE: *Gauge wire size refers to the size of the conductor, not the size of the complete wire. It is possible to have two wires of the same gauge with different diameters because one may have thicker insulation than the other.*

12 volt automotive electrical systems generally use 10, 12, 14, 16 and 18 gauge wire. Main power distribution circuits and larger accessories usually use 10 and 12 gauge wire. Battery cables are usually 4 or 6 gauge, although 1 and 2 gauge wires are occasionally used. Wire length must also be considered when making repairs to a circuit. As conductor length increases, so does resistance. An 18 gauge wire, for example, can carry a 10 amp load for 10 feet without excessive voltage drop; however if a 15 foot wire is required for the same 10 amp load, it must be a 16 gauge wire.

An electrical schematic shows the electrical current paths when a circuit is operating properly. It is essential to understand how a circuit works before trying to figure out why it doesn't. Schematics break the entire electrical system down into individual circuits and show only one particular circuit. In a schematic, no attempt is made to represent wiring and components as they physically appear on the vehicle; switches and other components are shown as simply as possible. Face views of harness connectors show the cavity or terminal locations in all multi-pin connectors to help locate test points.

If you need to backprobe a connector while it is on the component, the order of the terminals must be mentally reversed. The wire color code can help in this situation, as well as a keyway, lock tab or other reference mark.

NOTE: *Wiring diagrams are not included in this book. As trucks have become more complex and available with longer option lists, wiring diagrams have grown in size and complexity. It has become almost impossible to provide a readable reproduction of a wiring diagram in a book this size. Information on ordering wiring diagrams from the vehicle manufacturer can be found in the owner's manual.*

WIRING REPAIR

Soldering is a quick, efficient method of joining metals permanently. Everyone who has the occasion to make wiring repairs should know how to solder. Electrical connections that are soldered are far less likely to come apart and will conduct electricity much better than connections that are only "pig-tailed" together. The most popular (and preferred) method of soldering is with an electrical soldering gun. Soldering irons are available in many sizes and wattage ratings. Irons with higher wattage ratings deliver higher temperatures and recover lost heat faster. A small soldering iron rated for no more than 50 watts is recommended, especially on electrical systems where excess heat can damage the components being soldered.

There are three ingredients necessary for successful soldering; proper flux, good solder and sufficient heat. A soldering flux is necessary to clean the metal of tarnish, prepare it for soldering and to enable the solder to spread into tiny crevices. When soldering, always use a resin flux or resin core solder which is non-corrosive and will not attract moisture once the job is finished. Other types of flux (acid core) will leave a residue that will attract moisture and cause the wires to corrode. Tin is a unique metal with a low melting point. In a molten state, it dissolves and alloys easily with many metals. Solder is made by mixing tin with lead. The most common proportions are 40/60, 50/50 and 60/40, with the percentage of tin listed first. Low priced solders usually contain less tin, making them very difficult for a beginner to use because more heat is required to melt the solder. A common solder is 40/60 which is well suited for all-around general use, but 60/40 melts easier, has more tin for a better joint and is preferred for electrical work.

Soldering Techniques

Successful soldering requires that the metals to be joined be heated to a temperature that will melt the solder—usually 360-460°F (182-238°C). Contrary to popular belief, the purpose of the soldering iron is not to melt the solder itself, but to heat the parts being soldered to a temperature high enough to melt the solder when it is touched to the work. Melting flux-cored solder on the soldering iron will usually destroy the effectiveness of the flux.

NOTE: *Soldering tips are made of copper for good heat conductivity, but must be "tinned" regularly for quick transference of heat to the project and to prevent the solder from sticking to the iron. To "tin" the iron, simply heat it and touch the flux-cored solder to the tip; the solder will flow over the hot tip. Wipe the excess off with a clean rag, but be careful as the iron will be hot.*

After some use, the tip may become pitted. If so, simply dress the tip smooth with a smooth file and "tin" the tip again. An old saying holds that "metals well cleaned are half soldered." Flux-cored solder will remove oxides but rust, bits of insulation and oil or grease must be removed with a wire brush or emery cloth. For maximum strength in soldered parts, the joint must start off clean and tight. Weak joints will result in gaps too wide for the solder to bridge.

If a separate soldering flux is used, it should be brushed or swabbed on only those areas that are to be soldered. Most solders contain a core of flux and separate fluxing is unnecessary. Hold the work to be soldered firmly. It is best to solder on a wooden board, because a metal vise will only rob the piece to be soldered of heat and make it difficult to melt the solder. Hold the soldering tip with the broadest face against the work to be soldered. Apply solder under the tip close to the work, using enough solder to give a heavy film between the iron and the piece being soldered, while moving slowly and making sure the solder melts properly. Keep the work level or the solder will run to the lowest part and favor the thicker parts, because these require more heat to melt the solder. If the soldering tip overheats (the solder coating on the face of the tip burns up), it should be retinned. Once the soldering is completed, let the soldered joint stand until cool. Tape and seal all soldered wire splices after the repair has cooled.

Wire Harness and Connectors

The on-board computer (ECM) wire harness electrically connects the control unit to the various solenoids, switches and sensors used by the control system. Most connectors in the engine compartment or otherwise exposed to the elements are protected against moisture and dirt which could create oxidation and deposits on the terminals. This protection is important because of the very low voltage and current levels used by the computer and sensors. All connectors have a lock which secures the male and female terminals together, with a secondary lock

holding the seal and terminal into the connector. Both terminal locks must be released when disconnecting ECM connectors.

These special connectors are weather-proof and all repairs require the use of a special terminal and the tool required to service it. This tool is used to remove the pin and sleeve terminals. If removal is attempted with an ordinary pick, there is a good chance that the terminal will be bent or deformed. Unlike standard blade type terminals, these terminals cannot be straightened once they are bent. Make certain that the connectors are properly seated and all of the sealing rings in place when connecting leads. On some models, a hinge-type flap provides a backup or secondary locking feature for the terminals. Most secondary locks are used to improve the connector reliability by retaining the terminals if the small terminal lock tangs are not positioned properly.

Molded-on connectors require complete replacement of the connection. This means splicing a new connector assembly into the harness. All splices in on-board computer systems should be soldered to insure proper contact. Use care when probing the connections or replacing terminals in them as it is possible to short between opposite terminals. If this happens to the wrong terminal pair, it is possible to damage certain components. Always use jumper wires between connectors for circuit checking and never probe through weather-proof seals.

Open circuits are often difficult to locate by sight because corrosion or terminal misalignment are hidden by the connectors. Merely wiggling a connector on a sensor or in the wiring harness may correct the open circuit condition. This should always be considered when an open circuit or a failed sensor is indicated. Intermittent problems may also be caused by oxidized or loose connections. When using a circuit tester for diagnosis, always probe connections from the wire side. Be careful not to damage sealed connectors with test probes.

All wiring harnesses should be replaced with identical parts, using the same gauge wire and connectors. When signal wires are spliced into a harness, use wire with high temperature insulation only. With the low voltage and current levels found in the system, it is important that the best possible connection at all wire splices be made by soldering the splices together. It is seldom necessary to replace a complete harness. If replacement is necessary, pay close attention to insure proper harness routing. Secure the harness with suitable plastic wire clamps to prevent vibrations from causing the harness to wear in spots or contact any hot components.

NOTE: *Weatherproof connectors cannot be*

replaced with standard connectors. Instructions are provided with replacement connector and terminal packages. Some wire harnesses have mounting indicators (usually pieces of colored tape) to mark where the harness is to be secured.

In making wiring repairs, it's important that you always replace damaged wires with wires that are the same gauge as the wire being replaced. The heavier the wire, the smaller the gauge number. Wires are color-coded to aid in identification and whenever possible the same color coded wire should be used for replacement. A wire stripping and crimping tool is necessary to install solderless terminal connectors. Test all crimps by pulling on the wires; it should not be possible to pull the wires out of a good crimp.

Wires which are open, exposed or otherwise damaged are repaired by simple splicing. Where possible, if the wiring harness is accessible and the damaged place in the wire can be located, it is best to open the harness and check for all possible damage. In an inaccessible harness, the wire must be bypassed with a new insert, usually taped to the outside of the old harness.

When replacing fusible links, be sure to use fusible link wire, NOT ordinary automotive wire. Make sure the fusible segment is of the same gauge and construction as the one being replaced and double the stripped end when crimping the terminal connector for a good contact. The melted (open) fusible link segment of the wiring harness should be cut off as close to the harness as possible, then a new segment spliced in as described. In the case of a damaged fusible link that feeds two harness wires, the harness connections should be replaced with two fusible link wires so that each circuit will have its own separate protection.

NOTE: *Most of the problems caused in the wiring harness are due to bad ground connections. Always check all vehicle ground connections for corrosion or looseness before performing any power feed checks to eliminate the chance of a bad ground affecting the circuit.*

Repairing Hard Shell Connectors

Unlike molded connectors, the terminal contacts in hard shell connectors can be replaced. Weatherproof hard-shell connectors with the leads molded into the shell have non-replaceable terminal ends. Replacement usually involves the use of a special terminal removal tool that depress the locking tangs (barbs) on the connector terminal and allow the connector to be removed from the rear of the shell. The connector shell should be replaced if it shows any evidence of burning, melting, cracks, or breaks.

Replace individual terminals that are burnt, corroded, distorted or loose.

NOTE: *The insulation crimp must be tight to prevent the insulation from sliding back on the wire when the wire is pulled. The insulation must be visibly compressed under the crimp tabs, and the ends of the crimp should be turned in for a firm grip on the insulation.*

The wire crimp must be made with all wire strands inside the crimp. The terminal must be fully compressed on the wire strands with the ends of the crimp tabs turned in to make a firm grip on the wire. Check all connections with an ohmmeter to insure a good contact. There should be no measurable resistance between the wire and the terminal when connected.

Mechanical Test Equipment

Vacuum Gauge

Most gauges are graduated in inches of mercury (in.Hg), although a device called a manometer reads vacuum in inches of water (in. H_2O). The normal vacuum reading usually varies between 18 and 22 in.Hg at sea level. To test engine vacuum, the vacuum gauge must be connected to a source of manifold vacuum. Many engines have a plug in the intake manifold which can be removed and replaced with an adapter fitting. Connect the vacuum gauge to the fitting with a suitable rubber hose or, if no manifold plug is available, connect the vacuum gauge to any device using manifold vacuum, such as EGR valves, etc. The vacuum gauge can be used to determine if enough vacuum is reaching a component to allow its actuation.

Hand Vacuum Pump

Small, hand-held vacuum pumps come in a variety of designs. Most have a built-in vacuum gauge and allow the component to be tested without removing it from the vehicle. Operate the pump lever or plunger to apply the correct amount of vacuum required for the test specified in the diagnosis routines. The level of vacuum in inches of Mercury (in.Hg) is indicated on the pump gauge. For some testing, an additional vacuum gauge may be necessary.

Intake manifold vacuum is used to operate various systems and devices on late model vehicles. To correctly diagnose and solve problems in vacuum control systems, a vacuum source is necessary for testing. In some cases, vacuum can be taken from the intake manifold when the engine is running, but vacuum is normally provided by a hand vacuum pump. These hand vacuum pumps have a built-in vacuum gauge that allow testing while the device is still attached to the component. For some tests, an additional vacuum gauge may be necessary.

HEATING AND AIR CONDITIONING

Heater, Evaporator Core or Heater Air Conditioning Blower Motor

Service such as blower motor and heater core replacement require the removal of the Heater/Evaporator unit from the vehicle. Two persons will be required for the operation. Discharge, evacuation, recharge and leak testing of the refrigerant system is necessary.

Heater/Evaporator Unit

REMOVAL AND INSTALLATION

CAUTION: *The air conditioning system contains refrigerant under high pressure. Severe personal injury may result from improper service procedures. If the knowledge and necessary equipment are not on hand, have the system serviced by qualified service the refrigerant system completely.*

1. Discharge the air conditioning system. See the CAUTION notice above.
2. Block the vehicle wheels and apply the parking brake.
3. Disconnect the negative battery cable. Drain the cooling system.

CAUTION: *When draining the coolant, keep in mind that cats and dogs are attracted by the ethylene glycol antifreeze, and are quite likely to drink any that is left in an uncovered container or in puddles on the ground. This will prove fatal in sufficient quantity. Always drain the coolant into a sealable container. Coolant should be reused unless it is contaminated or several years old.*

4. Remove the passenger side lower instrument panel.
5. Remove the steering column lower cover.
6. Remove the right side cowl and sill trim.
7. Remove the mounting bolt from the right side instrument panel to the right cowl.
8. Loosen the (2) brackets supporting the lower edge to air conditioning and heater unit housing.
9. Remove the mid-reinforcement instrument panel trim moulding.
10. Remove the attaching screws from the right side to center of the steering column.
11. From the engine compartment; disconnect the vacuum line at brake booster and water valve.
12. Remove the hoses from the heater core. Plug the heater tubes.
13. Disconnect the air conditioning plumbing at the H-valve.
14. Remove the (4) nuts from engine compartment package mounting studs.
15. From the passenger compartment, pull the right side of lower instrument panel rearward until it reaches the passenger seat. Disconnect the electrical connectors and temperature control cable.
16. Remove the hangar strap from the unit assembly and bend rearward.
17. Carefully remove the unit assembly from the vehicle.
18. Place the heater/evaporator unit assembly on a work bench.
19. Remove the vacuum harness attaching screw and remove the harness through the access hole in the cover.
20. Remove the (13) attaching screws from the cover and remove the cover. The temperature control door will come out with the cover.
21. Remove the retaining bracket screws and the remove heater core assembly.
22. Remove the evaporator core assembly.
23. Disconnect the actuator linkage from the recirculation door and remove the vacuum line. Remove the actuator retaining screws and remove the actuator.
24. Remove the (4) attaching screws from the recirculation door cover to evaporator/heater assembly. Lift the cover from the unit and remove the recirculation door from its housing.
25. Remove the (5) attaching screws from the blower assembly sound helmet.
26. Remove the retaining clamp from the blower wheel hub and slide the blower wheel from the blower motor shaft.
27. Remove the blower motor (3) mounting screws from the helmet and remove the blower motor assembly.
28. Install the blower wheel to the blower motor shaft and secure it with the retaining clamp.
29. Feed the blower motor electrical wires through the access hole in the sound helmet and lower the blower motor into helmet.
30. Secure the blower motor with the (3) mounting screws.
31. Install the blower assembly and helmet into the fan scroll and secure it with (5) retaining screws.
32. Install the recirculation door into its housing. Place the recirculation door cover onto the unit and secure with the (4) retaining screws.
33. Install the actuator shaft onto the recirculation door and slide the actuator into its bracket. Secure the actuator assembly with (2) nuts.
34. Install the evaporator core into the unit.
35. Install the heater core into the unit and secure the core tube retaining bracket with attaching screws.
36. Install the unit cover and secure with (13) attaching screws.
37. Install the vacuum harness through the

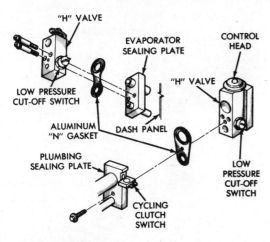

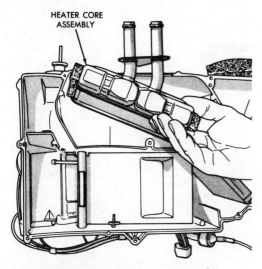

"H" valve assembly

Typical heater core removal/installation

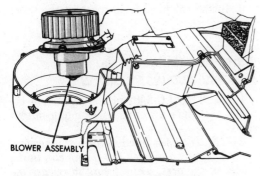

Typical blower motor removal/installation

40. Connect the temperature control cable, vacuum and electrical connectors.

41. Install the (4) retaining nuts to the unit mounting studs from the engine compartment.

42. Connect the air conditioning plumbing to the H-valve.

43. Connect the vacuum line at the brake booster and water valve.

44. Install the attaching screws from the right side to the center of the steering column.

45. Install the mid-reinforcement instrument panel trim moulding.

46. Tighten the (2) brackets supporting the lower edge to the heater/evaporator unit housing.

47. Install the mounting bolt from the right side of the instrument panel to the right cowl.

48. Install the right side cowl and sill trim.

49. Install the steering column lower cover.

50. Install the passenger side lower instrument panel

51. Connect the heater hoses to heater core in the engine compartment.

52. Connect the negative battery cable.

53. Fill the cooling system.

54. Evacuate, charge and leak test the air conditioning system.

RADIO

REMOVAL AND INSTALLATION

1. Remove the control knobs by pulling them from the mounting stalks. Remove the three (3) screws from the top of the radio trim bezel.

2. Remove the ash tray to gain access to the trim bezel lower screws.

3. Remove the two (2) screws from the lower portion of the trim bezel.

4. Pull outward on the left side of bezel to unsnap the mounting clips. Remove the bezel.

5. Remove the radio to instrument panel retaining screws.

6. Pull the radio through the front of the instrument panel and unplug the wiring harness, ground strap and antenna plug.

7. Connect the radio wiring harness, ground strap and antenna lead.

8. Position the radio into the instrument panel and install the retaining screws.

9. Install the trim bezel and secure it with the lower and upper retaining screws. Install the ash tray.

Antenna

REMOVAL AND INSTALLATION

1. Remove the radio.

2. Disconnect the antenna cable from the radio.

access hole in the cover and secure the vacuum harness.

38. Place the heater/evaporator assembly into the vehicle and position it against the dash panel.

39. Install the hangar strap.

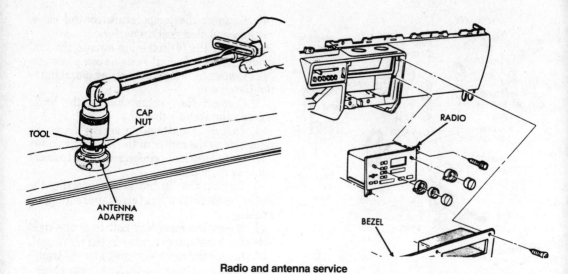

Radio and antenna service

3. Remove the antenna cable from the harness retaining clips.

4. Unscrew the antenna mast from the upper adapter.

5. Remove the cap mounting nut.

6. Remove the adapter and mounting gasket.

7. From beneath the fender remove the antenna lead and body assembly.

8. Install the new antenna body and cable assembly from under fender.

9. Install the adapter gasket, adapter and cap nut.

10. Install the antenna cable through harness mounting clips and install the cable into radio receiver.

11. Install the radio into the instrument panel.

WINDSHIELD WIPERS

Wiper Blade

Refer to Chapter 1 for removal and installation procedure.

Wiper Arm (Windshield)
REMOVAL AND INSTALLATION

1. Remove the head cover from the wiper arm base.

2. Remove the arm to pivot attaching nut.

3. Remove the wiper arm from pivot using a rocking motion.

4. With the wiper motor in Park position, position the arm on the pivot shaft. Choose a point where the tip of the left wiper arm is approximately 2 to 3 inches above the windshield cowl top, and the right arm 1 to 1.5 inches above the windshield cowl top.

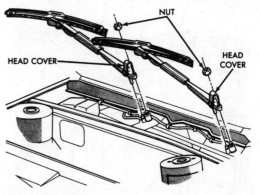

Wiper arm service

5. Install the attaching nut and torque to 120 in. lbs.

6. Install the pivot head cover on the wiper arm.

Wiper Arm (Liftgate)
REMOVAL AND INSTALLATION

1. Insert Tool C-3982 or the equivalent between the wiper arm and wiper motor output shaft.

NOTE: *The use of screwdrivers or other prying tool may damaged the spring clip in the base of the arm, while trying to release the arm. Damage of the spring clip will result in the arm coming off the shaft regardless of how carefully it is installed.*

2. Lift the arm and remove it from motor output shaft.

3. With motor in the Park position, position the arm on the motor output shaft. Choose a point where the tip of blade is about 38mm par-

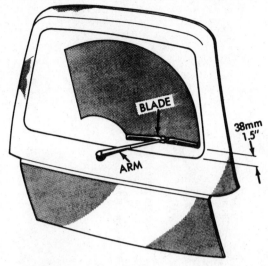

Liftgate wiper arm installation

allel with the bottom lower edge of liftgate glass. Push the wiper arm onto the motor shaft.

Windshield Wiper Motor

REMOVAL AND INSTALLATION

1. The motor and wiper linkage are serviced as a unit. Disconnect the negative battery cable. Remove the wiper arm and blade assemblies. Refer to the windshield wiper arm removal and installation procedure in this section.
2. Open the hood and remove the cowl plenum grille and plastic screen.
3. Remove the hoses from the turret connnector. Remove the pivot mounting screws.
4. Disconnect the motor wiring connector from the motor.
5. Remove the retaining nut from the wiper motor shaft to linkage drive crank, and remove the drive crank from the wiper motor shaft.
6. Remove the wiper motor assembly mounting screws and nuts, and remove the wiper motor.
7. Position the wiper motor against it's mounting surface and secure in position with the mounting screws and nuts Connect the wiring harness.
8. Install the linkage drive crank onto the wiper motor shaft and secure it with the retaining nut. Torque the nut to 95 in. lbs.
9. Install cowl plenum grille plastic screen.
10. Connect hoses to turret connector.
11. Install the cowl plenum grille. Connect the negative battery cable. Close the hood.
12. Install the windshield wiper arm and blade assemblies.

Liftgate Wiper Motor

REMOVAL AND INSTALLATION

1. Disconnect the negative battery cable. Remove the wiper arm and blade assembly.
2. Open the liftgate and remove the trim panel.
3. Remove the four (4) mounting screws from liftgate wiper motor and bracket assembly.
4. Disconnect the electrical harness connector and remove the liftgate motor.
5. Install the liftgate wiper motor and bracket assembly. Secure it with the mounting screws.
6. Connect the wiring harness to the wiper motor.
7. Install the liftgate trim panel and secure it with the mounting screws.
8. Install the liftgate wiper arm and blade assembly.

Windshield Wiper Linkage

Refer to the Wiper Motor procedures in this section.

INSTRUMENTS AND SWITCHES

Instrument Cluster Assembly

WARNING: *Before servicing the instrument cluster or components, disconnect the negative battery.*

REMOVAL AND INSTALLATION

1. Remove the cluster assembly bezel mounting (7) screws and remove the cluster bezel.
2. On vehicles equipped with an automatic transaxle, remove the steering column lower cover. Disconnect the shift indicator wire.
3. Remove the cluster assembly retaining screws.
4. Carefully pull the cluster assembly from the panel and disconnect the speedometer cable.
5. Remove the cluster assembly wiring harness.
6. Remove the cluster assembly past the right side of the steering column.
7. Position the cluster assembly to the dash from the right side of the steering column.
8. Connect the cluster wiring.
9. Connect the speedometer cable.
10. Install the cluster assembly and retaining screws.
11. On models equipped with an automatic transaxle, place the selector lever in (D) Drive position.

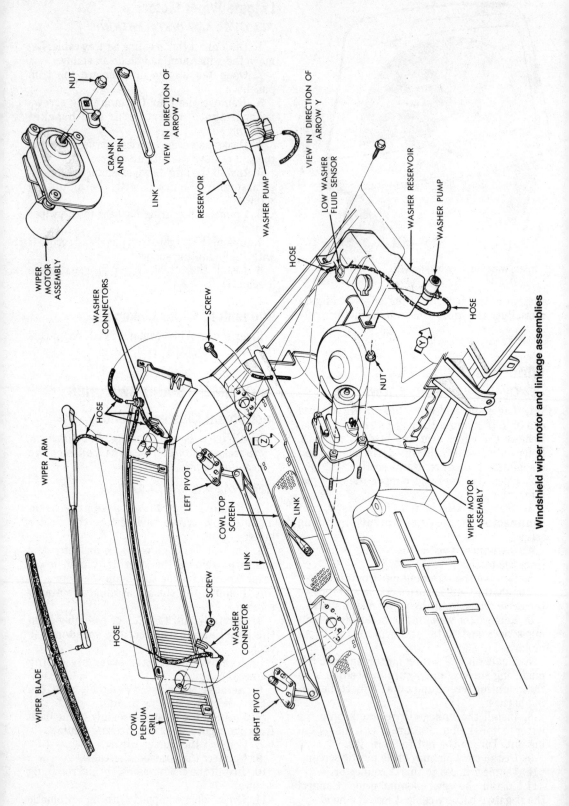

NUT

CRANK AND PIN

LINK

VIEW IN DIRECTION OF ARROW Z

WIPER MOTOR ASSEMBLY

RESERVOIR

WASHER PUMP

VIEW IN DIRECTION OF ARROW Y

LOW WASHER FLUID SENSOR

HOSE

WASHER RESERVOIR

WASHER PUMP

HOSE

WASHER CONNECTORS

SCREW

HOSE

WIPER ARM

LEFT PIVOT

COWL TOP SCREEN

LINK

LINK

NUT

WIPER MOTOR ASSEMBLY

WIPER BLADE

HOSE

SCREW

WASHER CONNECTOR

COWL PLENUM GRILL

RIGHT PIVOT

Windshield wiper motor and linkage assemblies

12. Connect the shift indicator wire to the steering column shift housing. Route the wire on the outside of slotted flange.

13. Place the shift lever in (P) Park position to make the indicator self-adjust.

14. Connect the shift indicator wire.

15. Install the steering column lower cover.

16. Install the cluster assembly bezel. Secure the bezel with the retaining screws.

Cluster Gauges

REMOVAL AND INSTALLATION

The following instruments can be serviced after removing the instrument cluster mask/lens. Do not completely remove the cluster assembly if only instrument service or cluster bulb replacement is necessary.

Fuel Gauge

1. Remove the cluster bezel retaining screws and remove the cluster bezel.

2. Remove the cluster mask/lens.

3. Remove the fuel gauge attaching screws to cluster assembly and remove the fuel gauge.

4. Position the replacement gauge to the cluster assembly and secure it with attaching screws.

5. Install the cluster mask/lens, bezel and bezel retaining screws.

Voltmeter

1. Remove the cluster bezel retaining screws and remove the cluster bezel.

2. Remove the cluster mask/lens.

3. Remove the voltmeter attaching screws to cluster assembly and remove the voltmeter.

4. Position the replacement voltmeter to cluster assembly and secure with the attaching screws.

5. Install the cluster mask/lens, bezel and bezel retaining screws.

Temperature Gauge

1. Remove the cluster bezel retaining screws and remove the cluster bezel.

2. Remove the cluster mask/lens.

3. Remove the temperature/oil pressure gauge attaching screws to cluster assembly and remove the temperature gauge.

4. Position the replacement temperature/oil pressure gauge to cluster assembly and secure with the attaching screws.

5. Install the cluster mask/lens, bezel and bezel retaining screws.

Oil Pressure Gauge

1. Remove the cluster bezel retaining screws and remove the cluster bezel.

2. Remove the cluster mask/lens.

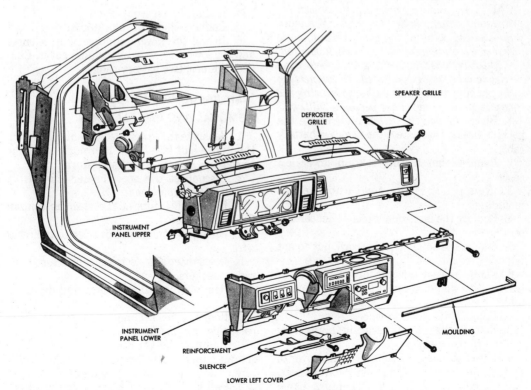

Instrument panel assembly

3. Remove the oil pressure/temperature gauge attaching screws to cluster assembly and remove the temperature gauge.

4. Position the replacement oil pressure/temperature gauge to cluster assembly and secure with the attaching screws.

5. Install the cluster mask/lens, bezel and bezel retaining screws.

Cluster Lamp Bulbs

1. Remove the cluster bezel retaining screws and remove the cluster bezel.

2. Remove the cluster mask/lens.

3. Remove the gauge assembly in front of blown bulbs and replace thebulbs.

4. Install the gauge to the cluster assembly.

5. Install the cluster mask/lens, bezel and bezel retaining screws.

Cluster Lamp Sockets

All cluster lamp sockets are twist out sockets and are removed from the rear of the instrument cluster. Refer to Instrument Cluster Removal and Installation procedure in this section.

Instrument Panel (Lower)

REMOVAL AND INSTALLATION

CAUTION: *Before servicing the lower instrument panel, chock the wheels. Servicing the steering column may cause an automatic transaxle to come out of the (P) Park position.*

Always release the parking brake before the release cable is disconnected. Disconnecting the parking brake cable without releasing the parking brake may cause personal injury.

1. Block the vehicle wheels and release the parking brake. Disconnect the negative battery cable.

2. Remove the steering column lower left cover.

3. Remove the side cowl and the sill moulding.

4. Remove the instrument panel silencer and reinforcement.

5. Loosen the bolt in the side cowl, but do not remove the bolt.

6. Place the gear selector into the (N) Neutral position and disconnect the shift indicator cable.

7. Remove the steering wheel.

8. Remove the (5) nuts securing the steering column to the support bracket.

9. Lower the steering column. Use a cover to protect the steering column and the front seat.

10. Remove the right side instrument panel trim moulding.

11. Remove the (9) screws securing the lower panel to the upper panel and mid-reinforcement.

12. Lower the instrument panel approximately six inches.

13. Disconnect the park brake release cable, heater attachment or air conditioning control cables, antenna and wiring connectors from the radio and fresh air ducts.

14. Disconnect the electrical connections and label them with tape for identification.

15. Pry the A-pillar garnish off the door opening weatherstrip at the panel bolt.

16. Pull the weatherstrip from the body and remove the lower panel from the vehicle.

17. Position the lower panel into the vehicle.

18. Install the weatherstrip and garnish moulding.

19. Connect the park brake release cable, heater attachment or air conditioning control cables, antenna and wiring connectors to the radio and fresh air ducts.

20. Connect all electrical connections.

21. Secure the lower instrument panel to upper panel and mid-reinforcement with (9) retaining screws.

22. Install the right side instrument panel trim moulding.

23. Raise the steering column and install the (5) nuts securing steering column to the support bracket.

24. Install the steering wheel.

25. Connect the shift indicator cable.

26. Install the lower reinforcement, silencer and the lower left steering column cover. Connect the negative battery cable.

Instrument Panel (Upper)

REMOVAL AND INSTALLATION

1. Separate the lower instrument panel from the upper half (see Steps 1 through 12 of the Lower Instrument Panel procedure).

2. Disconnect the speedometer cable from the engine compartment.

3. Remove (2) nuts at the steering column floating bracket.

4. Disconnect the gearshift selector indicator wire.

5. Disconnect the electrical connector at the radio speakers.

6. Remove the radio speaker and defroster grilles.

7. Remove the (2) mounting screws from each side cowl bracket.

8. Remove the (4) upper panel attaching screws from the defroster duct slots and the (2) screws next to the radio speakers.

9. Pull the panel and disconnect the speedometer cable from the speedometer.

10. Remove upper instrument panel from vehicle.

11. Position the upper instrument panel into the vehicle.

12. Connect the speedometer cable.

13. Install the (6) upper panel attaching screws.

14. Install the cowl bracket retaining screws.

15. Install the radio speaker and defroster grilles.

16. Connect the radio speaker wiring.

17. Connect the gearshift selector indicator wire.

18. Install the retaining nuts at the steering column floating bracket.

19. Connect the speedometer cable in the engine compartment.

20. Install the lower panel to the upper.

Forward Console

REMOVAL AND INSTALLATION

1. Remove the cigar lighter and ash receiver.

2. Remove the retaining screws securing the forward console to the upper mounting bracket.

3. Remove the retaining screws securing the forward console to the lower bracket.

4. Pull the console rearward and disconnect the cigar lighter and illumination electrical wiring connectors.

5. Remove the forward console from vehicle.

6. Position the forward console into the vehicle.

7. Connect the cigar lighter and illumination wiring connectors.

8. Install the console lower bracket retaining screws.

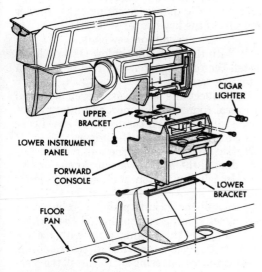

Forward console mounting

9. Install the console upper bracket retaining screws.

10. Install the cigar lighter and ash receiver.

Windshield Wiper Switch (Standard Column)

REMOVAL AND INSTALLATION

1. Disconnect negative battery cable.

2. Remove the steering wheel horn pad assembly.

3. Remove the lower steering column cover, silencer and reinforcement.

4. Remove the wiper switch wiring harness from the steering column retainer.

5. Remove the wash/wipe switch cover. Rotate the cover upward.

6. Disconnect the wipe/wash seven terminal electrical connector. Disconnect intermittent the wipe switch electrical connector or speed control electrical connector, if equipped.

7. Unlock the steering column and turn the wheel so that the access hole provided in the wheel base is in the 9 o'clock position.

8. Reach through the access hole using a small screwdriver and loosen the turn signal lever mounting screw.

9. Remove the wipe/wash switch assembly the from steering column.

10. Slide the circular hider up the control stalk and remove the (2) screws that attach the control stalk sleeve to wipe/wash switch.

11. Remove the wipe/wash switch control knob from the multifunction control stalk. Rotate the control stalk to full clockwise position and pull the shaft from the switch.

12. Install the stalk shaft into the wash/wipe switch and rotate full counterclockwise.

13. Install the wash/wipe switch control knob onto the end of the multifunction control stalk.

14. Install (2) retaining screws that secure the wipe/wash switch to the control stalk sleeve.

15. Install the wipe/wash switch assembly to the steering column.

16. Install and tighten the turn signal lever screw (through the access hole).

17. Connect the wipe/wash seven terminal electrical connector. Connect the intermittent wipe switch electrical connector or speed control electrical connector, if equipped.

18. Install the wash/wipe switch cover.

19. Secure the wiring harness into the steering column retainer.

20. Install the reinforcement, silencer and lower steering column cover.

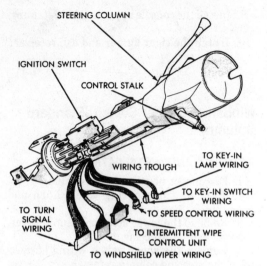

Column wiring connector identifcation

21. Install the steering wheel horn pad assembly.
21. Connect the negative batter cable.

Windshield Wiper Switch (Tilt Column)

REMOVAL AND INSTALLATION

1. Disconnect the negative battery cable.
2. Remove the horn cover pad from the steering wheel. Remove steering column cover. Remove the steering wheel nut.
3. Remove the steering wheel using puller C-3428B or equivalent.
4. Carefully remove the plastic cover from the locking plate. Install locking plate depressing tool C-4156 or equivalent onto the steering shaft. Depress the locking plate and remove the retaining ring from the mounting groove using a small screwdriver. To avoid difficulty when removing the retaining ring, the full load of the upper bearing spring should not be relieved. Remove the locking plate, canceling cam, and upper bearing spring.
5. Remove the switch stalk actuator screw and arm.
6. Remove the hazard warning knob.
7. Disconnect the wipe/wash seven terminal electrical connector. Disconnect the intermittent wipe switch electrical connector or speed control electrical connector, if equipped.
8. Remove the turn signal switch (3) retaining screws.
9. Tape the connectors at end of the wiring to prevent snagging when removing. Place the shift bowl in low (1st) position. Remove the switch and wiring.

10. Remove the ignition key lamp located next to the hazard warning knob.
11. Insert a thin screwdriver into the lock release slot next to the lock cylinder mounting and depress the spring latch at the bottom of the slot. Remove the lock cylinder.
12. Insert a straightened paper clip or similar piece of wire with a hook bent on one end into the exposed loop of the wedge spring of key buzzer switch. Pull on the clip to remove both spring and switch.

NOTE: *If the wedge spring is dropped, it could fall into steering column, requiring complete disassembly of the column.*

13. Remove the column housing cover (3) screws and remove the housing cover.
14. Use a punch, and tap the wiper switch pivot pin from the lock housing. Use tape to hold the dimmer switch rod in place.
15. Remove the wipe/wash switch assembly.
16. Slide the circular hider up the control stalk and remove the (2) screws that attach the control stalk sleeve to the wipe/wash switch.
17. Remove the wipe/wash switch control knob from the multifunction control stalk. Rotate the control stalk to full clockwise position and pull the shaft from the switch.
18. Install the stalk shaft into the wash/wipe switch and rotate full counterclockwise.
19. Install the wash/wipe switch control knob on the end of the multifunction control stalk.
20. Install the (2) retaining screws that secure the wipe/wash switch to the control stalk sleeve.
21. Install the wipe/wash switch assembly to the steering column.
22. Install the wiper switch pivot pin.
23. Install the housing cover and secure with retaining screws.
24. Install the lock cylinder.
25. Assemble the wedge spring to key buzzer and install the key buzzer switch.
26. Install the ignition key lamp.
27. With the shift bowl in low (1st) position, install the turn signal switch and secure with retaining screws.
28. Connect the wipe/wash seven terminal electrical connector. Connect the intermittent wipe switch electrical connector or speed control electrical connector, if equipped.
29. Secure thewiring harness in retainer.
30. Install the hazard warning knob.
31. Install the switch stalk actuator screw and arm.
32. Install the locking plate, canceling cam, and upper bearing spring. Install the locking plate. Depress the locking plate with tool C-4156 or equivalent and install the retaining ring in groove of steering shaft. Install the plastic cover on locking plate.

33. Install the reinforcement, silencer and lower steering column cover.

34. Install the steering wheel and steering shaft nut.

35. Install the horn contact, horn pad and install the horn pad retaining screws.

36. Connect the negative battery cable.

Headlamp and Accessory Switches

REMOVAL AND INSTALLATION

1. Remove the headlamp switch plate bezel.

2. Remove the switch plate (4) retaining screws and pull the switch plate rearward.

3. Disconnect the electrical connectors. Remove the headlamp switch knob and shaft by depressing button on the switch body. Pull the knob and shaft out of the switch.

4. Remove the (2) screws retaining the headlamp switch to switch plate assembly.

5. Remove the headlamp switch retainer.

6. Install the replacement switch into the headlamp switch plate with retainer.

7. Install the headlamp switch retaining screws to the switch plate assembly.

8. Install the headlamp switch knob and shaft.

9. Connect the electrical connectors.

10. Secure the headlamp switch plate with (4) attaching screws.

11. Install the headlamp switch plate bezel.

Headlamp Dimmer Switch

REMOVAL AND INSTALLATION

1. Remove the lower left steering column cover.

2. Tape the actuator control rod to prevent the rod from falling out.

3. Remove the dimmer switch retaining screws.

4. Disconnect the switch electrical connector and remove the switch.

5. Install a new switch and connect the electrical connector.

6. Position the actuator control rod into the dimmer switch and secure the switch onto the steering column.

7. Remove the tape from the actuator control rod.

8. Install the lower left steering column cover.

ADJUSTMENT

1. Loosen the dimmer switch retaining screws.

2. Insert a 24mm drill bit or pin in the adjusting pin hole. Push the switch lightly against the control rod to remove free play. Tighten the

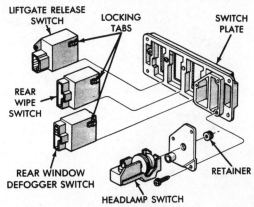

Headlight and accessory switches

switch retaining screws while maintaining light pressure on the dimmer switch.

3. Remove the drill bit or pin.

Speedometer Cable

REMOVAL AND INSTALLATION

1. Disconnect the speedometer cable in the engine compartment.

2. Remove the instrument cluster and disconnect the speedometer cable from the speedometer.

3. Service the cable as necessary. Connect the cable to the speedometer.

4. Install the instrument cluster. Connect the speedometer cable in the engine compartment.

LIGHTING

Headlights

REMOVAL AND INSTALLATION

Sealed Beam

1. Remove the headlight bezel retaining screws and remove the bezel.

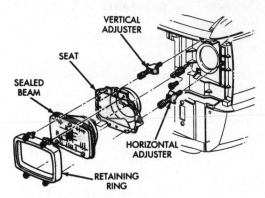

Sealed beam replacement

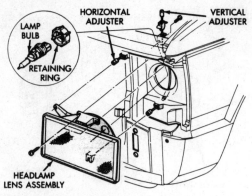

Aero lamp replacement

2. Remove the headlamp retaining ring screws and remove the retaining ring. Do not disturb the headlamp adjusting crews.
3. Pull the sealed beam forward and disconnect the electrical connector.
4. Install the replacement beam and connect the electrical connector.
5. Install the retaining ring.
6. Install the headlight bezel.

Aerodynamic Headlamp

1. From the engine compartment, remove the three wire connector behind the headlamp assembly.
2. Rotate the bulb retaining ring counterclockwise and remove the retaining ring and lamp bulb.
3. Install the replacement bulb and retaining ring assembly. Rotate the ring clockwise.
4. Connect the three wire connector.

Signal and Marker Lights

REMOVAL AND INSTALLATION

Front Park, Turn Signal and Side Marker

1. Remove the headlamp bezel retaining screws and remove the bezel.
2. Twist the bulb from the lamp socket.
3. Install the replacement bulb and twist into position.
4. Install the headlamp bezel and retaining screws.

Rear Tail, Stop, Turn Signal, Back Up and Side Marker

1. To replace the bulb, remove (4) attaching screws.
2. Pull out the lamp assembly. Twist the socket from the lamp and replace the bulb.
3. Install the replacement bulb and twist the socket into the lamp assembly.
4. Position the lamp assembly in place and secure with (4) attaching screws.

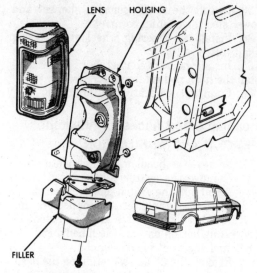

Lamp replacement

TRAILER WIRING

Wiring the truck for towing is fairly easy. There are a number of good wiring kits available and these should be used, rather than trying to design your own. All trailers will need brake lights and turn signals as well as tail lights and side marker lights. Most states require extra marker lights for overly wide trailers. Also, most states have recently required back-up lights for trailers, and most trailer manufacturers have been building trailers with back-up lights for several years.

Additionally, some Class I, most Class II and just about all Class III trailers will have electric brakes.

Add to this number an accessories wire, to operate trailer internal equipment or to charge the trailer's battery, and you can have as many as seven wires in the harness.

Determine the equipment on your trailer and buy the wiring kit necessary. The kit will contain all the wires needed, plus a plug adapter set which included the female plug, mounted on the bumper or hitch, and the male plug, wired into, or plugged into the trailer harness.

When installing the kit, follow the manufacturer's instructions. The color coding of the wires is standard throughout the industry.

One point to note, some domestic vehicles, and most imported vehicles, have separate turn signals. On most domestic vehicles, the brake lights and rear turn signals operate with the same bulb. For those vehicles with separate turn signals, you can purchase an isolation unit so that the brake lights won't blink whenever the turn signals are operated, or, you can go to your local electronics supply house and buy four diodes to wire in series with the brake and turn signal bulbs. Diodes will isolate the brake and turn signals. The choice is yours. The isolation units are simple and quick to install, but far more expensive than the diodes. The diodes, however, require more work to install properly, since they require the cutting of each bulb's wire and soldering in place of the diode.

One final point, the best kits are those with a spring loaded cover on the vehicle mounted socket. This cover prevents dirt and moisture from corroding the terminals. Never let the vehicle socket hang loosely. Always mount it securely to the bumper or hitch.

CIRCUIT PROTECTION

Fuse Block

The fuse block and relay bank is located on the driver's side under the lower instrument panel. The fuse block contains fuses for various circuits as well as circuit breakers, horn relay, ignition lamp thermal time delay, and the turn signal flasher. The hazard warning flasher is mounted into a bracket below the fuse block.

Fusible Links

The main wiring harnesses are equipped with fusible links to protect against harness damage should a short circuit develop.

Never replace a fusible link with standard wire. Only fusible link wire of the correct gauge with hypalon insulation should be used.

When a fusible link blows, it is very important to locate and repair the short. Do not just replace the link to correct the problem.

Always disconnect battery negative cable when servicing the electrical system.

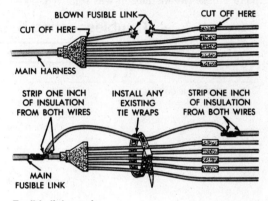

Fusible link repair

CAVITY	FUSE/COLOR	ITEMS FUSED	CAVITY	FUSE/COLOR	ITEMS FUSED
1	20 AMP YL	HAZARD FLASHER	13	5 AMP TN	FUEL VOLTAGE, OIL AND TEMPERATURE GAUGES, BRAKE WARNING LIFTGATE OPEN, SEAT BELT WARNING MODULE, UPSHIFT, AND CHECK ENGINE WARNING AND EMISSION MAINTENENCE REMINDER LAMPS; CHIMES AND SPEED CONTROL
2	20 AMP YL	BACK-UP LAMPS, A/C FAN AND CLUTCH RELAY, HEATED REAR WINDOW SWITCH, REAR SEAT HEATER AND A/C AND OVERHEAD CONSOLE	14	20 AMP YL	REAR WASH WIPE AND LIFTGATE RELEASE ELECTRONIC MODULE (MANUAL TRANSMISSION)
3	30 AMP C/BRKR SILVER CAN	POWER WINDOW MOTORS	15	10 AMP RD	UNDERSEAT STORAGE, LOWER CONSOLE, DOME, CARGO AND COURTESY LAMPS, TIME DELAY RELAY AND VANITY MIRRORS
4	30 AMP LG	A/C, OR HEATER BLOWER MOTOR	16	20 AMP YL	SPOTLIGHT
5	20 AMP YL	PARK, TAIL, SIDE MARKER AND LICENSE LAMPS; CLOCK, RADIO AND OVERHEAD CONSOLE DISPLAY INTENSITY			
6	20 AMP YL	STOP, DOME, CARGO, VANITY MIRROR, IGNITION SWITCH, DOOR COURTESY, READING, AND UNDERSEAT STORAGE LAMPS; IGNITION SWITCH LAMP TIME DELAY RELAY			
7	25 AMP NAT	CONSOLE AND EMISSION MAINTENANCE REMINDER LAMPS; HORNS, CIGAR LIGHTER, CLOCK AND RADIO MEMORY, CHIMES AND PREMIUM SPEAKER POWER AMPLIFIER FEED			
8	30 AMP C/BRKR SILVER CAN	POWER DOOR LOCKS, SEATS AND MIRRORS			
9	10 AMP RD	RADIO			
10	20 AMP YL	TURN SIGNAL LAMPS AND VAN CONVERSION RELAY			
11	20 AMP YL	WINDSHIELD WIPER AND WASHERS			
12	4 AMP PK	CLUSTER, A/C AND HEATER CONTROL, SWITCH TITLE, ASH RECEIVER, RADIO, CIGAR LIGHTER, OVERHEAD CONSOLE, REAR SEAT HEATER AND A/C SWITCH LAMPS			

AMPS	FUSE	COLOR CODE
3	VT	VIOLET
4	PK	PINK
5	TN	TAN
10	RD	RED
20	YL	YELLOW
25	NAT	NATURAL
30	LG	LIGHT GREEN

Typical fuse block

REPLACEMENT

1. Disconnect the negative battery cable.
2. Cut off the remaining portion of the blown fusible link flush with the multiple connection insulator. Take care not to cut any of the other fusible links.
3. Carefully remove about one inch of insulation from the main harness wire at a point one inch away from the connection insulator.
4. Remove one inch of insulation from the replacement fusible link wire and wrap the exposed area around the main harness wire at the point where the insulation was removed.

5. Heat the splice with a high temperature soldering gun and apply resin type solder until it runs freely. Remove the soldering gun and confirm that a "bright" solder joint has been made. Resolder if "cold" (dull) joint.
6. Cut the other end of the fusible link off at a point just behind the small single wire insulator. Strip one inch of insulation from fusible link and connection wires. Wrap and solder.
7. After the connections have cooled, wrap the splices with at least three layers of electrical tape.

Troubleshooting Basic Lighting Problems

Problem	Cause	Solution
Lights		
One or more lights don't work, but others do	• Defective bulb(s) • Blown fuse(s) • Dirty fuse clips or light sockets • Poor ground circuit	• Replace bulb(s) • Replace fuse(s) • Clean connections • Run ground wire from light socket housing to car frame
Lights burn out quickly	• Incorrect voltage regulator setting or defective regulator • Poor battery/alternator connections	• Replace voltage regulator • Check battery/alternator connections
Lights go dim	• Low/discharged battery • Alternator not charging • Corroded sockets or connections • Low voltage output	• Check battery • Check drive belt tension; repair or replace alternator • Clean bulb and socket contacts and connections • Replace voltage regulator
Lights flicker	• Loose connection • Poor ground • Circuit breaker operating (short circuit)	• Tighten all connections • Run ground wire from light housing to car frame • Check connections and look for bare wires
Lights "flare"—Some flare is normal on acceleration—if excessive, see "Lights Burn Out Quickly"	• High voltage setting	• Replace voltage regulator
Lights glare—approaching drivers are blinded	• Lights adjusted too high • Rear springs or shocks sagging • Rear tires soft	• Have headlights aimed • Check rear springs/shocks • Check/correct rear tire pressure
Turn Signals		
Turn signals don't work in either direction	• Blown fuse • Defective flasher • Loose connection	• Replace fuse • Replace flasher • Check/tighten all connections
Right (or left) turn signal only won't work	• Bulb burned out • Right (or left) indicator bulb burned out • Short circuit	• Replace bulb • Check/replace indicator bulb • Check/repair wiring
Flasher rate too slow or too fast	• Incorrect wattage bulb • Incorrect flasher	• Flasher bulb • Replace flasher (use a variable load flasher if you pull a trailer)
Indicator lights do not flash (burn steadily)	• Burned out bulb • Defective flasher	• Replace bulb • Replace flasher
Indicator lights do not light at all	• Burned out indicator bulb • Defective flasher	• Replace indicator bulb • Replace flasher

Troubleshooting Basic Turn Signal and Flasher Problems

Most problems in the turn signals or flasher system, can be reduced to defective flashers or bulbs, which are easily replaced. Occasionally, problems in the turn signals are traced to the switch in the steering column, which will require professional service.

F = Front   R = Rear   ● = Lights off   ○ = Lights on

Problem		Solution
Turn signals light, but do not flash		• Replace the flasher
No turn signals light on either side		• Check the fuse. Replace if defective. • Check the flasher by substitution • Check for open circuit, short circuit or poor ground
Both turn signals on one side don't work		• Check for bad bulbs • Check for bad ground in both housings
One turn signal light on one side doesn't work		• Check and/or replace bulb • Check for corrosion in socket. Clean contacts. • Check for poor ground at socket
Turn signal flashes too fast or too slow		• Check any bulb on the side flashing too fast. A heavy-duty bulb is probably installed in place of a regular bulb. • Check the bulb flashing too slow. A standard bulb was probably installed in place of a heavy-duty bulb. • Check for loose connections or corrosion at the bulb socket
Indicator lights don't work in either direction		• Check if the turn signals are working • Check the dash indicator lights • Check the flasher by substitution

One indicator light doesn't light		• On systems with 1 dash indicator:
		    See if the lights work on the same side. Often the filaments have been reversed in systems combining stoplights with taillights and turn signals.
		    Check the flasher by substitution
		• On systems with 2 indicators:
		    Check the bulbs on the same side
		    Check the indicator light bulb
		    Check the flasher by substitution

Troubleshooting Basic Dash Gauge Problems

Problem	Cause	Solution
Coolant Temperature Gauge		
Gauge reads erratically or not at all	• Loose or dirty connections • Defective sending unit	• Clean/tighten connections • Bi-metal gauge: remove the wire from the sending unit. Ground the wire for an instant. If the gauge registers, replace the sending unit.
	• Defective gauge	• Magnetic gauge: disconnect the wire at the sending unit. With ignition ON gauge should register COLD. Ground the wire; gauge should register HOT.
Ammeter Gauge—Turn Headlights ON (do not start engine). Note reaction		
Ammeter shows charge Ammeter shows discharge Ammeter does not move	• Connections reversed on gauge • Ammeter is OK • Loose connections or faulty wiring • Defective gauge	• Reinstall connections • Nothing • Check/correct wiring • Replace gauge
Oil Pressure Gauge		
Gauge does not register or is inaccurate	• On mechanical gauge, Bourdon tube may be bent or kinked	• Check tube for kinks or bends preventing oil from reaching the gauge
	• Low oil pressure	• Remove sending unit. Idle the engine briefly. If no oil flows from sending unit hole, problem is in engine.
	• Defective gauge	• Remove the wire from the sending unit and ground it for an instant with the ignition ON. A good gauge will go to the top of the scale.
	• Defective wiring	• Check the wiring to the gauge. If it's OK and the gauge doesn't register when grounded, replace the gauge.
	• Defective sending unit	• If the wiring is OK and the gauge functions when grounded, replace the sending unit
All Gauges		
All gauges do not operate	• Blown fuse • Defective instrument regulator	• Replace fuse • Replace instrument voltage regulator
All gauges read low or erratically	• Defective or dirty instrument voltage regulator	• Clean contacts or replace
All gauges pegged	• Loss of ground between instrument voltage regulator and car • Defective instrument regulator	• Check ground • Replace regulator
Warning Lights		
Light(s) do not come on when ignition is ON, but engine is not started	• Defective bulb • Defective wire	• Replace bulb • Check wire from light to sending unit
	• Defective sending unit	• Disconnect the wire from the sending unit and ground it. Replace the sending unit if the light comes on with the ignition ON.
Light comes on with engine running	• Problem in individual system • Defective sending unit	• Check system • Check sending unit (see above)

Troubleshooting the Heater

Problem	Cause	Solution
Blower motor will not turn at any speed	• Blown fuse • Loose connection • Defective ground • Faulty switch • Faulty motor • Faulty resistor	• Replace fuse • Inspect and tighten • Clean and tighten • Replace switch • Replace motor • Replace resistor
Blower motor turns at one speed only	• Faulty switch • Faulty resistor	• Replace switch • Replace resistor
Blower motor turns but does not circulate air	• Intake blocked • Fan not secured to the motor shaft	• Clean intake • Tighten security
Heater will not heat	• Coolant does not reach proper temperature • Heater core blocked internally • Heater core air-bound • Blend-air door not in proper position	• Check and replace thermostat if necessary • Flush or replace core if necessary • Purge air from core • Adjust cable
Heater will not defrost	• Control cable adjustment incorrect • Defroster hose damaged	• Adjust control cable • Replace defroster hose

Troubleshooting Basic Windshield Wiper Problems

Problem	Cause	Solution
Electric Wipers		
Wipers do not operate— Wiper motor heats up or hums	• Internal motor defect • Bent or damaged linkage • Arms improperly installed on linking pivots	• Replace motor • Repair or replace linkage • Position linkage in park and reinstall wiper arms
Wipers do not operate— No current to motor	• Fuse or circuit breaker blown • Loose, open or broken wiring • Defective switch • Defective or corroded terminals • No ground circuit for motor or switch	• Replace fuse or circuit breaker • Repair wiring and connections • Replace switch • Replace or clean terminals • Repair ground circuits
Wipers do not operate— Motor runs	• Linkage disconnected or broken	• Connect wiper linkage or replace broken linkage
Vacuum Wipers		
Wipers do not operate	• Control switch or cable inoperative • Loss of engine vacuum to wiper motor (broken hoses, low engine vacuum, defective vacuum/fuel pump) • Linkage broken or disconnected • Defective wiper motor	• Repair or replace switch or cable • Check vacuum lines, engine vacuum and fuel pump • Repair linkage • Replace wiper motor
Wipers stop on engine acceleration	• Leaking vacuum hoses • Dry windshield • Oversize wiper blades • Defective vacuum/fuel pump	• Repair or replace hoses • Wet windshield with washers • Replace with proper size wiper blades • Replace pump

Drive Train

7

UNDERSTANDING THE MANUAL TRANSMISSION

Because of the way an internal combustion engine breathes, it can produce torque, or twisting force, only within a narrow speed range. Most modern, overhead valve engines must turn at about 2,500 rpm to produce their peak torque. By 4,500 rpm they are producing so little torque that continued increases in engine speed produce no power increases.

The torque peak on overhead camshaft engines is, generally, much higher, but much narrower.

The manual transmission and clutch are employed to vary the relationship between engine speed and the speed of the wheels so that adequate engine power can be produced under all circumstances. The clutch allows engine torque to be applied to the transmission input shaft gradually, due to mechanical slippage. The car can, consequently, be started smoothly from a full stop.

The transmission changes the ratio between the rotating speeds of the engine and the wheels by the use of gears. 4-speed or 5-speed transmissions are most common. The lower gears allow full engine power to be applied to the wheels during acceleration at low speeds.

The clutch drive plate is a thin disc, the center of which is splined to the transmission input shaft. Both sides of the disc are covered with a layer of material which is similar to brake lining and which is capable of allowing slippage without roughness or excessive noise.

The clutch cover is bolted to the engine flywheel and incorporates a diaphragm spring which provides the pressure to engage the clutch. The cover also houses the pressure plate. The driven disc is sandwiched between the pressure plate and the smooth surface of the flywheel when the clutch pedal is released, thus forcing it to turn at the same speed as the engine crankshaft.

The transmission contains a mainshaft which passes all the way through the transmission, from the clutch to the halfshafts. This shaft is separated at one point, so that front and rear portions can turn at different speeds.

Power is transmitted by a countershaft in the lower gears and reverse. The gears of the countershaft mesh with gears on the mainshaft, allowing power to be carried from one to the other. All the countershaft gears are integral with that shaft, while several of the mainshaft gears can either rotate independently of the shaft or be locked to it. Shifting from one gear to the next causes one of the gears to be freed from rotating with the shaft and locks another to it. Gears are locked and unlocked by internal dog clutches which slide between the center of the gear and the shaft. The forward gears usually employ synchronizers; friction members which smoothly bring gear and shaft to the same speed before the toothed dog clutches are engaged.

The clutch is operating properly if:

1. It will stall the engine when released with the vehicle held stationary.

2. The shift lever can be moved freely between 1st and reverse gears when the vehicle is stationary and the clutch disengaged.

A clutch pedal free-play adjustment is incorporated in the linkage. If there is about 1-2″ (25-50mm) of motion before the pedal begins to release the clutch, it is adjusted properly. Inadequate free-play wears all parts of the clutch releasing mechanisms and may cause slippage. Excessive free-play may cause inadequate release and hard shifting of gears.

Some clutches use a hydraulic system in place of mechanical linkage. If the clutch fails to release, fill the clutch master cylinder with fluid to the proper level and pump the clutch pedal to fill the system with fluid. Bleed the system in the same way as a brake system. If leaks are located, tighten loose connections or overhaul the master or slave cylinder as necessary.

Front wheel drive cars do not have conventional rear axles or drive shafts. Instead, power is transmitted from the engine to a transaxle, or a combination of transmission and drive axle, in one unit. Both the transmission and drive axle accomplish the same function as their counterparts in a front engine/rear drive axle design. The difference is in the location of the components.

In place of a conventional driveshaft, a front-wheel-drive design uses two driveshafts, sometimes called halfshafts, which couple the drive axle portion of the transaxle to the wheels. Universal joints or constant velocity joints are used just as they would in a rear-wheel drive design.

Manual Transaxle

Identification

Three manual transaxles, built by Chrysler, are used; a 4-speed, A-460 and two 5-speeds, A-520 and A-525. The transmission and differential are contained together in a single die-cast aluminum case. All of the transmissions are fully synchronized in all gears. Dexron® II automatic transmission type fluid (models through 1986) or 5W-30 motor oil (1987 and later models) is used for lubrication. The transaxle model, build date and final drive ratio are stamped on a tag that is attached to the top of the transaxle. Always give the tag information when odering parts for the unit.

Adjustments

SHIFT LINKAGE

NOTE: *If a hard shifting situation is experienced, determine if the cables are binding and need replacement, or if a linkage adjustment is necessary. Disconnect both cables at the transaxle and move the selector through the various positions. If the selector moves freely an adjustment may be all that is necessary; if not, cable replacement might be indicated.*

1. Working over the left front fender, unscrew the lock pin, from the transaxle selector shaft housing.

2. Reverse the lock pin so that the long end faces down and insert into the same threaded hole it was removed from. Push the selector shaft into the selector housing while inserting the pin. A hole in the selector shaft will align with the lock pin, allowing the pin to be threaded into the housing. This will lock the selector shaft into the neutral position.

3. From inside the vehicle, remove the gear-

shift knob by pulling straight up. Remove the reverse pull up ring by first removing the retaining nut and then pull the ring up and off of the lever.

4. Remove the shift lever boot. Remove the console.

5. For models built through 1987: Fabricate two adjusting lock pins out of $^{3}/_{16}$" rod. Total length of the pins should be five inches with a hook shaped on one end.

6. Loosen the selector and cross-over cable end adjusting/retainer bolts. Be sure the transaxle end of the cables are connected.

7. Install one adjusting lock pin on the side of the lever bracket in hole provided while moving lever slightly to help alignment. Install the other lock pin at the rear of the lever bracket (cross-over cable). Be sure that both cable end pieces are free to move.

8. After pins are inserted, the cable ends will be positioned to the correct adjustment point.

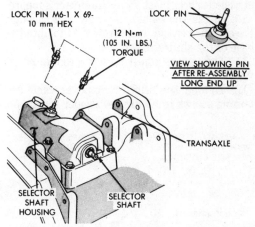

Transaxle pinned in the 1–2/neutral position to adjust the gearshift linkage—MT

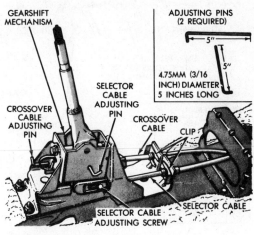

Cable adjusting pins—MT

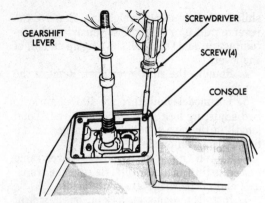

Console removal/installation

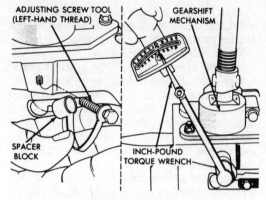

Installing the adjusting screw tool

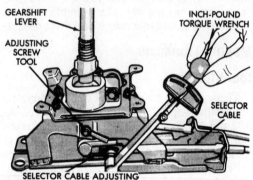

Adjusting the selector cable

SELECTOR CABLE ADJUSTING
SCREW—TORQUE=8 N·m (70 IN. LBS.)

Tighten the adjustment/retainer bolts to 55 inch lbs.

9. On model built in late 1986 and later: Loosen the selector and crossover cable adjusting screws.Remove tne adjusting screw tool and attached spacer block from the shifter support.

10. Install the adjusting screw tool through the attached spacer, and screw the tool into the base of the shifter tower base.

11. Tighten the adjusting screw tool to 20 in. lbs.

12. Tighten the selector/crossover cable retaining screws to 55 in. lbs. Proper torque on

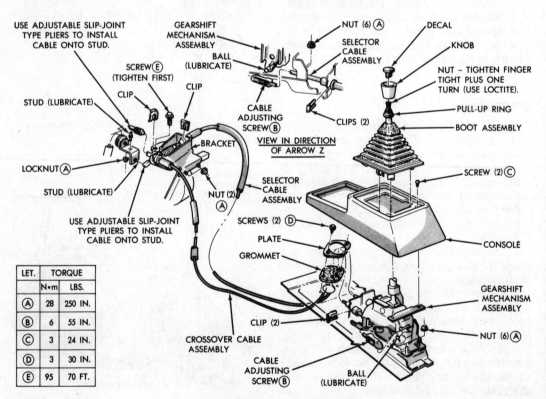

LET.	TORQUE	
	N·m	LBS.
Ⓐ	28	250 IN.
Ⓑ	6	55 IN.
Ⓒ	3	24 IN.
Ⓓ	3	30 IN.
Ⓔ	95	70 FT.

Cable operated gearshift linkage—MT

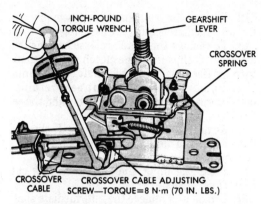

Adjusting the cross-over cable

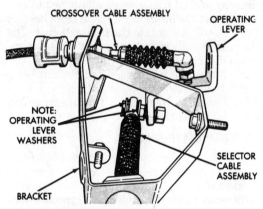

Cable connection at the transaxle

the selector/crossover cable bracket is very important for proper operation.

13. Remove the adjusting screw tool and attach it to the bracket.

14. Check the gearshift cables for proper connection to the transaxle.

15. Install console and remainder of the removed parts.

16. Remove the selector housing lock pin at the transaxle and install it in the reversed position (see Step 1). Tighten the lock pin to 105 inch lbs. check gear shift operation.

Back-up Light Switch

The back-up light switch is located at the upper left side of the transaxle case. The switch is screwed into the transaxle and serviced by replacement. No adjustment is possible.

Transaxle

REMOVAL AND INSTALLATION

NOTE: *Transaxle removal does not require engine removal.*

1. Disconnect the negative battery cable from the battery.

2. Install a sling or lifting bracket to the No. 4 cylinder exhaust manifold mounting bolt (through 1987), or the the battery ground strap bolt (1988 and later). Place an engine support device across the engine compartment and connect to the sling. Tighten until slight upward pressure is applied to the engine.

3. Disconnect the gearshift operating control from the transaxle selector lever. Disconnect the throttle control cable, if automatic.

4. Loosen the wheel lug nuts slightly. Raise and support the front of the vehicle.

5. Remove both front wheel and tire assemblies. Remove the left front engine splash shield. Drain the fluid from the transaxle.

6. Remove the left front mount from the transaxle. Remove the speedometer cable adapter and pinion from the transaxle.

7. Disconnect the front sway bar. Disconnect the anti-rotational link (anti-hop damper) from the crossmember bracket, do not remove the bracket fom the transaxle. Remove both lower ball joint-to-steering knuckle mounting bolts. Pry the ball joint from the steering knuckle. Remove the halfshaft from the drive wheel hub.

8. Remove the halfshafts from the differential.

9. If equipped with an automatic transaxle, remove the converter access cover. Mark the torque converter and driveplate for installation reference. Remove the access plug in the right front splash shield, turn the engine with proper tool to place the converter mounting bolts in position for removal. Remove bolts.

10. If automatic, remove the neutral safety switch connector.

11. Remove the engine mount bracket from the front crossover.

12. Remove the front mount insulator through bolt. Place a suitable floor jack or transmission jack under the transaxle and raise to gently support.

13. Remove the top bell housing bolts.

14. Remove the left engine mount at rear cover plate. Remove the starter motor.

15. Secure the transaxle to the jack and re-

Support fixture installed

move the lower bell housing bolts. Check that all transaxle support mounts or through bolts are removed. Slide the jack and transaxle away from the engine and lower assembly. If an automatic, push the convertor back on transaxle shaft and secure in position with wire.

16. To install the transaxle; make two locating pins for extra same thread bolts that are slightly longer than the mounting bolts. Cut the heads off with a hacksaw, remove any burrs or sharp edges with a file. Install the bolts into the rear of the engine and guide the transaxle over them. After the transaxle is in position, remove the guide bolts and install mounting bolts.

17. Raise the transaxle into position (align the converter to flexplate or mainshaft to clutch disc) and slide it over the locating pins. Install the top bell housing bolts.

18. Install the front mount insulator through bolt. Install the left engine mount and the starter motor.

19. Connect the converter mounting bolts and neutral safety switch harnesss if automatic. Install the halfshafts (halfshafts).

20. Connect the swaybar and anti-hop/rotation link. Install the front wheels and lower the vehicle.

21. Install the speedometer drive and cable. Connect the throttle and shift linkage. Remove the engine support and connect the negative battery cable. Fill the transaxle with the correct lubrication fluid.

A-460 4-Speed Overhaul

TRANSAXLE CASE DISASSEMBLY

1. Remove the transaxle from the vehicle and position on suitable holding fixture.
2. Remove the differential cover bolts and the stud nuts, then remove the cover.
3. Remove the differential bearing retainer bolts.
4. Using tool No. L-4435 or equivalent spanner, rotate the differential bearing retainer to remove it.
5. Remove the extension housing bolts, differential assembly and extension housing.
6. Unbolt and remove the selector shaft housing.
7. Remove the stud nuts and the bolts from the rear end cover then pry off the rear end cover.
8. Remove the large snapring from the intermediate shaft rear ball bearing.
9. Remove the bearing retainer plate by tapping it with a plastic hammer.
10. Remove the 3rd/4th shift fork rail.
11. Remove the reverse idler gear shaft and gear.

12. Remove the input shaft gear assembly and the intermediate shaft gear assembly.
13. To remove the clutch release bearing, remove the E-clips from the clutch release shaft, then disassemble the clutch shaft components.
14. Remove the input shaft seal retainer bolts, the seal, the retainer assembly and the select shim.
15. Remove the reverse shift lever E-clip and flat washer and disassemble the reverse shift lever components.
16. Press the input shaft front bearing cup from the transaxle case.
17. Unbolt and remove the intermediate shaft front bearing retaining strap.
18. Remove the intermediate shaft front bearing and oil feeder using a bearing puller.
19. Press the intermediate shaft front bearing with the oil feeder into the transaxle case. The bearing identification letters must be facing upward during installation.
20. Install the intermediate shaft front bearing retaining strap.
21. Press the input shaft front bearing cup into the transaxle case.

INTERMEDIATE SHAFT

NOTE: *The 1st/2nd, the 3rd/4th shift forks are interchangeable, however, the synchronizer stop rings are not. The 1st and 2nd synchronizer stop rings have a larger diameter than the other stop rings.*

1. Remove the intermediate shaft rear bearing snapring.
2. Remove the intermediate shaft rear bearing with a bearing puller.
3. Remove the 3rd/4th synchronizer hub snapring.
4. Matchmark then remove the 3rd/4th synchronizer hub and the 3rd speed gear using a puller.
5. Install the 1st speed gear thrust washer, 1st speed gear, stop ring and 1-2 synchronizer assembly
6. Install the 1-2 synchronizer snapring.
7. Install the 2nd speed gear and stop ring.
8. Install the retaining ring and split thrust washer. Install the 3rd speed gear and the 3-4 synchronizer. Install the hub snapring.
9. Install the intermediate shaft rear bearing and retaining snapring.
10. Install the intermediate shaft front bearing.

NOTE: *Pay attention to the following when servicing the intermediate shaft: When assembling the intermediate shaft, make sure the speed gears turn freely and have a minimum of 0.076mm endplay. When installing the 1st speed gear thrust washer make sure the chamfered edge is facing the pinion gear.*

When installing the 1st/2nd synchronizer make sure the relief faces the 2nd speed gear. Use an arbor press to install the intermediate shaft rear bearing, the 3rd/4th synchronizer hub and the 3rd speed gear. When installing the 3-4 synchronizer hub and 3rd speed gear, index the snapring 90 degrees to the split washer. During the installation of synchronizer ring assemblies, make sure that all the matchmarks are aligned.

SELECTOR SHAFT HOUSING

1. Remove the snapring from the selector shaft boot and remove the boot.
2. Pry the shaft oil seal from the selector shaft housing.
3. With a small prybar positioned against the gearshift selector, compress the crossover and push the E-clip from the selector shaft. Remove the E-clip to release the selector shaft.
4. Withdraw the selctor shaft from the selector housing.
5. Remove the plate stop retaining bolts and remove the stop.
6. Disassemble the selector shaft housing components.
7. Assemble the selector shaft housing components in the reverse order of removal. Use a new back-up lamp switch gasket if needed.
8. Install the plate stop with the retaining bolts.
9. Insert the selector shaft into the housing.
10. Compress the gearshift selector and install the E-clip.
11. Clean the bore and drive a new oil seal into the housing using the proper tool.
12. Place the boot onto the shaft and retain with the snapring.

DIFFERENTIAL BEARING RETAINER

1. Pry the oil seal from the retainer.
2. Remove the retainer cup with a pulller. Be careful not to damage the oil baffle and the select shim .
3. Remove the oil baffle and the select shim from the retainer cup.
4. Drive the oil baffle and select shim into the retainer cup using the proper tool.
5. Drive the retainer cup into the retainer using the proper tool.
6. Drive in a new retainer oil seal.

EXTENSION HOUSING

1. Pry the oil seal from the extension housing.
2. Pull the extension cup from the extension housing using the proper tool.
3. Remove the O-ring and oil baffle from the housing.

4. Install a new O-ring into the groove on the outside of the housing.
5. Press the oil baffle in the housing using the proper tool.
6. Press the bearing cup into the extension housing using the proper tool.
7. Install a new housing oil seal.

INPUT SHAFT

1. Remove the input shaft rear and front bearing cones using a suitable puller.
2. Mount the bearing retainer plate on wood blocks and press the input shaft rear bearing cup from the plate.
3. Before pressing in the bearing cup, bolt the support plate onto the retainer plate.
4. With the support plate in place, press the bearing cup into the retainer plate.
5. Press the front and rear bearing cones onto the input shaft using the proper tool.

Bearing Endplay Adjustment

Shim thickness calculation and endplay adjustment need only be done if any of the following parts are replaced: transaxle case, input shaft seal retainer, bearing retainer plate, rear end cover, input shaft or input shaft bearings.

If any of the above ́components were replaced, use the folwing procedure to adjust the bearing preload and proper bearing turning torque.

1. Select a gauging shim which will give 0.025-0.250mm of endplay.
NOTE: *Measure the original shim from the input shaft seal retainer and select a shim 0.25mm thinner than the original for the gauging shim.*
2. Install the gauging shim on the bearing cup and the input shaft seal retainer.
3. Alternately tighten the input shaft seal retainer bolts until the retainer is bottomed against the case. Torque the bolts to 21 ft. lbs.
NOTE: *The input shaft seal retainer is used to draw the input shaft front bearing cup the proper distance into the case bore.*
4. Oil the input shaft bearings with A.T.F. (1984-87) or SAE 5W-30 engine oil (1988-89) and install the input shaft in the case. Install the bearing retainer plate with the input shaft rear bearing cup pressed in and the end cover installed. Torque all bolts and nuts to 21 ft. lbs.
5. Position the dial indicator to check the input shaft endplay. Apply moderate load, by hand, to the input shaft splines. Push toward the rear while rotating the input shaft back and forth a number of times and to settle out the bearings. Zero the dial indicator. Pull the input shaft toward the front while rotating the input shaft back and forth a number of times to settle out the bearings. Record the endplay.

6. The shim required for proper bearing preload is the total of the gauging shim thickness, plus endplay, plus (constant) preload of 0.050-0.076mm. Combine shims, if necessary, to obtain a shim within 0.04mm of the required shim.

7. Remove the input shaft seal retainer and gauging shim. Install the shim(s) selected in Step 6 and install the input shaft seal retainer with a $\frac{1}{16}$" bead of R.T.V. sealant.

NOTE: *Keep R.T.V. sealant out of the oil slot.*

8. Tighten the input shaft seal retainer bolts to 21 ft. lbs.

NOTE: *The input shaft seal retainer is used to draw the input shaft front bearing cup the proper distance into the case bore.*

9. Using special tool L-4508 and an inch lb. torque wrench, check the input shaft turning torque. The turning torque should be 1-5 inch lbs. for new bearings or a minimum of 1 inch lb. for used bearings. If the turning torque is too high, install a 0.04mm thinner shim. If the turning torque is too low, install a 0.04mm thicker shim.

10. Check the input shaft turning torque. Repeat Step 9 until the proper bearing turning torque is obtained.

DIFFERENTIAL

1. Remove the bearing cone from the differential case.

2. Remove the ring gear bolts and separate the gear from the differential case. The ring gear bolts are epoxy patch type bolts and not to be reused.

3. Using a steel punch and hammer, knock the pinion shaft split pin from the ring gear and differential case.

4. Withdraw the pinion shaft(s) from the differential case.

5. Rotate the side gears to align them with the case opening and remove the thrust washers, side gears and pinion gears.

NOTE: *Shim thickness calculation and bearing preload adjustment need only be done if any of the following parts are re-placed: transaxle case, input shaft seal retainer, bearing retainer plate, rear end cover, input shaft or input shaft bearings. If any of the those components were replaced, refer to the appropriate section to adjust the bearing preload, proper bearing turning torque or side gear endplay.*

1. In their original order, install the side gears, pinion gears and pinion gear washers.

2. Insert the pinion shaft(s) into the differential case making sure that the hole in the shaft is aligned with the roll pin opening in the case.

3. Insert the pinion shaft roll pin(s) into the notched opening(s) on the side of the differential case and drive them into place.

4. Connect the ring gear to the differential case using new bolts. Torque the bolts in a criss-cross pattern to the proper specification.

5. Attach special tool L-4410 to a suitable extension handle and press the bearing cone onto the diffential case.

6. Refer to the appropriate section to check and adjust the bearing preload, if necessary.

Bearing Preload Adjustment Procedure

1. Remove the bearing cup and existing shim from the differential bearing retainer.

2. Select a gauging shim which will give 0.025-0.250mm endplay.

NOTE: *Measure the original shim from the differentail bearing retainer and select a shim 0.38mm thinner than the original for the gauging shim.*

3. Install the gauging shim in the differential bearing retainer and press in the bearing cup. Installation of the oil baffle is not necessary when checking differential assembly endplay.

4. Lubricate the differential bearings with A.T.F. (1984-87) or SAE 5W-30 engine oil (1988-89) and install the differential assemby in the transaxle case.

5. Inspect the extension housing for damage and replace it as necessary. Apply a $\frac{1}{16}$" bead of RTV sealant to the extension flange. Install the extension housing and differential bearing retainer. Tighten the bolts to 21 ft. lbs.

1. Selector shaft	12. Detent selector	23. Insert 5th speed
2. Snap ring	13. Retainer clip	24. 5th speed shift rail
3. Seal	14. Crossover spring	25. Pin
4. Seal	15. Reverse shift lever and plate	26. Shifter
5. Housing	16. Blocker	27. Pin
6. 1st/2nd shift adjusting plug	17. 5th speed load spring	28. Shifter 5th speed fork
7. Backup light switch	18. Pin	29. 3rd and 4th shift fork
8. Gasket	19. Spring stop plate	30. Insert 3rd and 4th speed
9. Gearshift fork stop lever and plate	20. Operating lever	31. 1st and 2nd shift fork
10. Mounting bolt	21. Set screw	32. Insert 1st and 2nd speed
11. Selector stop pin	22. Fork w/inserts for 5th gear	33. Pin

Transaxle internal controls

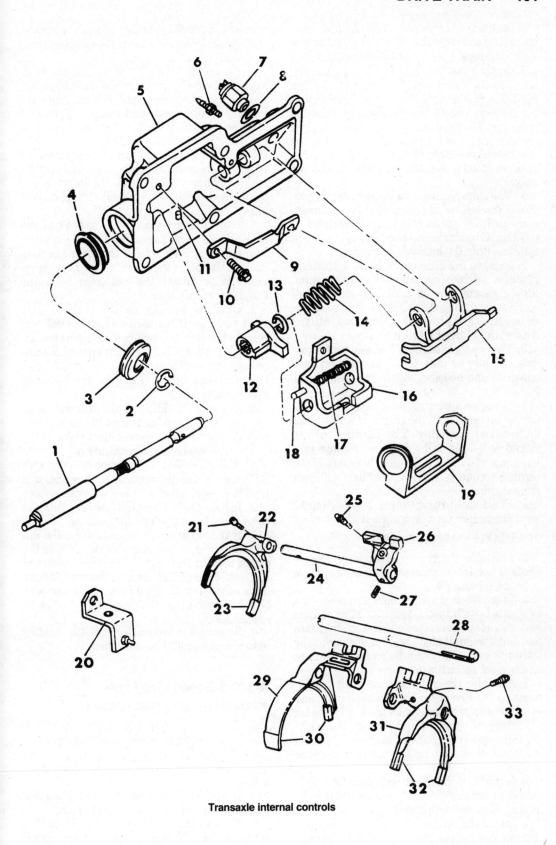

Transaxle internal controls

6. Position the transaxle with the bell housing facing down on the workbench and secure with C-clamps. Position the dial indicator.

7. Apply a medium load to the ring gear, by hand, in the downward direction while rolling the differential assembly back and forth a number of times to settle the bearings. Zero the dial indicator. To obtain endplay readings, apply a medium load upward by hand while rolling the differential assembly back and forth a number of times to settle out the bearings. Record the endplay.

8. The shim required for proper bearing preload is the total of the gauging shim thickness, plus endplay, plus (constant) preload of 0.25mm. Combine shims if necessary, to obtain a shim within 0.05mm of the shim(s).

9. Remove the differential bearing retainer. Remove the bearing cup and gauging shim. Properly install the oil baffle. Be sure the oil baffle is not damaged. Install the shim(s) selected in Step 8 and press the bearing cup into the differential bearing retainer.

10. Using a $\frac{1}{16}''$ bead of R.T.V. sealant for gaskets, install the differential bearing retainer and extension housing. Tighten the bolts to 21 ft. lbs.

11. Using an appropriate tool and an inch lb. torque wrench, check the turning torque of the differential assembly. The turning torque should be 9-14 inch lbs. for new bearings or a minimum of 6 inch lbs. for used bearings. If the turning torque is too low, install a 0.05mm thicker shim.

12. Check the turning torque. Repeat Step 11 until the proper turning torque is obtained.

TRANSAXLE CASE ASSEMBLY

1. Assemble the reverse shift lever components to the transaxle case and lock it in place with the E-clip.

2. Clean the input shaft bore and press in a new oil seal with special tool C-4674 or equivalent. Place the select shim into the retainer race and bolt the input shaft seal retainer onto the transaxle case. The drain hole on the retainer sleeve must be facing downward.

3. Assemble the clutch release shaft components in the reverse order of disassembly and secure the release lever with the E-clip. Insert the release shaft spline end through the bushing and engage it with the release shaft fork. Install the E-clip on the shaft groove to secure the shaft.

4. Install the shift fork and shift fork pads onto the intermediate shaft gear set. Install the intermediate and input shaft gear sets.

5. Install the reverse idler gear (with plastic stop) so that the roll pin on the end of the gear shaft aligns with the roll pin notch in the transaxle case. Lock the gear and engage the reverse shift lever. Make sure the plastic stop is firmly seated on the gear.

6. Install the 3-4 shift fork rail into the locating hole above the intermediate shaft assembly.

7. Remove all the excess sealant from the bearing retainer plate and run an $\frac{1}{8}''$ bead of RTV around the plate's seating surface. Keep the RTV away from the bolt holes. Align the locating dowel on the plate with the dowel on the transaxle case and install by tapping the plate with a rubber mallet. Install the intermediate shaft rear bearing snapring once the plate is in place.

8. Clean the excess sealant from the end cover and make sure the oil feeder hole is clear. Run a bead of RTV around the cover's seating surface and place the cover on the bearing retainer plate. Install the end cover bolts and torque to specification.

9. Clean the excess sealant from the selector shaft housing. If the back-up light switch was removed, install the switch with a new gasket. Run a $\frac{1}{16}''$ bead of RTV sealant around the cover's seating surface and install the housing with the housing bolts. Torque the bolts to specification.

10. Connect the differential to the extension housing. Use a new extension housing O-ring seal. Attach the housing with the housing bolts and torque the bolts to specification.

11. Seal the differential bearing retainer with RTV and tighten the retainer with special tool L-4435 or equivalent spanner wrench.

12. Install the differential bearing retainer bolts and torque them to specifcation.

13. If the magnet was removed from the differential cover, install it at this time. Clean the excess sealant from the differential cover and run a $\frac{1}{8}''$ bead of RTV around the cover's seating surface. Install the differential cover with the cover bolts. Torque the bolts to specification.

14. Remove the transaxle from the holding fixture and install it in the vehicle.

A-520 5-Speed Overhaul
TRANSAXLE CASE DISASEMBLY

1. Remove the transaxle from the vehicle and position on suitable holding fixture.

2. Remove the extension outer bolts.

3. Remove the differential retainer outer bolts.

4. Remove the differential cover bolts and gently pry the cover from the extension.

5. Remove the extension housing bolts then separate the differential assembly and extension housing. Remove the O-ring seal and clean

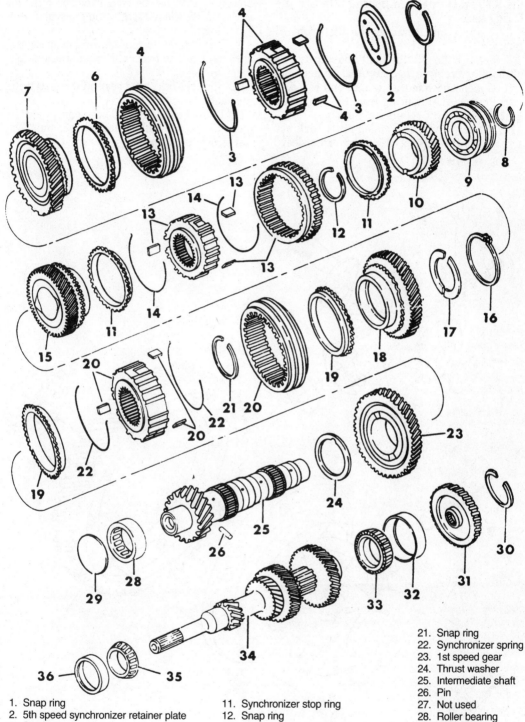

1. Snap ring
2. 5th speed synchronizer retainer plate
3. Spring
4. 5th speed synchronizer
5. not used
6. Stop ring
7. 5th speed gear
8. Snap ring
9. Intermediate shaft bearing
10. 4th speed gear
11. Synchronizer stop ring
12. Snap ring
13. Synchronizer stop ring
14. Synchronizer spring
15. 3rd speed gear
16. Snap ring
17. Thrust washer
18. 2nd speed gear
19. Synchronizer stop ring
20. 1st and 2nd gear synchronizer
21. Snap ring
22. Synchronizer spring
23. 1st speed gear
24. Thrust washer
25. Intermediate shaft
26. Pin
27. Not used
28. Roller bearing
29. Oil feeder
30. Snap ring
31. 5th speed gear
32. Bearing cup
33. Bearing cone
34. Input shaft
35. Bearing cone
36. Bearing cup

Transaxle gear train

the RTV from extension housing. Discard the O-ring seal.

6. Unbolt and remove the differential retainer.

7. Remove the selector shaft housing assembly bolts and remove the selector shaft housing.

8. Unbolt and remove the rear end cover.

9. Remove the snapring from the 5th speed synchronizer strut retainer plate.

10. Unscrew the 5th speed shift fork set screw. Lift the 5th speed synchronizer sleeve and shift fork off the synchronizer hub. Retrieve the (3) winged struts and top synchronizer spring.

11. Use a puller to remove the 5th speed synchronizer hub. Retrieve the remaining synchronizer spring.

12. Slide the 5th speed gear off the intermediate shaft.

13. Using holding tool 6252 or equivalent, remove the input shaft 5th speed gear nut. This nut is not to be reused.

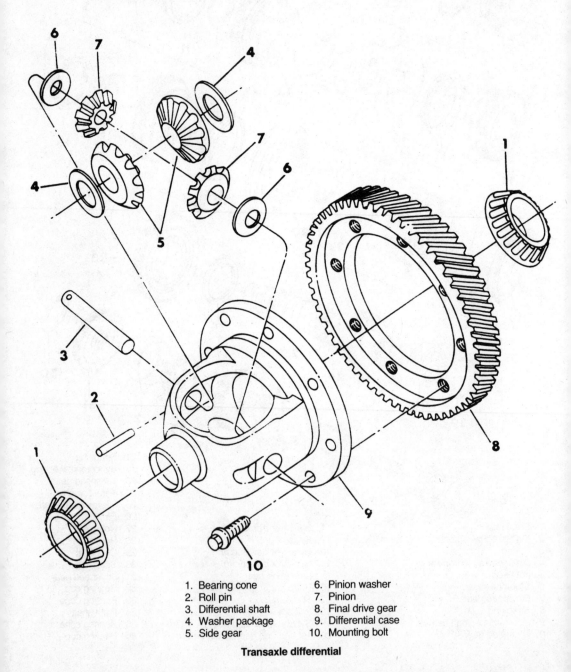

1. Bearing cone	6. Pinion washer
2. Roll pin	7. Pinion
3. Differential shaft	8. Final drive gear
4. Washer package	9. Differential case
5. Side gear	10. Mounting bolt

Transaxle differential

14. Remove the remaining bearing support plate bolts. Gently pry off the bearing support plate.

15. Remove the large snapring from the intermediate shaft rear ball bearing. Then, gently tap the lower surface of the bearing retainer plate with a plastic hammer to free it and lift it off the transaxle case. Clean the RTV sealer from both surfaces.

16. Unscrew the 5th speed shifter guide pin. Do the same with the 1st/2nd shift fork setscrew. Withdraw the 1st/2nd, 3rd/4th shift fork rail.

17. Slide out the reverse idler gear shaft, gear, and plastic stop.

18. Rotate the 3rd/4th shift fork to the left, and the 5th gear shifter to the right. Pull out the 5th speed shift rail. Pull out the input shaft and intermediate shaft assemblies.

19. Remove the 1st/2nd, 3rd/4th, and 5th speed shift forks.

20. To remove the clutch release bearing, remove the E-clips from the clutch release shaft, then disassemble the clutch shaft components.

21. Remove the input shaft seal retainer bolts, the seal, the retainer assembly and the select shim.

22. Remove the reverse shift lever E-clip and flat washer and disassemble the reverse shift lever components.

23. Press the input shaft front bearing cup from the transaxle case.

24. Unbolt and remove the intermediate shaft front bearing retaining strap.

25. Remove the intermediate shaft front bearing and oil feeder using a bearing puller.

26. Press the intermediate shaft front bearing with the oil feeder into the transaxle case. The bearing identification letters must be facing upward during installation.

27. Install the intermediate shaft front bearing retaining strap.

28. Press the input shaft front bearing cup into the transaxle case.

INTERMEDIATE SHAFT

NOTE: *The 1st/2nd, the 3rd/4th shift forks are interchangeable, however, the synchronizer stop rings are not. The 1st and 2nd synchronizer stop rings have a larger diameter than the other stop rings.*

1. Remove the intermediate shaft rear bearing snapring.

2. Remove the intermediate shaft rear bearing with a bearing puller.

3. Remove the 3rd/4th synchronizer hub snapring.

4. Matchmark then remove the 3rd/4th syn-

chronizer hub and the 3rd speed gear using a puller.

5. Remove the 2nd speed gear from the intermediate shaft and remove the 1-2 synchronizer hub snapring.

6. Pull the 1st speed gear and 1-2 synchronizer assembly from the intermediate shaft.

NOTE: *The 1-2 synchronizer assembly components are not interchangable with other synnchronizers.*

7. Install the 1st speed gear thrust washer, 1st speed gear, stop ring and 1-2 synchronizer assembly

8. Install the 1-2 synchronizer snapring.

9. Install the 2nd speed gear and stop ring.

10. Install the retaining ring and split thrust washer. Install the 3rd speed gear and the 3-4 synchronizer. Install the hub snapring.

11. Install the intermediate shaft rear bearing and retaining snapring.

12. Install the intermediate shaft front bearing.

NOTE: *Pay attention to the following when servicing the intermediate shaft: When assembling the intermediate shaft, make sure the speed gears turn freely and have a minimum of 0.076mm endplay. When installing the 1st speed gear thrust washer make sure the chamfered edge is facing the pinion gear. When installing the 1st/2nd synchronizer make sure the relief faces the 2nd speed gear. Use an arbor press to install the intermediate shaft rear bearing, the 3rd/4th synchronizer hub and the 3rd speed gear. When installing the 3-4 synchronizer hub and 3rd speed gear, index the snapring 90 degrees to the split washer. During the installation of synchronizer ring assemblies, make sure that all he matchmarks are aligned.*

SELECTOR SHAFT HOUSING

1. Remove the snapring from the selector shaft boot and remove the boot.

2. Pry the shaft oil seal from the selector shaft housing.

3. With a small prybar positioned against the gearshift selector, compress the crossover and 5th speed load spring and push the E-clip from the selector shaft. Remove the E-clip to release the selector shaft.

4. Withdraw the selctor shaft from the selector housing.

5. Remove the plate stop retaining bolts and remove the stop.

6. Disassemble the selector shaft housing components.

7. Assemble the selector shaft housing components in the reverse order of removal. Use a new back-up lamp switch gasket if needed.

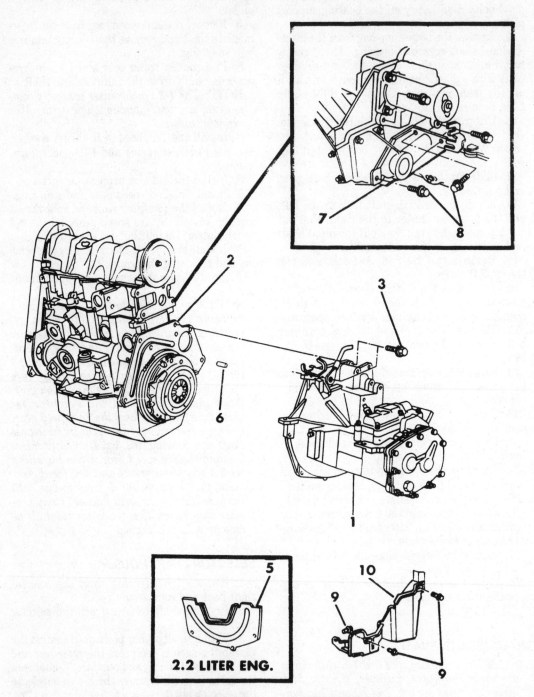

2.2 LITER ENG.

1. Transaxle assembly
2. Upper case cover
3. Retaining bolt
4. Not used
5. Lower case cover
6. Alignment dowel
7. Strut
8. Mounting bolt
9. Mounting bolt
10. Shield

Transaxle to engine mounting

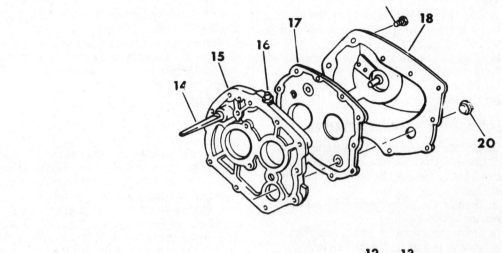

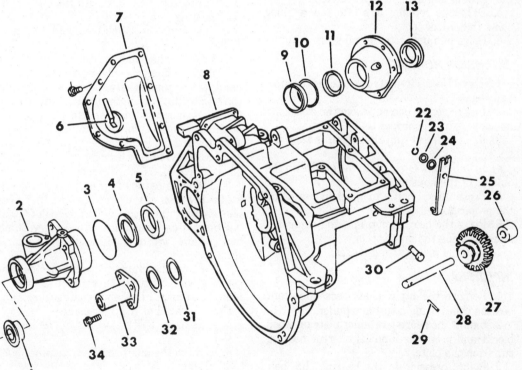

1. Extension seal
2. Extension with bushing
3. Extension O-ring seal
4. Retainer
5. Bearing cup
6. Magnet
7. Differential cover
8. Transaxle case
9. Bearing cup
10. Final drive spacer
11. Oil feed baffle
12. Bearing retainer

13. Seal
14. Oil scoop
15. Retainer plate
16. Vent
17. Bearing plate
18. Oil feed cover
19. not used
20. Drain plug
21. not used
22. Lock clip
23. Wave washer

24. Pivot washer
25. Reverse lever
26. Reverse idler spacer
27. Reverse idler gear
28. Reverse idler gear shaft
29. Spring pin
30. Clevis pin
31. Input shaft spacer
32. Input shaft seal
33. Retainer
34. Retainer bolt

Transaxle case components

8. Install the plate stop with the retaining bolts.

9. Insert the selector shaft into the housing.

10. Compress the gearshift selector and install the E-clip.

11. Clean the bore and drive a new oil seal into the housing using the proper tool.

12. Place the boot onto the shaft and retain with the snapring.

DIFFERENTIAL BEARING RETAINER

1. Pry the oil seal from the retainer.

2. Remove the retainer cup with a pulller. Be careful not to damage the oil baffle and the select shim .

3. Remove the oil baffle and the select shim from the retainer cup.

4. Drive the oil baffle and select shim into the retainer cup using the proper tool.

5. Drive the retainer cup into the retainer using the proper tool.

6. Drive in a new retainer oil seal.

EXTENSION HOUSING

1. Pry the oil seal from the extension housing.

2. Pull the extension cup from the extension housing using the proper tool.

3. Remove the O-ring and oil baffle from the housing.

4. Install a new O-ring into the groove on the outside of the housing.

5. Press the oil baffle in the housing using the proper tool.

6. Press the bearing cup into the extension housing using the proper tool.

7. Install a new housing oil seal.

INPUT SHAFT

1. Remove the input shaft rear and front bearing cones using a suitable puller.

2. Mount the bearing retainer plate on wood blocks and press the input shaft rear bearing cup from the plate.

3. Before pressing in the bearing cup, bolt the support plate onto the retainer plate.

4. With the support plate in place, press the bearing cup into the retainer plate.

5. Press the front and rear bearing cones onto the input shaft using the proper tool.

Bearing Endplay Adjustment

Shim thickness calculation and endplay adjustment need only be done if any of the following parts are replaced: transaxle case, input shaft seal retainer, bearing retainer plate, rear end cover, input shaft or input shaft bearings.

If any of the above components were replaced, use the folwing procedure to adjust the bearing preload and proper bearing turning torque.

1. Select a gauging shim which will give 0.025-0.250mm of endplay.

NOTE: *Measure the original shim from the input shaft seal retainer and select a shim 0.25mm thinner than the original for the gauging shim.*

2. Install the gauging shim on the bearing cup and the input shaft seal retainer.

3. Alternately tighten the input shaft seal retainer bolts until the retainer is bottomed against the case. Torque the bolts to 21 ft. lbs.

NOTE: *The input shaft seal retainer is used to draw the input shaft front bearing cup the proper distance into the case bore.*

4. Oil the input shaft bearings with A.T.F. (1984-87) or SAE 5W-30 engine oil (1988-89) and install the input shaft in the case. Install the bearing retainer plate with the input shaft rear bearing cup pressed in and the support plate installed. Torque all bolts and nuts to 21 ft. lbs.

5. Position the dial indicator to check the input shaft endplay. Apply moderate load, by hand, to the input shaft splines. Push toward the rear while rotating the input shaft back and forth a number of times and to settle out the bearings. Zero the dial indicator. Pull the input shaft toward the front while rotating the input shaft back and forth a number of times to settle out the bearings. Record the endplay.

6. The shim required for proper bearing preload is the total of the gauging shim thickness, plus endplay, plus (constant) preload of 0.050-0.076mm. Combine shims, if necessary, to obtain a shim within 0.04mm of the required shim.

7. Remove the input shaft seal retainer and gauging shim. Install the shim(s) selected in Step 6 and install the input shaft seal retainer with a $^1/_{16}$″ bead of R.T.V. sealant.

NOTE: *Keep R.T.V. sealant out of the oil slot.*

8. Tighten the input shaft seal retainer bolts to 21 ft. lbs.

NOTE: *The input shaft seal retainer is used to draw the input shaft front bearing cup the proper distance into the case bore.*

9. Using special tool L-4508 and an inch lb. torque wrench, check the input shaft turning torque. The turning torque should be 1-5 inch lbs. for new bearings or a minimum of 1 inch lb. for used bearings. If the turning torque is too high, install a 0.04mm thinner shim. If the turning torque is too low, install a 0.04mm thicker shim.

10. Check the input shaft turning torque. Repeat Step 9 until the proper bearing turning torque is obtained.

DIFFERENTIAL

1. Remove the bearing cone from the differential case.

2. Remove the ring gear bolts and separate the gear from the differential case. The ring gear bolts are epoxy patch type bolts and not to be reused.

3. Using a steel punch and hammer, knock the pinion shaft split pin from the ring gear and differential case.

4. Withdraw the pinion shaft(s) from the differential case.

5. Rotate the side gears to align them with the case opening and remove the thrust washers, side gears and pinion gears.

NOTE: *Shim thickness calculation and bearing preload adjustment need only be done if any of the following parts are replaced: transaxle case, input shaft seal retainer, bearing retainer plate, rear end cover, input shaft or input shaft bearings. If any of the those components were replaced, refer to the appropriate section to adjust the bearing preload, proper bearing turning torque or side gear endplay.*

1. In their original order, install the side gears, pinion gears and pinion gear washers. Leave the thrust washer out until after the side gear endplay is adjusted.

2. Insert the pinion shaft(s) into the differential case making sure that the hole in the shaft is aligned with the roll pin opening in the case.

3. Insert the pinion shaft roll pin(s) into the notched opening(s) on the side of the differential case and drive them into place.

4. Connect the ring gear to the differential case using new bolts. Torque the bolts in a criss-cross pattern to the proper specification.

5. Attach special tool L-4410 to a suitable extension handle and press the bearing cone onto the diffential case.

6. Refer to the appropriate section to check and adjust the bearing preload, if necessary. Check the side gear endplay and select the proper dimension thrust washer.

Side Gear Endplay Adjustment

1. Once assembled, rotate the gears 2 complete revolutions in both a clockwise and counterclockwise direction.

2. Install special tool C-4996 on the bearing cone and mount a dial indicator so that the stylus of the dial rests on the surface of the tool.

3. Move one of the side gears up and down by hand and record the endplay.

4. Zero the dial and rotate the side gear in 90 degree increments an repeat Step 3.

5. Use the smallest endplay reading recorded

and shim the side gear to within 0.025-0.330mm. For shimming, 4 select thrust washer sizes are available: 0.8mm, 0.9mm, 1.0mm, and 1.2mm.

6. Repeat Steps 1-4 for the other side gear.

Bearing Preload Adjustment Procedure

1. Remove the bearing cup and existing shim from the differential bearing retainer.

2. Select a gauging shim which will give 0.025-0.250mm endplay.

NOTE: *Measure the original shim from the differentail bearing retainer and select a shim 0.38mm thinner than the original for the gauging shim.*

3. Install the gauging shim in the differential bearing retainer and press in the bearing cup. Installation of the oil baffle is not necessary when checking differential assembly endplay.

4. Lubricate the differential bearings with A.T.F. (1984-87) or SAE 5W-30 engine oil (1988-89) and install the differential assemby in the transaxle case.

5. Inspect the extension housing for damage and replace it as necessary. Apply a $1/16''$ bead of RTV sealant to the extension flange. Install the extension housing and differential bearing retainer. Tighten the bolts to 21 ft. lbs.

6. Position the transaxle with the bell housing facing down on the workbench and secure with C-clamps. Position the dial indicator.

7. Apply a medium load to the ring gear, by hand, in the downward direction while rolling the differential assembly back and forth a number of times to settle the bearings. Zero the dial indicator. To obtain endplay readings, apply a medium load upward by hand while rolling the differential assembly back and forth a number of times to settle out the bearings. Record the endplay.

8. The shim required for proper bearing preload is the total of the gauging shim thickness, plus endplay, plus (constant) preload of 0.25mm. Combine shims if necessary, to obtain a shim within 0.05mm of the shim(s).

9. Remove the differential bearing retainer. Remove the bearing cup and gauging shim. Properly install the oil baffle. Be sure the oil baffle is not damaged. Install the shim(s) selected in Step 8 and press the bearing cup into the differential bearing retainer.

10. Using a $1/16''$ bead of R.T.V. sealant for gaskets, install the differential bearing retainer and extension housing. Tighten the bolts to 21 ft. lbs.

11. Using an appropriate tool and an inch lb. torque wrench, check the turning torque of the differential assembly. The turning torque should be 9-14 inch lbs. for new bearings or a

minimum of 6 inch lbs. for used bearings. If the turning torque is too low, install a 0.05mm thicker shim.

12. Check the turning torque. Repeat Step 11 until the proper turning torque is obtained.

TRANSAXLE CASE ASSEMBLY

1. Assemble the reverse shift lever components to the transaxle case and lock it in place with the E-clip.

2. Clean the input shaft bore and press in a new oil seal with special tool C-4674 or equivalent. Place the select shim into the retainer race and bolt the input shaft seal retainer onto the transaxle case. The drain hole on the retainer sleeve must be facing downward.

3. Assemble the clutch release shaft components in the reverse order of disassembly and secure the release lever with the E-clip. Insert the release shaft spline end through the bushing and engage it with the release shaft fork. Install the E-clip on the shaft groove to secure the shaft.

4. Install the shift forks and shift rails onto the intermediate gear shaft assembly.

5. Install the intermediate and input shaft gear sets into the transaxle case and make sure that the gears are in proper mesh. Once the gear sets are in place, rotate the 5th speed shifter to the right and the 1-2 and 3-4 shift forks to the left.

6. Install the reverse idler gear (with plastic stop) so that the roll pin on the end of the gear shaft aligns with the roll pin notch in the transaxle case. Lock the gear and engage the reverse shift lever. Make sure the plastic stop is firmly seated on the gear.

7. Install the 1-2, 3-4 and 5th speed shift fork rails into their respective locating holes.

8. Install and tighten the 1-2 shift fork set screw and 5th speed selector guide pin.

9. Remove all the excess sealant from the bearing retainer plate and run an 1/8" bead of RTV around the plate's seating surface. Keep the RTV away from the bolt holes. Align the plate with the transaxle case and install it. The plate will align with the oil trough and the 5th speed shift rail. Install the intermediate shaft rear bearing snapring once the plate is in place and seated.

10. Install the bearing support plate with the retaining bolts. Torque the bolts to specification.

11. Install the 5th speed gear onto the input shaft. Install a new gear nut with special holding tool 6252. The holding tool must be used to install the gear nut and the old nut must not be reused. Torque the nut to 190 ft. lbs. and remove the holding tool.

12. Install the intermediate shaft 5th speed gear, synchronizer hub and struts using special tool C-4888 or equivalent gear installer.

13. Position the 5th speed synchronizer sleeve and shift fork over the 5th speed shift rail and install it using the alignment marks for reference. Lock the fork to the rail with the set screw.

14. Install the 5th speed synchronizer strut retainer plate with the snapring.

15. Clean the excess sealant from the end cover and make sure the oil fill plug hole is clear. Run a bead of RTV around the cover's seating surface and place the cover on the bearing retainer plate. Install the end cover bolts and torque to specification.

16. Clean the excess sealant from the selector shaft housing. If the back-up light switch was removed, install the switch with a new gasket. Run a 1/16" bead of RTV sealant around the cover's seating surface and install the housing with the housing bolts. Torque the bolts to specification.

17. Apply RTV sealant to the portion of the differential bearing retainer that bolts to the ring gear to form a gasket.

18. Position the differential in the support saddles.

19. Connect the bearing retainer to the differential with the inner bolts and torque the bolts to specification.

20. Remove the O-ring seal from the extension housing and replace it with a new one. Remove the old sealant from the base of the extension and run a bead of new sealant.

21. Connect the extension to the other side of the differential with the outer bolts. Torque the bolts to specification.

22. Clean the excess sealant from the differential cover and run a 1/8" bead of RTV around the cover's seating surface. Install the differential cover with the cover bolts. Torque the bolts to specification.

23. Install the remaining extension and differential bearing retainer (outer) bolts and torque them to specifcation.

24. Remove the transaxle from the holding fixture and install it in the vehicle.

A-525 Overhaul

CASE DISASSEMBLY

1. Remove the transaxle from the vehicle and position on suitable holding fixture.

2. Remove the extension housing bolts then remove the differential assembly and extension housing.

3. Remove the differential cover bolts, stud nuts and remove the cover.

4. Remove the differential bearing retainer bolts.

5. Using the L-4435 or equivalent spanner wrench, rotate the differential bearing retainer to remove it.

6. Remove the selector shaft housing assembly bolts and remove the selector shaft housing assembly. On 1984-85 transaxles, remove the 5th speed shifter pin bolt and rear end cover fill plug.

7. Unbolt and remove the rear end cover.

8. Using snapring pliers, remove the snapring from the 5th speed synchronizer strut retainer plate to remove it, if installed.

9. Unscrew the 5th speed shift fork set screw. Lift the 5th speed synchronizer sleeve and shift fork off the synchronizer hub. Retrieve the 3 winged struts and top synchronizer spring.

10. Use a puller to remove the 5th speed synchronizer hub. Retrieve the remaining synchronizer spring.

11. Slide the 5th speed gear off the intermediate shaft. Remove the copper colored snapring retaining the 5th speed gear to the input shaft. Using a pulley puller, pull the 5th speed gear off the input shaft.

12. Remove the remaining bearing support plate bolts. Gently pry off the bearing support plate.

13. Remove the large snapring from the intermediate shaft rear ball bearing. Gently tap the lower surface of the bearing retainer plate with a plastic hammer to free it and lift it off the transaxle case. Clean the RTV sealer from both surfaces.

14. Unscrew the 5th speed shifter guide pin. Then, remove it. Do the same with the 1st/2nd shift fork setscrew. Withdraw the 1st/2nd, 3rd/4th shift fork rail.

15. Withdraw the reverse idler gear shaft, gear, and plastic stop.

16. Rotate the 3rd/4th shift fork to the left, and the 5th gear shifter to the right. Pull out the 5th speed shift rail. Withdraw the input shaft and intermediate shaft assemblies.

17. Remove the 1st/2nd, 3rd/4th, and 5th speed shift forks.

18. To remove the clutch release bearing, remove the E-clips from the clutch release shaft, then disassemble the clutch shaft components.

19. Remove the input shaft seal retainer bolts, seal, retainer assembly and the select shim.

20. Remove the reverse shift lever E-clip and flat washer and disassemble the reverse shift lever components.

21. Press the input shaft front bearing cup from the transaxle case.

22. Unbolt and remove the intermediate shaft front bearing retaining strap.

23. Remove the intermediate shaft front bearing and oil feeder using a bearing puller.

24. Press the intermediate shaft front bearing with the oil feeder into the transaxle case. The bearing identification letters must be facing upward during installation.

25. Install the intermediate shaft front bearing retaining strap.

26. Press the input shaft front bearing cup into the transaxle case.

INTERMEDIATE SHAFT

NOTE: *The 1st/2nd, the 3rd/4th shift forks are interchangeable, however, the synchronizer stop rings are not. The 1st and 2nd synchronizer stop rings have a larger diameter than the other stop rings.*

1. Remove the intermediate shaft rear bearing snapring.

2. Remove the intermediate shaft rear bearing with a bearing puller.

3. Remove the 3rd/4th synchronizer hub snapring.

4. Matchmark then remove the 3rd/4th synchronizer hub and the 3rd speed gear using a puller.

NOTE: *The 1-2 synchronizer assembly components are not interchangable with other synchronizers.*

5. Install the 1st speed gear thrust washer, 1st speed gear, stop ring and 1-2 synchronizer assembly

6. Install the 1-2 synchronizer snapring.

7. Install the 2nd speed gear and stop ring.

8. Install the retaining ring and split thrust washer. Install the 3rd speed gear and the 3-4 synchronizer. Install the hub snapring.

9. Install the intermediate shaft rear bearing and retaining snapring.

10. Install the intermediate shaft front bearing.

NOTE: *Pay attention to the following when servicing the intermediate shaft: When assembling the intermediate shaft, make sure the speed gears turn freely and have a minimum of 0.076mm endplay. When installing the 1st speed gear thrust washer make sure the chamfered edge is facing the pinion gear. When installing the 1st/2nd synchronizer make sure the relief faces the 2nd speed gear. Use an arbor press to install the intermediate shaft rear bearing, the 3rd/4th synchronizer hub and 3rd speed gear. When installing the 3-4 synchronizer hub and 3rd speed gear, index the snapring 90 degrees to the split washer. During the installation of synchro-*

nizer ring assemblies, make sure that all he matchmarks are aligned.

SELECTOR SHAFT HOUSING

1. Remove the snapring from the selector shaft boot and remove the boot.
2. Pry the shaft oil seal from the selector shaft housing.
3. With a small prybar positioned against the gearshift selector, compress the crossover and 5th speed load spring and push the E-clip from the selector shaft. Remove the E-clip to release the selector shaft.
4. Withdraw the selctor shaft from the selector housing.
5. Remove the plate stop retaining bolts and remove the stop.
6. Disassemble the selector shaft housing components.
7. Assemble the selector shaft housing components in the reverse order of removal. Use a new back-up lamp switch gasket if needed.
8. Install the plate stop with the retaining bolts.
9. Insert the selector shaft into the housing.
10. Compress the gearshift selector and install the E-clip.
11. Clean the bore and drive a new oil seal into the housing using the proper tool.
12. Place the boot onto the shaft and retain with the snapring.

DIFFERENTIAL BEARING RETAINER

1. Pry the oil seal from the retainer.
2. Remove the retainer cup with a pulller. Be careful not to damage the oil baffle and the select shim .
3. Remove the oil baffle and the select shim from the retainer cup.
4. Drive the oil baffle and select shim into the retainer cup using the proper tool.
5. Drive the retainer cup into the retainer using the proper tool.
6. Drive in a new retainer oil seal.

EXTENSION HOUSING

1. Pry the oil seal from the extension housing.
2. Pull the extension cup from the extension housing using the proper tool.
3. Remove the O-ring and oil baffle from the housing.
4. Install a new O-ring into the groove on the outside of the housing.
5. Press the oil baffle in the housing using the proper tool.
6. Press the bearing cup into the extension housing using the proper tool.
7. Install a new housing oil seal.

INPUT SHAFT

1. Remove the input shaft rear and front bearing cones using a suitable puller.
2. Mount the bearing retainer plate on wood blocks and press the input shaft rear bearing cup from the plate.
3. Before pressing in the bearing cup, bolt the support plate onto the retainer plate.
4. With the support plate in place, press the bearing cup into the retainer plate.
5. Press the front and rear bearing cones onto the input shaft using the proper tool.

Bearing Endplay Adjustment

Shim thickness calculation and endplay adjustment need only be done if any of the following parts are replaced: transaxle case, input shaft seal retainer, bearing retainer plate, rear end cover, input shaft or input shaft bearings.

If any of the above components were replaced, use the folwing procedure to adjust the bearing preload and proper bearing turning torque.

1. Select a gauging shim which will give 0.025-0.250mm of endplay.
NOTE: *Measure the original shim from the input shaft seal retainer and select a shim 0.25mm thinner than the original for the gauging shim.*
2. Install the gauging shim on the bearing cup and the input shaft seal retainer.
3. Alternately tighten the input shaft seal retainer bolts until the retainer is bottomed against the case. Torque the bolts to 21 ft. lbs.
NOTE: *The input shaft seal retainer is used to draw the input shaft front bearing cup the proper distance into the case bore.*
4. Oil the input shaft bearings with A.T.F. (1984-87) or SAE 5W-30 engine oil (1988-89) and install the input shaft in the case. Install the bearing retainer plate with the input shaft rear bearing cup pressed in and the support plate installed. Torque all bolts and nuts to 21 ft. lbs.
5. Position the dial indicator to check the input shaft endplay. Apply moderate load, by hand, to the input shaft splines. Push toward the rear while rotating the input shaft back and forth a number of times and to settle out the bearings. Zero the dial indicator. Pull the input shaft toward the front while rotating the input shaft back and forth a number of times to settle out the bearings. Record the endplay.
6. The shim required for proper bearing preload is the total of the gauging shim thickness, plus endplay, plus (constant) preload of 0.050-0.076mm. Combine shims, if necessary, to obtain a shim within 0.04mm of the required shim.

7. Remove the input shaft seal retainer and gauging shim. Install the shim(s) selected in Step 6 and install the input shaft seal retainer with a $\frac{1}{16}$″ bead of R.T.V. sealant.

NOTE: *Keep R.T.V. sealant out of the oil slot.*

8. Tighten the input shaft seal retainer bolts to 21 ft. lbs.

NOTE: *The input shaft seal retainer is used to draw the input shaft front bearing cup the proper distance into the case bore.*

9. Using special tool L-4508 and an inch lb. torque wrench, check the input shaft turning torque. The turning torque should be 1-5 inch lbs. for new bearings or a minimum of 1 inch lb. for used bearings. If the turning torque is too high, install a 0.04mm thinner shim. If the turning torque is too low, install a 0.04mm thicker shim.

10. Check the input shaft turning torque. Repeat Step 9 until the proper bearing turning torque is obtained.

DIFFERENTIAL

1. Remove the bearing cone from the differential case.

2. Remove the ring gear bolts and separate the gear from the differential case. The ring gear bolts are epoxy patch type bolts and not to be reused.

3. Using a steel punch and hammer, knock the pinion shaft split pin from the ring gear and differential case.

4. Withdraw the pinion shaft(s) from the differential case.

5. Rotate the side gears to align them with the case opening and remove the thrust washers, side gears and pinion gears.

NOTE: *Shim thickness calculation and bearing preload adjustment need only be done if any of the following parts are replaced: transaxle case, input shaft seal retainer, bearing retainer plate, rear end cover, input shaft or input shaft bearings. If any of the those components were replaced, refer to the appropriate section to adjust the bearing preload, proper bearing turning torque or side gear endplay.*

1. In their original order, install the side gears, pinion gears and pinion gear washers.

2. Insert the pinion shaft(s) into the differential case making sure that the hole in the shaft is aligned with the roll pin opening in the case.

3. Insert the pinion shaft roll pin(s) into the notched opening(s) on the side of the differential case and drive them into place.

4. Connect the ring gear to the differential case using new bolts. Torque the bolts in a criss-cross pattern to the proper specification.

5. Attach special tool L-4410 to a suitable extension handle and press the bearing cone onto the diffential case.

6. Refer to the appropriate section to check and adjust the bearing preload, if necessary.

Bearing Preload Adjustment Procedure

1. Remove the bearing cup and existing shim from the differential bearing retainer.

2. Select a gauging shim which will give 0.025-0.250mm endplay.

NOTE: *Measure the original shim from the differentail bearing retainer and select a shim 0.38mm thinner than the original for the gauging shim.*

3. Install the gauging shim in the differential bearing retainer and press in the bearing cup. Installation of the oil baffle is not necessary when checking differential assembly endplay.

4. Lubricate the differential bearings with A.T.F. (1984-87) or SAE 5W-30 engine oil (1988-89) and install the differential assemby in the transaxle case.

5. Inspect the extension housing for damage and replace it as necessary. Apply a $\frac{1}{16}$″ bead of RTV sealant to the extension flange. Install the extension housing and differential bearing retainer. Tighten the bolts to 21 ft. lbs.

6. Position the transaxle with the bell housing facing down on the workbench and secure with C-clamps. Position the dial indicator.

7. Apply a medium load to the ring gear, by hand, in the downward direction while rolling the differential assembly back and forth a number of times to settle the bearings. Zero the dial indicator. To obtain endplay readings, apply a medium load upward by hand while rolling the differential assembly back and forth a number of times to settle out the bearings. Record the endplay.

8. The shim required for proper bearing preload is the total of the gauging shim thickness, plus endplay, plus (constant) preload of 0.25mm. Combine shims if necessary, to obtain a shim within 0.05mm of the shim(s).

9. Remove the differential bearing retainer. Remove the bearing cup and gauging shim. Properly install the oil baffle. Be sure the oil baffle is not damaged. Install the shim(s) selected in Step 8 and press the bearing cup into the differential bearing retainer.

10. Using a $\frac{1}{16}$″ bead of R.T.V. sealant for gaskets, install the differential bearing retainer and extension housing. Tighten the bolts to 21 ft. lbs.

11. Using an appropriate tool and an inch lb. torque wrench, check the turning torque of the differential assembly. The turning torque should be 9-14 inch lbs. for new bearings or a minimum of 6 inch lbs. for used bearings. If the

turning torque is too low, install a 0.05mm thicker shim.

12. Check the turning torque. Repeat Step 11 until the proper turning torque is obtained.

TRANSAXLE CASE ASSEMBLY

1. Assemble the reverse shift lever components to the transaxle case and lock it in place with the E-clip.

2. Clean the input shaft bore and press in a new oil seal with special tool C-4674 or equivalent. Place the select shim into the retainer race and bolt the input shaft seal retainer onto the transaxle case. The drain hole on the retainer sleeve must be facing downward.

3. Assemble the clutch release shaft components in the reverse order of disassembly and secure the release lever with the E-clip. Insert the release shaft spline end through the bushing and engage it with the release shaft fork. Install the E-clip on the shaft groove to secure the shaft.

4. Install the shift forks and shift rails onto the intermediate gear shaft assembly.

5. Install the intermediate and input shaft gear sets into the transaxle case and make sure that the gears are in proper mesh. Once the gear sets are in place, rotate the 5th speed shifter to the right and the 1-2 and 3-4 shift forks to the left.

6. Install the reverse idler gear (with plastic stop) so that the roll pin on the end of the gear shaft aligns with the roll pin notch in the transaxle case. Lock the gear and engage the reverse shift lever. Make sure the plastic stop is firmly seated on the gear.

7. Install the 1-2, 3-4 and 5th speed shift fork rails into their respective locating holes.

8. Install and tighten the 1-2 shift fork set screw and 5th speed selector guide pin.

9. Remove all the excess sealant from the bearing retainer plate and run an 1/8" bead of RTV around the plate's seating surface. Keep the RTV away from the bolt holes. Align the plate with the transaxle case and install it. The plate will align with the oil trough and the 5th speed shift rail. Install the intermediate shaft rear bearing snapring once the plate is in place and seated.

10. Install the bearing support plate with the retaining bolts. Torque the bolts to specification.

11. Install the input shaft 5th speed gear using special tool C-4810 or suitable gear installer. Retain the gear with the snapring.

12. Install the intermediate shaft 5th speed gear, synchronizer hub and struts using special tool C-4888 or equivalent gear installer.

13. Position the 5th speed synchronizer sleeve and shift fork over the 5th speed shift rail and install it. Lock the fork to the rail with the set screw. Install the 5th speed synchronizer strut retainer plate with the snapring.

14. Clean the excess sealant from the end cover and make sure the oil fill plug hole is clear. Run a bead of RTV around the cover's seating surface and place the cover on the bearing retainer plate. Install the end cover bolts and torque to specification.

15. Clean the excess sealant from the selector shaft housing. If the back-up light switch was removed, install the switch with a new gasket. Run a 1/16" bead of RTV sealant around the cover's seating surface and install the housing with the housing bolts. Torque the bolts to specification.

16. Connect the differential to the extension housing. Use a new extension housing O-ring seal. Attach the housing with the housing bolts and torque the bolts to specification.

17. Seal the differential bearing retainer with RTV and tighten the retainer with special tool L-4435 or equivalent spanner wrench.

18. Install the differential bearing retainer bolts and torque them to specifcation.

18. If the magnet was removed from the differential cover, install it at this time. Clean the excess sealant from the differential cover and run a 1/8" bead of RTV around the cover's seating surface. Install the differential cover with the cover bolts. Torque the bolts to specification.

19. Remove the transaxle from the holding fixture and install it in the vehicle.

Halfshafts

The halfshafts used on your vehicle are of three piece construction, and are unequal in length and material composition. A short solid interconnecting shaft is used on the left side and a longer tubular interconnecting shaft is installed on the right side.

The halfshaft assemblies are three piece units. Each shaft has a Tripod joint on the transaxle side, an interconnecting shaft and a Rzeppa joint on the wheel side. The Rzeppa joint mounts a splined stub shaft that connects with the wheel hub. The inner Tripod joint mounts a spring that maintains constant spline engagement with the transaxle. The design enables the halfshaft to be removed without dismantling the transaxle.

REMOVAL AND INSTALLATION

1. Remove the cotter pin, lock and spring washer from the front axle ends.

2. Have a helper apply the service brakes and loosen the front axle hub retaining nut.

3. Raise and support the front of the vehicle on jackstands.

4. Remove the hub nut, washer and wheel assembly. Drain transaxle fluid.

NOTE: *The speedometer drive pinion must be removed from the transaxle housing before the right side driveaxle can be removed. Remove the retaining bolts and lift the pinion with cable connected from the housing.*

5. Remove the clamp bolt that secures the ball joint stud with the steering knuckle.

6. Separate the ball joint from the knuckle by prying downward against the knuckle connecting point and the control arm. Take care not to damage the rubber boot.

7. Separate the outer CV (constant velocity) joint splines from the steering knuckle hub by holding the CV housing and pushing the knuckle out and away. If resistance is encountered, use a brass drift and hammer to gently tap the outer hub end of the axle. Do not pry on the outer wear sleeve of the CV joint.

8. After the outboard end of the drive axle has been removed from the steering knuckle, support the assembly and pull outward on the inner CV joint housing to remove the assembly from the transaxle.

WARNING: *Do not pull on the shaft or the assembly will disconnect. Pull only on the inner CV joint housing.*

9. Remove the halfshaft from under the vehicle and service as necessary.

10. To install the halfshaft; Hold the inner joint assembly by its housing, align and guide the shaft into the transaxle or intermediate shaft assembly.

11. Lubricate the outer wear sleeve and seal with multi-purpose grease. Push the steering knuckle outward and install the splined outer shaft into the drive hub. Install the steering knuckle assembly. Torque the ball joint clamp bolt to 70 ft. lbs. Hub nut (splined shaft nut) torque to 180 ft. lbs. Refill the transaxle with the proper lubrication fluid.

NOTE: *If after install the axle assembly, the inboard boot appears collapsed, vent the boot by inserting a thin round rod between the boot and the shaft. Message the boot until is expands. Install a new clamp to prevent dirt from entering the boot.*

CV-JOINT OVERHAUL

Inner Joint

1. With the halfshaft assembly removed from the vehicle, remove the clamps and boot.

2. Depending on the unit (GKN or Citroen) separate the tripod assembly from the housing as follows: Citroen type: Since the trunion ball rollers are not retained on bearing studs a re-

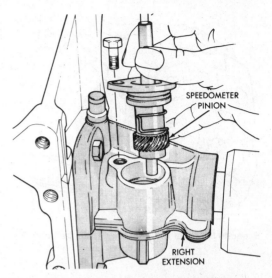
Remove the speedometer pinion from rightside

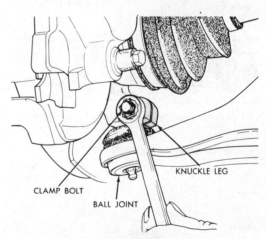
Remove the ball joint to steering knuckle clamp bolt

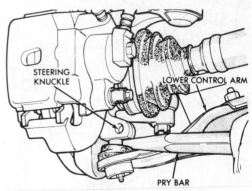
Separate the ball joint from the steering knuckle

taining ring is used to prevent accidental tripod/housing separation, which would allow roller and needle bearings to fall away.

In the case of the spring loaded inner CV-joints, if it weren't for the retaining ring, the

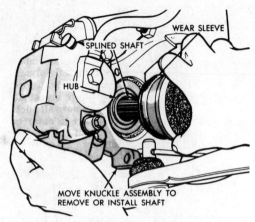

Separate the outer C/V joint shaft from the hub

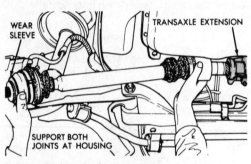

Remove the driveaxle assembly

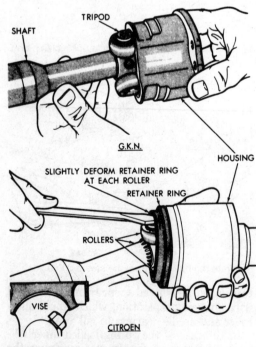

Separate tripod from hosing

spring would automatically force the tripod out of the housing whenever the shaft was not installed in the vehicle.

Separate the tripod from the housing by slightly deforming the retaining ring in 3 places, with a suitable tool.

WARNING: *Secure the rollers to the studs during separation. With the tripod out of the housing secure the assembly with tape.*

3. GKN type: Spring loaded GKN inboard CV-joints have tabs on the can cover that prevent the spring from forcing the tripod out of the housing. These tabs must be bent back with a pair of pliers before the tripod can be removed. Under normal conditions it is not necessary to secure the GKN rollers to their studs during separation due to the presence of a retainer ring on the end of each stud. This retention force can easily be overcome if the rollers are pulled or impacted. It is also possible to pull the rollers off by removing or installing the tripod with the connecting shaft at too high an angle, relative to the housing.

4. Remove the snapring from the shaft end groove, then remove the tripod with a brass punch.

INSPECTION

Remove as much grease as possible from the assembly. Look at the ball housing races, and the components for excessive wear. DO NOT CLEAN THE INNER HOUSING WITH MINERAL SPIRITS OR SOLVENT. Solvents will destroy the rubber seals that are hidden in the housing and permit grease leakage. If wear is excessive, replace as necessary.

ASSEMBLY

1. Fasten the new boot onto the interconnecting shaft. Install the tripod on the shaft as follows: G.K.N. type: Slide the tripod onto the shaft with the non-chamfered end facing the tripod retaining ring groove. Citroen type: Slide the tripod onto the shaft (both sides are the same).

2. Install the retainer snapring into the groove on the interconnecting shaft locking the tripod in position.

3. On G.K.N. type: Put two of the three packets of grease into the boot and the remaining pack into the housing. On Citroen type: Put two thirds of the packet of grease into the boot and the remaining grease into the housing.

4. Position the spring into the housing spring pocket with the cup attached to the exposed end of the spring. Place a small amount of grease in the spring cup.

5. On G.K.N type: Slip the tripod into the housing and bend down the retaining tabs. Make sure the tabs are holding the housing

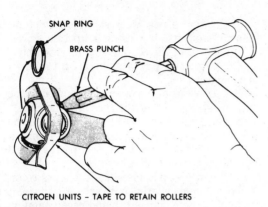

CITROEN UNITS – TAPE TO RETAIN ROLLERS

Remove snapring—then tripod

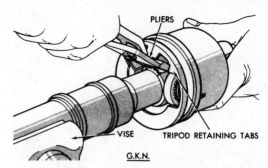

G.K.N.

Separate the tripod from the housing—GKN

firmly. On Citroen type: Remove the tape holding the rollers and needle bearings in place. Hold the rollers and needles in place and install the housing. Install the retaining ring into the machined groove in the housing with a punch and plastic hammer. Hold the retaining collar in positon with two C-clamps while installing the retainer ring.

WARNING: *When installing the tripod, the spring must be centered in the housing to insure proper positioning.*

6. Position the boot over the retaining groove in the housing and clamp in position.

Outer Joint

1. Remove the boot clamps and discard them.

2. Wipe away the grease to expose the joint.

3. Support the shaft in a vise (Cushion the vise jaws to prevent shaft damage). Hold the outer joint, and using a plastic hammer, give a sharp tap to the top of the joint body to dislodge it from the internal circlip.

4. If the shaft is bent carefully pry the wear sleeve from the CV-joint machined ledge.

5. Remove the circlip from the shaft and discard it.

NOTE: *Replacement boot kits will contain this circlip.*

6. Unless the shaft is damaged do not remove the heavy spacer ring from the shaft.

NOTE: *If the shaft must be replaced, care must be taken that the new shaft is of the proper construction, depending on whether the inner joint is spring loaded or not. If the*

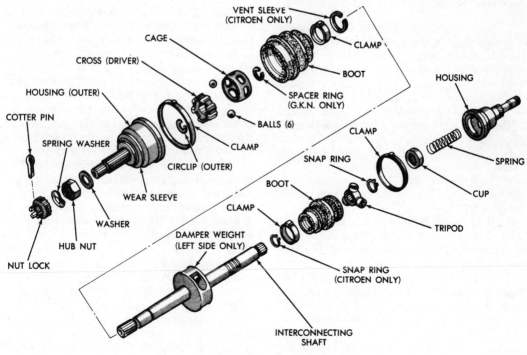

Driveaxle components

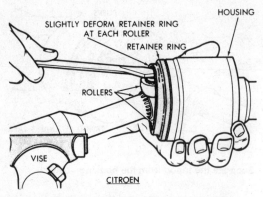

Separate the tripod from the housing—Citroen

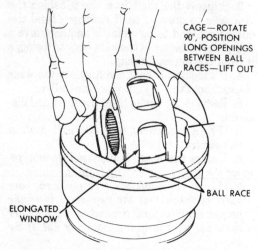

Removing cage and cross assembly from housing

CV-joint was operating satisfactorily, and the grease down not appear contaminated, just replace the boot. If the outer joint is noisy or badly worn, replace the entire unit. The repair kit will include boot, clamps, retaining ring (circlip) and lubricant.

7. Wipe off the grease and mark the position of the inner cross, cage and housing with a dab of paint.

8. Hold the joint vertically in a vise. Do not crush the splines on the shaft.

9. Press down on one side of the inner race to tilt the cage and remove the balls from the opposite side.

10. If the joint is tight, use a hammer and brass drift pin to tap the inner race. Repeat this step until all balls have been removed. DO NOT hit the cage.

11. Tilt the cage and inner race assembly vertically and position the two opposing, elongated cage windows in the area between the ball grooves. Pull the cage out of the housing.

12. Turn the inner cross 90 degrees and align the race lands with an elongated hole in the cage. Remove the inner race.

13. Position a new wear sleeve on the joint housing and install it using a suitable driver. Lubricate all of the components be assembly.

14. Align the parts according to paint markings.

15. Install one of the inner race lands into the cage window and feed the race into the cage.

16. Turn the cross 90 degrees and align the opposing cage windows with the land, pivot another 90 degrees and complete land installation.

17. When properly installed, the cross counterbore should be facing outward from the joint on G.K.N. type. The cross and cage chamfers will be facing out on Citroen type.

18. Apply the grease to the ball races. Install the balls into the raceway by tilting the cage and inner race assembly.

19. Fasten the boot to the shaft. Install the new retainer circlip provided. Position the outer joint on the splined end of the stubshaft, engage the splines and tap sharply to engage the circlip. Attempt to pull the shafts apart to see if the circlip is properly seated.

20. Position the large end of the boot and secure with a clamp.

CLUTCH

Understanding the Clutch

The purpose of the clutch is to disconnect and connect engine power from the transmission. A car at rest requires a lot of engine torque to get all that weight moving. An internal combustion engine does not develop a high starting torque (unlike steam engines), so it must be allowed to operate without any load until it builds up enough torque to move the car. Torque increases with engine rpm. The clutch allows the engine to build up torque by physically disconnecting the engine from the transmission, relieving the engine of any load or resistance. The transfer of engine power to the transmission (the load) must be smooth and gradual; if it weren't, drive line components would wear out or break quickly. This gradual power transfer is made possible by gradually releasing the clutch pedal. The clutch disc and pressure plate are the connecting link between the engine and transmission. When the clutch pedal is released, the disc and plate contact each other (clutch engagement), physically joining the engine and transmission. When the pedal is pushed in, the disc and plate separate (the clutch is disengaged), disconnecting the engine from the transmission.

The clutch assembly consists of the flywheel, the clutch disc, the clutch pressure plate, the throwout bearing and fork, the actuating linkage and the pedal. The flywheel and clutch pressure plate (driving members) are connected to the engine crankshaft and rotate with it. The clutch disc is located between the flywheel and pressure plate, and splined to the transmission shaft. A driving member is one that is attached to the engine and transfers engine power to a driven member (clutch disc) on the transmission shaft. A driving member (pressure plate) rotates (drives) a driven member (clutch disc) on contact and, in so doing, turns the transmission shaft. There is a circular diaphragm spring within the pressure plate cover (transmission side). In a relaxed state (when the clutch pedal is fully released), this spring is convex; that is, it is dished outward toward the transmission. Pushing in the clutch pedal actuates an attached linkage rod. Connected to the other end of this rod is the throwout bearing fork. The throwout bearing is attached to the fork. When the clutch pedal is depressed, the clutch linkage pushes the fork and bearing forward to contact the diaphragm spring of the pressure plate. The outer edges of the spring are secured to the pressure plate and are pivoted on rings so that when the center of the spring is compressed by the throwout bearing, the outer edges bow outward and, by so doing, pull the pressure plate in the same direction - away from the clutch disc. This action separates the disc from the plate, disengaging the clutch and allowing the transmission to be shifted into another gear. A coil type clutch return spring attached to the clutch pedal arm permits full release of the pedal. Releasing the pedal pulls the throwout bearing away from the diaphragm spring resulting in a reversal of spring position. As bearing pressure is gradually released from the spring center, the outer edges of the spring bow outward, pushing the pressure plate into closer contact with the clutch disc. As the disc and plate move closer together, friction between the two increases and slippage is reduced until, when full spring pressure is applied (by fully releasing the pedal), The speed of the disc and plate are the same. This stops all slipping, creating a direct connection between the plate and disc which results in the transfer of power from the engine to the transmission. The clutch disc is now rotating

Troubleshooting Basic Clutch Problems

Problem	Cause
Excessive clutch noise	Throwout bearing noises are more audible at the lower end of pedal travel. The usual causes are: • Riding the clutch • Too little pedal free-play • Lack of bearing lubrication A bad clutch shaft pilot bearing will make a high pitched squeal, when the clutch is disengaged and the transmission is in gear or within the first 2″ of pedal travel. The bearing must be replaced. Noise from the clutch linkage is a clicking or snapping that can be heard or felt as the pedal is moved completely up or down. This usually requires lubrication. Transmitted engine noises are amplified by the clutch housing and heard in the passenger compartment. They are usually the result of insufficient pedal free-play and can be changed by manipulating the clutch pedal.
Clutch slips (the car does not move as it should when the clutch is engaged)	This is usually most noticeable when pulling away from a standing start. A severe test is to start the engine, apply the brakes, shift into high gear and SLOWLY release the clutch pedal. A healthy clutch will stall the engine. If it slips it may be due to: • A worn pressure plate or clutch plate • Oil soaked clutch plate • Insufficient pedal free-play
Clutch drags or fails to release	The clutch disc and some transmission gears spin briefly after clutch disengagement. Under normal conditions in average temperatures, 3 seconds is maximum spin-time. Failure to release properly can be caused by: • Too light transmission lubricant or low lubricant level • Improperly adjusted clutch linkage
Low clutch life	Low clutch life is usually a result of poor driving habits or heavy duty use. Riding the clutch, pulling heavy loads, holding the car on a grade with the clutch instead of the brakes and rapid clutch engagement all contribute to low clutch life.

with the pressure plate at engine speed and, because it is splined to the transmission shaft, the shaft now turns at the same engine speed. Understanding clutch operation can be rather difficult at first; if you're still confused after reading this, consider the following analogy. The action of the diaphragm spring can be compared to that of an oil can bottom. The bottom of an oil can is shaped very much like the clutch diaphragm spring and pushing in on the can bottom and then releasing it produces a similar effect. As mentioned earlier, the clutch pedal return spring permits full release of the pedal and reduces linkage slack due to wear. As the linkage wears, clutch free-pedal travel will increase and free-travel will decrease as the clutch wears. Free-travel is actually throwout bearing lash.

The diaphragm spring type clutches used are available in two different designs: flat diaphragm springs or bent spring. The bent fingers are bent back to create a centrifugal boost ensuring quick re-engagement at higher engine speeds. This design enables pressure plate load to increase as the clutch disc wears and makes low pedal effort possible even with a heavy-duty clutch. The throwout bearing used with the bent finger design is 1¼" long and is shorter than the bearing used with the flat finger design. These bearings are not interchangeable. If the longer bearing is used with the bent finger clutch, free-pedal travel will not exist. This results in clutch slippage and rapid wear.

The transmission varies the gear ratio between the engine and drive wheels. It can be shifted to change engine speed as driving conditions and loads change. The transmission allows disengaging and reversing power from the engine to the wheels.

CAUTION: *The clutch driven disc contains asbestos, which has been determined to be a cancer causing agent. Never clean clutch surfaces with compressed air! Avoid inhaling any dust from any clutch surface! When cleaning clutch surfaces, use a commerically available brake cleaning fluid.*

Adjustments

All models are equipped with a self-adjusting clutch. No free-play adjustment is possible.

Driven Disc and Pressure Plate

NOTE: *Chrysler recommends the use of special tool #C4676 for disc alignment.*

REMOVAL AND INSTALLATION

1. Remove the transaxle.
2. Matchmark the clutch cover and flywheel for easy reinstallation.
3. Insert special tool C4676 or its equivalent to hold the clutch disc in place.
4. Loosen the cover attaching bolts. Do this procedure in a diagonal manner, a few turns at a time to prevent warping the cover.
5. Remove the cover assembly and disc from the flywheel.
6. Remove the clutch release shaft and slide the release bearing off the input shaft seal retainer.
7. Remove the fork from the release bearing thrust plate.

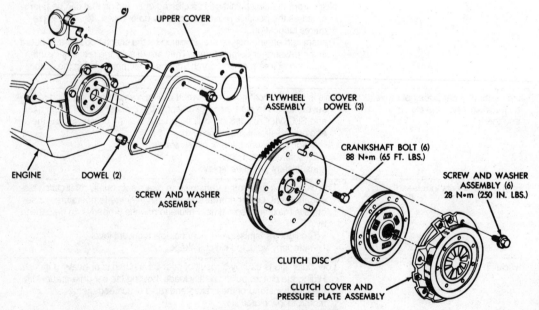

Clutch components (typical)

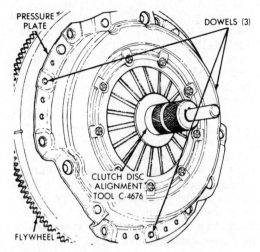

Use a clutch aligning tool

8. Inspect the components. Replace as necessary.

9. Install the throwout bearing, fork and component parts.

10. Mount the clutch assembly on the flywheel (Mate the matchmarks if old unit is used). Install the clutch disc alignment tool. Hold the alignment tool in position and loosely install the pressure plate retaining bolts.

11. Tighten the bolts a few turns at a time in rotation. Tighten to 250 in. lbs.

LINKAGE

The clutch release cable cannot be adjusted. When the cable is properly installed, a spring in the clutch pedal adjusts the cable to the proper position, regardless of clutch disc wear.

AUTOMATIC TRANSAXLE

Understanding Automatic Transmissions

The automatic transmission allows engine torque and power to be transmitted to the drive wheels within a narrow range of engine operating speeds. The transmission will allow the engine to turn fast enough to produce plenty of power and torque at very low speeds, while keeping it at a sensible rpm at high vehicle speeds. The transmission performs this job entirely without driver assistance. The transmission uses a light fluid as the medium for the transmission of power. This fluid also works in the operation of various hydraulic control circuits and as a lubricant. Because the transmission fluid performs all of these three functions, trouble within the unit can easily travel from one part to another. For this reason, and because of the complexity and unusual operating principles of the transmission, a very sound understanding of the basic principles of operation will simplify troubleshooting.

THE TORQUE CONVERTER

The torque converter replaces the conventional clutch. It has three functions:

1. It allows the engine to idle with the vehicle

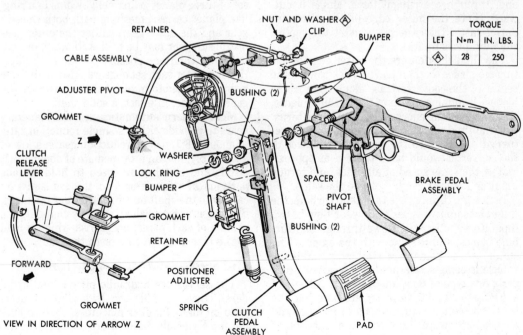

TORQUE		
LET	N•m	IN. LBS.
Ⓐ	28	250

VIEW IN DIRECTION OF ARROW Z

Clutch cable components

at a standstill, even with the transmission in gear.

2. It allows the transmission to shift from range to range smoothly, without requiring that the driver close the throttle during the shift.

3. It multiplies engine torque to an increasing extent as vehicle speed drops and throttle opening is increased. This has the effect of making the transmission more responsive and reduces the amount of shifting required.

The torque converter is a metal case which is shaped like a sphere that has been flattened on opposite sides. It is bolted to the rear end of the engine's crankshaft. Generally, the entire metal case rotates at engine speed and serves as the engine's flywheel.

The case contains three sets of blades. One set is attached directly to the case. This set forms the torus or pump. Another set is directly connected to the output shaft, and forms the turbine. The third set is mounted on a hub which, in turn, is mounted on a stationary shaft through a one-way clutch. This third set is known as the stator.

A pump, which is driven by the converter hub at engine speed, keeps the torque converter full of transmission fluid at all times. Fluid flows continuously through the unit to provide cooling.

Under low speed acceleration, the torque converter functions as follows:

The torus is turning faster than the turbine. It picks up fluid at the center of the converter and, through centrifugal force, slings it outward. Since the outer edge of the converter moves faster than the portions at the center, the fluid picks up speed.

The fluid then enters the outer edge of the turbine blades. It then travels back toward the center of the converter case along the turbine blades. In impinging upon the turbine blades, the fluid loses the energy picked up in the torus.

If the fluid were now to immediately be returned directly into the torus, both halves of the converter would have to turn at approximately the same speed at all times, and torque input and output would both be the same.

In flowing through the torus and turbine, the fluid picks up two types of flow, or flow in two separate directions. It flows through the turbine blades, and it spins with the engine. The stator, whose blades are stationary when the vehicle is being accelerated at low speeds, converts one type of flow into another. Instead of allowing the fluid to flow straight back into the torus, the stator's curved blades turn the fluid almost 90° toward the direction of rotation of the engine. Thus the fluid does not flow as fast toward the torus, but is already spinning when

the torus picks it up. This has the effect of allowing the torus to turn much faster than the turbine. This difference in speed may be compared to the difference in speed between the smaller and larger gears in any gear train. The result is that engine power output is higher, and engine torque is multiplied.

As the speed of the turbine increases, the fluid spins faster and faster in the direction of engine rotation. As a result, the ability of the stator to redirect the fluid flow is reduced. Under cruising conditions, the stator is eventually forced to rotate on its one-way clutch in the direction of engine rotation. Under these conditions, the torque converter begins to behave almost like a solid shaft, with the torus and turbine speeds being almost equal.

THE PLANETARY GEARBOX

The ability of the torque converter to multiply engine torque is limited. Also, the unit tends to be more efficient when the turbine is rotating at relatively high speeds. Therefore, a planetary gearbox is used to carry the power output of the turbine to the halfshafts.

Planetary gears function very similarly to conventional transmission gears. However, their construction is different in that three elements make up one gear system, and, in that all three elements are different from one another. The three elements are: an outer gear that is shaped like a hoop, with teeth cut into the inner surface; a sun gear, mounted on a shaft and located at the very center of the outer gear; and a set of three planet gears, held by pins in a ring-like planet carrier, meshing with both the sun gear and the outer gear. Either the outer gear or the sun gear may be held stationary, providing more than one possible torque multiplication factor for each set of gears. Also, if all three gears are forced to rotate at the same speed, the gearset forms, in effect, a solid shaft.

Most modern automatics use the planetary gears to provide either a single reduction ratio of about 1.8:1, or two reduction gears: a low of about 2.5:1, and an intermediate of about 1.5:1. Bands and clutches are used to hold various portions of the gearsets to the transmission case or to the shaft on which they are mounted. Shifting is accomplished, then, by changing the portion of each planetary gearset which is held to the transmission case or to the shaft.

THE SERVOS AND ACCUMULATORS

The servos are hydraulic pistons and cylinders. They resemble the hydraulic actuators used on many familiar machines, such as bulldozers. Hydraulic fluid enters the cylinder, under pressure, and forces the piston to move to engage the band or clutches.

The accumulators are used to cushion the engagement of the servos. The transmission fluid must pass through the accumulator on the way to the servo. The accumulator housing contains a thin piston which is sprung away from the discharge passage of the accumulator. When fluid passes through the accumulator on the way to the servo, it must move the piston against spring pressure, and this action smooths out the action of the servo.

THE HYDRAULIC CONTROL SYSTEM

The hydraulic pressure used to operate the servos comes from the main transmission oil pump. This fluid is channeled to the various servos through the shift valves. There is generally a manual shift valve which is operated by the transmission selector lever and an automatic shift valve for each automatic upshift the transmission provides: i.e., 2-speed automatics have a low/high shift valve, while 3-speeds have a 1-2 valve, and a 2-3 valve.

There are two pressures which effect the operation of these valves. One is the governor pressure which is affected by vehicle speed. The other is the modulator pressure which is affected by intake manifold vacuum or throttle position. Governor pressure rises with an increase in vehicle speed, and modulator pressure rises as the throttle is opened wider. By responding to these two pressures, the shift valves cause the upshift points to be delayed with increased throttle opening to make the best use of the engine's power output.

Most transmissions also make use of an auxiliary circuit for downshifting. This circuit may be actuated by the throttle linkage or the vacuum line which actuates the modulator, or by a cable or solenoid. It applies pressure to a special downshift surface on the shift valve or valves.

The transmission modulator also governs the line pressure, used to actuate the servos. In this way, the clutches and bands will be actuated with a force matching the torque output of the engine.

The three speed automatic transmission and differential are combined in a single housing and share the same Dexron®II type lubricant. Filter, fluid changes, and band adjustments are not require for average vehicle use. However, if the vehicle is used for constant heavy duty hauling, commercial use or more than 50 % operation in heavy traffic, the fluid and filter should be changed every 15,000 miles.

FLUID AND FILTER CHANGE

1. Raise and support the front of the vehicle on jackstands.
2. Remove the splash shield if it will interfere with the fluid pan removal.
3. Place a suitable container that will hold at least four quarts of fluid under the oil pan. Loosen all of the pan bolts slightly until the fluid stats to drain. Loosen the bolts around the point where the fluid is draining to increase the flow.
4. When the bulk of the fluid has drained, remove the oil pan. Clean the dirt from the pan and magnet. Remove RTV sealant or gasket material from the pan and case mounting surfaces.

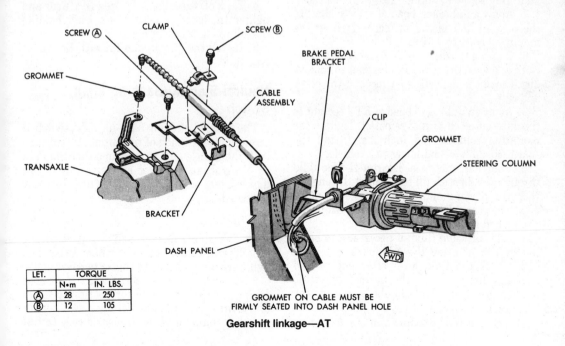

LET.	TORQUE	
	N•m	IN. LBS.
Ⓐ	28	250
Ⓑ	12	105

GROMMET ON CABLE MUST BE FIRMLY SEATED INTO DASH PANEL HOLE

Gearshift linkage—AT

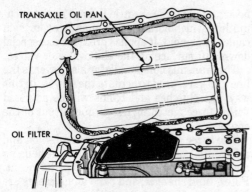

Automatic transaxle pan removal (out of vehicle view)

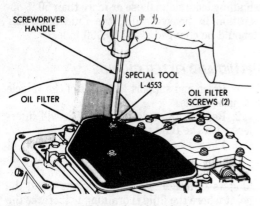

Filter removal—AT (out of vehicle view)

5. Remove the filter from the bottom of the valve body.

6. Install a new filter and gasket. Tighten the mounting screw to 40 inch lbs.

7. Apply a unbroken bead of RTV sealant to the oil pan and install on case. Tighten the mounting bolts to 165 inch lbs.

8. Remove the differential cover. Use a clean cloth and wipe the cover and magnet to remove dirt. Clean the mounting surfaces of the cover and case.

9. Apply an unbroken bead of RTV sealant to the differential cover and reinstall. Tighten the mounting bolts to 165 inch lbs. Install the splash shield, etc. and lower the vehicle.

10. Pour four quarts of Dexron II type fluid through the dipstick fill tube. Start the engine, with the parking and service brakes applied, move the gear selector through the various positions ending up in Park.

11. Add sufficient fluid, if necessary, to bring the level to 1/8″ below the Add mark.

12. Check the fluid level after engine and transaxle have reached the normal operating temperature. The level should be within the Hot range on the dipstick.

NOTE: *Always make sure that the dipstick is fully seated in its tube to prevent dirt from entering the transaxle.*

Adjustments
KICKDOWN CABLE

1. Run the engine until the normal operating temperature is reached. Be sure the choke is fully opened.

2. Loosen the adjustment bracket lock bolt mounted on transaxle to engine flange.

3. Be sure that the adjustment bracket can slide freely. Clean as necessary.

4. Slide the bracket toward the engine as far as possible. Release the bracket and move the throttle lever to the right as far as it will go. tighten the adjustment lock bolt to 105 inch lbs.

KICKDOWN BAND (FRONT)

The kickdown band adjusting screw is located on left top front side of the transaxle case.

1. Clean the locknut, adjusting screw and area around with safe solvent and brush. Loosen the locknut and back it off about five turns.

2. Tighten the band adjusting screw to 72 inch lbs. Back the adjustment screw off 2½ turns. Hold the adjustment screw in position and tighten the locknut to 35 ft. lbs.

LOW/REVERSE BAND (REAR)

1. Drain the fluid and remove the oil pan from the transaxle.

2. Loosen and back off the locknut about five turns.

3. Tighten the band adjusting screw to 41 inch lbs.

4. Back off the adjusting screw 3½ turns and tighten the locknut to 10 ft. lbs. while holding the adjusting screw in position.

5. Install the oil pan and fill with Dexron II type fluid.

Neutral Starting/Back-up Light Switch

The neutral starting/back-up light switch is screwed into the side of the automatic transaxle. If the vehicle fails to start in either the Park or Neutral positions, or starts in any of the drive gears a problem with the switch is indicated.

TESTING

1. The Neutral/Park sensing part of the switch is the center terminal, while the back-up lights are controlled by the outer two terminals.

2. Remove the wiring connector from the switch. Use an ohmmeter or continuity tester and connect the leads between the center switch terminal and the transaxle case to test

the Neutral/Park circuit. Continuity should exist only when the gearshift is either in the Park or Neutral positions. Check the gearshift cable adjustment first before replacing the switch.

3. Connect an ohmmeter or continuity tester connected between the outer two terminals of the switch to check the back-up light. Continuity should be present when the gearshift selector is in the Reverse position.

REMOVAL AND INSTALLATION

1. Remove the wiring connector. Place a container under the switch to catch transaxle fluid and unscrew the switch.

2. Move the gearshift selector to the Park and Neutral positions and check to see that the switch operating fingers center in the case opening.

3. Screw the new switch and new mounting seal into the transaxle case. Tighten to 24 ft. lbs. Retest switch operation. Add transaxle fluid if needed.

Transaxle and Halfshaft

REMOVAL AND INSTALLATION

Refer to the procedures following the manual transaxle section in this chapter.

Suspension and Steering

FRONT SUSPENSION

MacPherson Struts

A MacPherson Type front suspension, with vertical shock absorbers attached to the upper fender reinforcement and the steering knuckle, is used. Lower control arms, attached inboard to a crossmember and outboard to the steering knuckle through a ball joint, provide lower steering knuckle position. During steering maneuvers, the upper strut and steering knuckle turn as an assembly.

REMOVAL AND INSTALLATION

1. Loosen the front wheel lug nuts slightly. Raise and support the front of the vehicle on jackstands.

Troubleshooting Basic Steering and Suspension Problems

Problem	Cause	Solution
Hard steering (steering wheel is hard to turn)	• Low or uneven tire pressure • Loose power steering pump drive belt • Low or incorrect power steering fluid • Incorrect front end alignment • Defective power steering pump • Bent or poorly lubricated front end parts	• Inflate tires to correct pressure • Adjust belt • Add fluid as necessary • Have front end alignment checked/adjusted • Check pump • Lubricate and/or replace defective parts
Loose steering (too much play in the steering wheel)	• Loose wheel bearings • Loose or worn steering linkage • Faulty shocks • Worn ball joints	• Adjust wheel bearings • Replace worn parts • Replace shocks • Replace ball joints
Car veers or wanders (car pulls to one side with hands off the steering wheel)	• Incorrect tire pressure • Improper front end alignment • Loose wheel bearings • Loose or bent front end components • Faulty shocks	• Inflate tires to correct pressure • Have front end alignment checked/adjusted • Adjust wheel bearings • Replace worn components • Replace shocks
Wheel oscillation or vibration transmitted through steering wheel	• Improper tire pressures • Tires out of balance • Loose wheel bearings • Improper front end alignment • Worn or bent front end components	• Inflate tires to correct pressure • Have tires balanced • Adjust wheel bearings • Have front end alignment checked/adjusted • Replace worn parts
Uneven tire wear	• Incorrect tire pressure • Front end out of alignment • Tires out of balance	• Inflate tires to correct pressure • Have front end alignment checked/adjusted • Have tires balanced

2. Remove the wheel and tire assemblies.

NOTE: *If the original strut assemblies are to be installed, mark the camber eccentric bolt and strut for installment in same position.*

3. Remove the lower camber bolt and nut(at the steering knuckle), and the knuckle bolt and nut. Remove the brake hose to strut bracket mounting bolt.

4. Remove the upper mounting nuts and washers on the fender shield in the engine compartment. Remove the strut assembly from the vehicle.

5. Inspect the strut assembly for signs of leakage. A slight amount of seepage is normal, fluid streaking down the side of the strut is not. Replacer the strut if leakage is evident. Service the strut and spring assembly as required.

6. Position the strut assembly under the fender well and loosely install the upper washers and nuts. Position the lower mount over the steering knuckle and loosely install the mounting and camber bolts and nuts. Attach the brake hose retaining bracket and tighten the mounting bolts to 10 ft. lbs.

7. Tighten the upper mount nuts to 20 ft. lbs. Index the camber bolt to reference mark and snug the nut. Install the nut on the mounting bolt and tighten slightly.

8. Mount a 4″ C-clamp over the inner edge of the strut and outer edge of the steering knuckle. Tighten the clamp just enough to eliminate any looseness between the knuckle and the strut. check the alignment of the camber bolt and strut reference marks. Tighten the mounting and camber nuts to 75 ft. lbs. plug ¼ turn more. Remove the C-clamp.

9. Install the wheel and tire assembly and lower the vehicle.

Strut Spring

REMOVAL AND INSTALLATION

NOTE: *A coil spring compressor Chrysler Tool C-4838 or equivalent is required.*

1. Remove the strut and spring assembly from the vehicle.

2. Compress the coil spring with Chrysler Tool C-4838 or equivalent. Make sure the compressor is mounted correctly and tighten jaws evenly. If the spring slips from the compressor, bodily injury could occur.

3. Hold the strut center rod from turning and remove the assembly nut.

NOTE: *The coil springs on each are rated*

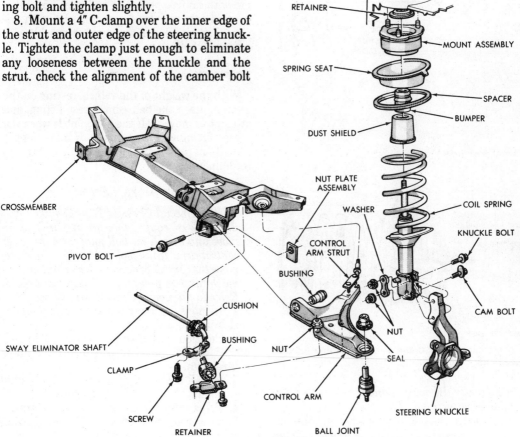

Front suspension

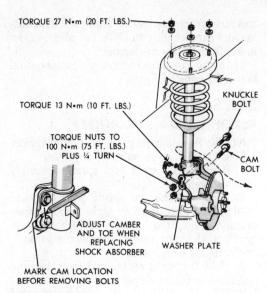

TORQUE 27 N•m (20 FT. LBS.)

TORQUE 13 N•m (10 FT. LBS.)

KNUCKLE BOLT

TORQUE NUTS TO 100 N•m (75 FT. LBS.) PLUS ¼ TURN

CAM BOLT

ADJUST CAMBER AND TOE WHEN REPLACING SHOCK ABSORBER

WASHER PLATE

MARK CAM LOCATION BEFORE REMOVING BOLTS

Strut removal

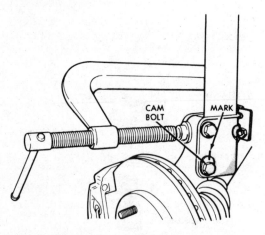

CAM BOLT

MARK

Clamp positioning for strut installation

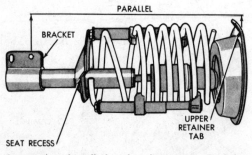

PARALLEL

BRACKET

UPPER RETAINER TAB

SEAT RECESS

Compressor installed and spring seat and retainer positions

differently. Be sure to mark the spring for side identification.

4. Remove the mount assembly and the coil spring. Inspect the assembly for rubber isolator deterioration, distortion, cracks and bonding

failure. Replace as necessary. Check the mount bearings for binding and the retainers for bends and cracks. Replace as necessary.

5. Install the spring on the strut in compressed mode. Install the upper mount assembly. The spring seat tab and the end of the coil spring must be aligned. install assembly nut and tighten while holding the center strut rod in position. Tighten the nut to 60 ft. lbs.

6. Release the coil spring compressor.

7. Install the strut assembly on the vehicle.

8. Misalignment of the upper coil spring seat can cause interference between the coil spring and the inside of the mounting tower. A scraping noise on turns will be an indication if the problem. To correct, raise and support the vehicle to take the weight off of the front wheels. Use two wrenches, one on the top of the center strut rod and one on the assembly nut. Turn both the strut rod and nut in the same direction. The spring will wind up and snap into position. Check the torque on the assembly nut (60 ft. lbs.).

Lower Ball Joint

The lower front suspension ball joints operate with no free play. The ball joint housing is pressed into the lower control arm with the joint stud retained in the steering knuckle with a (clamp) bolt.

INSPECTION

With the weight of the vehicle resting on the ground, grasp the ball joint grease fitting, and attempt to move it. If the ball joint is worn the grease fitting will move easily. If movement is noted, replacement of the ball joint is recommended.

REMOVAL AND INSTALLATION

NOTE: *Special Chrysler Tools C-4699-1 and C-4699-2 or equivalents are required to remove and install the ball joint form the lower control arm. If the tools are not on hand, remove the control arm and have an automotive machine shop press the ball joint out and in. Refer to the Lower Control Arm Section.*

1. Remove the lower control arm. Pry off the seal from the ball joint.

2. Position a receiving cup, special tool C-4699-2 or its equivalent to support the lower control arm.

3. Install a 1¹⁄₁₆″ deep socket over the stud and against the joint upper housing.

4. Press the joint assembly from the arm.

5. To install, position the ball joint housing into the control arm cavity.

6. Position the assembly in a press with spe-

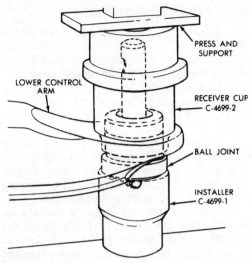

Installing ball joint

cial tool C-4699-1 or its equivalent, supporting the control arm.

7. Align the ball joint assembly, then press it until the housing ledge stops against the control arm cavity down flange.

8. To install a new seal, support the ball joint housing with tool #C-4699-2 and place a new seal over the stud, against the housing.

9. With a 1½" socket, press the seal onto the joint housing with the seat against the control arm. Install control arm.

Lower Control Arm
REMOVAL AND INSTALLATION

1. Jack up the vehicle and support it with jackstands.

2. Remove the front inner pivot through bolt, the rear stub strut nut, retainer and bushing, and the ball joint-to-steering knuckle clamp bolts.

3. Separate the ball joint stud from the steering knuckle by prying between the ball stud retainer on the knuckle and the lower control arm.

WARNING: *Pulling the steering knuckle out from the vehicle after releasing it from the ball joint can separate the inner CV joint.*

4. Remove the sway bar-to-control arm nut and reinforcement and rotate the control arm over the sway bar. Remove the rear stub strut bushing, sleeve and retainer. Remove the control arm.

NOTE: *The substitution of fasteners other than those of the grade originally used is not recommended.*

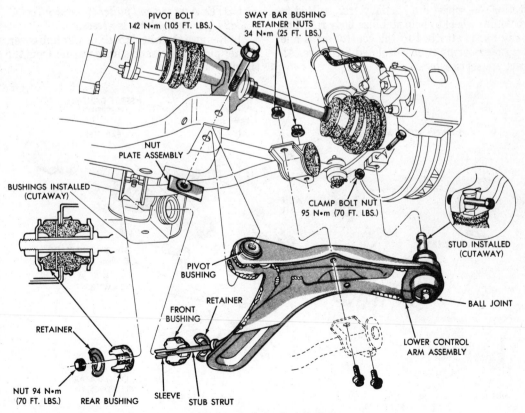

Lower control arm installation

5. Install the retainer, bushing and sleeve on the stub strut.

6. Position the control arm over the sway bar and install the rear stub strut and front pivot into the crossmember.

7. Install the front pivot bolt and loosely install the nut.

8. Install the stub strut bushing and retainer and loosely assembly the nut.

9. Position the sway bar bracket and stud through the control arm and install the retainer nut. Tighten the nuts to 25 ft. lbs.

10. Install the ball joint stud into the steering knuckle and install the clamp bolt. Torque the clamp bolt to 70 ft. lbs.

11. Lower the vehicle, weight on wheels, and tighten the front pivot bolt to 105 ft. lbs. Tighten the rear stub strut nut to 70 ft. lbs.

Pivot Bushing

The front pivot bushing of the lower control arm can be replaced. Remove the control arm and have an automotive machine shop press the bushing out and in.

Sway Bar

The sway bar connects the control arms together and attaches to the front crossmember of the vehicle, Bumps, jounce and rebound affecting one wheel are partially transmitted to the other wheel to help stabilize body roll. The sway bar is attached to the control arms and crossmember by rubber-isolated bushings. All part are serviceable.

REMOVAL AND INSTALLATION

1. Raise and support the front of the vehicle on jackstands.

2. Remove the nuts, bolts and retainer connecting the sway bar to the control arms.

3. Remove the bolt that mount the sway bar to the crossmember. Remove the sway bar and crossmember mounting clamps from the vehicle.

4. Inspect the bushings for wear. Replace as necessary. End bushings are replaced by cutting or driving them from the retainer. Center bushings are split and are removed by opening the split and sliding from the sway bar.

5. Force the new end bushings into the retainers, allow about ½" to protrude. Install the sway bar. Tighten the center bracket bolts to 25 ft. lbs. Place a jack under the control arm and raise the arm to normal design height. Tighten the outer bracket bolts to 25 ft. lbs. Lower the vehicle.

Steering Knuckle

The front suspension steering knuckle provides for steering, braking, front end alignment and supports the front driving hub and axle assembly.

REMOVAL AND INSTALLATION

NOTE: *A tie rod end puller (Chrysler Tool C-3894A or equivalent) is necessary.*

1. Remove the wheel cover, center hub cover, cotter pin, nut lock and spring washer from the front wheel.

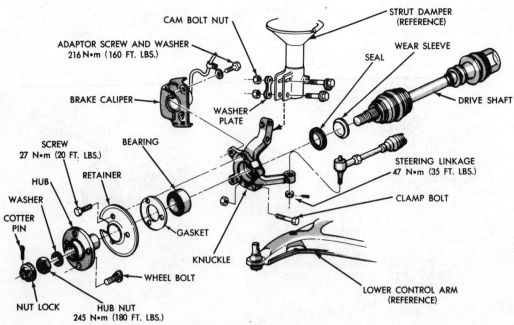

Steering knuckle installation

2. Loosen the front hub nut and wheel lug nuts. Raise the front of the vehicle and support on jackstands.

3. Remove the wheel and tire assembly. Remove the center hub nut.

4. Disconnect the tie rod end from the steering knuckle arm with Tool C-3894A or equivalent. Disconnect the front brake hose bracket from the strut.

5. Remove the caliper assembly and support it with a piece of wire. Do not permit the caliper to hang from the brake hose. Remove the disc brake rotor, inner pad and caliper mounting adapter.

6. Remove the clamp bolt that secures the ball joint and steering knuckle together.

7. Insure that the splined halfshaft is loose in the hub by tapping lightly with a brass drift and hammer. Separate the ball joint and steering knuckle. Pull the knuckle assembly out and away from the halfshaft. Remove the steering knuckle from the strut assembly.

8. Service hub, bearing, seal and steering knuckle as necessary.

9. Install the steering knuckle to the strut assembly. Install the halfshaft through the hub and steering knuckle. Connect the ball joint to the knuckle and tighten the clamp bolt to 70 ft. lbs.

10. Install the tie rod end and tighten the retaining nut to 35 ft. lbs. Install and bend the cotter pin.

11. Install the brake adapter, pads, rotor and caliper. Connect the brake hose bracket to the strut (see Chapter 8).

12. Install the center hub washer and retaining nut. Apply the brakes and tighten the nut to 180 ft. lbs. Install the spring washer, nut and new cotter pin. Install the wheel and tire assembly. Tighten the lug nuts to 95 ft. lbs. Lower the vehicle.

Front Hub and Bearing
REMOVAL AND INSTALLATION
Press In Type

NOTE: *A special set of tools, C-4811 or the equivalent, is required to remove and install the hub and bearing. If the special tool is not on hand, remove the steering knuckle and take it to an automotive machine shop for bearing replacement.*

1. Remove the cotter pin, nut lock and spring from the front halfshaft hub nut. Loosen the hub nut. Loosen the wheel lug nuts slightly.

2. Raise and safely support the vehicle on jackstands.

3. Remove the wheel assembly. Remove the center hub nut.

4. Disconnect the tie rod end from the steering arm. Disconnect the brake hose from the strut retainer. Remove the ball joint clamp nut.

5. Remove the brake caliper, suspend it with wire so that no strain is put on the brake hose. Remove the disc rotor.

6. Separate the knuckle from the control arm ball joint.

7. Pull the knuckle from the halfshaft. Tap the halfshaft with a brass hammer to loosen it if necessary. Use care so that the inner CV joint doen not separate. Support the halfshaft.

8. Using tool C-4811, or equivalent. Back out one of the bearing and 9install the tool adapter bolt into the retainer threads.

9. Position the tool at the back of the knuckle and install two mounting bolts in the brake caliper mounting holes. Center the tool and tighten the caliper adapter mounting bolts and the retainer bolt.

10. Tighten the center threaded driver on the tool and push the hub from the knuckle.

11. Remove the tool from the front side of the knuckle. Carefully pry the grease seal from the knuckle. Press the bearing from the knuckle using tool C-48ll.

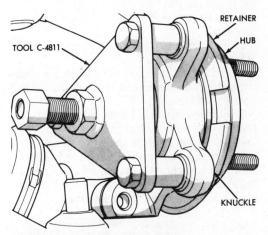

Removing the hub from the knuckle

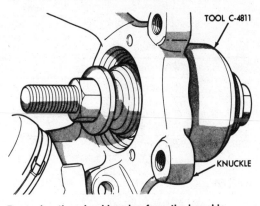

Removing the wheel bearing from the knuckle

12. Install a new bearing by using the puller adapter of tool C-4811. Install a new seal and lubricate. Install the bearing retainer and bolts, torque the bolts to 20 ft. lbs.

13. Press the hub into the bearing. Install a new wear/wipe seal. Install the halfshaft. Attach the ball joint and tie rod end. Install the brake rotor and caliper. Secure the brake hose. Tighten the clamp bolt to 70 ft. lbs. Tighten the tie rod end nut to 35 ft. lbs.

14. Install the washer and hub nut. Tighten the nut firmly. Install the wheel assemblies and tighten the lug nuts firmly.

15. Lower the vehicle. Tighten the center hub nut to 180 ft. lbs. Yighten the wheel lugs to 95 ft. lbs.

Bolt-In Type

Starting with 1988 eight-passenger model vehicles, a bolt in knuckle bearing is used. The bearing unit is serviced as a complete assembly. and is attached to the steering knuckle by four mounting bolts that are removed through a provided access hole in the hub flange.

1. Loosen the center splined retaining hub nut while the vehicle is on the ground. Loosen the wheel lug nuts slightly.

2. Raise and safely support the vehicle on jackstands.

3. Remove the wheel assembly. Remove the hub nut and washer.

4. Disconnect the tie rod end from the steering arm and the clamp bolt that retains the ball joint to the knuckle.

5. Remove the disc brake caliper and suspend it with wire so that there is no strain on the brake hose. Remove the rotor.

6. Separate the knuckle from the ball joint. Pull the knuckle assembly away from halfshaft. Take care not separate the halfshaft inner CV joint. Support the halfshaft.

7. Remove the four hub and bearing retaining bolts. Remove the assembly.

8. Install the new bearing assembly and tighten the mounting bolts in a criss-cross manner to 45 ft. lbs..

9. Install a new wear sleeve seal. Lubricate the sealing surfaces with multi-purpose grease. Install the halfshaft through the hub.

10. Install the steering knuckle onto the lower control arm. Torque the clamp bolt to 70 ft. lbs..

11. Install the tie rod end. Tighten the nut to 35 ft. lbs. Install the brake dics rotor and caliper assembly.

12. Install and tighten the hub nut reasonably tight. Install the wheel assembly, tighten the lug nuts fairly tight. Lower the vehicle and tighten the hub nut to 180 ft. lbs. and the wheel lugs to 85 ft. lbs.

Front End Alignment

Front wheel alignment is the proper adjustment of all the interrelated suspension angles affecting the running and steering of the front wheels.

There are six basic factors which are the foundation of front wheel alignment, height, caster, camber, toe-in, steering axis inclination, and toe-out turns. of these basic factors, only camber and toe are mechanically adjustable. Any checks and required adjustments should be made to the camber first, then to the toe.

CAMBER

Camber is the number of degrees or inches the top of the wheel is tilted inward or outward from true vertical. Outward tilt is positive camber, inward-negative camber. Excessive camber (inward or outward) can cause poor handling, pulling and excessive tire wear.

Wheel Alignment

Year	Model	Caster Range (deg.)	Caster Preferred Setting (deg.)	Camber Range (deg.)	Camber Preferred Setting (deg.)	Toe-in (in.)	Steering Axis Inclination (deg.)
1984	Mini Vans (Front)	—	3/8P	1/4N–3/4P	5/16P	1/16P	—
	Mini Vans (Rear)	—	—	1 1/8N–1/8N	1/2N	0	—
1985	Mini Vans (Front)	—	3/8P	1/4N–3/4P	5/16P	1/16P	—
	Mini Vans (Rear)	—	—	1 1/8N–1/8N	1/2N	0	—
1986	Mini Vans (Front)	—	3/8P	1/4N–3/4P	5/16P	1/16P	—
	Mini Vans (Rear)	—	—	1 3/8N–1/4N	13/16N	0	—
1987–88	Mini Vans (Front)	—	3/8P	1/4N–3/4P	5/16P	1/16P	—
	Mini Vans (Rear)	—	—	1 3/8N–1/4N	13/16N	0	—

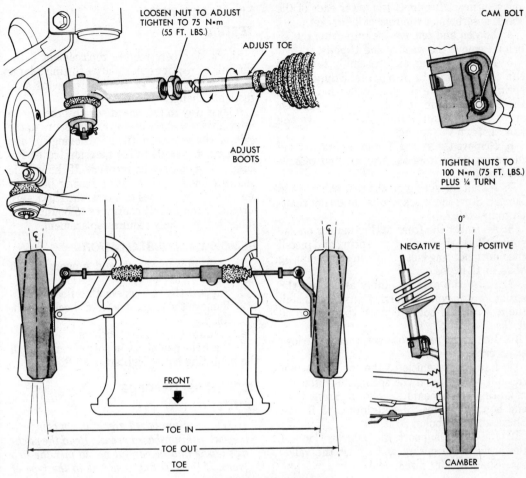

Camber and toe adjustment

TOE

Toe is measured in degrees or inches and is the distance that the front edges of the tires are closer or further apart then the rear edges. Front wheel drive vehicles usually have toe out which means that the outer edges are further apart than the inner. Incorrect toe adjustment will also cause poor handling and excessive tire wear.

REAR SUSPENSION

The rear suspension consists of a tube and casting axle, shock absorbers and leaf springs. Stub axles are mounted to the axle and spring by U-bolts. It is possible to align both the camber and toe of the rear wheels.

The rear leaf springs are mounted by shackles and a fixed end bushing. the shackle angles have been selected to provide increasing suspension rates as the vehicle is loaded. These angles provide a comfortable unloaded ride and ample suspension travel when the vehicle is loaded.

The rear shock absorbers are mounted at an angle, forward at the top and parallel to the springs. Greater stability and ride control are provided by this design.

WARNING: *Do not install aftermarket load leveling devices, air shocks or helper springs on your vehicle. These devices will cause the rear brake height sensing valve to adjust for a lighter lead than actually is contained.*

Rear Springs

REMOVAL AND INSTALLATION

1. Raise and support the rear of the vehicle on jackstands. Locate the jackstands under the frame contact points just ahead of the rear spring fixed ends.

2. Raise the rear axle just enough to relieve the weight on the springs and support on jackstands.

3. Disconnect the rear brake proportioning

valve spring. Disconnect the lower ends of the shock absorbers at the rear axle bracket.

4. Loosen and remove the nuts from the U-bolts. Remove the washer and U-bolts.

5. Lower the rear axle assembly to permit the rear springs to hang free. Support the spring and remove the four bolts that mount the fixed end spring bracket. Remove the rear spring shackle nuts and plate. Remove the shackle from the spring.

6. Remove the spring. Remove the fixed end mounting bolts from the bracket and remove the bracket.

7. Install the spring on the rear shackle and hanger. Start the shackle nuts but do not tighten completely.

8. Assembly the front spring hanger on the spring. Raise the front of the spring and install the four mounting bolts. Tighten the mounting bolts to 45 ft. lbs.

9. Raise the axle assembly and align the spring center bolts in correct position. Install the mounting U-bolts. Tighten the nuts to 60 ft. lbs.

10. Install the rear shock absorber to the lower brackets.

11. Lower the vehicle to the ground so that the full weight is on the springs. Tighten the mounting components as follows: Front fixed end bolt; 95 ft. lbs. Shackle nuts; 35 ft. lbs. Shock absorber bolts; 50 ft. lbs.

12. Raise and support the vehicle. Connect the brake valve spring and adjust the valve. (See Chapter 8 for directions).

Shock Absorbers

TESTING

Shock absorbers require replacement if the car fails to recover quickly after hitting a large bump or if it sways excessively following a directional change.

A good way to test the shock absorbers is to intermittently apply downward pressure to the side of the vehicle until it is moving up and down for almost its full suspension travel. Release it and observe its recovery. If the vehicle bounces once or twice after having been released and then comes to a rest, the shocks are alright. If the vehicle continues to bounce, the shock will probably require replacement.

REMOVAL AND INSTALLATION

1. Jack up your vehicle and support it with jackstands.

2. Support the rear axle with a floor jack.

3. Remove the top and bottom shock absorber bolts.

4. Remove the shock absorbers.

5. Place the new shock in position and install the mounting bolts. Tighten to 80 ft. lbs.

Rear Wheel Bearings

SERVICING

NOTE: *Sodium-based grease is not compatible with lithium-based grease. Read the package labels and be careful not to mix the two types. If there is any doubt as to the type of*

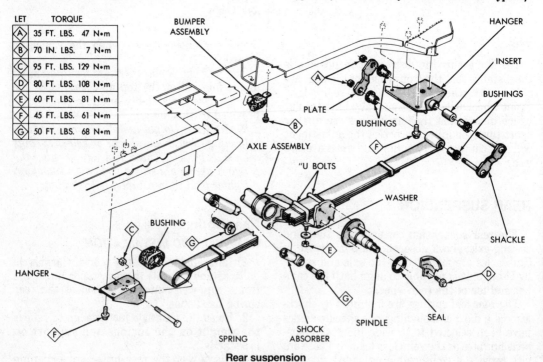

LET	TORQUE	
Ⓐ	35 FT. LBS.	47 N•m
Ⓑ	70 IN. LBS.	7 N•m
Ⓒ	95 FT. LBS.	129 N•m
Ⓓ	80 FT. LBS.	108 N•m
Ⓔ	60 FT. LBS.	81 N•m
Ⓕ	45 FT. LBS.	61 N•m
Ⓖ	50 FT. LBS.	68 N•m

Rear suspension

grease used, completely clean the old grease from the bearing and hub before replacing.

Before handling the bearings, there are a few things that you should remember to do and not to do.

Remember to DO the following:

- Remove all outside dirt from the housing before exposing the bearing.
- Treat a used bearing as gently as you would a new one.
- Work with clean tools in clean surroundings.
- Use clean, dry canvas gloves, or at least clean, dry hands.
- Clean solvents and flushing fluids are a must.
- Use clean paper when laying out the bearings to dry.
- Protect disassembled bearings from rust and dirt. Cover them up.
- Use clean rags to wipe bearings.
- Keep the bearings in oil-proof paper when they are to be stored or are not in use.
- Clean the inside of the housing before replacing the bearing.

Do NOT do the following:

- Don't work in dirty surroundings.
- Don't use dirty, chipped or damaged tools.
- Try not to work on wooden work benches or use wooden mallets.
- Don't handle bearings with dirty or moist hands.
- Do not use gasoline for cleaning; use a safe solvent.
- Do not spin-dry bearings with compressed air. They will be damaged.
- Do not spin dirty bearings.
- Avoid using cotton waste or dirty cloths to wipe bearings.
- Try not to scratch or nick bearing surfaces.
- Do not allow the bearing to come in contact with dirt or rust at any time.

The rear wheel bearings should be inspected and relubricated whenever the rear brakes are serviced or at least every 30,000 miles. Repack the bearings with high temperature multi-purpose grease.

Check the lubricant to see if it is contaminated. If it contains dirt or has a milky appearance indicating the presence of water, the bearings should be cleaned and repacked.

Clean the bearings in kerosene, mineral spirits or other suitable cleaning fluid. Do not dry them by spinning the bearings. Allow them to air dry.

1. Raise and support the vehicle with the rear wheels off the floor.

2. Remove the wheel grease cap, cotter pin, nut-lock and bearing adjusting nut.

3. Remove the thrust washer and bearing.

4. Remove the drum from the spindle.

5. Thoroughly clean the old lubricant from the bearings and hub cavity. Inspect the bearing rollers for pitting or other signs of wear. Light discoloration is normal.

6. Repack the bearings with high temperature multi-purpose EP grease and add a small amount of new grease to the hub cavity. Be sure to force the lubricant between all rollers in the bearing.

7. Install the drum on the spindle after coating the polished spindle surfaces with wheel bearing lubricant.

8. Install the outer bearing cone, thrust washer and adjusting nut.

9. Tighten the adjusting nut to 20-25 ft. lbs. while rotating the wheel.

10. Back off the adjusting nut to completely release the preload from the bearing.

11. Tighten the adjusting nut finger-tight.

12. Position the nut-lock with one pair of slots in line with the cotter pin hole. Install the cotter pin.

13. Clean and install the grease cap and wheel.

14. Lower the vehicle.

Rear Axle Alignment

Camber and Toe adjustment are possible through the use of shims. Shims are added or subtracted between the spindle mounting surface and the axle mounting plate. Each shim equals a wheel angle change of 0.3 degrees.

STEERING

Steering Wheel

REMOVAL AND INSTALLATION

NOTE: *A steering wheel puller (Chrysler tool C3428B or the equivalent) is required.*

1. Disconnect the negative battery cable at the battery.

2. Remove the center horn pad assembly. On standard steering wheels the horn pad is retained by two screws which are removed from underneath the wheel. Premium steering wheels require that the horn pad be pried from internal retainers. Pry the horn pad up from the bottom edges of the steering wheel.

3. Disconnect the horn wires from the center pad. Remove the pad.

4. Mark the column shaft and wheel for reinstallation reference and remove the steering wheel retaining nut.

5. Remove the steering wheel using a steer-

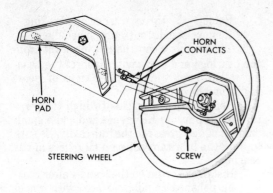

Horn/steering wheel pad removal

ing wheel puller (Chrysler Tool C3428B or the equivalent).

6. Line up the reference marks on the steering wheel and column shaft. Push wheel on to the shaft and draw into position with the mounting nut. Tighten the nut to 45 ft. lbs. Install the center horn pad after connecting the horn connectors. Connect the negative battery cable.

Turn Signal Switch

REMOVAL AND INSTALLATION

1. Disconnect the negative battery cable at the battery.

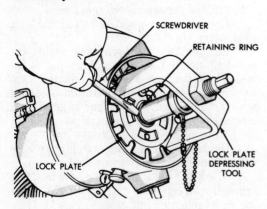

Depressing the lock plate

2. Remove the steering wheel. Remove the lower steering column cover, silencer panel and reinforcement.

3. The wiring harness is contained by a trough that is mounted on the side of the steering column. Remove the trough by prying the connectors from the column. New connectors may be required for installation.

4. Disconnect the turn signal wiring harness connector at the bottom of the steering column.

5. Disassemble the steering column for switch removal as follows:

6. On standard columns; remove the screw holding the wiper-washer switch to the turn signal switch. Allow the control stalk and switch to remain in position. Remove the three screws that attach the bearing retainer and turn signal switch to the upper bearing housing. Remove the turn signal and hazard warning switch assembly by gently pulling the switch up from the column while straightening the wires and guiding them up through the column opening. Be sure to disconnect the ground connector.

7. On models with tilt wheel; remove the plastic cover (if equipped) from the lock plate. Depress the lock plate and pry the retaining ring form mounting groove. (Chrysler Tool C4156 or equivalent is used to compress the lock plate). Remove the lock plate, canceling cam and upper bearing spring. Place the turn signal switch in right turn position. Remove the screw that attaches the link between the turn signal and wiper-washer switches. Remove the screw that attaches the hazard warning switch knob. Remove the three screws attaching the turn signal switch to the steering column. Remove the turn signal and hazard warning switch assembly by gently pulling the switch up from the column while straightening and guid-

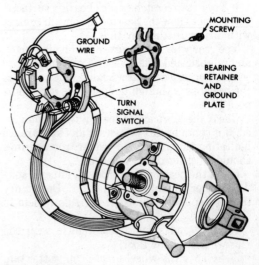

Turn signal switch

Troubleshooting the Steering Column

Problem	Cause	Solution
Will not lock	• Lockbolt spring broken or defective	• Replace lock bolt spring
High effort (required to turn ignition key and lock cylinder)	• Lock cylinder defective	• Replace lock cylinder
	• Ignition switch defective	• Replace ignition switch
	• Rack preload spring broken or deformed	• Replace preload spring
	• Burr on lock sector, lock rack, housing, support or remote rod coupling	• Remove burr
	• Bent sector shaft	• Replace shaft
	• Defective lock rack	• Replace lock rack
	• Remote rod bent, deformed	• Replace rod
	• Ignition switch mounting bracket bent	• Straighten or replace
	• Distorted coupling slot in lock rack (tilt column)	• Replace lock rack
Will stick in "start"	• Remote rod deformed	• Straighten or replace
	• Ignition switch mounting bracket bent	• Straighten or replace
Key cannot be removed in "off-lock"	• Ignition switch is not adjusted correctly	• Adjust switch
	• Defective lock cylinder	• Replace lock cylinder
Lock cylinder can be removed without depressing retainer	• Lock cylinder with defective retainer	• Replace lock cylinder
	• Burr over retainer slot in housing cover or on cylinder retainer	• Remove burr
High effort on lock cylinder between "off" and "off-lock"	• Distorted lock rack	• Replace lock rack
	• Burr on tang of shift gate (automatic column)	• Remove burr
	• Gearshift linkage not adjusted	• Adjust linkage
Noise in column	• One click when in "off-lock" position and the steering wheel is moved (all except automatic column)	• Normal—lock bolt is seating
	• Coupling bolts not tightened	• Tighten pinch bolts
	• Lack of grease on bearings or bearing surfaces	• Lubricate with chassis grease
	• Upper shaft bearing worn or broken	• Replace bearing assembly
	• Lower shaft bearing worn or broken	• Replace bearing. Check shaft and replace if scored.
	• Column not correctly aligned	• Align column
	• Coupling pulled apart	• Replace coupling
	• Broken coupling lower joint	• Repair or replace joint and align column
	• Steering shaft snap ring not seated	• Replace ring. Check for proper seating in groove.
	• Shroud loose on shift bowl. Housing loose on jacket—will be noticed with ignition in "off-lock" and when torque is applied to steering wheel.	• Position shroud over lugs on shift bowl. Tighten mounting screws.
High steering shaft effort	• Column misaligned	• Align column
	• Defective upper or lower bearing	• Replace as required
	• Tight steering shaft universal joint	• Repair or replace
	• Flash on I.D. of shift tube at plastic joint (tilt column only)	• Replace shift tube
	• Upper or lower bearing seized	• Replace bearings
Lash in mounted column assembly	• Column mounting bracket bolts loose	• Tighten bolts
	• Broken weld nuts on column jacket	• Replace column jacket
	• Column capsule bracket sheared	• Replace bracket assembly

Troubleshooting the Steering Column (cont.)

Problem	Cause	Solution
Lash in mounted column assembly (cont.)	· Column bracket to column jacket mounting bolts loose	· Tighten to specified torque
	· Loose lock shoes in housing (tilt column only)	· Replace shoes
	· Loose pivot pins (tilt column only)	· Replace pivot pins and support
	· Loose lock shoe pin (tilt column only)	· Replace pin and housing
	· Loose support screws (tilt column only)	· Tighten screws
Housing loose (tilt column only)	· Excessive clearance between holes in support or housing and pivot pin diameters	· Replace pivot pins and support
	· Housing support-screws loose	· Tighten screws
Steering wheel loose—every other tilt position (tilt column only)	· Loose fit between lock shoe and lock shoe pivot pin	· Replace lock shoes and pivot pin
Steering column not locking in any tilt position (tilt column only)	· Lock shoe seized on pivot pin	· Replace lock shoes and pin
	· Lock shoe grooves have burrs or are filled with foreign material	· Clean or replace lock shoes
	· Lock shoe springs weak or broken	· Replace springs
Noise when tilting column (tilt column only)	· Upper tilt bumpers worn	· Replace tilt bumper
	· Tilt spring rubbing in housing	· Lubricate with chassis grease
One click when in "off-lock" position and the steering wheel is moved	· Seating of lock bolt	· None. Click is normal characteristic sound produced by lock bolt as it seats.
High shift effort (automatic and tilt column only)	· Column not correctly aligned	· Align column
	· Lower bearing not aligned correctly	· Assemble correctly
	· Lack of grease on seal or lower bearing areas	· Lubricate with chassis grease
Improper transmission shifting— automatic and tilt column only	· Sheared shift tube joint	· Replace shift tube
	· Improper transmission gearshift linkage adjustment	· Adjust linkage
	· Loose lower shift lever	· Replace shift tube

Troubleshooting the Ignition Switch

Problem	Cause	Solution
Ignition switch electrically inoperative	· Loose or defective switch connector	· Tighten or replace connector
	· Feed wire open (fusible link)	· Repair or replace
	· Defective ignition switch	· Replace ignition switch
Engine will not crank	· Ignition switch not adjusted properly	· Adjust switch
Ignition switch wil not actuate mechanically	· Defective ignition switch	· Replace switch
	· Defective lock sector	· Replace lock sector
	· Defective remote rod	· Replace remote rod
Ignition switch cannot be adjusted correctly	· Remote rod deformed	· Repair, straighten or replace

ing the wires up through the column opening.

8. On models with the standard column; lubricate the turn signal switch pivot hole with a white lube (such as Lubriplate). Thread the connector and wires through the column hole carefully. Position the turn signal switch and bearing retainer in place on the upper bearing housing and install the three mounting screws. Position the turn signal lever to turn signal pivot and secure with the mounting screws. Be sure the dimmer switch rod is in mounting pocket.

Troubleshooting the Manual Steering Gear

Problem	Cause	Solution
Hard or erratic steering	• Incorrect tire pressure	• Inflate tires to recommended pressures
	• Insufficient or incorrect lubrication	• Lubricate as required (refer to Maintenance Section)
	• Suspension, or steering linkage parts damaged or misaligned	• Repair or replace parts as necessary
	• Improper front wheel alignment	• Adjust incorrect wheel alignment angles
	• Incorrect steering gear adjustment	• Adjust steering gear
	• Sagging springs	• Replace springs
Play or looseness in steering	• Steering wheel loose	• Inspect shaft spines and repair as necessary. Tighten attaching nut and stake in place.
	• Steering linkage or attaching parts loose or worn	• Tighten, adjust, or replace faulty components
	• Pitman arm loose	• Inspect shaft splines and repair as necessary. Tighten attaching nut and stake in place
	• Steering gear attaching bolts loose	• Tighten bolts
	• Loose or worn wheel bearings	• Adjust or replace bearings
	• Steering gear adjustment incorrect or parts badly worn	• Adjust gear or replace defective parts
Wheel shimmy or tramp	• Improper tire pressure	• Inflate tires to recommended pressures
	• Wheels, tires, or brake rotors out-of-balance or out-of-round	• Inspect and replace or balance parts
	• Inoperative, worn, or loose shock absorbers or mounting parts	• Repair or replace shocks or mountings
	• Loose or worn steering or suspension parts	• Tighten or replace as necessary
	• Loose or worn wheel bearings	• Adjust or replace bearings
	• Incorrect steering gear adjustments	• Adjust steering gear
	• Incorrect front wheel alignment	• Correct front wheel alignment
Tire wear	• Improper tire pressure	• Inflate tires to recommended pressures
	• Failure to rotate tires	• Rotate tires
	• Brakes grabbing	• Adjust or repair brakes
	• Incorrect front wheel alignment	• Align incorrect angles
	• Broken or damaged steering and suspension parts	• Repair or replace defective parts
	• Wheel runout	• Replace faulty wheel
	• Excessive speed on turns	• Make driver aware of conditions
Vehicle leads to one side	• Improper tire pressures	• Inflate tires to recommended pressures
	• Front tires with uneven tread depth, wear pattern, or different cord design (i.e., one bias ply and one belted or radial tire on front wheels)	• Install tires of same cord construction and reasonably even tread depth, design, and wear pattern
	• Incorrect front wheel alignment	• Align incorrect angles
	• Brakes dragging	• Adjust or repair brakes
	• Pulling due to uneven tire construction	• Replace faulty tire

9. On models with tilt wheel; thread connector and wire harness through column hole. Position the turn signal switch in the upper column housing. Place the switch in the right turn position. Install the three mounting screws. Install the link between the turn signal switch and the wiper-washer switch pivot and secure mounting screw. Install the lock plate bearing spring, canceling cam and new retainer clip using Tool C4156 or equivalent. Install the hazard warning knob, screw.

10. Connect the wiring harness plug. Install

Troubleshooting the Turn Signal Switch

Problem	Cause	Solution
Turn signal will not cancel	• Loose switch mounting screws • Switch or anchor bosses broken • Broken, missing or out of position detent, or cancelling spring	• Tighten screws • Replace switch • Reposition springs or replace switch as required
Turn signal difficult to operate	• Turn signal lever loose • Switch yoke broken or distorted • Loose or misplaced springs • Foreign parts and/or materials in switch • Switch mounted loosely	• Tighten mounting screws • Replace switch • Reposition springs or replace switch • Remove foreign parts and/or material • Tighten mounting screws
Turn signal will not indicate lane change	• Broken lane change pressure pad or spring hanger • Broken, missing or misplaced lane change spring • Jammed wires	• Replace switch • Replace or reposition as required • Loosen mounting screws, reposition wires and retighten screws
Turn signal will not stay in turn position	• Foreign material or loose parts impeding movement of switch yoke • Defective switch	• Remove material and/or parts • Replace switch
Hazard switch cannot be pulled out	• Foreign material between hazard support cancelling leg and yoke	• Remove foreign material. No foreign material impeding function of hazard switch—replace turn signal switch.
No turn signal lights	• Inoperative turn signal flasher • Defective or blown fuse • Loose chassis to column harness connector • Disconnect column to chassis connector. Connect new switch to chassis and operate switch by hand. If vehicle lights now operate normally, signal switch is inoperative • If vehicle lights do not operate, check chassis wiring for opens, grounds, etc.	• Replace turn signal flasher • Replace fuse • Connect securely • Replace signal switch • Repair chassis wiring as required
Instrument panel turn indicator lights on but not flashing	• Burned out or damaged front or rear turn signal bulb • If vehicle lights do not operate, check light sockets for high resistance connections, the chassis wiring for opens, grounds, etc. • Inoperative flasher • Loose chassis to column harness connection • Inoperative turn signal switch • To determine if turn signal switch is defective, substitute new switch into circuit and operate switch by hand. If the vehicle's lights operate normally, signal switch is inoperative.	• Replace bulb • Repair chassis wiring as required • Replace flasher • Connect securely • Replace turn signal switch • Replace turn signal switch
Stop light not on when turn indicated	• Loose column to chassis connection • Disconnect column to chassis connector. Connect new switch into system without removing old.	• Connect securely • Replace signal switch

Troubleshooting the Turn Signal Switch (cont.)

Problem	Cause	Solution
Stop light not on when turn indicated (cont.)	Operate switch by hand. If brake lights work with switch in the turn position, signal switch is defective. • If brake lights do not work, check connector to stop light sockets for grounds, opens, etc.	 • Repair connector to stop light circuits using service manual as guide
Turn indicator panel lights not flashing	• Burned out bulbs • High resistance to ground at bulb socket • Opens, ground in wiring harness from front turn signal bulb socket to indicator lights	• Replace bulbs • Replace socket • Locate and repair as required
Turn signal lights flash very slowly	• High resistance ground at light sockets • Incorrect capacity turn signal flasher or bulb • If flashing rate is still extremely slow, check chassis wiring harness from the connector to light sockets for high resistance • Loose chassis to column harness connection • Disconnect column to chassis connector. Connect new switch into system without removing old. Operate switch by hand. If flashing occurs at normal rate, the signal switch is defective.	• Repair high resistance grounds at light sockets • Replace turn signal flasher or bulb • Locate and repair as required • Connect securely • Replace turn signal switch
Hazard signal lights will not flash— turn signal functions normally	• Blow fuse • Inoperative hazard warning flasher • Loose chassis-to-column harness connection • Disconnect column to chassis connector. Connect new switch into system without removing old. Depress the hazard warning lights. If they now work normally, turn signal switch is defective. • If lights do not flash, check wiring harness "K" lead for open between hazard flasher and connector. If open, fuse block is defective	• Replace fuse • Replace hazard warning flasher in fuse panel • Conect securely • Replace turn signal switch • Repair or replace brown wire or connector as required

the cover through wiring cover to the steering column.

11. Install the steering wheel and retaining nut. Connect battery cable and test the switch for operation.

Ignition Switch and Keylock
REMOVAL AND INSTALLATION
Without Tilt Wheel

1. Follow the turn signal switch removal procedure previously described.

2. Unclip the horn and key light ground wires.

3. Remove the retaining screw and move the ignition key lamp assembly out of the way.

4. Remove the four screws that hold the bearing housing to the lock housing.

5. Remove the snap ring from the upper end of the steering shaft.

6. Remove the bearing housing from the shaft.

7. Remove the lock plate spring and lock plate from the steering shaft.

Troubleshooting the Power Steering Gear

Problem	Cause	Solution
Hissing noise in steering gear	• There is some noise in all power steering systems. One of the most common is a hissing sound most evident at standstill parking. There is no relationship between this noise and performance of the steering. Hiss may be expected when steering wheel is at end of travel or when slowly turning at standstill.	• Slight hiss is normal and in no way affects steering. Do not replace valve unless hiss is extremely objectionable. A replacement valve will also exhibit slight noise and is not always a cure. Investigate clearance around flexible coupling rivets. Be sure steering shaft and gear are aligned so flexible coupling rotates in a flat plane and is not distorted as shaft rotates. Any metal-to-metal contacts through flexible coupling will transmit valve hiss into passenger compartment through the steering column.
Rattle or chuckle noise in steering gear	• Gear loose on frame	• Check gear-to-frame mounting screws. Tighten screws to 88 N·m (65 foot pounds) torque.
	• Steering linkage looseness	• Check linkage pivot points for wear. Replace if necessary.
	• Pressure hose touching other parts of car	• Adjust hose position. Do not bend tubing by hand.
	• Loose pitman shaft over center adjustment **NOTE:** A slight rattle may occur on turns because of increased clearance off the "high point." This is normal and clearance must not be reduced below specified limits to eliminate this slight rattle.	• Adjust to specifications
	• Loose pitman arm	• Tighten pitman arm nut to specifications
Squawk noise in steering gear when turning or recovering from a turn	• Damper O-ring on valve spool cut	• Replace damper O-ring
Poor return of steering wheel to center	• Tires not properly inflated	• Inflate to specified pressure
	• Lack of lubrication in linkage and ball joints	• Lube linkage and ball joints
	• Lower coupling flange rubbing against steering gear adjuster plug	• Loosen pinch bolt and assemble properly
	• Steering gear to column misalignment	• Align steering column
	• Improper front wheel alignment	• Check and adjust as necessary
	• Steering linkage binding	• Replace pivots
	• Ball joints binding	• Replace ball joints
	• Steering wheel rubbing against housing	• Align housing
	• Tight or frozen steering shaft bearings	• Replace bearings
	• Sticking or plugged valve spool	• Remove and clean or replace valve
	• Steering gear adjustments over specifications	• Check adjustment with gear out of car. Adjust as required.
	• Kink in return hose	• Replace hose
Car leads to one side or the other (keep in mind road condition and wind. Test car in both directions on flat road)	• Front end misaligned	• Adjust to specifications
	• Unbalanced steering gear valve **NOTE:** If this is cause, steering effort will be very light in direction of lead and normal or heavier in opposite direction	• Replace valve

Troubleshooting the Power Steering Gear (cont.)

Problem	Cause	Solution
Momentary increase in effort when turning wheel fast to right or left	• Low oil level • Pump belt slipping • High internal leakage	• Add power steering fluid as required • Tighten or replace belt • Check pump pressure. (See pressure test)
Steering wheel surges or jerks when turning with engine running especially during parking	• Low oil level • Loose pump belt • Steering linkage hitting engine oil pan at full turn • Insufficient pump pressure • Pump flow control valve sticking	• Fill as required • Adjust tension to specification • Correct clearance • Check pump pressure. (See pressure test). Replace relief valve if defective. • Inspect for varnish or damage, replace if necessary
Excessive wheel kickback or loose steering	• Air in system • Steering gear loose on frame • Steering linkage joints worn enough to be loose • Worn poppet valve • Loose thrust bearing preload adjustment • Excessive overcenter lash	• Add oil to pump reservoir and bleed by operating steering. Check hose connectors for proper torque and adjust as required. • Tighten attaching screws to specified torque • Replace loose pivots • Replace poppet valve • Adjust to specification with gear out of vehicle • Adjust to specification with gear out of car
Hard steering or lack of assist	• Loose pump belt • Low oil level **NOTE:** Low oil level will also result in excessive pump noise • Steering gear to column misalignment • Lower coupling flange rubbing against steering gear adjuster plug • Tires not properly inflated	• Adjust belt tension to specification • Fill to proper level. If excessively low, check all lines and joints for evidence of external leakage. Tighten loose connectors. • Align steering column • Loosen pinch bolt and assemble properly • Inflate to recommended pressure
Foamy milky power steering fluid, low fluid level and possible low pressure	• Air in the fluid, and loss of fluid due to internal pump leakage causing overflow	• Check for leak and correct. Bleed system. Extremely cold temperatures will cause system aeriation should the oil level be low. If oil level is correct and pump still foams, remove pump from vehicle and separate reservoir from housing. Check welsh plug and housing for cracks. If plug is loose or housing is cracked, replace housing.
Low pressure due to steering pump	• Flow control valve stuck or inoperative • Pressure plate not flat against cam ring	• Remove burrs or dirt or replace. Flush system. • Correct
Low pressure due to steering gear	• Pressure loss in cylinder due to worn piston ring or badly worn housing bore • Leakage at valve rings, valve body-to-worm seal	• Remove gear from car for disassembly and inspection of ring and housing bore • Remove gear from car for disassembly and replace seals

Troubleshooting the Power Steering Pump

Problem	Cause	Solution
Chirp noise in steering pump	• Loose belt	• Adjust belt tension to specification
Belt squeal (particularly noticeable at full wheel travel and stand still parking)	• Loose belt	• Adjust belt tension to specification
Growl noise in steering pump	• Excessive back pressure in hoses or steering gear caused by restriction	• Locate restriction and correct. Replace part if necessary.
Growl noise in steering pump (particularly noticeable at stand still parking)	• Scored pressure plates, thrust plate or rotor • Extreme wear of cam ring	• Replace parts and flush system • Replace parts
Groan noise in steering pump	• Low oil level • Air in the oil. Poor pressure hose connection.	• Fill reservoir to proper level • Tighten connector to specified torque. Bleed system by operating steering from right to left—full turn.
Rattle noise in steering pump	• Vanes not installed properly • Vanes sticking in rotor slots	• Install properly • Free up by removing burrs, varnish, or dirt
Swish noise in steering pump	• Defective flow control valve	• Replace part
Whine noise in steering pump	• Pump shaft bearing scored	• Replace housing and shaft. Flush system.
Hard steering or lack of assist	• Loose pump belt • Low oil level in reservoir **NOTE:** Low oil level will also result in excessive pump noise • Steering gear to column misalignment • Lower coupling flange rubbing against steering gear adjuster plug • Tires not properly inflated	• Adjust belt tension to specification • Fill to proper level. If excessively low, check all lines and joints for evidence of external leakage. Tighten loose connectors. • Align steering column • Loosen pinch bolt and assemble properly • Inflate to recommended pressure
Foaming milky power steering fluid, low fluid level and possible low pressure	• Air in the fluid, and loss of fluid due to internal pump leakage causing overflow	• Check for leaks and correct. Bleed system. Extremely cold temperatures will cause system aeriation should the oil level be low. If oil level is correct and pump still foams, remove pump from vehicle and separate reservoir from body. Check welsh plug and body for cracks. If plug is loose or body is cracked, replace body.
Low pump pressure	• Flow control valve stuck or inoperative • Pressure plate not flat against cam ring	• Remove burrs or dirt or replace. Flush system. • Correct
Momentary increase in effort when turning wheel fast to right or left	• Low oil level in pump • Pump belt slipping • High internal leakage	• Add power steering fluid as required • Tighten or replace belt • Check pump pressure. (See pressure test)
Steering wheel surges or jerks when turning with engine running especially during parking	• Low oil level • Loose pump belt • Steering linkage hitting engine oil pan at full turn • Insufficient pump pressure	• Fill as required • Adjust tension to specification • Correct clearance • Check pump pressure. (See pressure test). Replace flow control valve if defective.

Troubleshooting the Power Steering Pump (cont.)

Problem	Cause	Solution
Steering wheel surges or jerks when turning with engine running especially during parking (cont.)	• Sticking flow control valve	• Inspect for varnish or damage, replace if necessary
Excessive wheel kickback or loose steering	• Air in system	• Add oil to pump reservoir and bleed by operating steering. Check hose connectors for proper torque and adjust as required.
Low pump pressure	• Extreme wear of cam ring	• Replace parts. Flush system.
	• Scored pressure plate, thrust plate, or rotor	• Replace parts. Flush system.
	• Vanes not installed properly	• Install properly
	• Vanes sticking in rotor slots	• Freeup by removing burrs, varnish, or dirt
	• Cracked or broken thrust or pressure plate	• Replace part

8. Remove the ignition key, then remove the screw and lift out the buzzer/chime switch.

9. Remove the two screws attaching the ignition switch to the column jacket.

10. Remove the ignition switch by rotating the switch 90 degrees on the rod then sliding off the rod.

11. Remove the two mounting screws from the dimmer switch and disengage the switch from the actuator rod.

12. Remove the two screws that mount the bellcrank and slide the bellcrank up in the lock housing until it can be disconnect from the ignition switch actuator rod.

13. To remove the lock cylinder and lock levers place the cylinder in the lock position and remove the key.

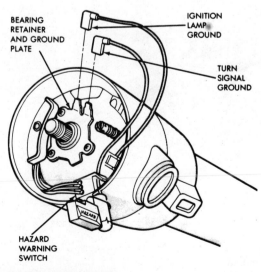

BEARING RETAINER AND GROUND PLATE

IGNITION LAMP GROUND

TURN SIGNAL GROUND

HAZARD WARNING SWITCH

Hazard warning switch

14. Insert a small diameter screwdriver or similar tool into the lock cylinder release holes and push into the release spring loaded lock retainers. At the same time pull the lock cylinder out of the housing bore.

15. Grasp the lock lever and spring assembly and pull straight out of the housing.

16. If necessary the lock housing may be removed from the column jacket by removing the hex head retaining screws.

17. Installation is the reverse of removal. If the lock housing was removed tighten the lock housing screws to 90 inch pounds.

18. To install the dimmer switch, firmly seat the push rod into the switch. Compress the switch until two $\frac{3}{32}''$ drill shanks can be inserted into the alignment holes. Reposition the upper end of the push rod in the pocket of the wash/wipe switch. With a light rearward pressure on the switch, install the two screws.

19. Grease and assemble the two lock levers, lock lever spring and pin.

20. Install the lock lever assembly in the lock housing. Seat the pin firmly into the bottom of the slots and make sure the lock lever spring leg is firmly in place in the lock casting notch.

21. Install the ignition switch actuator rod from the bottom through the oblong hole in the lock housing and attach it to the bellcrank onto its mounting surface. The gearshift lever should be in the park position.

22. Place the ignition switch on the ignition switch actuator rod and rotate it 90 degrees to lock the rod into position.

23. To install the ignition lock, turn the key to the lock position and remove the key. Insert the cylinder far enough into the housing to contact the switch actuator. Insert the key and press inward and rotate the cylinder.

With Tilt Wheel

Due to the complexity of the ignition switch removal procedure and the necessity of special tools it is recommended that the switch be replaced by a qualified repair shop.

Lock Cylinder

REMOVAL AND INSTALLATION

With Tilt Wheel

1. Remove the turn signal switch as previously described.

2. Place the lock cylinder in the lock position.

3. Insert a thin tool into the slot next to the switch mounting screwing boss (right hand slot) and depress the spring latch at the bottom of the slot and remove the lock.

4. Install the new switch. Refer to the assembly of the turn signal switch as previously described. Turn the ignition lock to the **Lock** position and remove the key. Insert the cylinder until the spring leaded retainer snaps into place.

Steering Column

REMOVAL AND INSTALLATION

1. Disconnect the negative battery cable from the battery. If the vehicle is equipped with a column mounted shift, pry the shift cable rod from the lever grommet at the bottom of the steering column. Remove the cable clip and cable from lower bracket.

2. Disconnect the wiring harness connector at the bottom of the steering column.

3. Remove the instrument panel lower steering column cover and disconnect the bezel. On models with floorshift, unsnap and remove shroud cover extensions.

4. If automatic, remove the selector indicator set screw and pointer from the shift housing.

5. Remove the nuts that attach the steering column mounting bracket to the instrument panel support and lower the bracket.

NOTE: *Do not remove the roll pin from the steering column assembly connector.*

6. Pull the steering column rearward, disconnecting the lower stub shaft from the steering gear connector. If the vehicle is equipped with speed control and a manual transmission, take care not to damage the control switch mounted on the clutch pedal.

7. Install the anti-rattle coupling spring into the lower coupling tube. Be sure that the spring snaps into the slot in the coupling.

8. Align the column lower shaft stub with coupling and insert. Raise the column and place bracket into position on the mounting studs. Loosely install the mounting nuts. Pull the column rearward and tighten the nuts to 105 inch lbs. Tighten stub shaft connector.

9. Connect and adjust the linkage. Connect all harnesses. Connect ths shift indicator and adjust as required. Connect the gear shift indicator operating cable into the slot on the shift housing. Slowly move the gearshift from 1 to P. The pointer will now be properly adjusted. Install the instrument steering column cover.

Steering Linkage

REMOVAL AND INSTALLATION

Tie Rod Ends

1. Jack up the front of the vehicle and support on jackstands.

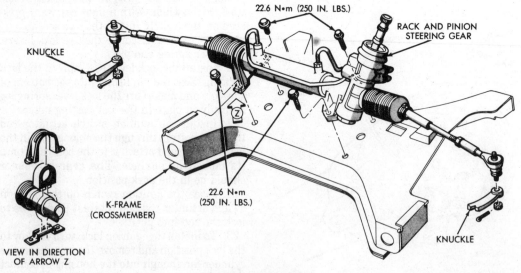

Steering gear mounting

2. Loosen the jam nut which connects the tie rod end to the rack.

3. Mark the tie rod position on the threads.

4. Remove the tie rod cotter pin and nut.

5. Using a puller, remove the tie rod from the steering knuckle.

NOTE: *Count the number of turns when removing tie rod end. Install the new end the same amount of turns.*

6. Unscrew the tie rod end from the rack.

7. Install a new tie rod end, screw in the same number of turns as removal. Tighten the jam nut.

8. Check the wheel alignment.

Steering Gear

The steering system (either manual or power) used on these vehicles is of the rack and pinion design.

The manual steering gear assembly consists of a tube which contains a toothed rack and a housing containing a straddle mounted, helical-cut pinion gear. Tie rods are connected to each end of the rack and an adjustable end (on each side) connects to the steering knuckles. A double universal joint attaches the pinion to the steering column shaft. Steering wheel movement is transmitted by the column shaft and the rack and pinion converts the rotational movement of the pinion to transverse movement of the rack. The manual steering gear is permanently lubricated at the factory and periodic lubrication is not necessary. The manual steering gear cannot be adjusted or serviced. If a malfunction occurs, the entire assembly must be replaced.

The power steering gear is similar to appearance, except for a rotary valve assembly and two fluid hose assemblies. The rotary valve assembly directs fluid from the power steering pump, through hoses, to either side of an internal rack piston. As steering wheel effort is applied, an internal torsion bar twists causing the rotary valve to direct the fluid behind an internal rack piston, which in turn builds up hydraulic pressure and assists in the turning effort.

Rubber boots seal the tie rods and rack assembly. Inspect the boots periodically for cuts, tears or leakage. Replace the boots as necessary.

REMOVAL AND INSTALLATION

1. Loosen the wheel lugs slightly. Raise and support the front of the vehicle at the frame point below the front doors, not on the front crossmember. Use jackstands for supporting.

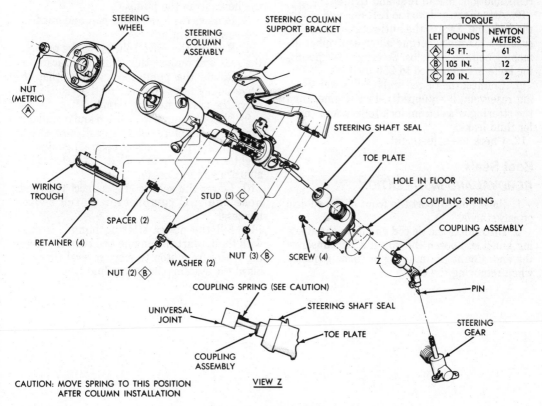

TORQUE		
LET	POUNDS	NEWTON METERS
A	45 FT.	61
B	105 IN.	12
C	20 IN.	2

CAUTION: MOVE SPRING TO THIS POSITION AFTER COLUMN INSTALLATION

VIEW Z

Standard steering column

2. Remove the front wheels and tire assemblies.

3. Remove the tie rod ends from the steering knuckles.

4. Lower and disconnect the steering column from the steering gear pinion shaft.

5. If equipped, remove the anti-rotation link from the crossmember and the air diverter valve from the left side of the crossmember.

6. Place a transmission jack, or floor jack with a wide lifting flange, under the front suspension K-crossmember. Support the crossmember and remove the four crossmember to frame attaching bolts. Slowly lower the crossmember until enough room is gained to remove the steering gear assembly. Place stands under the crossmember, if available.

7. Remove the splash and boot shields. If equipped with power steering, disconnect the power steering hoses.

8. Remove the bolts that attach the steering gear assembly to the crossmember. Remove the assembly from the left side of the vehicle.

9. Line up the gear pinion with the column. Installation is in the reverse order of removal. On models with manual steering, be sure the master serration of the steering gear aligns with the steering column connector. the right rear crossmember bolt is the alignment pilot for reinstallation. Install first and tighten.

10. Attach the gear to the K-frame and secure the K-frame. Secure the anti-rotation link. Secure the K-frame. Torque all crossmember attaching bolts to 90 ft. lbs. Steering gear mounting bolts are tightened to 250 inch lbs.

11. Connect the tie rod ends. Fill power steering reservoir (if equipped), start engine, turn the steering wheel from lock to lock and check for fluid leaks.

12. Check toe adjustment.

Boot Seals

REMOVAL AND INSTALLATION

1. Raise and support the front of the vehicle on jackstands.

2. Disconnect the tie rod end from the steering knuckle. Loosen the jam nut and unscrew the end. Count the number of turns required when removing the end.

3. Cut the inner boot clamp, use pliers to expand the outer clamp and remove.

4. Locate and mark for reinstallation, the location of the breather tube.

5. Use a small tool to lift the boot from inner mounting groove and slide boot from the shaft.

6. Install the new boot and clamps. Locate breather tube to reference mark. Lubricate boot and mounting groove with silicone type lubricant. Install the tie rod end the same number of turns as counted when removing.

Power Steering Pump

REMOVAL AND INSTALLATION

1. Disconnect the negative battery cable from the battery. Disconnect the vapor hose (canister) from the carburetor. Disconnect the A/C compressor clutch wire harness connector at the compressor.

2. Remove the power steering pump adjustment bolt. Remove the power steering hose bracket from mounting.

3. Raise and support the front of the vehicle on jackstands.

4. Disconnect the return hose from the steering gear and drain the fluid into a container.

5. Remove the right side splash shield if it interferes with pump removal. After the fluid has drained from the pump, disconnect and plug the hoses from the pump.

6. Remove the lower pivot bolt and nut from the pump mounting.

7. Remove the drive belt. Move the pump to the rear and remove the adjusting bracket.

8. Rotate the pump clockwise so that the drive pulley faces the rear of the vehicle. Remove the power steering pump.

9. Place the pump in position and install it in reverse order of removal. Install new O-ring seal on the pump hoses before installation. Tighten the tube nuts to 25 ft. lbs. Refer to belt abjustments in Chapter 1.

10. Lower the vehicle and connect the vapor hose and A/C compressor clutch switch harness.

11. Fill the power steering pump reservoir with fluid. Start the engine and turn the steering wheel from stop to stop, several times, to bleed the system. check the fluid level.

BRAKE SYSTEMS

Hydraulic System

BASIC OPERATING PRINCIPLES

Hydraulic systems are used to actuate the brakes of all modern automobiles. The system transports the power required to force the frictional surfaces of the braking system together from the pedal to the individual brake units at each wheel. A hydraulic system is used for two reasons. First, fluid under pressure can be carried to all parts of an automobile by small hoses-some of which are flexible-without taking up a significant amount of room or posing routing problems. Second, a great mechanical advantage can be given to the brake pedal end of the system, and the foot pressure required to actuate the brakes can be reduced by making the surface area of the master cylinder pistons smaller than that of any of the pistons in the wheel cylinders or calipers.

The master cylinder consists of a fluid reservoir and either a single or double cylinder and piston assembly. Double type master cylinders are designed to separate the front and rear braking systems hydraulically in case of a leak.

Steel lines carry the brake fluid to a point on the vehicle's frame near each of the vehicle's wheels. The fluid is then carried to the wheel cylinders by flexible tubes in order to allow for suspension and steering movements.

Each wheel cylinder contains two pistons, one at either end, which push outward in opposite directions. In disc brake systems, the cylinders are part of the calipers. One or four cylinders are used to force the brake pads against the disc, but all cylinders contain one piston only. All pistons employ some type of seal, usually made of rubber, to minimize fluid leakage. A rubber dust boot seals the outer end of the cylinder against dust and dirt. The boot fits around the outer end of the piston on disc brake calipers, and around the brake actuating rod on wheel cylinders.

The hydraulic system operates as follows: When at rest, the entire system, from the piston(s) in the master cylinder to those in the wheel cylinders or calipers, is full of brake fluid. Upon application of the brake pedal, fluid trapped in front of the master cylinder piston(s) is forced through the lines to the wheel cylinders. Here, it forces the pistons outward, in the case of drum brakes, and inward toward the disc, in the case of disc brakes. The motion of the pistons is opposed by return springs mounted outside the cylinders in drum brakes, and by internal springs or spring seals, in disc brakes.

Upon release of the brake pedal, a spring located inside the master cylinder immediately returns the master cylinder pistons to the normal position. The pistons contain check valves and the master cylinder has compensating ports drilled in it. These are uncovered as the pistons reach their normal position. The piston check valves allow fluid to flow toward the wheel cylinders or calipers as the pistons withdraw. Then, as the return springs force the brake pads or shoes into the released position, the excess fluid reservoir through the compensating ports. It is during the time the pedal is in the released position that any fluid that has leaked out of the system will be replaced through the compensating ports.

Dual circuit master cylinders employ two pistons, located one behind the other, in the same cylinder. The primary piston is actuated directly by mechanical linkage from the brake pedal. The secondary piston is actuated by fluid trapped between the two pistons. If a leak develops in front of the secondary piston, it moves forward until it bottoms against the front of the master cylinder, and the fluid trapped between the pistons will operate the rear brakes. If the rear brakes develop a leak, the primary piston will move forward until direct contact with the secondary piston takes place, and it will force the secondary piston to actuate the front brakes. In either case, the brake pedal moves farther when the brakes are applied, and less braking power is available.

All dual-circuit systems use a switch to warn the driver when only half of the brake system is operational. This switch is located in a valve body which is mounted on the firewall or the frame below the master cylinder. A hydraulic piston receives pressure from both circuits, each circuit's pressure being applied to one end of the piston. When the pressures are in balance, the piston remains stationary. When one circuit has a leak, however, the greater pressure in that circuit during application of the brakes will push the piston to one side, closing the switch and activating the brake warning light.

In disc brake systems, this valve body also contains a metering valve and, in some cases, a proportioning valve. The metering valve keeps pressure from traveling to the disc brakes on the front wheels until the brake shoes on the rear wheels have contacted the drums, ensuring that the front brakes will never be used alone. The proportioning valve controls the pressure to the rear brakes to avoid rear wheel lock-up during very hard braking.

Warning lights may be tested by depressing the brake pedal and holding it while opening one of the wheel cylinder bleeder screws. If this does not cause the light to go on, substitute a new lamp, make continuity checks, and, finally, replace the switch as necessary.

The hydraulic system may be checked for leaks by applying pressure to the pedal gradually and steadily. If the pedal sinks very slowly to the floor, the system has a leak. This is not to be confused with a springy or spongy feel due to the compression of air within the lines. If the system leaks, there will be a gradual change in the position of the pedal with a constant pressure.

Check for leaks along all lines and at wheel cylinders. If no external leaks are apparent, the problem is inside the master cylinder.

Disc Brakes

BASIC OPERATING PRINCIPLES

Instead of the traditional expanding brakes that press outward against a circular drum, disc brake systems utilize a disc (rotor) with brake pads positioned on either side of it. Braking effect is achieved in a manner similar to the way you would squeeze a spinning phonograph record between your fingers. The disc (rotor) is a casting with cooling fins between the two braking surfaces. This enables air to circulate between the braking surfaces making them less sensitive to heat buildup and more resistant to fade. Dirt and water do not affect braking action since contaminants are thrown off by the centrifugal action of the rotor or scraped off the by the pads. Also, the equal clamping action of the two brake pads tends to ensure uniform, straightline stops. Disc brakes are inherently self-adjusting.

There are three general types of disc brake:

1. A fixed caliper.
2. A floating caliper.
3. A sliding caliper.

The fixed caliper design uses two pistons mounted on either side of the rotor (in each side of the caliper). The caliper is mounted rigidly and does not move.

The sliding and floating designs are quite similar. In fact, these two types are often lumped together. In both designs, the pad on the inside of the rotor is moved into contact with the rotor by hydraulic force. The caliper, which is not held in a fixed position, moves slightly, bringing the outside pad into contact with the rotor. There are various methods of attaching floating calipers. Some pivot at the bottom or top, and some slide on mounting bolts. In any event, the end result is the same.

Drum Brakes

BASIC OPERATING PRINCIPLES

Drum brakes employ two brake shoes mounted on a stationary backing plate. These shoes are positioned inside a circular drum which rotates with the wheel assembly. The shoes are held in place by springs; this allows them to slide toward the drums (when they are applied) while keeping the linings and drums in alignment. The shoes are actuated by a wheel cylinder which is mounted at the top of the backing plate. When the brakes are applied, hydraulic pressure forces the wheel cylinder's actuating links outward. Since these links bear directly against the top of the brake shoes, the tops of the shoes are then forced against the inner side of the drum. This action forces the bottoms of the two shoes to contact the brake drum by rotating the entire assembly slightly (known as servo action). When pressure within the wheel cylinder is relaxed, return springs pull the shoes back away from the drum.

Most modern drum brakes are designed to self-adjust themselves during application when the vehicle is moving in reverse. This motion causes both shoes to rotate very slightly with the drum, rocking an adjusting lever, thereby causing rotation of the adjusting screw.

Power Boosters

Power brakes operate just as standard brake systems except in the actuation of the master cylinder pistons. A vacuum diaphragm is located on the front of the master cylinder and assists the driver in applying the brakes, reducing both the effort and travel he must put into moving the brake pedal.

The vacuum diaphragm housing is connected to the intake manifold by a vacuum hose. A check valve is placed at the point where the hose enters the diaphragm housing, so that during periods of low manifold vacuum brake assist vacuum will not be lost.

Depressing the brake pedal closes off the vacuum source and allows atmospheric pressure to enter on one side of the diaphragm. This causes the master cylinder pistons to move and apply the brakes. When the brake pedal is released, vacuum is applied to both sides of the diaphragm, and return springs return the diaphragm and master cylinder pistons to the released position. If the vacuum fails, the brake pedal rod will butt against the end of the master cylinder actuating rod, and direct mechanical application will occur as the pedal is depressed.

The hydraulic and mechanical problems that apply to conventional brake systems also apply to power brakes, and should be checked for if the tests below do not reveal the problem.

Test for a system vacuum leak as described below:

1. Operate the engine at idle without touching the brake pedal for at least one minute.
2. Turn off the engine, and wait one minute.
3. Test for the presence of assist vacuum by depressing the brake pedal and releasing it several times. Light application will produce less and less pedal travel, if vacuum was present. If there is no vacuum, air is leaking into the system somewhere.

Test for system operation as follows:

1. Pump the brake pedal (with engine off) until the supply vacuum is entirely gone.
2. Put a light, steady pressure on the pedal.
3. Start the engine, and operate it at idle. If the system is operating, the brake pedal should fall toward the floor if constant pressure is maintained on the pedal.

Power brake systems may be tested for hydraulic leaks just as ordinary systems are tested.

Your vehicle is equipped with pin slider type caliper front disc brakes and automatic adjuster equipped rear drum brakes. The brake system is diagonally split, with the left front and right rear brakes on one hydraulic system and the right front and left rear on the other. Should one side of the split system fail, the other should provide enough braking power to bring the vehicle to a stop. Other components included in the brake system are: A brake warning switch, master cylinder, a lead sensing dual proportioning valve, a brake booster and the necessary hoses and lines.

Adjustments

Periodic brake adjustment is not necessary as the front calipers are inherently self-adjusting, and the rear brakes are equipped with self-adjusters. In the event of a brake reline or component service requiring brake shoe removal, initial manual adjustment of the rear brake shoes will speed up servicing time. Front brake pads adjust themselves as the brake pedal is applied. After installing new front brake pads pump the brake pedal several times until a firm feeling is obtained. The pads will be incorrect adjustment.

DRUM BRAKES

1. To make an initial rear brake shoe adjustment, raise and support the rear of the vehicle on jackstands, so that both wheels are off the ground and can turn freely.
2. Remove the adjusting hole cover at the back of the brake mounting plates.
3. Be sure the parking brake is fully released and that there is slack in the brake cables.
4. Insert a brake adjusting tool through the hole in the backing plate until the adjuster starwheel is engaged. move the adjusting tool upward to turn the starwheel. Continue until a slight drag is felt when the wheel is rotated.
5. Insert a thin screwdriver or piece of stiff rod through the backing plate slot and push the adjuster lock tab away from the starwheel. Move the adjusting tool down while holding the locking tab out of the way. Back off the starwheel until the wheel turns freely without any brake drag. Install the adjusting slot cover.
6. Repeat the procedure for the other rear wheel. Adjust the parking brake after initial rear brake adjustment is finished. Check parking brake adjustment after applying several times, insure freedom from brake drag.

Brake Light Switch

The brake light switch is a self adjusting unit installed on the brake pedal shaft pivot pin.

REMOVAL AND INSTALLATION

1. Remove the old switch from the retaining bracket.
2. Install the new brake light switch into the bracket and push the switch as far forward as it will go.

3. The brake pedal will move forward slightly when the switch is pushed forward.

4. Pull back on the brake pedal gently. As the brake pedal is pulled back, the switch striker will move toward the switch. When the brake pedal can not be pull back any further, the switch will ratchet to the correct position. Very little movement is required, and no further adjustment is required.

Master Cylinder

The master cylinder is of tandem design, having an anondized aluminum body and a glass reinforced nylon reservoir. If the cylinder bore is pitted or scratched, the body must be replaced as honing will remove the anodized surface. The reservoir is indexed to prevent incorrect installation and the cap diaphragms are slotted to allow internal pressure to equalize. A secondary outlet tube leading from the master cylinder is connected to the differential valve mounted underneath the master cylinder. The front part of the valve supplied the right rear and left front brakes. The rear portion supplied the right rear and left front. The rear portion of the valve is connect to the primary outlet tube of the master cylinder.

REMOVAL AND INSTALLATION

1. Disconnect the primary and secondary brake lines at the master cylinder. Tape or plug the ends of the lines.

2. Remove the nuts attaching the master cylinder to the power brake booster.

3. Wrap a rag around the brake line tilting holes, slide the master straight away from the booster and remove from the vehicle. Take care not to spill any brake fluid on the finish. Flush off with water if any fluid is spilled.

4. Bench bleed the master cylinder. (See the Bleeding section). Install the master cylinder over the mounting studs. After aligning the master cylinder pushrod and mounting studs, hold the cylinder in position and start the attaching nuts but do not tighten completely. In-

stall the brake lines but do not tighten completely.

5. After the brake lines are installed, tighten the cylinder mounting nuts fully and then the brake lines.

6. Finish bleeding the brake system.

OVERHAUL

The aluminum master cylinder cannot be rebuilt; service is limited to replacement.

Fluid Reservoir

REMOVAL AND INSTALLATION

1. Remove the master cylinder from the vehicle. Clean the outside of the reservoir and cylinder.

2. Remove the reservoir caps and empty the brake fluid. Do not reuse the old fluid.

3. Position the master cylinder in a vise. Pad the vise jaws and do not overtighten.

4. Rock the reservoir from side to side to loosen and lift up to remove from the master cylinder. Do not pry the reservoir with an tools. Damage to the reservoir will result.

5. Remove the old housing to reservoir mounting grommets. Clean the cylinder and reservoir grommet mounting surfaces.

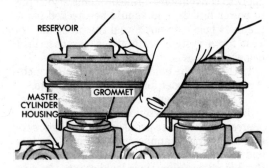

Removing/installing the fluid reservoir

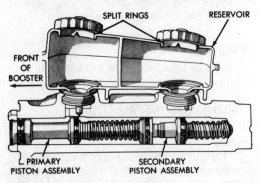

Cutaway view of the master cylinder

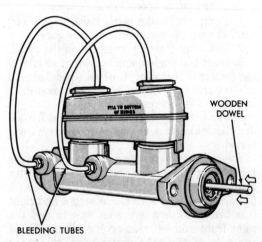

Bleeding the master cylinder

6. Install new mounting grommets in the master cylinder housing.

7. Lubricate the mounting surfaces of the grommets with brake fluid.

8. Place the reservoir in position over the grommets and seat it into the grommets using a rocking motion.

9. Be sure that the reservoir is fully seated on the master cylinder and the bottom of the reservoir touches the top of the grommets.

10. Fill the reservoir with fresh brake fluid and bench bleed the master cylinder.

Power Brake Booster

REMOVAL AND INSTALLATION

1. Remove the nuts that attach the master cylinder to the power brake booster. Slowly and carefully slide the master cylinder away from the booster, off the mounting studs. Allow the cylinder to rest against the fender shield.

2. Disconnect the vacuum hose from the brake booster.

3. From the inside of the vehicle under the instrument panel, locate the point where the booster linkage connects to the brake pedal. Use a small tool and position between the center tang of the booster linkage to brake pedal retaining clip. Rotate the tool and pull the retainer from the pin. disconnect the brake pedal.

4. Remove the brake booster mounting nuts and unfasten the brackets mounting the steel water line at the firewall and left frame rail. On models equipped with a manual transmission, unfasten the clutch cable bracket at the shock tower and move it to the side.

5. The booster mounting bracket holes are slotted, slide the booster up and to the left. Tilt the booster inboard and up to remove from the engine compartment.

6. Position the power booster over the firewall mounting studs. Install the mounting nuts and tighten to 200-300 inch lbs.

7. install the steel heater line bracket and clutch cable bracket, if equipped.

8. Carefully install the master cylinder and tighten the mounting bolts to 200-300 inch lbs.

9. Connect the vacuum line to the power brake booster.

10. Connect the pedal linkage to the booster push rod after lubricating the pivot point with white grease. Install a new retainer clip. Check brake and stoplight operation.

Pressure Differential Switch/Warning Light

As mentioned before, the hydraulic brake system on your vehicle is diagonally split; the left front and right rear are part of one system

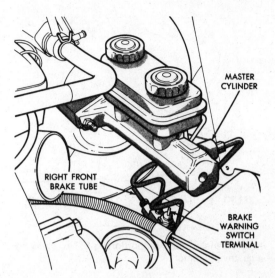

Brake warning switch location

and the right front and left rear part of the other. Both systems are routed through a pressure differential switch (located under the master cylinder) which is designed to warn the driver should a failure occur. If hydraulic pressure is lost in one side of the split system the switch will activate a warning light on the instrument panel, indicating that the brake system should be checked and repaired, if necessary. After repairs to the system have been made, the switch will automatically recenter itself and the light will go out.

TESTING

To test the warning switch system, raise the front or rear of the vehicle and safely support with jackstands. Open a caliper or wheel cylinder bleeder valve while a helper holds pressure on the brake pedal. As fluid is lost through the bleeder, the dash lamp should light. If the lamp fails to light, check for a burned out bulb, disconnected socket, or a broken or disconnected wire at the switch. Replace the warning switch if the rest of the circuit members check out. Be sure to fill the master cylinder and bleed the brakes after repairs have been completed.

Height Sensing Proportioning Valve

All vehicles are equipped with a height sensing dual proportioning valve. The valve is located under the rear floor pan just forward of the rear axle. The valve automatically provides the proper brake balance between the front and rear brakes regardless of the vehicle load condition. the valve modulates the rear brakes sensing the loading condition of the vehicle through

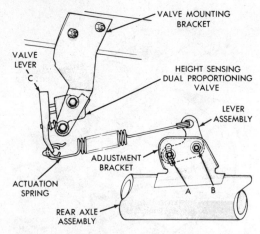

VALVE MOUNTING BRACKET

VALVE LEVER
C

HEIGHT SENSING DUAL PROPORTIONING VALVE

LEVER ASSEMBLY

ADJUSTMENT BRACKET

ACTUATION SPRING

A B

REAR AXLE ASSEMBLY

Height sensing dual proportioning valve, showing adjustment points

relative height movement between the rear axle and load floor.

The valve is mounted on a crossmember and connected to an adjustable lever on the rear axle by a large spring. When the vehicle is unloaded or lightly leaded, the hydraulic line pressure is minimized. As the vehicle is more heavily loaded and the ride height lowers, the spring moves the valve control arm to allow higher rear brake pressure.

NOTE: *Because ride height determines rear brake pressure, the use of aftermarket load leveling or capacity increasing devices should be avoided.*

The proportioning section of the valve transmits full input pressure up to a certain point, called the split point. Beyond the split point the valve reduces the amount of pressure increase to the rear brakes according to a certain ratio. This means that on light brake pedal application equal pressure will be transmitted to the front and rear brakes. On harder pedal application, pressure transmitted to the rear brakes will be lower to prevent rear wheel lock-up and skid.

TESTING

NOTE: *Two pressure gauges and adapter fittings (tool set C4007A or equivalent) are required of the following test.*

If premature rear wheel lock-up and skid is experienced frequently, it could be an indication that the fluid pressure to the rear brakes is excessive and that a malfunction has occurred in the proportioning valve or an adjustment is necessary.

1. If a pressure gauge and adapter fittings are on hand, proceed with the following test.

2. Disconnect the external spring at the valve lever.

3. Install one pressure gauge and T-fitting in

line from either master cylinder port to the brake valve assembly.

4. Install the second gauge to either rear brake outlet port between the valve assembly and the rear brake line. Bleed the rear brakes.

5. Have a helper apply and hold pedal pressure to get a reading on the valve inlet gauge and outlet gauge. The inlet pressure should be 500 psi and the outlet pressure should be 100-200 psi. If the required pressures are not present, replace the valve. If the test pressures are alright, adjust the external spring and arm.

VALVE INSTALLATION AND ADJUSTMENT

1. Raise and support the rear of the vehicle. Position jackstands at the rear contact pads so that the rear axle will hang free with the tires off the ground.

2. Loosen the rear axle mounted adjustable lever assembly and remove the actuating spring. Remove the brake lines from the proportioning valve and remove the valve.

3. Install the brake lines loosely in the proportioning valve and mount valve in position.

4. Tighten the brake lines, fill the master cylinder to the correct fluid level and bleed the brakes.

5. Confirm that the axle is hanging free and at full rebound position with the wheels and tires mounted.

6. Confirm that the actuating spring is connected between the proportioning valve and axle adjusting lever. the axle adjusting lever mounting bolts should be loose so that the bracket can be moved.

7. Push the control lever on the proportioning valve towards the valve until it is against the body and hold it in that position.

8. Move the axle lever up and away to apply tension to the spring. When all free play is taken out of the spring, but the spring is not stretched, tighten the mounting bolt that goes through the slotted side of the adjustment bracket. Tighten the anchor bolt. Both mounting bolts should be tightened to 150 inch lbs.

Brake Hoses
REMOVAL AND INSTALLATION

1. Right and left brake hoses are not interchangeable. Remove the connecter at the caliper, then remove the mounting bracket from the strut support and finally, remove the the from the upper body mount and disconnect the hose from the steel line.

2. Always use a flare wrench to prevent rounding of the line fittings.

3. Install the new hose to the caliper first. Always use a new copper washer after making

sure the mounting surfaces are clean. Tighten the caliper hose fitting. Install the strut bracket next, then attach the steel line fitting. Position the upper keyed end of the hose to the body bracket and secure it.

4. Rear brake hoses should be attached first to the trailing arm bracket and the to the floor pan tubes.

5. Keep the hose as straight as possible, avoid twisting.

6. Bleed the brake system.

Bleeding the Brake System

The purpose of bleeding the brakes is to expel air trapped in the hydraulic system. The system must be bled whenever the pedal feels spongy, indicating that compressible air has entered the system. It must also be bled whenever the system has been opened or repaired. You will need a helper to help bleed the system. Always use fresh brake fluid.

BENCH BLEEDING

Always bench bleed the master cylinder before installin it on the vehicle.

1. Place the master cylinder in a vise.

2. Connect two lines to the fluid outlet orifices, bend the lines upwards and insert the opened ends into the reservoir.

3. Fill the reservoir with brake fluid.

4. Using a wooden dowel, depress the pushrod slowly, allowing the pistons to return. do this several times until the air bubbles are all expelled.

5. Remove the bleeding tubes from the master cylinder, plug the outlets and install the caps.

NOTE: *It is not necessary to bleed the entire system after replacing the master cylinder, provided that master cylinder has been bled and filled upon installation. However, if a soft pedal is experienced, bleed the entire system.*

SYSTEM BLEEDING

CAUTION: *Do not allow brake fluid to spill on the vehicle's finish; it will remove the paint. In case of a spill, flush the area with water.*

1. The sequence for bleeding is right rear, left front, left rear and right front. If the vehicle is equipped with power brakes, remove the vacuum by applying the brakes several times. Do not run the engine while bleeding the brakes.

2. Clean all the bleeder screws. You may want to give each one a shot of penetrating solvent to help loosen the fitting. Seizure is a common problem with bleeder screws, which then

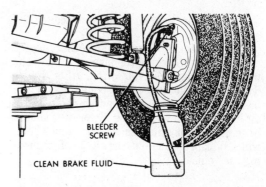

Bleeding the brake system

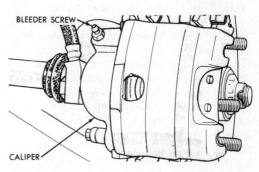

Open the bleeder screw at least one full turn on calipers

brake off, sometimes requiring replacement of the part to which they are attached.

3. Check the fluid level in the master cylinder and fill with DOT 3 brake fluid, if necessary.

NOTE: *Brake fluid absorbs moisture from the air. Don't leave the master cylinder or the fluid container uncovered any longer than necessary. Be careful handling the brake fluid,it is a great paint remover. If any brake fluid spills on the vehicle's finish, flush off with water immediately. Check the level of the fluid often when bleeding, and refill the reservoirs as necessary. Don't let them run dry, or you will have to repeat the process.*

4. Attach a length of clear vinyl tubing to the bleeder screw at the wheel cylinder or caliper. Insert the other end of the tube into a clear, clean jar half filled with brake fluid. Start at a rear cylinder first, then bleed the opposite side front cylinder.

5. Have your assistant slowly depress the brake pedal. As this is done, open the bleeder screw $\frac{1}{3}$-$\frac{1}{2}$ of a turn on wheel cylinders and at least one turn on calipers, and allow the fluid to run through the tube. Then close the bleeder screw before the pedal reaches the end of its travel. Have your assistant slowly release the pedal after the bleeder screw is closed. Repeat

this process until no air bubbles appear in the expelled fluid.

6. Repeat the procedure on the other calipers and cylinders, checking the level of fluid in the master cylinder reservoir often. After you're done, there should be no sponginess in the brake pedal feel. If there is, either there is still air in the line, in which case the process should be repeated, or there is a leak somewhere, which of course must be corrected before moving the vehicle.

FRONT DISC BRAKES

CAUTION: *Brake shoes contain asbestos, which has been determined to be a cancer causing agent. Never clean the brake surfaces with compressed air! Avoid inhaling any dust from any brake surface! When cleaning brake surfaces, use a commerically available brake cleaning fluid.*

The front disc brakes are of the single position, floating caliper type. The caliper "floats" through a rubber bushing, inserted into the inboard portion of the caliper, via a guide pin that is threaded into the mounting adapter. the mounting adapter for the caliper if fitted with two machined abutments that position and align the caliper. The guide pin and bushing, on the Kelsey-Hayes type caliper, control the movement of the caliper when the brakes are applied, providing a clamping force. The A.T.E. type caliper, uses two steel guide pins and mounting bushings to control the movement of the caliper upon brake application.

Disc Brake Pads

INSPECTION

1. Loosen the front wheel lug nuts slightly. Raise and support the front of the vehicle safely on jackstands. Remove the front wheel.

2. When the front wheels are off, the cutout built into the caliper housing will be exposed. Look through the opening and check the lining thickness of the inner and outer pads.

3. If a visual inspection does not give a clear picture of lining wear, a physical check will be necessary.

4. Refer to the following section covering pad removal and installation for instructions.

REMOVAL AND INSTALLATION

Kelsey-Hayes Type

NOTE: *Three anti-rattle clips are provided on each brake caliper, take note of locations for installation purposes.*

1. The Kelsey Hayes caliper uses one mounting pin. Loosen the wheel lug nuts slightly.

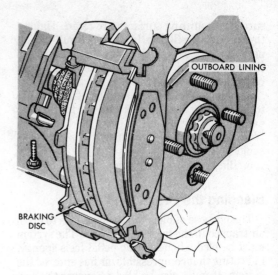

Removal/installation of the outboard brake pad

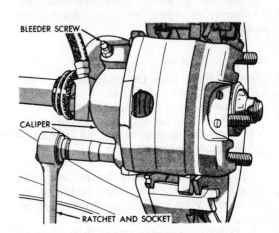

Removing/installing the guide pin

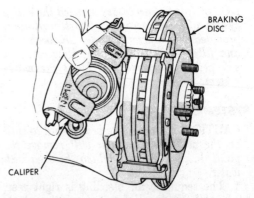

Removing/installing the brake caliper

Raise and safely support the front of the vehicle on jackstands. Remove the front wheel and tire assemblies.

2. Siphon about one quarter of the brake fluid from the master cylinder and replace the cover caps.

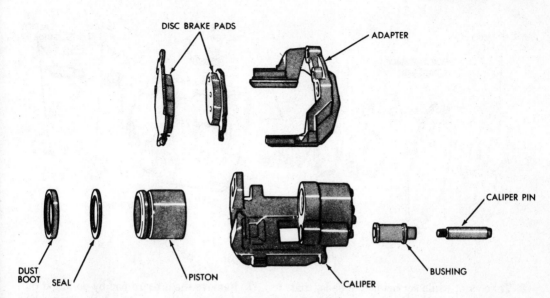

Kelsey Hayes disc brake caliper

3. Use the proper size socket wrench and remove the threaded caliper guide pin.

4. Insert a small prybar between the front edge of the caliper and the adapter rail. Apply steady upward pressure to loosen the adhesive seals. Remove the caliper by slowly sliding it up and off the adapter and disc rotor.

5. Support the caliper by hanging it out of the way on wire. Do not allow the caliper to be supported by the brake hose.

6. Observe the location of the anti-rattle clips. One clip is on the top of the inboard (closes to axle) brake pad. Another clip is on the bottom of the outboard brake pad, and the third is installed on the top finger of the caliper.

7. Slide the outboard brake pad from the adapter. Remove the brake disc rotor and remove the inboard pad.

8. Measure the brake lining and pad thickness. If the combined thickness at the thinnest point of the is $5/16"$ or less replace both front wheel brake pad assemblies.

9. Check around the caliper piston and boot for signs of brake fluid leakage. Inspect the dust boot around the caliper piston for cuts and breaks. If the boot is damaged or fluid leakage is visible, the caliper should be serviced. Check the adapter and caliper mounting surfaces for rust and dirt, clean them with a wire brush.

10. Remove the protective paper from the gaskets mounted on the metal part of the brake pads. Install the anti-rattle clips in position. Install inner brake pad on the adapter.

11. Install the brake disc rotor and outer brake pad.

12. Press the caliper back into the caliper until it bottoms. If may be necessary to place a small piece of wood on the piston and use a C-clamp to retract the piston. If so, tighten the clamp with slow steady pressure. Stop when resistance is felt.

13. Lower the caliper over the brake pads and disc rotor. Install the caliper guide pin and tighten to 25-35 ft. lbs. Take care not to cross thread the guide pin.

14. After both calipers have been installed, fill the master cylinder and bleed the brakes if the caliper were rebuilt. If the calipers were not serviced, pump the brakes until a firm brake pedal is obtained.

15. Install the front wheels and lower the vehicle. After the vehicle is lowered, check the lug nut torque and tighten to required specification to 95 ft. lbs. Road test the vehicle and make several firm but not hard stops to wear off any dirt from the pads or rotor.

A.T.E. Type

NOTE: *The caliper is equipped with one holddown spring running across the outboard fingers of the caliper, and is also equipped with an inner shoe to piston mounting clip.*

1. The A.T.E. caliper uses two mounting pins. Loosen the wheel lugs slightly. Raise and safely support the front of the vehicle.

2. Remove the wheel and tire assembly.

3. Loosen, but do not remove the two steel caliper guide pins. Back the pins out until the caliper can be moved freely.

4. Pull the lower end of the caliper out from the stering knuckle support. Roll the caliper up and away from the disc rotor. The disc brake pads will remain located in their caliper positions.

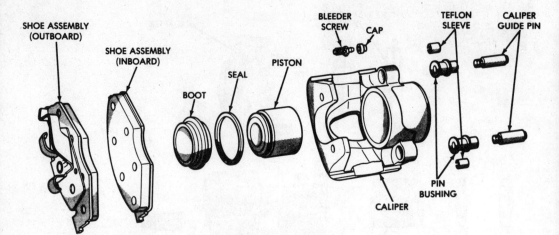

ATE disc brake caliper

5. Take care, while servicing the pads, that strain is not put on the brake hose.

6. Pry the outboard pad toward the bottom opened end of the caliper. The pad is retained by a captured clip. Remove the pad.

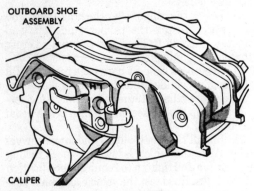

Removing the outboard pad—ATE

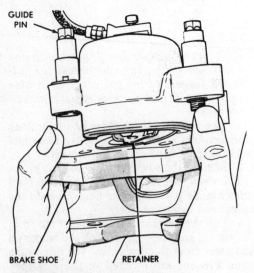

Removing the inboard pad—ATE

7. Remove the inboard pad by pulling it outward from the caliper piston. It is retained by a captive clip.

8. Inspect the caliper. Check for piston seal leaks and boot damage. Service the caliper as required.

9. Press the caliper piston slowly back into the caliper bore. Use a small block of wood and a C-clamp, if necessary. Tighten the clamp slowly, and make sure the piston is not cocked. Gently bottom the piston in the caliper.

10. The inboard pads are interchangeable, the outboard pads are marked with an **L** or **R** relating to the side of the vehicle they are to be used on.

11. Place the inboard pad clip into the caliper piston and push into position on the piston.

12. Place the outboard pad retaininer clip over the ears of the caliper and slide the pad into position. If the replacement pads are equipped with a noise suppression gasket, remove the protective paper from the gasket before installation.

13. Lower the caliper over the disc rotor and align the holddown spring under the machined surface of the steering knuckle. Install the caliper mounting pins, take care not to crossthread and tighten the pins to 18-26 ft. lbs. Pump the brake pedal several times to move the pads against the rotor. If the caliper has been rebuilt, or other system service completed, bleed the brake system.

14. Install the wheel and tire assembly. Lower the vehicle. Do not move the vehicle until a firm brake pedal is verified.

Caliper
OVERHAUL

1. Remove the caliper as described in the previous section.

CHILTON'S
AUTO BODY
REPAIR TIPS

**Tools and Materials • Step-by-Step Illustrated Procedures
How To Repair Dents, Scratches and Rust Holes
Spray Painting and Refinishing Tips**

With a little practice, basic body repair procedures can be mastered by any do-it-yourself mechanic. The step-by-step repairs shown here can be applied to almost any type of auto body repair.

TOOLS & MATERIALS

You may already have basic tools, such as hammers and electric drills. Other tools unique to body repair — body hammers, grinding attachments, sanding blocks, dent puller, half-round plastic file and plastic spreaders — are relatively inexpensive and can be obtained wherever auto parts or auto body repair parts are sold. Portable air compressors and paint spray guns can be purchased or rented.

Auto Body Repair Kits

The best and most often used products are available to the do-it-yourselfer in kit form, from major manufacturers of auto body repair products. The same manufacturers also merchandise the individual products for use by pros.

Kits are available to make a wide variety of repairs, including holes, dents and scratches and fiberglass, and offer the advantage of buying the materials you'll need for the job. There is little waste or chance of materials going bad from not being used. Many kits may also contain basic body-working tools such as body files, sanding blocks and spreaders. Check the contents of the kit before buying your tools.

BODY REPAIR TIPS

Safety

Many of the products associated with auto body repair and refinishing contain toxic chemicals. Read all labels before opening containers and store them in a safe place and manner.

• Wear eye protection (safety goggles) when using power tools or when performing any operation that involves the removal of any type of material.

• Wear lung protection (disposable mask or respirator) when grinding, sanding or painting.

Sanding

1 Sand off paint before using a dent puller. When using a non-adhesive sanding disc, cover the back of the disc with an overlapping layer or two of masking tape and trim the edges. The disc will last considerably longer.

2 Use the circular motion of the sanding disc to grind *into* the edge of the repair. Grinding or sanding away from the jagged edge will only tear the sandpaper.

3 Use the palm of your hand flat on the panel to detect high and low spots. Do not use your fingertips. Slide your hand slowly back and forth.

WORKING WITH BODY FILLER

Mixing The Filler

Cleanliness and proper mixing and application are extremely important. Use a clean piece of plastic or glass or a disposable artist's palette to mix body filler.

1 Allow plenty of time and follow directions. No useful purpose will be served by adding more hardener to make it cure (set-up) faster. Less hardener means more curing time, but the mixture dries harder; more hardener means less curing time but a softer mixture.

2 Both the hardener and the filler should be thoroughly kneaded or stirred before mixing. Hardener should be a solid paste and dispense like thin toothpaste. Body filler should be smooth, and free of lumps or thick spots.

Getting the proper amount of hardener in the filler is the trickiest part of preparing the filler. Use the same amount of hardener in cold or warm weather. For contour filler (thick coats), a bead of hardener twice the diameter of the filler is about right. There's about a 15% margin on either side, but, if in doubt use less hardener.

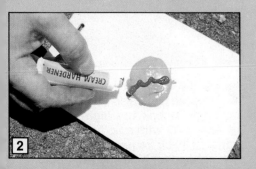

3 Mix the body filler and hardener by wiping across the mixing surface, picking the mixture up and wiping it again. Colder weather requires longer mixing times. Do not mix in a circular motion; this will trap air bubbles which will become holes in the cured filler.

Applying The Filler

1 For best results, filler should not be applied over 1/4" thick.

Apply the filler in several coats. Build it up to above the level of the repair surface so that it can be sanded or grated down.

The first coat of filler must be pressed on with a firm wiping motion.

Apply the filler in one direction only. Working the filler back and forth will either pull it off the metal or trap air bubbles.

REPAIRING DENTS

Before you start, take a few minutes to study the damaged area. Try to visualize the shape of the panel before it was damaged. If the damage is on the left fender, look at the right fender and use it as a guide. If there is access to the panel from behind, you can reshape it with a body hammer. If not, you'll have to use a dent puller. Go slowly and work the metal a little at a time. Get the panel as straight as possible before applying filler.

1 This dent is typical of one that can be pulled out or hammered out from behind. Remove the headlight cover, headlight assembly and turn signal housing.

2 Drill a series of holes ½ the size of the end of the dent puller along the stress line. Make some trial pulls and assess the results. If necessary, drill more holes and try again. Do not hurry.

3 If possible, use a body hammer and block to shape the metal back to its original contours. Get the metal back as close to its original shape as possible. Don't depend on body filler to fill dents.

4 Using an 80-grit grinding disc on an electric drill, grind the paint from the surrounding area down to bare metal. Use a new grinding pad to prevent heat buildup that will warp metal.

5 The area should look like this when you're finished grinding. Knock the drill holes in and tape over small openings to keep plastic filler out.

6 Mix the body filler (see Body Repair Tips). Spread the body filler evenly over the entire area (see Body Repair Tips). Be sure to cover the area completely.

7 Let the body filler dry until the surface can just be scratched with your fingernail. Knock the high spots from the body filler with a body file ("Cheesegrater"). Check frequently with the palm of your hand for high and low spots.

8 Check to be sure that trim pieces that will be installed later will fit exactly. Sand the area with 40-grit paper.

9 If you wind up with low spots, you may have to apply another layer of filler.

10 Knock the high spots off with 40-grit paper. When you are satisfied with the contours of the repair, apply a thin coat of filler to cover pin holes and scratches.

11 Block sand the area with 40-grit paper to a smooth finish. Pay particular attention to body lines and ridges that must be well-defined.

12 Sand the area with 400 paper and then finish with a scuff pad. The finished repair is ready for priming and painting (see Painting Tips).

Materials and photos courtesy of Ritt Jones Auto Body, Prospect Park, PA.

REPAIRING RUST HOLES

There are many ways to repair rust holes. The fiberglass cloth kit shown here is one of the most cost efficient for the owner because it provides a strong repair that resists cracking and moisture and is relatively easy to use. It can be used on large and small holes (with or without backing) and can be applied over contoured areas. Remember, however, that short of replacing an entire panel, no repair is a guarantee that the rust will not return.

1 Remove any trim that will be in the way. Clean away all loose debris. Cut away all the rusted metal. But be sure to leave enough metal to retain the contour or body shape.

2 Grind away all traces of rust with a 24-grit grinding disc. Be sure to grind back 3-4 inches from the edge of the hole down to bare metal and be sure all traces of paint, primer and rust are removed.

3 Block sand the area with 80 or 100 grit sandpaper to get a clear, shiny surface and feathered paint edge. Tap the edges of the hole inward with a ball peen hammer.

4 If you are going to use release film, cut a piece about 2-3″ larger than the area you have sanded. Place the film over the repair and mark the sanded area on the film. Avoid any unnecessary wrinkling of the film.

5 Cut 2 pieces of fiberglass matte to match the shape of the repair. One piece should be about 1″ smaller than the sanded area and the second piece should be 1″ smaller than the first. Mix enough filler and hardener to saturate the fiberglass material (see Body Repair Tips).

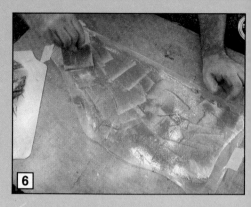

6 Lay the release sheet on a flat surface and spread an even layer of filler, large enough to cover the repair. Lay the smaller piece of fiberglass cloth in the center of the sheet and spread another layer of filler over the fiberglass cloth. Repeat the operation for the larger piece of cloth.

7 Place the repair material over the repair area, with the release film facing outward. Use a spreader and work from the center outward to smooth the material, following the body contours. Be sure to remove all air bubbles.

8 Wait until the repair has dried tack-free and peel off the release sheet. The ideal working temperature is 60°-90° F. Cooler or warmer temperatures or high humidity may require additional curing time. Wait longer, if in doubt.

9

9 Sand and feather-edge the entire area. The initial sanding can be done with a sanding disc on an electric drill if care is used. Finish the sanding with a block sander. Low spots can be filled with body filler; this may require several applications.

10

10 When the filler can just be scratched with a fingernail, knock the high spots down with a body file and smooth the entire area with 80-grit. Feather the filled areas into the surrounding areas.

11

11 When the area is sanded smooth, mix some topcoat and hardener and apply it directly with a spreader. This will give a smooth finish and prevent the glass matte from showing through the paint.

12

12 Block sand the topcoat smooth with finishing sandpaper (200 grit), and 400 grit. The repair is ready for masking, priming and painting (see Painting Tips).

Materials and photos courtesy Marson Corporation, Chelsea, Massachusetts

PAINTING TIPS

Preparation

1 SANDING — Use a 400 or 600 grit wet or dry sandpaper. Wet-sand the area with a ¼ sheet of sandpaper soaked in clean water. Keep the paper wet while sanding. Sand the area until the repaired area tapers into the original finish.

2 CLEANING — Wash the area to be painted thoroughly with water and a clean rag. Rinse it thoroughly and wipe the surface dry until you're sure it's completely free of dirt, dust, fingerprints, wax, detergent or other foreign matter.

3 MASKING — Protect any areas you don't want to overspray by covering them with masking tape and newspaper. Be careful not get fingerprints on the area to be painted.

4 PRIMING — All exposed metal should be primed before painting. Primer protects the metal and provides an excellent surface for paint adhesion. When the primer is dry, wet-sand the area again with 600 grit wet-sandpaper. Clean the area again after sanding.

4

Painting Techniques

Paint applied from either a spray gun or a spray can (for small areas) will provide good results. Experiment on an old piece of metal to get the right combination before you begin painting.

SPRAYING VISCOSITY (SPRAY GUN ONLY) — Paint should be thinned to spraying viscosity according to the directions on the can. Use only the recommended thinner or reducer and the same amount of reduction regardless of temperature.

AIR PRESSURE (SPRAY GUN ONLY) — This is extremely important. Be sure you are using the proper recommended pressure.

TEMPERATURE — The surface to be painted should be approximately the same temperature as the surrounding air. Applying warm paint to a cold surface, or vice versa, will completely upset the paint characteristics.

THICKNESS — Spray with smooth strokes. In general, the thicker the coat of paint, the longer the drying time. Apply several thin coats about 30 seconds apart. The paint should remain wet long enough to flow out and no longer; heavier coats will only produce sags or wrinkles. Spray a light (fog) coat, followed by heavier color coats.

DISTANCE — The ideal spraying distance is 8″-12″ from the gun or can to the surface. Shorter distances will produce ripples, while greater distances will result in orange peel, dry film and poor color match and loss of material due to overspray.

OVERLAPPING — The gun or can should be kept at right angles to the surface at all times. Work to a wet edge at an even speed, using a 50% overlap and direct the center of the spray at the lower or nearest edge of the previous stroke.

RUBBING OUT (BLENDING) FRESH PAINT — Let the paint dry thoroughly. Runs or imperfections can be sanded out, primed and repainted.

Don't be in too big a hurry to remove the masking. This only produces paint ridges. When the finish has dried for at least a week, apply a small amount of fine grade rubbing compound with a clean, wet cloth. Use lots of water and blend the new paint with the surrounding area.

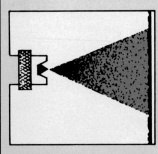

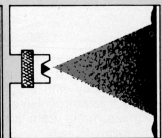

WRONG

Thin coat. Stroke too fast, not enough overlap, gun too far away.

CORRECT

Medium coat. Proper distance, good stroke, proper overlap.

WRONG

Heavy coat. Stroke too slow, too much overlap, gun too close.

2. Place rags on the upper control arm and place the caliper on top of the rags. Take care not to put strain on the brake hose. Place a small block of wood between the caliper piston and outer fingers.

3. Have a helper slowly depress the brake pedal to push the piston from the caliper bore using hydraulic pressure. If both front caliper pistons are to be removed, disconnect the brake hose, to the first caliper, at the frame bracket; plug the brake tube and repeat Steps 2 and 3. Never use air pressure to blow the pistons from their bores. The pistons are made of a plastic composition and can damage easily, or can fly out and cause personal injury.

4. Disconnect the flexible brake line from the caliper and remove the caliper to work area.

5. Position the caliper between padded jaws of a bench vise. Do not overtighten since excessive pressure can distort the caliper bore. Remove the dust boot.

6. Use a plastic tool and work the piston seal from the mounting groove. Do not use a metal tool; damage can result to the bore or burrs can be created on the edges of the machined seal groove.

7. Remove the guide pin bushing from the caliper. A wooden dowel makes a good tool for this purpose.

8. Clean all parts using a safe solvent or alcohol and blow dry if compressed air is on hand.

9. Inspect the piston bore for pitting or scores. Light scratches or pitting can be cleaned with crocus cloth and brake fluid. Deep scratches or pitting require honing.

10. Caliper hones are available from an auto parts supplier. Do not remove more than 0.001" of material from the bore. Deep scratches or pitting require caliper replacement.

11. After cleaning up the caliper bore with crocus cloth or hone, remove all the dirt and grit by flushing the caliper with brake fluid. After flushing, wipe dry with a lintless rag. Flush the caliper a second time and dry.

12. Carefully reclamp the caliper in the padded vise jaws. Dip the new piston seal in clean brake fluid and install in caliper bore mounting groove. Use your fingers to work the seal into the groove until properly seated.

13. Coat the caliper piston and piston boot with clean brake fluid. Install the boot on the caliper piston. Install the piston into the caliper bore. Push the piston past the seal until bottomed in the caliper bore. Use even pressure around the edges of the piston to avoid cocking when installing the piston.

14. Position the lip of the dust boot into the counterbore of the caliper. Use a seal driver or suitable tool to install the boot edge.

15. Compress the edges of the new guide pin

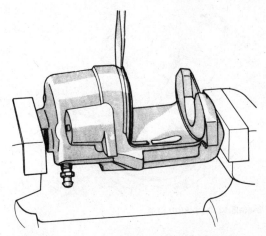

Remove the dust seal from the caliper piston

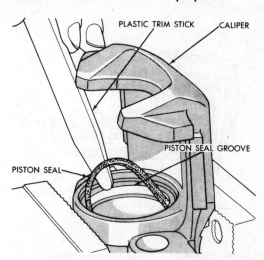

Removing the piston seal

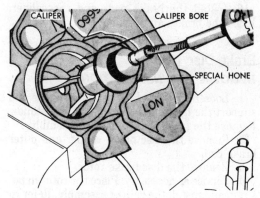

Honing the caliper bore

bushing with your fingers and install into position on the caliper. Press in on the bushing while working it into the caliper until fully seated. Be sure the bushing flanges extend evenly over the caliper casting on both sides when installed.

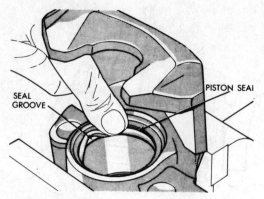

SEAL GROOVE

PISTON SEAL

Installing the piston seal

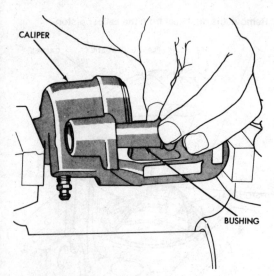

CALIPER

BUSHING

Installing bushings

16. Install the brake pads and the caliper. Bleed the brakes after caliper service.

Brake Disc (Rotor)

REMOVAL AND INSTALLATION

1. Loosen the wheel lugs slightly. Raise and support the front of the vehicle on jackstands. Remove the front wheel and tire assembly.
2. Remove the disc brake caliper and outer brake pad.
3. Remove the disc brake rotor.
4. Service as necessary. Place the rotor in position and install the caliper assembly. Refer to Brake Pad Removal and Installation for detailed procedures, if necessary.

INSPECTION

If excessive runout, wobble or thickness variation is present, feedback through the brake pedal will be felt when the brakes are applied. Pedal pulsation, chatter, surge and increased pedal travel can be caused when the disc rotor is worn unevenly or deeply scored. Remove the rotor and have an automotive machine shop measure the wear and check for runout. The machine shop can refinish the braking surfaces if replacement is not necessary.

REAR DRUM BRAKES

CAUTION: *Brake shoes contain asbestos, which has been determined to be a cancer causing agent. Never clean the brake surfaces with compressed air! Avoid inhaling any dust from any brake surface! When cleaning brake surfaces, use a commerically available brake cleaning fluid.*

Brake Drums

REMOVAL AND INSTALLATION

1. Raise and support the rear of the vehicle on jackstands. Remove the wheels and tire assemblies.
2. Remove the brake shoe adjusting slot cover from the rear of backing plate.
3. Insert a thin tool through the adjusting slot and hold the adjusting lever away from the starwheel. Insert an adjusting tool and back off the starwheel by prying downward with the tool.
4. Remove the center hub dust cover, nut, washer, brake drum, hub and wheel bearings.
5. Inspect the brake lining and drum for wear. Inspect the wheel cylinder for leakage. Service as required.
6. Remove, clean, inspect and repack the wheel bearings. Install the brake drum. Tighten the hub nut to 240-300 inch lbs. and back off the nut until bearing pressure is released. Retighten the nut finger tight, align the cotter pin hole and install the cotter pin.
7. Adjust the rear brakes as described in the beginning of this Chapter.

INSPECTION

Check the brake drum for any cracks, scores, grooves, or an out-of-round condition. Slight scores can be removed with Emory cloth, while extensive scoring or grooves will require machining. Have an automotive machine shop measure the wear and check the drum for runout. The shop will be able to turn the drum on a lathe, if necessary. Never have a drum turned more than 0.060". If the drum is cracked, or worn more than the limit, replace.

Brake Shoes

REMOVAL AND INSTALLATION

NOTE: *A pair of brake springs pliers or spring removal/installation tool and a retain-*

er cap spring tool are good tools to have on hand for this job.

1. Raise and support the rear of the vehicle on jackstands. Remove the rear wheels and brake drums.

NOTE: *Remove and install the brake shoes on one side at a time. Use the assembled side for reference.*

CAUTION: *Brake shoes contain asbestos, which has been determined to be a cancer causing agent. Never clean the brake surfaces with compressed air! Avoid inhaling any dust from any brake surface! When cleaning brake surfaces, use a commercially available brake cleaning fluid.*

2. Use a pair of brake spring pliers or appropriate tool and remove the shoe return springs from the top anchor. Take note that the secondary shoe spring is on top of the primary shoe spring. Install in the same position at installation time.

3. Slide the closed eye of the adjuster cable off of the anchor stud. Unhook the spring end and remove the cable, overload spring, cable guide and anchor plate.

4. Remove the adjusting lever from the spring by sliding forward to clear the pivot. Work the lever out from under the spring. Remove the spring from the pivot.

5. Unhook the bottom shoe-to-shoe spring from the secondary (back) shoe and disengage from the primary (front) shoe.

6. Spread the bottom of the brake shoes apart and remove the starwheel adjuster. Remove the parking brake strut and spring assembly.

7. Locate the shoe retainer nail head at the rear of the brake backing plate. Support the nail head with a finger, press in and twist the spring retainer washer with the special retainer tool or a pair of pliers. If you are using pliers, take care not to slip and pinch your fingers.

8. Remove the retainer, spring, inner washer and nail from both shoes. Remove the parking brake lever from the secondary brake shoe. Remove the shoes from the backing plate. Disconnect the parking brake lever from the brake cable.

9. Clean the backing plate with a safe solvent. Inspect the raised show support pads for rough or rusted contact areas. Clean and smooth as necessary. Clean and inspect the adjuster starwheels, apply a thin film of lubricant to the threads, socket and washer. Replace the starwheel if rust or threads show damage.

10. Inspect the holddown springs, return springs and adjuster spring. If the springs have been subjected to overheating or if their strength is questionable, replace the spring.

11. Inspect the wheel cylinder. If signs of leakage are present (a small amount of fluid inside the end boot is normal) rebuild or replace the cylinder.

12. Lubricate the shoe contact area pads on the backing plate with high temperature resistant white lube.

13. Engage the parking brake lever with the cable and install the lever on the secondary brake shoe. Engage the end of the brake shoe with the wheel cylinder piston and the top anchor. Install the retainer nail, washer, spring and retainer.

14. Position the primary shoe in like manner and install holddown pin assembly. Install the top anchor plate.

15. Install the parking brake strut and spring in position, press the lower part of the brake.

16. Straighten the adjuster cable and install

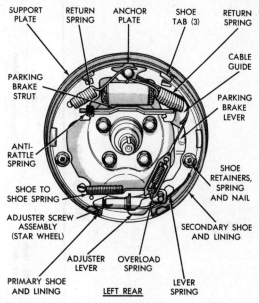

Rear wheel brake assembly

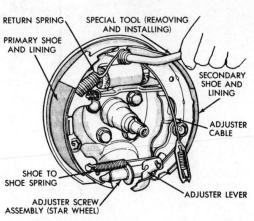

Removing the return springs

Brake Specifications

Year, Make, Model	Brake Shoe * Minimum Lining Thickness	Brake Drum Diameter Standard Size	Brake Drum Diameter Machine To	Brake Pad Minimum Lining Thickness	Brake Rotor Min. Thickness Machine To	Brake Rotor Min. Thickness Discard At	Brake Rotor Variation From Parallelism	Brake Rotor Runout T.I.R.	Caliper Guide Pins	Wheel Lugs or Nuts Torque (ft. lbs.)	Wheel Bearing Setting Step 1 Tighten Spindle Nut (ft. lbs.)	Wheel Bearing Setting Step 2 Back Off Retorque (in. lbs.)	Wheel Bearing Setting Step 3 Lock, or Back Off and Lock
84–88 Caravan, Mini Ram Van, Voyager	.030	9.000	9.060	.030*	.833	.803	.0005	.005	①	95	20–25	Handtight	Step 2

① Kelsey Hayes: 25–35 ft. lbs.
   A.T.E.: 18–26 ft. lbs.

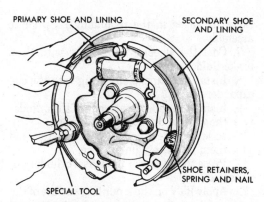

PRIMARY SHOE AND LINING

SECONDARY SHOE AND LINING

SHOE RETAINERS, SPRING AND NAIL

SPECIAL TOOL

Removing the shoe retainers

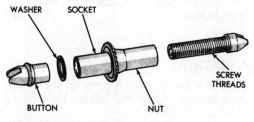

WASHER SOCKET

SCREW THREADS

BUTTON NUT

Adjuster screw assembly

the eye end over the top anchor. Be sure the lower spring end hook is facing inward.

17. Install the primary (front) shoe return spring. Place the cable guide in position on the secondary (rear) shoe (keep cable out of the way) and install the return spring. Check the cable guide and ensure proper mounting position. Squeeze the anchor ends of the return springs with pliers until they are parallel.

18. Carefully install the starwheel between the brake shoes. The wheel end goes closest the secondary (back) shoe. Wind out the starwheel until snug contact between the brake shoes will hold it in position.

19. Install the adjusting lever spring over the

pivot pin on the lower shoe web of the secondary shoe. Install the adjuster lever under the spring and over the pivot pin. Slide the lever rearward until it locks in position.

20. Thread the adjuster cable over the guide and hook the end of the overload spring on the adjuster lever. Make sure the cable is float on the guide and the eye end is against the anchor.

21. Check the operation of the adjuster by pulling the cable rearward. The starwheel should rotate upward as the adjuster lever engages the teeth.

22. Back off the starwheel, if necessary, and install the hub and drum. Adjust the brakes.

23. Repeat the procedures on the other rear wheel.

Wheel Cylinders

REMOVAL AND INSTALLATION

1. Jack up the rear of the vehicle and support it with jackstands.

2. Remove the brake drums as previously outlined.

3. Visually inspect the wheel cylinder boots for signs of excessive leakage. Replace any boots that are torn or broken.

NOTE: *A slight amount of fluid on the boots may not be a leak but may be a preservative fluid used at the factory.*

4. If a leak has been discovered, remove the brake shoes and check for contamination. Replace the linings if they are soaked with grease or brake fluid.

5. Disconnect the brake line from the wheel cylinder.

6. Remove the wheel cylinder attaching bolts, then pull the wheel cylinder out of its support.

7. Position the wheel cylinder onto the backing plate and loosely install the mounting bolts. Start the brake line into the cylinder. Tighten

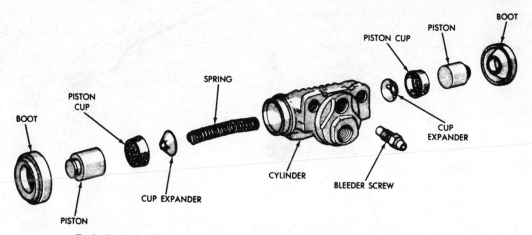

BOOT

PISTON CUP

BOOT

PISTON

SPRING

PISTON CUP

PISTON

CUP EXPANDER

CYLINDER

BLEEDER SCREW

CUP EXPANDER

Typical wheel cylinder (cup expanders may not be present on original equipment)

the mounting bolts and the brake line. Install the brake shoes and brake drum. Adjust the brake shoes.

8. Bleed the brake system.

OVERHAUL

1. Pry the boots away from the cylinder and remove the boots and pistons.

2. Disengage the boot from the piston.

3. Slide the piston into the cylinder bore and press inward to remove the other boot, piston and spring.

4. Wash all parts (except rubber parts) in clean brake fluid thoroughly. Do not use a rag; lint will adhere to the bore.

5. Inspect the cylinder bores. Light scoring can usually be cleaned up with crocus cloth. Heavier scores can be cleaned up with a cylinder hone. Black stains are caused by the piston cups and are no cause of concern. Bad scoring or pitting means that the wheel cylinder should be replaced.

6. Dip the pistons and new cups in clean brake fluid, or apply lubricant that is some-times packaged in the rebuilding kit prior to assembly.

7. Coat the wheel cylinder bore with clean brake fluid.

8. Install the expansion spring with the cup expanders.

9. Install the cups in each end of the cylinder with the open ends facing each other.

10. Assemble new boots on the piston and slide them into the cylinder bore.

11. Press the boot over the wheel cylinder until seated.

12. Apply RTV on the mounting surface of the backing plate. Install the wheel cylinder, and connect brake lines.

13. Install brake shoes, and drum. Adjust and bleed brakes.

Parking Brake
ADJUSTMENT

1. Raise and support the rear of the vehicle on jackstands. Apply and release the parking brake several times.

LET	TIGHTENING TORQUE	
⬦	40 IN. LBS.	5 N•m

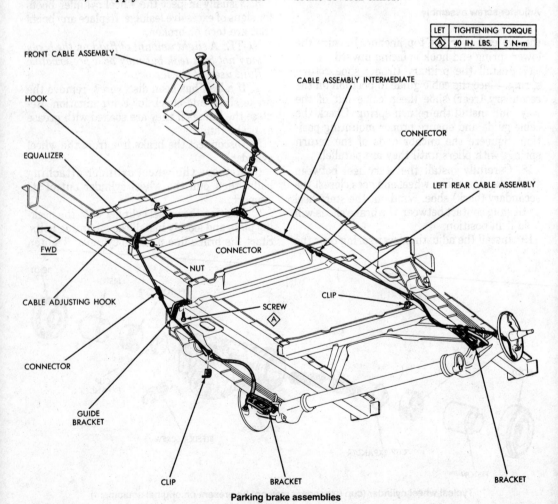

FRONT CABLE ASSEMBLY

CABLE ASSEMBLY INTERMEDIATE

HOOK

CONNECTOR

EQUALIZER

LEFT REAR CABLE ASSEMBLY

FWD

CONNECTOR

NUT

CABLE ADJUSTING HOOK

CLIP

SCREW

CONNECTOR

GUIDE BRACKET

CLIP

BRACKET

BRACKET

Parking brake assemblies

2. Clean the parking park adjustment bolts with a wire brush and lubricate the threads. Back off the adjusting nut until there is slack in the cable.

3. Check the rear brake adjustment, adjust as necessary.

4. Tighten the parking brake cable adjuster until the slight drag is felt when turning the rear wheel.

5. Loosen the cable until no drag is felt on either rear wheel. Back off adjusting nut two full turns more.

6. Apply and release the parking brake several times to ensure there is not rear wheel drag. Lower the vehicle.

REMOVAL AND INSTALLATION

Front Cable

1. Raise and support the front of the vehicle on jackstands.

2. Back off the adjuster nut until the cable can be released from the connectors.

3. Lift the floor mat for access to the floor pan. Force the seal surrounding the cable from the floor.

4. Pull the cable forward and disconnect from lever clevis. Remove the front cable from support bracket and vehicle.

5. Feed the new cable through the floor pan

hole. Attach the front end of the cable to the parking brake lever clevis and support.

6. Engage intermediate cable and adjust.

Intermediate Cable

1. Back off the parking brake adjuster. Disengage the front cable and rear cables from the intermediate cable connector.

2. Remove the intermediate cable. Install the new cable and adjust.

Rear Cables

1. Raise and support the rear of the vehicle on jackstands.

2. Back off the cable adjustment and disconnect the rear cable (that is to be replaced) from the intermediate cable. Remove the rear cable from the mounting clips.

3. Remove the rear wheel and the brake shoes from the side requiring replacement.

4. Disconnect the cable from the rear brake apply lever. Compress the cable lock with a mini-hose clamp and pull the cable from the backing plate.

5. Install the new cable through the brake backing plate. Engage the locks. Attach the cable to the apply lever. Install the brake shoes, drum and wheel assembly.

6. Adjust the service brakes and parking brake.

Body

10

EXTERIOR

Front Doors

REMOVAL AND INSTALLATION

1. Open the front door and remove the inner door panel covering. Disconnect the interior light wiring harness and feed it through the access hole. Disconnect the door swing stop.

2. Open the door wide enough to gain access to the hinge bolts. Place a padded support under the door edge that will hold the door in a level position when the hinges have been unbolted from the frame.

3. Scribe around the door hinge on the door frame. Remove the hinge mounting bolts, lower hinge first, then the upper, from the door frame.

4. Remove the door.

5. Place the door on the padded support and install the hinge mounting bolts until they are

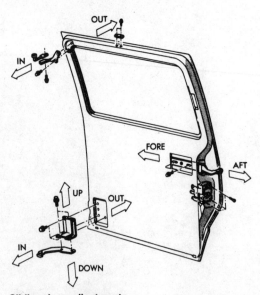

Sliding door adjustments

snug enough to support the door, but not tight enough to prevent door adjustment. Adjust the door position until correctly aligned and tighten the hinge bolts. Adjust the striker as necessary. Connect the door stop and interior light harness. Install the inner trim panel.

ALIGNMENT

The front doors should be adjusted so that there is a one quarter inch gap between the edge of the front fender and the edge of the door, and a one quarter inch gap between the back edge of the door and the lock pillar. Adjust the door to position and raise or lower it so that the stamped edge line matches the body panel line. Secure the door in proper position after necessary adjustments.

Sliding Door

ALIGNMENT

1. The gap between the back edge of the front door and the front edge of the sliding door should be five sixteenths of an inch. The gap between the sliding door edge and the quarter panel should be one quarter of and inch. The stamped edge line of the front door the sliding door and the quarter panel should be in line.

2. Remove the hinge trim panels and adjust the sliding door in the direction(s) required. Refer to the illustration provided for adjustment direction.

Liftgate

REMOVAL AND INSTALLATION

1. Support the liftgate in the full opened position.

2. Scribe a mark on the liftgate to mark the hinge positions.

3. Place masking tape on the roof edge and

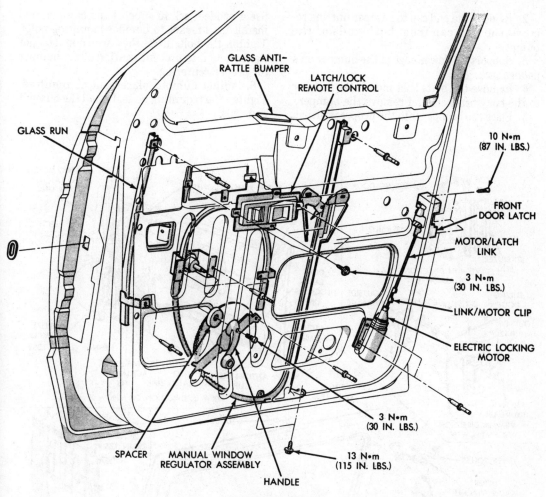

GLASS ANTI-RATTLE BUMPER

LATCH/LOCK REMOTE CONTROL

GLASS RUN

10 N•m (87 IN. LBS.)

FRONT DOOR LATCH

MOTOR/LATCH LINK

3 N•m (30 IN. LBS.)

LINK/MOTOR CLIP

ELECTRIC LOCKING MOTOR

3 N•m (30 IN. LBS.)

13 N•m (115 IN. LBS.)

SPACER   MANUAL WINDOW REGULATOR ASSEMBLY

HANDLE

Front door assembly

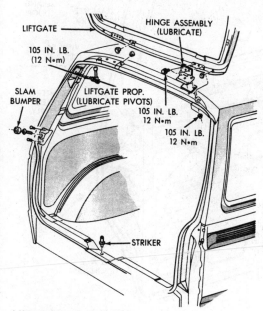

LIFTGATE

HINGE ASSEMBLY (LUBRICATE)

105 IN. LB. (12 N•m)

SLAM BUMPER

LIFTGATE PROP. (LUBRICATE PIVOTS)

105 IN. LB. 12 N•m

105 IN. LB. 12 N•m

STRIKER

Liftgate hinges and props

liftgate edge to protect the paint surfaces during removal and installation.

4. Remove the liftgate prop fasteners and remove the props.

5. Have a helper on hand to support the liftgate. Remove the hinge mounting bolts and remove the liftgate.

6. Raise the liftgate into position and install the hinge mounting bolts. Tighten the bolts until they are snug, but not tight enough to prevent liftgate adjustment.

7. Shift the liftgate until the hinge scribe marks are in position and tighten the hinge mounting bolts.

8. Attach and secure the liftgate props.

Bumpers

REMOVAL AND INSTALLATION

1. Remove the end cap to bumper mounting screw and the two end cap to fender nuts from both ends of the bumper.

2. Remove the end cap to bumper nut and remove the end cap from both ends of the bumper.

3. Support the lower edge of the bumper on a padded jack.

4. Remove the bolts that mount the bumper to the body brackets and remove the bumper.

5. Place the bumper into the proper position, use a padded jack to support the bumper, and install the bracket to bumper mounting bolts. Tighten the bolts until they are snug. but not tight enough to prevent shifting of the bumper for proper centering.

6. Adjust bumper placement as required. Tighten the mounting bolts. Install the bumper end caps.

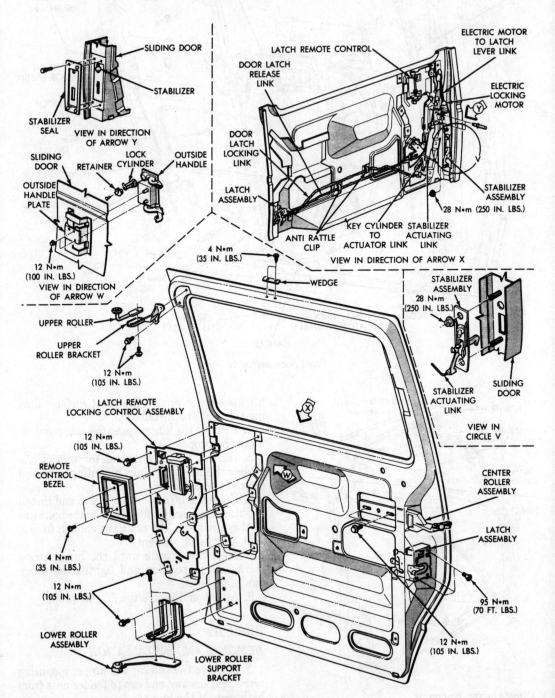

Sliding door components

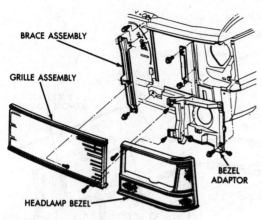

Grille removal and installation

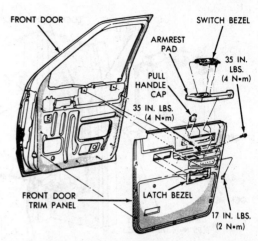

Door trim panel removal/installation

Grille

REMOVAL AND INSTALLATION

1. Remove the screws from the headlamp bezels. Remove the screws from the sides of the grille.
2. Remove the screws from the grille to center support bracket.
3. Remove the grille.
4. Place the grille into position. Install the center support screws and the outer mounting screws. Center the grille and tighten the mounting screws.
5. Install the headlamp bezel screws.

Outside Mirrors

REMOVAL AND INSTALLATION

1. Remove the door trim panel.
2. Remove the adjustment knob with an Allen wrench. Remove the screw cover plug and the mirror inner bezel mounting screws. Remove the bezel.
3. Remove the mirror mounting nuts and the mirror.
4. Place the mirror into position and install the mounting nuts.
5. Place the bezel into position and install the mounting screws and cover plug.
6. Install the control knob and trim panel.

Antenna

Refer to Chapter 6 for antenna servicing under the Radio section.

INTERIOR

Door Panels

REMOVAL AND INSTALLATION

1. Lower the door glass until it is 3″ from the full down position.

2. Unlock the door and remove the remote door latch control handle bezel by prying the front of the bezel out and rearward.
3. Remove the armrest mounting screw, and on models with electric controls, pry out the power window switch bezel.
4. Remove the window crank handle on models with manual window regulators.
5. Remove the two edge inserts that cover the mounting screws for the door pull strap, and remove the mounting screws and strap.
6. Insert a wide flat tool between the panel and door frame and carefully twist the tool to unfasten the retainer clips from the door.
7. If the vehicle is equipped with power locks, slide the switch bezel through the trim panel.
8. Disconnect the courtesy lamp connector. Remove the door trim panel.
9. Remove the inner plastic cover and service the components as required.
10. Place sealer along the edges of the plastic liner and put the liner onto the door frame.
11. Postion the trim panel, slide the power lock bezel through the panel, connect the courtesy lamp.
12. Postion the panel clips over their mounting holes and push the panel against the door frame to lock the clips.
13. Install the pull strap, the armrest, widow handle/power switch, remote latch control/bezel.

Door Locks/Latch

REMOVAL AND INSTALLATION

1. Remove the door trim panel and inner cover.
2. Raise the window to the full up position.
3. Disconnect all the locking clips from the remote linkage at the latch.

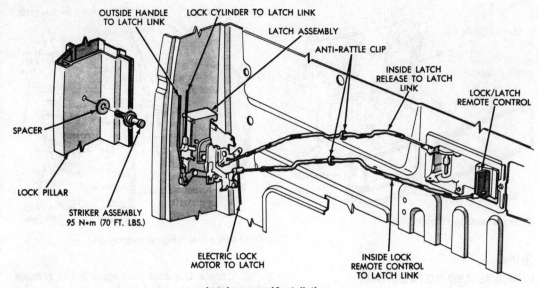

Latch removal/installation

4. Remove the retaining screws at the door edge and remove the latch assembly.

5. Position the latch to the door frame and secure it with the retaining screws.

6. Connect all of the remote linkage to the latch levers.

7. Check latch operation. Install the inner cover and door trim panel.

Door Glass Regulator

REMOVAL AND INSTALLATION

1. Remove the door trim panel and inner liner.

2. Remove the window glass from the regulator and the door.

3. If equipped with power windows, disconnect the wiring harness and remove the retainer clip.

4. Drill out the regulator mounting rivets. Their are five on vehicles equipped with electric

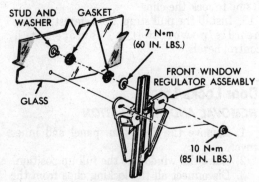

Door glass removal/installation

windows, and six if equipped with manual windows.

5. Remove the regulator through the larger access hole. Rotate the regulator through the hole as required for removal.

6. Install the regulator to the mounting holes using ¼-20 × ½" screws and nuts. Tighten the screws to 90 in. lbs.

7. Install the window glass, connect the motor wiring harness, and install the inner liner and door trim panel.

NOTE: *The window glass is mounted to the regulator by two mounting studs and nuts. Raise the glass until the mounting nuts align with the large access hole. Remove the nuts. Raise the glass up through the door frame. Rotate the glass so that the mounting studs pass through the notch at the rear of the door and remove the glass from the door.*

Electric Window Motor

REMOVAL AND INSTALLATION

1. Remove the window regulator. See procedure.

2. Remove the electric motor mounting screws and the motor.

3. Place the window motor into the door and secure the mounting screws.

4. Install the windoe regulator.

Inside Rear View Mirror

REMOVAL AND INSTALLATION

1. Loosen the mounting set screw on the mounting arm.

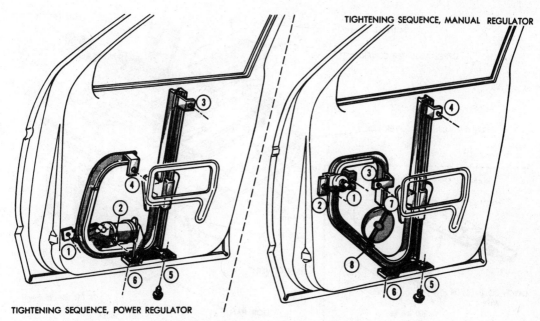

TIGHTENING SEQUENCE, MANUAL REGULATOR

TIGHTENING SEQUENCE, POWER REGULATOR

Window regulator removal/installation

2. Slide the mirror off of the windshield mounting button.

3. Slide the mirror mounting arm over the mounting button and secure the set screw.

Seats

REMOVAL AND INSTALLATION

1. To remove the right front seat; raise and safely support the vehicle.

2. Remove the four nuts and washer that attach the seat to the fllor pan.

3. Remove the seat.

4. Position the seat over and through the floor pan holes. Secure the seat with the nuts and washers.

5. To remove the left front seat: tilt the seat reward. Reach under the front of the seat and grab the cable near the clip that retains the cable to the lever. Pull the cable toward the driv-

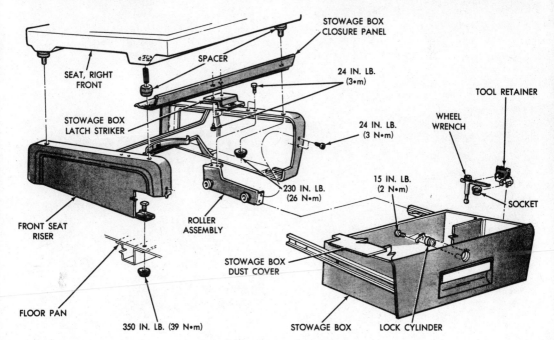

Right front seat components

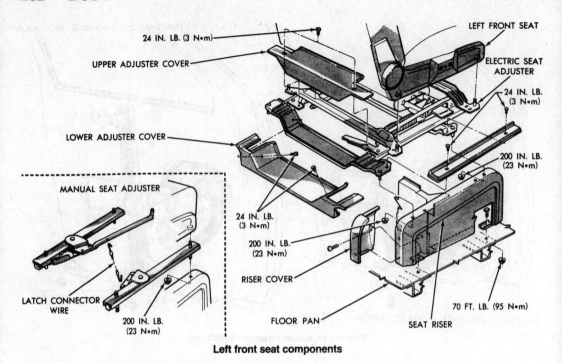

24 IN. LB. (3 N•m)

UPPER ADJUSTER COVER

LOWER ADJUSTER COVER

MANUAL SEAT ADJUSTER

LATCH CONNECTOR WIRE

200 IN. LB. (23 N•m)

24 IN. LB. (3 N•m)

200 IN. LB. (23 N•m)

RISER COVER

FLOOR PAN

LEFT FRONT SEAT

ELECTRIC SEAT ADJUSTER

24 IN. LB. (3 N•m)

200 IN. LB. (23 N•m)

70 FT. LB. (95 N•m)

SEAT RISER

Left front seat components

er's door until it is released from the lever assembly.

6. Turn the cable ninety degrees and push it inward to seperate the cable from the lever assembly.

7. Disconnect the electrical connectors. Re-

move the mounting nuts and washers and remove the seat.

8. Position the seat over the mounting holes and lowwer through the holes. Secure the seat with the nuts and washers. Connect the electrical wiring and cable.

Mechanic's Data

1":254mm
TAX
10.16mm
Liter
Parts
Overhaul

General Conversion Table

Multiply By	To Convert	To	
		LENGTH	
2.54	Inches	Centimeters	.3937
25.4	Inches	Millimeters	.03937
30.48	Feet	Centimeters	.0328
.304	Feet	Meters	3.28
.914	Yards	Meters	1.094
1.609	Miles	Kilometers	.621
		VOLUME	
.473	Pints	Liters	2.11
.946	Quarts	Liters	1.06
3.785	Gallons	Liters	.264
.016	Cubic inches	Liters	61.02
16.39	Cubic inches	Cubic cms.	.061
28.3	Cubic feet	Liters	.0353
		MASS (Weight)	
28.35	Ounces	Grams	.035
.4536	Pounds	Kilograms	2.20
—	To obtain	From	Multiply by

Multiply By	To Convert	To	
		AREA	
.645	Square inches	Square cms.	.155
.836	Square yds.	Square meters	1.196
		FORCE	
4.448	Pounds	Newtons	.225
.138	Ft./lbs.	Kilogram/meters	7.23
1.36	Ft./lbs.	Newton-meters	.737
.112	In./lbs.	Newton-meters	8.844
		PRESSURE	
.068	Psi	Atmospheres	14.7
6.89	Psi	Kilopascals	.145
		OTHER	
1.104	Horsepower (DIN)	Horsepower (SAE)	.9861
.746	Horsepower (SAE)	Kilowatts (KW)	1.34
1.60	Mph	Km/h	.625
.425	Mpg	Km/1	2.35
—	To obtain	From	Multiply by

Tap Drill Sizes

National Coarse or U.S.S.

Screw & Tap Size	Threads Per Inch	Use Drill Number
No. 5	40	39
No. 6	32	36
No. 8	32	29
No. 10	24	25
No. 12	24	17
1/4	20	8
5/16	18	F
3/8	16	5/16
7/16	14	U
1/2	13	27/64
9/16	12	31/64
5/8	11	17/32
3/4	10	21/32
7/8	9	49/64

National Coarse or U.S.S.

Screw & Tap Size	Threads Per Inch	Use Drill Number
1	8	7/8
1 1/8	7	63/64
1 1/4	7	1 7/64
1 1/2	6	1 11/32

National Fine or S.A.E.

Screw & Tap Size	Threads Per Inch	Use Drill Number
No. 5	44	37
No. 6	40	33
No. 8	36	29
No. 10	32	21

National Fine or S.A.E.

Screw & Tap Size	Threads Per Inch	Use Drill Number
No. 12	28	15
1/4	28	3
6/16	24	1
3/8	24	Q
7/16	20	W
1/2	20	29/64
9/16	18	33/64
5/8	18	37/64
3/4	16	11/16
7/8	14	13/16
1 1/8	12	1 3/64
1 1/4	12	1 11/64
1 1/2	12	1 27/64

Drill Sizes In Decimal Equivalents

Inch	Decimal	Wire	mm
1/64	.0156		.39
	.0157		.4
	.0160	78	
	.0165		.42
	.0173		.44
	.0177		.45
	.0180	77	
	.0181		.46
	.0189		.48
	.0197		.5
	.0200	76	
	.0210	75	
	.0217		.55
	.0225	74	
	.0236		.6
	.0240	73	
	.0250	72	
	.0256		.65
	.0260	71	
	.0276		.7
	.0280	70	
	.0292	69	
	.0295		.75
	.0310	68	
1/32	.0312		.79
	.0315		.8
	.0320	67	
	.0330	66	
	.0335		.85
	.0350	65	
	.0354		.9
	.0360	64	
	.0370	63	
	.0374		.95
	.0380	62	
	.0390	61	
	.0394		1.0
	.0400	60	
	.0410	59	
	.0413		1.05
	.0420	58	
	.0430	57	
	.0433		1.1
	.0453		1.15
3/64	.0465	56	
	.0469		1.19
	.0472		1.2
	.0492		1.25
	.0512		1.3
	.0520	55	
	.0531		1.35
	.0550	54	
	.0551		1.4
	.0571		1.45
	.0591		1.5
	.0595	53	
1/16	.0610		1.55
	.0625		1.59
	.0630		1.6
	.0635	52	
	.0650		1.65
	.0669		1.7
	.0670	51	
	.0689		1.75
	.0700	50	
	.0709		1.8
	.0728		1.85

Inch	Decimal	Wire	mm
	.0730	49	
	.0748		1.9
	.0760	48	
	.0768		1.95
5/64	.0781		1.98
	.0785	47	
	.0787		2.0
	.0807		2.05
	.0810	46	
	.0820	45	
	.0827		2.1
	.0846		2.15
	.0860	44	
	.0866		2.2
	.0886		2.25
	.0890	43	
	.0906		2.3
	.0925		2.35
	.0935	42	
3/32	.0938		2.38
	.0945		2.4
	.0960	41	
	.0965		2.45
	.0980	40	
	.0981		2.5
	.0995	39	
	.1015	38	
	.1024		2.6
	.1040	37	
	.1063		2.7
	.1065	36	
	.1083		2.75
7/64	.1094		2.77
	.1100	35	
	.1102		2.8
	.1110	34	
	.1130	33	
	.1142		2.9
	.1160	32	
	.1181		3.0
	.1200	31	
	.1220		3.1
1/8	.1250		3.17
	.1260		3.2
	.1280		3.25
	.1285	30	
	.1299		3.3
	.1339		3.4
	.1360	29	
	.1378		3.5
	.1405	28	
9/64	.1406		3.57
	.1417		3.6
	.1440	27	
	.1457		3.7
	.1470	26	
	.1476		3.75
	.1495	25	
	.1496		3.8
	.1520	24	
	.1535		3.9
	.1540	23	
5/32	.1562		3.96
	.1570	22	
	.1575		4.0
	.1590	21	
	.1610	20	

Inch	Decimal	Wire & Letter	mm
	.1614		4.1
	.1654		4.2
	.1660	19	
	.1673		4.25
	.1693		4.3
	.1695	18	
11/64	.1719		4.36
	.1730	17	
	.1732		4.4
	.1770	16	
	.1772		4.5
	.1800	15	
	.1811		4.6
	.1820	14	
	.1850	13	
	.1850		4.7
	.1870		4.75
3/16	.1875		4.76
	.1890		4.8
	.1890	12	
	.1910	11	
	.1929		4.9
	.1935	10	
	.1960	9	
	.1969		5.0
	.1990	8	
	.2008		5.1
	.2010	7	
13/64	.2031		5.16
	.2040	6	
	.2047		5.2
	.2055	5	
	.2067		5.25
	.2087		5.3
	.2090	4	
	.2126		5.4
	.2130	3	
	.2165		5.5
7/32	2188		5.55
	.2205		5.6
	.2210	2	
	.2244		5.7
	.2264		5.75
	.2280	1	
	.2283		5.8
	.2323		5.9
	.2340	A	
15/64	.2344		5.95
	.2362		6.0
	.2380	B	
	.2402		6.1
	.2420	C	
	.2441		6.2
	.2460	D	
	.2461		6.25
	.2480		6.3
1/4	.2500	E	6.35
	.2520		6.
	.2559		6.5
	.2570	F	
	.2598		6.6
	.2610	G	
	.2638		6.7
17/64	.2656		6.74
	.2657		6.75
	.2660	H	
	.2677		6.8

Inch	Decimal	Letter	mm
	.2717		6.9
	.2720	I	
	.2756		7.0
	.2770	J	
	.2795		7.1
	.2810	K	
9/32	.2812		7.14
	.2835		7.2
	.2854		7.25
	.2874		7.3
	.2900	L	
	.2913		7.4
	.2950	M	
	.2953		7.5
19/64	.2969		7.54
	.2992		7.6
	.3020	N	
	.3031		7.7
	.3051		7.75
	.3071		7.8
	.3110		7.9
5/16	.3125		7.93
	.3150		8.0
	.3160	O	
	.3189		8.1
	.3228		8.2
	.3230	P	
	.3248		8.25
	.3268		8.3
21/64	.3281		8.33
	.3307		8.4
	.3320	Q	
	.3346		8.5
	.3386		8.6
	.3390	R	
	.3425		8.7
11/32	.3438		8.73
	.3445		8.75
	.3465		8.8
	.3480	S	
	.3504		8.9
	.3543		9.0
	.3580	T	
	.3583		9.1
23/64	.3594		9.12
	.3622		9.2
	.3642		9.25
	.3661		9.3
	.3680	U	
	.3701		9.4
	.3740		9.5
3/8	.3750		9.52
	.3770	V	
	.3780		9.6
	.3819		9.7
	.3839		9.75
	.3858		9.8
	.3860	W	
	.3898		9.9
25/64	.3906		9.92
	.3937		10.0
	.3970	X	
	.4040	Y	
13/32	.4062		10.31
	.4130	Z	
	.4134		10.5
27/64	.4219		10.71

Inch	Decimal	mm
	.4331	11.0
7/16	.4375	11.11
	.4528	11.5
29/64	.4531	11.51
15/32	.4688	11.90
	.4724	12.0
31/64	.4844	12.30
	.4921	12.5
1/2	.5000	12.70
	.5118	13.0
33/64	.5156	13.09
17/32	.5312	13.49
	.5315	13.5
35/64	.5469	13.89
	.5512	14.0
9/16	.5625	14.28
	.5709	14.5
37/64	.5781	14.68
	.5906	15.0
19/32	.5938	15.08
39/64	.6094	15.47
	.6102	15.5
5/8	.6250	15.87
	.6299	16.0
41/64	.6406	16.27
	.6496	16.5
21/32	.6562	16.66
	.6693	17.0
43/64	.6719	17.06
11/16	.6875	17.46
	.6890	17.5
45/64	.7031	17.85
	.7087	18.0
23/32	.7188	18.25
	.7283	18.5
47/64	.7344	18.65
	.7480	19.0
3/4	.7500	19.05
49/64	.7656	19.44
	.7677	19.5
25/32	.7812	19.84
	.7874	20.0
51/64	.7969	20.24
	.8071	20.5
13/16	.8125	20.63
	.8268	21.0
53/64	.8281	21.03
27/32	.8438	21.43
	.8465	21.5
55/64	.8594	21.82
	.8661	22.0
7/8	.8750	22.22
	.8858	22.5
57/64	.8906	22.62
	.9055	23.0
29/32	.9062	23.01
59/64	.9219	23.41
	.9252	23.5
15/16	.9375	23.81
	.9449	24.0
61/64	.9531	24.2
	.9646	24.5
31/64	.9688	24.6
	.9843	25.0
63/64	.9844	25.0
1	1.0000	25.4

AIR/FUEL RATIO: The ratio of air to gasoline by weight in the fuel mixture drawn into the engine.

AIR INJECTION: One method of reducing harmful exhaust emissions by injecting air into each of the exhaust ports of an engine. The fresh air entering the hot exhaust manifold causes any remaining fuel to be burned before it can exit the tailpipe.

ALTERNATOR: A device used for converting mechanical energy into electrical energy.

AMMETER: An instrument, calibrated in amperes, used to measure the flow of an electrical current in a circuit. Ammeters are always connected in series with the circuit being tested.

AMPERE: The rate of flow of electrical current present when one volt of electrical pressure is applied against one ohm of electrical resistance.

ANALOG COMPUTER: Any microprocessor that uses similar (analogous) electrical signals to make its calculations.

ARMATURE: A laminated, soft iron core wrapped by a wire that converts electrical energy to mechanical energy as in a motor or relay. When rotated in a magnetic field, it changes mechanical energy into electrical energy as in a generator.

ATMOSPHERIC PRESSURE: The pressure on the Earth's surface caused by the weight of the air in the atmosphere. At sea level, this pressure is 14.7 psi at 32°F (101 kPa at 0°C).

ATOMIZATION: The breaking down of a liquid into a fine mist that can be suspended in air.

AXIAL PLAY: Movement parallel to a shaft or bearing bore.

BACKFIRE: The sudden combustion of gases in the intake or exhaust system that results in a loud explosion.

BACKLASH: The clearance or play between two parts, such as meshed gears.

BACKPRESSURE: Restrictions in the exhaust system that slow the exit of exhaust gases from the combustion chamber.

BAKELITE: A heat resistant, plastic insulator material commonly used in printed circuit boards and transistorized components.

BALL BEARING: A bearing made up of hardened inner and outer races between which hardened steel ball roll.

BALLAST RESISTOR: A resistor in the primary ignition circuit that lowers voltage after the engine is started to reduce wear on ignition components.

BEARING: A friction reducing, supportive device usually located between a stationary part and a moving part.

BIMETAL TEMPERATURE SENSOR: Any sensor or switch made of two dissimilar types of metal that bend when heated or cooled due to the different expansion rates of the alloys. These types of sensors usually function as an on/off switch.

BLOWBY: Combustion gases, composed of water vapor and unburned fuel, that leak past the piston rings into the crankcase during normal engine operation. These gases are removed by the PCV system to prevent the build-up of harmful acids in the crankcase.

BRAKE PAD: A brake shoe and lining assembly used with disc brakes.

BRAKE SHOE: The backing for the brake lining. The term is, however, usually applied to the assembly of the brake backing and lining.

BUSHING: A liner, usually removable, for a bearing; an anti-friction liner used in place of a bearing.

BYPASS: System used to bypass ballast resistor during engine cranking to increase voltage supplied to the coil.

CALIPER: A hydraulically activated device in a disc brake system, which is mounted straddling the brake rotor (disc). The caliper contains at least one piston and two brake pads. Hydraulic pressure on the piston(s) forces the pads against the rotor.

CAMSHAFT: A shaft in the engine on which are the lobes (cams) which operate the valves. The camshaft is driven by the crankshaft, via a belt, chain or gears, at one half the crankshaft speed.

CAPACITOR: A device which stores an electrical charge.

CARBON MONOXIDE (CO): a colorless, odorless gas given off as a normal byproduct of combustion. It is poisonous and extremely dangerous in confined areas, building up slowly to toxic levels without warning if adequate ventilation is not available.

CARBURETOR: A device, usually mounted on the intake manifold of an engine, which mixes the air and fuel in the proper proportion to allow even combustion.

CATALYTIC CONVERTER: A device installed in the exhaust system, like a muffler, that converts harmful byproducts of combustion into carbon dioxide and water vapor by means of a heat-producing chemical reaction.

CENTRIFUGAL ADVANCE: A mechanical method of advancing the spark timing by using flyweights in the distributor that react to centrifugal force generated by the distributor shaft rotation.

CHECK VALVE: Any one-way valve installed to permit the flow of air, fuel or vacuum in one direction only.

CHOKE: A device, usually a moveable valve, placed in the intake path of a carburetor to restrict the flow of air.

CIRCUIT: Any unbroken path through which an electrical current can flow. Also used to describe fuel flow in some instances.

CIRCUIT BREAKER: A switch which protects an electrical circuit from overload by opening the circuit when the current flow exceeds a predetermined level. Some circuit breakers must be reset manually, while other reset automatically

COIL (IGNITION): A transformer in the ignition circuit which steps of the voltage provided to the spark plugs.

COMBINATION MANIFOLD: An assembly which includes both the intake and exhaust manifolds in one casting.

COMBINATION VALVE: A device used in some fuel systems that routes fuel vapors to a charcoal storage canister instead of venting

them into the atmosphere. The valve relieves fuel tank pressure and allows fresh air into the tank as fuel level drops to prevent a vapor lock situation.

COMPRESSION RATIO: The comparison of the total volume of the cylinder and combustion chamber with the piston at BDC and the piston at TDC.

CONDENSER: 1. An electrical device which acts to store an electrical charge, preventing voltage surges.
2. A radiator-like device in the air conditioning system in which refrigerant gas condenses into a liquid, giving off heat.

CONDUCTOR: Any material through which an electrical current can be transmitted easily.

CONTINUITY: Continuous or complete circuit. Can be checked with an ohmmeter.

COUNTERSHAFT: An intermediate shaft which is rotated by a mainshaft and transmits, in turn, that rotation to a working part.

CRANKCASE: The lower part of an engine in which the crankshaft and related parts operate.

CRANKSHAFT: The main driving shaft of an engine which receives reciprocating motion from the pistons and converts it to rotary motion.

CYLINDER: In an engine, the round hole in the engine block in which the piston(s) ride.

CYLINDER BLOCK: The main structural member of an engine in which is found the cylinders, crankshaft and other principal parts.

CYLINDER HEAD: The detachable portion of the engine, fastened, usually, to the top of the cylinder block, containing all or most of the combustion chambers. On overhead valve engines, it contains the valves and their operating parts. On overhead cam engines, it contains the camshaft as well.

DEAD CENTER: The extreme top or bottom of the piston stroke.

DETONATION: An unwanted explosion of the air fuel mixture in the combustion chamber caused by excess heat and compression, advanced timing, or an overly lean mixture. Also referred to as "ping".

DIAPHRAGM: A thin, flexible wall separating two cavities, such as in a vacuum advance unit.

DIESELING: A condition in which hot spots in the combustion chamber cause the engine to run on after the key is turned off.

DIFFERENTIAL: A geared assembly which allows the transmission of motion between drive axles, giving one axle the ability to turn faster than the other.

DIODE: An electrical device that will allow current to flow in one direction only.

DISC BRAKE: A hydraulic braking assembly consisting of a brake disc, or rotor, mounted on an axle, and a caliper assembly containing, usually two brake pads which are activated by hydraulic pressure. The pads are forced against the sides of the disc, creating friction which slows the vehicle.

DISTRIBUTOR: A mechanically driven device on an engine which is responsible for electrically firing the spark plug at a predetermined point of the piston stroke.

DOWEL PIN: A pin, inserted in mating holes in two different parts allowing those parts to maintain a fixed relationship.

DRUM BRAKE: A braking system which consists of two brake shoes and one or two wheel cylinders, mounted on a fixed backing plate, and a brake drum, mounted on an axle, which revolves around the assembly. Hydraulic action applied to the wheel cylinders forces the shoes outward against the drum, creating friction and slowing the vehicle.

DWELL: The rate, measured in degrees of shaft rotation, at which an electrical circuit cycles on and off.

ELECTRONIC CONTROL UNIT (ECU): Ignition module, module, amplifier or igniter. See Module for definition.

ELECTRONIC IGNITION: A system in which the timing and firing of the spark plugs is controlled by an electronic control unit, usually called a module. These systems have not points or condenser.

ENDPLAY: The measured amount of axial movement in a shaft.

ENGINE: A device that converts heat into mechanical energy.

EXHAUST MANIFOLD: A set of cast passages or pipes which conduct exhaust gases from the engine.

FEELER GAUGE: A blade, usually metal, of precisely predetermined thickness, used to measure the clearance between two parts. These blades usually are available in sets of assorted thicknesses.

F-Head: An engine configuration in which the intake valves are in the cylinder head, while the camshaft and exhaust valves are located in the cylinder block. The camshaft operates the intake valves via lifters and pushrods, while it operates the exhaust valves directly.

FIRING ORDER: The order in which combustion occurs in the cylinders of an engine. Also the order in which spark is distributed to the plugs by the distributor.

FLATHEAD: An engine configuration in which the camshaft and all the valves are located in the cylinder block.

FLOODING: The presence of too much fuel in the intake manifold and combustion chamber which prevents the air/fuel mixture from firing, thereby causing a no-start situation.

FLYWHEEL: A disc shaped part bolted to the rear end of the crankshaft. Around the outer perimeter is affixed the ring gear. The starter drive engages the ring gear, turning the flywheel, which rotates the crankshaft, imparting the initial starting motion to the engine.

FOOT POUND (ft.lb. or sometimes, ft. lbs.): The amount of energy or work needed to raise an item weighing one pound, a distance of one foot.

FUSE: A protective device in a circuit which prevents circuit overload by breaking the circuit when a specific amperage is present. The device is constructed around a strip or wire of a lower amperage rating than the circuit it is designed to protect. When an amperage higher than that stamped on the fuse is present in the circuit, the strip or wire melts, opening the circuit.

GEAR RATIO: The ratio between the number of teeth on meshing gears.

GENERATOR: A device which converts mechanical energy into electrical energy.

HEAT RANGE: The measure of a spark plug's ability to dissipate heat from its firing end. The higher the heat range, the hotter the plug fires.

HUB: The center part of a wheel or gear.

HYDROCARBON (HC): Any chemical compound made up of hydrogen and carbon. A major pollutant formed by the engine as a byproduct of combustion.

HYDROMETER: An instrument used to measure the specific gravity of a solution.

INCH POUND (in.lb. or sometimes, in. lbs.): One twelfth of a foot pound.

INDUCTION: A means of transferring electrical energy in the form of a magnetic field. Principle used in the ignition coil to increase voltage.

INJECTION PUMP: A device, usually mechanically operated, which meters and delivers fuel under pressure to the fuel injector.

INJECTOR: A device which receives metered fuel under relatively low pressure and is activated to inject the fuel into the engine under relatively high pressure at a predetermined time.

INPUT SHAFT: The shaft to which torque is applied, usually carrying the driving gear or gears.

INTAKE MANIFOLD: A casting of passages or pipes used to conduct air or a fuel/air mixture to the cylinders.

JOURNAL: The bearing surface within which a shaft operates.

KEY: A small block usually fitted in a notch between a shaft and a hub to prevent slippage of the two parts.

MANIFOLD: A casting of passages or set of pipes which connect the cylinders to an inlet or outlet source.

MANIFOLD VACUUM: Low pressure in an engine intake manifold formed just below the throttle plates. Manifold vacuum is highest at idle and drops under acceleration.

MASTER CYLINDER: The primary fluid pressurizing device in a hydraulic system. In automotive use, it is found in brake and hydraulic clutch systems and is pedal activated, either directly or, in a power brake system, through the power booster.

MODULE: Electronic control unit, amplifier or igniter of solid state or integrated design which controls the current flow in the ignition primary circuit based on input from the pickup coil. When the module opens the primary circuit, the high secondary voltage is induced in the coil.

NEEDLE BEARING: A bearing which consists of a number (usually a large number) of long, thin rollers.

OHM: (Ω) The unit used to measure the resistance of conductor to electrical flow. One ohm is the amount of resistance that limits current flow to one ampere in a circuit with one volt of pressure.

OHMMETER: An instrument used for measuring the resistance, in ohms, in an electrical circuit.

OUTPUT SHAFT: The shaft which transmits torque from a device, such as a transmission.

OVERDRIVE: A gear assembly which produces more shaft revolutions than that transmitted to it.

OVERHEAD CAMSHAFT (OHC): An engine configuration in which the camshaft is mounted on top of the cylinder head and operates the valve either directly or by means of rocker arms.

OVERHEAD VALVE (OHV): An engine configuration in which all of the valves are located in the cylinder head and the camshaft is located in the cylinder block. The camshaft operates the valves via lifters and pushrods.

OXIDES OF NITROGEN (NOx): Chemical compounds of nitrogen produced as a byproduct of combustion. They combine with hydrocarbons to produce smog.

OXYGEN SENSOR: Used with the feedback system to sense the presence of oxygen in the exhaust gas and signal the computer which can reference the voltage signal to an air/fuel ratio.

PINION: The smaller of two meshing gears.

PISTON RING: An open ended ring which fits into a groove on the outer diameter of the piston. Its chief function is to form a seal between the piston and cylinder wall. Most automotive pistons have three rings: two for compression sealing; one for oil sealing.

PRELOAD: A predetermined load placed on a bearing during assembly or by adjustment.

PRIMARY CIRCUIT: Is the low voltage side of the ignition system which consists of the ignition switch, ballast resistor or resistance wire, bypass, coil, electronic control unit and pick-up coil as well as the connecting wires and harnesses.

PRESS FIT: The mating of two parts under pressure, due to the inner diameter of one being smaller than the outer diameter of the other, or vice versa; an interference fit.

RACE: The surface on the inner or outer ring of a bearing on which the balls, needles or rollers move.

REGULATOR: A device which maintains the amperage and/or voltage levels of a circuit at predetermined values.

RELAY: A switch which automatically opens and/or closes a circuit.

RESISTANCE: The opposition to the flow of current through a circuit or electrical device, and is measured in ohms. Resistance is equal to the voltage divided by the amperage.

RESISTOR: A device, usually made of wire, which offers a preset amount of resistance in an electrical circuit.

RING GEAR: The name given to a ring-shaped gear attached to a differential case, or affixed to a flywheel or as part a planetary gear set.

ROLLER BEARING: A bearing made up of hardened inner and outer races between which hardened steel rollers move.

ROTOR: 1. The disc-shaped part of a disc brake assembly, upon which the brake pads bear; also called, brake disc.
2. The device mounted atop the distributor shaft, which passes current to the distributor cap tower contacts.

SECONDARY CIRCUIT: The high voltage side of the ignition system, usually above 20,000 volts. The secondary includes the ignition coil, coil wire, distributor cap and rotor, spark plug wires and spark plugs.

SENDING UNIT: A mechanical, electrical, hydraulic or electromagnetic device which transmits information to a gauge.

SENSOR: Any device designed to measure engine operating conditions or ambient pressures and temperatures. Usually electronic in nature and designed to send a voltage signal to an on-board computer, some sensors may operate as a simple on/off switch or they may provide a variable voltage signal (like a potentiometer) as conditions or measured parameters change.

SHIM: Spacers of precise, predetermined thickness used between parts to establish a proper working relationship.

SLAVE CYLINDER: In automotive use, a device in the hydraulic clutch system which is activated by hydraulic force, disengaging the clutch.

SOLENOID: A coil used to produce a magnetic field, the effect of which is produce work.

SPARK PLUG: A device screwed into the combustion chamber of a spark ignition engine. The basic construction is a conductive core inside of a ceramic insulator, mounted in an outer conductive base. An electrical charge from the spark plug wire travels along the conductive core and jumps a preset air gap to a grounding point or points at the end of the conductive base. The resultant spark ignites the fuel/air mixture in the combustion chamber.

SPLINES: Ridges machined or cast onto the outer diameter of a shaft or inner diameter of a bore to enable parts to mate without rotation.

TACHOMETER: A device used to measure the rotary speed of an engine, shaft, gear, etc., usually in rotations per minute.

THERMOSTAT: A valve, located in the cooling system of an engine, which is closed when cold and opens gradually in response to engine heating, controlling the temperature of the coolant and rate of coolant flow.

TOP DEAD CENTER (TDC): The point at which the piston reaches the top of its travel on the compression stroke.

TORQUE: The twisting force applied to an object.

TORQUE CONVERTER: A turbine used to transmit power from a driving member to a driven member via hydraulic action, providing changes in drive ratio and torque. In automotive use, it links the driveplate at the rear of the engine to the automatic transmission.

TRANSDUCER: A device used to change a force into an electrical signal.

TRANSISTOR: A semi-conductor component which can be actuated by a small voltage to perform an electrical switching function.

TUNE-UP: A regular maintenance function, usually associated with the replacement and adjustment of parts and components in the electrical and fuel systems of a vehicle for the purpose of attaining optimum performance.

TURBOCHARGER: An exhaust driven pump which compresses intake air and forces it into the combustion chambers at higher than atmospheric pressures. The increased air pressure allows more fuel to be burned and results in increased horsepower being produced.

VACUUM ADVANCE: A device which advances the ignition timing in response to increased engine vacuum.

VACUUM GAUGE: An instrument used to measure the presence of vacuum in a chamber.

VALVE: A device which control the pressure, direction of flow or rate of flow of a liquid or gas.

VALVE CLEARANCE: The measured gap between the end of the valve stem and the rocker arm, cam lobe or follower that activates the valve.

VISCOSITY: The rating of a liquid's internal resistance to flow.

VOLTMETER: An instrument used for measuring electrical force in units called volts. Voltmeters are always connected parallel with the circuit being tested.

WHEEL CYLINDER: Found in the automotive drum brake assembly, it is a device, actuated by hydraulic pressure, which, through internal pistons, pushes the brake shoes outward against the drums.

ABBREVIATIONS AND SYMBOLS

A: Ampere

AC: Alternating current

A/C: Air conditioning

A-h: Ampere hour

AT: Automatic transmission

ATDC: After top dead center

μA: Microampere

bbl: Barrel

BDC: Bottom dead center

bhp: Brake horsepower

BTDC: Before top dead center

BTU: British thermal unit

C: Celsius (Centigrade)

CCA: Cold cranking amps

cd: Candela

cm^2: Square centimeter

cm^3, cc: Cubic centimeter

CO: Carbon monoxide

CO_2: Carbon dioxide

cu.in., in^3: Cubic inch

CV: Constant velocity

Cyl.: Cylinder

DC: Direct current

ECM: Electronic control module

EFE: Early fuel evaporation

EFI: Electronic fuel injection

EGR: Exhaust gas recirculation

Exh.: Exhaust

F: Fahrenheit

F: Farad

pF: Picofarad

μF: Microfarad

FI: Fuel injection

ft.lb., ft. lb., ft. lbs.: foot pound(s)

gal: Gallon

g: Gram

HC: Hydrocarbon

HEI: High energy ignition

HO: High output

hp: Horsepower

Hyd.: Hydraulic

Hz: Hertz

ID: Inside diameter

in.lb.; in. lb.; in. lbs: inch pound(s)

Int.: Intake

K: Kelvin

kg: Kilogram

kHz: Kilohertz

km: Kilometer

km/h: Kilometers per hour

kΩ: Kilohm

kPa: Kilopascal

kV: Kilovolt

kW: Kilowatt

l: Liter

l/s: Liters per second

m: Meter

mA: Milliampere

mg: Milligram

mHz: Megahertz

mm: Millimeter

mm^2: Square millimeter

m^3: Cubic meter

MΩ: Megohm

m/s: Meters per second

MT: Manual transmission

mV: Millivolt

μm: Micrometer

N: Newton

N-m: Newton meter

NOx: Nitrous oxide

OD: Outside diameter

OHC: Over head camshaft

OHV: Over head valve

Ω: Ohm

PCV: Positive crankcase ventilation

psi: Pounds per square inch

pts: Pints

qts: Quarts

rpm: Rotations per minute

rps: Rotations per second

R-12: A refrigerant gas (Freon)

SAE: Society of Automotive Engineers

SO$_2$: Sulfur dioxide

T: Ton

t: Megagram

TBI: Throttle Body Injection

TPS: Throttle Position Sensor

V: 1. Volt; 2. Venturi

μV: Microvolt

W: Watt

∞: Infinity

$<$: Less than

$>$: Greater than

Index

Chilton's Repair & Tune-Up Guides

The Complete line covers domestic cars, imports, trucks, vans, RV's and 4-wheel drive vehicles.

RTUG Title	Part No.
AMC 1975-82	7199
Covers all U.S. and Canadian models	
Aspen/Volare 1976-80	6637
Covers all U.S. and Canadian models	
Audi 1970-73	5902
Covers all U.S. and Canadian models.	
Audi 4000/5000 1978-81	7028
Covers all U.S. and Canadian models including turbocharged and diesel engines	
Barracuda/Challenger 1965-72	5807
Covers all U.S. and Canadian models	
Blazer/Jimmy 1969-82	6931
Covers all U.S. and Canadian 2- and 4-wheel drive models, including diesel engines	
BMW 1970-82	6844
Covers U.S. and Canadian models	
Buick/Olds/Pontiac 1975-85	7308
Covers all U.S. and Canadian full size rear wheel drive models	
Cadillac 1967-84	7462
Covers all U.S. and Canadian rear wheel drive models	
Camaro 1967-81	6735
Covers all U.S. and Canadian models	
Camaro 1982-85	7317
Covers all U.S. and Canadian models	
Capri 1970-77	6695
Covers all U.S. and Canadian models	
Caravan/Voyager 1984-85	7482
Covers all U.S. and Canadian models	
Century/Regal 1975-85	7307
Covers all U.S. and Canadian rear wheel drive models, including turbocharged engines	
Champ/Arrow/Sapporo 1978-83	7041
Covers all U.S. and Canadian models	
Chevette/1000 1976-86	6836
Covers all U.S. and Canadian models	
Chevrolet 1968-85	7135
Covers all U.S. and Canadian models	
Chevrolet 1968-79 Spanish	7082
Chevrolet/GMC Pick-Ups 1970-82 Spanish	7468
Chevrolet/GMC Pick-Ups and Suburban 1970-86	6936
Covers all U.S. and Canadian 1/2, 3/4 and 1 ton models, including 4-wheel drive and diesel engines	
Chevrolet LUV 1972-81	6815
Covers all U.S. and Canadian models	
Chevrolet Mid-Size 1964-86	6840
Covers all U.S. and Canadian models of 1964-77 Chevelle, Malibu and Malibu SS; 1974-77 Laguna; 1978-85 Malibu; 1970-86 Monte Carlo; 1964-84 El Camino, including diesel engines	
Chevrolet Nova 1986	7658
Covers all U.S. and Canadian models	
Chevy/GMC Vans 1967-84	6930
Covers all U.S. and Canadian models of 1/2, 3/4, and 1 ton vans, cutaways, and motor home chassis, including diesel engines	
Chevy S-10 Blazer/GMC S-15 Jimmy 1982-85	7383
Covers all U.S. and Canadian models	
Chevy S-10/GMC S-15 Pick-Ups 1982-85	7310
Covers all U.S. and Canadian models	
Chevy II/Nova 1962-79	6841
Covers all U.S. and Canadian models	
Chrysler K- and E-Car 1981-85	7163
Covers all U.S. and Canadian front wheel drive models	
Colt/Challenger/Vista/Conquest 1971-85	7037
Covers all U.S. and Canadian models	
Corolla/Carina/Tercel/Starlet 1970-85	7036
Covers all U.S. and Canadian models	
Corona/Cressida/Crown/Mk.II/Camry/Van 1970-84	7044
Covers all U.S. and Canadian models	

RTUG Title	Part No.
Corvair 1960-69	6691
Covers all U.S. and Canadian models	
Corvette 1953-62	6576
Covers all U.S. and Canadian models	
Corvette 1963-84	6843
Covers all U.S. and Canadian models	
Cutlass 1970-85	6933
Covers all U.S. and Canadian models	
Dart/Demon 1968-76	6324
Covers all U.S. and Canadian models	
Datsun 1961-72	5790
Covers all U.S. and Canadian models of Nissan Patrol; 1500, 1600 and 2000 sports cars; Pick-Ups; 410, 411, 510, 1200 and 240Z	
Datsun 1973-80 Spanish	7083
Datsun/Nissan F-10, 310, Stanza, Pulsar 1977-86	7196
Covers all U.S. and Canadian models	
Datsun/Nissan Pick-Ups 1970-84	6816
Covers all U.S. and Canadian models	
Datsun/Nissan Z & ZX 1970-86	6932
Covers all U.S. and Canadian models	
Datsun/Nissan 1200, 210, Sentra 1973-86	7197
Covers all U.S. and Canadian models	
Datsun/Nissan 200SX, 510, 610, 710, 810, Maxima 1973-84	7170
Covers all U.S. and Canadian models	
Dodge 1968-77	6554
Covers all U.S. and Canadian models	
Dodge Charger 1967-70	6486
Covers all U.S. and Canadian models	
Dodge/Plymouth Trucks 1967-84	7459
Covers all 1/2, 3/4, and 1 ton 2- and 4-wheel drive U.S. and Canadian models, including diesel engines	
Dodge/Plymouth Vans 1967-84	6934
Covers all 1/2, 3/4, and 1 ton U.S. and Canadian models of vans, cutaways and motor home chassis	
D-50/Arrow Pick-Up 1979-81	7032
Covers all U.S. and Canadian models	
Fairlane/Torino 1962-75	6320
Covers all U.S. and Canadian models	
Fairmont/Zephyr 1978-83	6965
Covers all U.S. and Canadian models	
Fiat 1969-81	7042
Covers all U.S. and Canadian models	
Fiesta 1978-80	6846
Covers all U.S. and Canadian models	
Firebird 1967-81	5996
Covers all U.S. and Canadian models	
Firebird 1982-85	7345
Covers all U.S. and Canadian models	
Ford 1968-79 Spanish	7084
Ford Bronco 1966-83	7140
Covers all U.S. and Canadian models	
Ford Bronco II 1984	7408
Covers all U.S. and Canadian models	
Ford Courier 1972-82	6983
Covers all U.S. and Canadian models	
Ford/Mercury Front Wheel Drive 1981-85	7055
Covers all U.S. and Canadian models Escort, EXP, Tempo, Lynx, LN-7 and Topaz	
Ford/Mercury/Lincoln 1968-85	6842
Covers all U.S. and Canadian models of FORD Country Sedan, Country Squire, Crown Victoria, Custom, Custom 500, Galaxie 500, LTD through 1982, Ranch Wagon; and XL; MERCURY Colony Park, Commuter, Marquis through 1982, Gran Marquis, Monterey and Park Lane; LINCOLN Continental and Towne Car	
Ford/Mercury/Lincoln Mid-Size 1971-85	6696
Covers all U.S. and Canadian models of FORD Elite, 1983-85 LTD, 1977-79 LTD II, Ranchero, Torino, Gran Torino, 1977-85 Thunderbird; MERCURY 1972-85 Cougar,	

continued on next page

RTUG Title	Part No.	RTUG Title	Part No.
1983-85 Marquis, Montego, 1980-85 XR-7; LINCOLN 1982-85 Continental, 1984-85 Mark VII, 1978-80 Versailles		Mercedes-Benz 1974-84 Covers all U.S. and Canadian models	6809
Ford Pick-Ups 1965-86 Covers all 1/2, 3/4 and 1 ton, 2- and 4-wheel drive U.S. and Canadian pick-up, chassis cab and camper models, including diesel engines	6913	**Mitsubishi, Cordia, Tredia, Starion, Galant 1983-85** Covers all U.S. and Canadian models	7583
Ford Pick-Ups 1965-82 Spanish	7469	**MG 1961-81** Covers all U.S. and Canadian models	6780
Ford Ranger 1983-84 Covers all U.S. and Canadian models	7338	**Mustang/Capri/Merkur 1979-85** Covers all U.S. and Canadian models	6963
Ford Vans 1961-86 Covers all U.S. and Canadian 1/2, 3/4 and 1 ton van and cutaway chassis models, including diesel engines	6849	**Mustang/Cougar 1965-73** Covers all U.S. and Canadian models	6542
		Mustang II 1974-78 Covers all U.S. and Canadian models	6812
GM A-Body 1982-85 Covers all front wheel drive U.S. and Canadian models of BUICK Century, CHEVROLET Celebrity, OLDSMOBILE Cutlass Ciera and PONTIAC 6000	7309	**Omni/Horizon/Rampage 1978-84** Covers all U.S. and Canadian models of DODGE omni, Miser, 024, Charger 2.2; PLYMOUTH Horizon, Miser, TC3, TC3 Tourismo; Rampage	6845
GM C-Body 1985 Covers all front wheel drive U.S. and Canadian models of BUICK Electra Park Avenue and Electra T-Type, CADILLAC Fleetwood and deVille, OLDSMOBILE 98 Regency and Regency Brougham	7587	**Opel 1971-75** Covers all U.S. and Canadian models	6575
		Peugeot 1970-74 Covers all U.S. and Canadian models	5982
		Pinto/Bobcat 1971-80 Covers all U.S. and Canadian models	7027
GM J-Car 1982-85 Covers all U.S. and Canadian models of BUICK Skyhawk, CHEVROLET Cavalier, CADILLAC Cimarron, OLDSMOBILE Firenza and PONTIAC 2000 and Sunbird	7059	**Plymouth 1968-76** Covers all U.S. and Canadian models	6552
		Pontiac Fiero 1984-85 Covers all U.S. and Canadian models	7571
GM N-Body 1985-86 Covers all U.S. and Canadian models of front wheel drive BUICK Somerset and Skylark, OLDSMOBILE Calais, and PONTIAC Grand Am	7657	**Pontiac Mid-Size 1974-83** Covers all U.S. and Canadian models of Ventura, Grand Am, LeMans, Grand LeMans, GTO, Phoenix, and Grand Prix	7346
		Porsche 924/928 1976-81 Covers all U.S. and Canadian models	7048
GM X-Body 1980-85 Covers all U.S. and Canadian models of BUICK Skylark, CHEVROLET Citation, OLDSMOBILE Omega and PONTIAC Phoenix	7049	**Renault 1975-85** Covers all U.S. and Canadian models	7165
		Roadrunner/Satellite/Belvedere/GTX 1968-73 Covers all U.S. and Canadian models	5821
GM Subcompact 1971-80 Covers all U.S. and Canadian models of BUICK Skyhawk (1975-80), CHEVROLET Vega and Monza, OLDSMOBILE Starfire, and PONTIAC Astre and 1975-80 Sunbird	6935	**RX-7 1979-81** Covers all U.S. and Canadian models	7031
		SAAB 99 1969-75 Covers all U.S. and Canadian models	5988
Granada/Monarch 1975-82 Covers all U.S. and Canadian models	6937	**SAAB 900 1979-85** Covers all U.S. and Canadian models	7572
Honda 1973-84 Covers all U.S. and Canadian models	6980	**Snowmobiles 1976-80** Covers Arctic Cat, John Deere, Kawasaki, Polaris, Ski-Doo and Yamaha	6978
International Scout 1967-73 Covers all U.S. and Canadian models	5912	**Subaru 1970-84** Covers all U.S. and Canadian models	6982
Jeep 1945-87 Covers all U.S. and Canadian CJ-2A, CJ-3A, CJ-3B, CJ-5, CJ-6, CJ-7, Scrambler and Wrangler models	6817	**Tempest/GTO/LeMans 1968-73** Covers all U.S. and Canadian models	5905
		Toyota 1966-70 Covers all U.S. and Canadian models of Corona, MkII, Corolla, Crown, Land Cruiser, Stout and Hi-Lux	5795
Jeep Wagoneer, Commando, Cherokee, Truck 1957-86 Covers all U.S. and Canadian models of Wagoneer, Cherokee, Grand Wagoneer, Jeepster, Jeepster Commando, J-100, J-200, J-300, J-10, J20, FC-150 and FC-170	6739	**Toyota 1970-79 Spanish**	7467
		Toyota Celica/Supra 1971-85 Covers all U.S. and Canadian models	7043
		Toyota Trucks 1970-85 Covers all U.S. and Canadian models of pickups, Land Cruiser and 4Runner	7035
Laser/Daytona 1984-85 Covers all U.S. and Canadian models	7563	**Valiant/Duster 1968-76** Covers all U.S. and Canadian models	6326
Maverick/Comet 1970-77 Covers all U.S. and Canadian models	6634	**Volvo 1956-69** Covers all U.S. and Canadian models	6529
Mazda 1971-84 Covers all U.S. and Canadian models of RX-2, RX-3, RX-4, 808, 1300, 1600, Cosmo, GLC and 626	6981	**Volvo 1970-83** Covers all U.S. and Canadian models	7040
		VW Front Wheel Drive 1974-85 Covers all U.S. and Canadian models	6962
Mazda Pick-Ups 1972-86 Covers all U.S. and Canadian models	7659	**VW 1949-71**	5796
Mercedes-Benz 1959-70 Covers all U.S. and Canadian models	6065	**VW 1970-79 Spanish**	7081
Mereceds-Benz 1968-73 Covers all U.S. and Canadian models	5907	**VW 1970-81** Covers all U.S. and Canadian Beetles, Karmann Ghia, Fastback, Squareback, Vans, 411 and 412	6837

Chilton's Repair & Tune-Up Guides are available at your local retailer or by mailing a check or money order for **$13.95** plus **$3.25** to cover postage and handling to:

Chilton Book Company
Dept. DM
Radnor, PA 19089

NOTE: When ordering be sure to include your name & address, book part No. & title.